学ぶ人は、変えてゆく人だ。

目の前にある問題はもちろん、

人生の問いや、

社会の課題を自ら見つけ、

挑み続けるために、人は学ぶ。

「学び」で、

少しずつ世界は変えてゆける。

いつでも、どこでも、誰でも、

学ぶことができる世の中へ。

旺文社

2024年度版

文部科学省後援

英検®

準1級

過去6回
全問題集

旺文社

2023年度　第2回
準1級　二次試験・A日程
(2023.11.5 実施)

問題カード

この問題カードは切り取って、本番の面接
の練習用にしてください。
質問は本文p.53にありますので、参考にし
てください。

You have **one minute** to prepare.

This is a story about a couple who liked traveling.

You have **two minutes** to narrate the story.

Your story should begin with the following sentence:

One day, a couple was talking at a café.

問題カード

この問題カードは切り取って、本番の面接の練習用にしてください。
質問は本文p.55にありますので、参考にしてください。

You have **one minute** to prepare.

This is a story about a couple whose son liked sports.

You have **two minutes** to narrate the story.

Your story should begin with the following sentence:

One day, a family was at home.

問題カード

この問題カードは切り取って、本番の面接の練習用にしてください。
質問は本文p.81にありますので、参考にしてください。

You have **one minute** to prepare.

This is a story about a university student who lived with his family.

You have **two minutes** to narrate the story.

Your story should begin with the following sentence:

One day, a university student was watching TV with his mother and grandfather.

問題カード

You have **one minute** to prepare.

This is a story about a woman who worked at a dentist's office.

You have **two minutes** to narrate the story.

Your story should begin with the following sentence:

One day, a woman was working at the reception desk of a dentist's office.

2022年度 第3回
準1級 二次試験・A日程
(2023.2.19 実施)

問題カード

この問題カードは切り取って、本番の面接
の練習用にしてください。
質問は本文 p.109 にありますので、参考に
してください。

You have **one minute** to prepare.

This is a story about a president of a small company.
You have **two minutes** to narrate the story.

Your story should begin with the following sentence:
One day, a company president was walking around the office.

2022年度 第3回
準1級 二次試験・C日程
(2023.3.5 実施)

問題カード

この問題カードは切り取って、本番の面接
の練習用にしてください。
質問は本文 p.111 にありますので、参考に
してください。

You have **one minute** to prepare.

This is a story about a girl who wanted to learn to skateboard.

You have **two minutes** to narrate the story.

Your story should begin with the following sentence:
One day, a girl was walking home from school.

2023年度第2回　英検準1級　解答用紙

【注意事項】

①解答にはHBの黒鉛筆（シャープペンシルも可）を使用し、解答を訂正する場合には消しゴムで完全に消してください。

②解答用紙は絶対に汚したり折り曲げたり、所定以外のところへの記入はしないでください。

③マーク例

良い例	悪い例
●	

これ以下の濃さのマークは読めません。

筆記解答欄

問題番号	1	2	3	4
(1)	①	②	③	④
(2)	①	②	③	④
(3)	①	②	③	④
(4)	①	②	③	④
(5)	①	②	③	④
(6)	①	②	③	④
(7)	①	②	③	④
(8)	①	②	③	④
(9)	①	②	③	④
(10)	①	②	③	④
(11)	①	②	③	④
(12)	①	②	③	④
(13)	①	②	③	④
(14)	①	②	③	④
(15)	①	②	③	④
(16)	①	②	③	④
(17)	①	②	③	④
(18)	①	②	③	④
(19)	①	②	③	④
(20)	①	②	③	④
(21)	①	②	③	④
(22)	①	②	③	④
(23)	①	②	③	④
(24)	①	②	③	④
(25)	①	②	③	④

（筆記解答欄は 1）

筆記解答欄

問題番号	1	2	3	4
(26)	①	②	③	④
(27)	①	②	③	④
(28)	①	②	③	④
(29)	①	②	③	④
(30)	①	②	③	④
(31)	①	②	③	④

（筆記解答欄は 2）

筆記解答欄

問題番号	1	2	3	4
(32)	①	②	③	④
(33)	①	②	③	④
(34)	①	②	③	④
(35)	①	②	③	④
(36)	①	②	③	④
(37)	①	②	③	④
(38)	①	②	③	④
(39)	①	②	③	④
(40)	①	②	③	④
(41)	①	②	③	④

（筆記解答欄は 3）

※筆記4の解答欄はこの裏にあります。

リスニング解答欄

	問題番号	1	2	3	4
Part 1	No.1	①	②	③	④
	No.2	①	②	③	④
	No.3	①	②	③	④
	No.4	①	②	③	④
	No.5	①	②	③	④
	No.6	①	②	③	④
	No.7	①	②	③	④
	No.8	①	②	③	④
	No.9	①	②	③	④
	No.10	①	②	③	④
	No.11	①	②	③	④
	No.12	①	②	③	④
Part 2	A No.13	①	②	③	④
	A No.14	①	②	③	④
	B No.15	①	②	③	④
	B No.16	①	②	③	④
	C No.17	①	②	③	④
	C No.18	①	②	③	④
	D No.19	①	②	③	④
	D No.20	①	②	③	④
	E No.21	①	②	③	④
	E No.22	①	②	③	④
	F No.23	①	②	③	④
	F No.24	①	②	③	④
Part 3	G No.25	①	②	③	④
	H No.26	①	②	③	④
	I No.27	①	②	③	④
	J No.28	①	②	③	④
	K No.29	①	②	③	④

※実際の解答用紙に似せていますが、デザイン・サイズは異なります。

・指示事項を守り、文字は、はっきり分かりやすく書いてください。
・太枠に囲まれた部分のみが採点の対象です。

4 English Composition

Write your English Composition in the space below.

5

10

15

20

2023年度第1回　英検準1級　解答用紙

【注意事項】

①解答にはHBの黒鉛筆(シャープペンシルも可)を使用し、解答を訂正する場合には消しゴムで完全に消してください。

②解答用紙は絶対に汚したり折り曲げたり、所定以外のところへの記入はしないでください。

③マーク例

良い例	悪い例
●	

これ以下の濃さのマークは読めません。

筆記解答欄

問題番号	1	2	3	4
(1)	①	②	③	④
(2)	①	②	③	④
(3)	①	②	③	④
(4)	①	②	③	④
(5)	①	②	③	④
(6)	①	②	③	④
(7)	①	②	③	④
(8)	①	②	③	④
(9)	①	②	③	④
(10)	①	②	③	④
(11)	①	②	③	④
(12)	①	②	③	④
(13)	①	②	③	④
(14)	①	②	③	④
(15)	①	②	③	④
(16)	①	②	③	④
(17)	①	②	③	④
(18)	①	②	③	④
(19)	①	②	③	④
(20)	①	②	③	④
(21)	①	②	③	④
(22)	①	②	③	④
(23)	①	②	③	④
(24)	①	②	③	④
(25)	①	②	③	④

（解答欄 **1**）

筆記解答欄

問題番号	1	2	3	4
(26)	①	②	③	④
(27)	①	②	③	④
(28)	①	②	③	④
(29)	①	②	③	④
(30)	①	②	③	④
(31)	①	②	③	④

（解答欄 **2**）

筆記解答欄

問題番号	1	2	3	4
(32)	①	②	③	④
(33)	①	②	③	④
(34)	①	②	③	④
(35)	①	②	③	④
(36)	①	②	③	④
(37)	①	②	③	④
(38)	①	②	③	④
(39)	①	②	③	④
(40)	①	②	③	④
(41)	①	②	③	④

（解答欄 **3**）

※筆記4の解答欄はこの裏にあります。

リスニング解答欄

	問題番号	1	2	3	4
Part 1	No.1	①	②	③	④
	No.2	①	②	③	④
	No.3	①	②	③	④
	No.4	①	②	③	④
	No.5	①	②	③	④
	No.6	①	②	③	④
	No.7	①	②	③	④
	No.8	①	②	③	④
	No.9	①	②	③	④
	No.10	①	②	③	④
	No.11	①	②	③	④
	No.12	①	②	③	④
Part 2	A No.13	①	②	③	④
	No.14	①	②	③	④
	B No.15	①	②	③	④
	No.16	①	②	③	④
	C No.17	①	②	③	④
	No.18	①	②	③	④
	D No.19	①	②	③	④
	No.20	①	②	③	④
	E No.21	①	②	③	④
	No.22	①	②	③	④
	F No.23	①	②	③	④
	No.24	①	②	③	④
Part 3	G No.25	①	②	③	④
	H No.26	①	②	③	④
	I No.27	①	②	③	④
	J No.28	①	②	③	④
	K No.29	①	②	③	④

※実際の解答用紙に似せていますが、デザイン・サイズは異なります。

・指示事項を守り、文字は、はっきり分かりやすく書いてください。
・太枠に囲まれた部分のみが採点の対象です。

4 English Composition

Write your English Composition in the space below.

5

10

15

20

2022年度第3回　英検準1級　解答用紙

【注意事項】

①解答にはHBの黒鉛筆（シャープペンシルも可）を使用し、解答を訂正する場合には消しゴムで完全に消してください。

②解答用紙は絶対に汚したり折り曲げたり、所定以外のところへの記入はしないでください。

③マーク例

良い例	悪い例
●	◑ ✗ ◖

 これ以下の濃さのマークは読めません。

筆記解答欄

問題番号	1	2	3	4
(1)	①	②	③	④
(2)	①	②	③	④
(3)	①	②	③	④
(4)	①	②	③	④
(5)	①	②	③	④
(6)	①	②	③	④
(7)	①	②	③	④
(8)	①	②	③	④
(9)	①	②	③	④
(10)	①	②	③	④
(11)	①	②	③	④
(12)	①	②	③	④
(13)	①	②	③	④
(14)	①	②	③	④
(15)	①	②	③	④
(16)	①	②	③	④
(17)	①	②	③	④
(18)	①	②	③	④
(19)	①	②	③	④
(20)	①	②	③	④
(21)	①	②	③	④
(22)	①	②	③	④
(23)	①	②	③	④
(24)	①	②	③	④
(25)	①	②	③	④

（筆記欄番号 1）

筆記解答欄

問題番号	1	2	3	4
(26)	①	②	③	④
(27)	①	②	③	④
(28)	①	②	③	④
(29)	①	②	③	④
(30)	①	②	③	④
(31)	①	②	③	④

（筆記欄番号 2）

筆記解答欄

問題番号	1	2	3	4
(32)	①	②	③	④
(33)	①	②	③	④
(34)	①	②	③	④
(35)	①	②	③	④
(36)	①	②	③	④
(37)	①	②	③	④
(38)	①	②	③	④
(39)	①	②	③	④
(40)	①	②	③	④
(41)	①	②	③	④

（筆記欄番号 3）

※筆記4の解答欄はこの裏にあります。

リスニング解答欄

	問題番号	1	2	3	4
Part 1	No.1	①	②	③	④
	No.2	①	②	③	④
	No.3	①	②	③	④
	No.4	①	②	③	④
	No.5	①	②	③	④
	No.6	①	②	③	④
	No.7	①	②	③	④
	No.8	①	②	③	④
	No.9	①	②	③	④
	No.10	①	②	③	④
	No.11	①	②	③	④
	No.12	①	②	③	④
Part 2 A	No.13	①	②	③	④
	No.14	①	②	③	④
B	No.15	①	②	③	④
	No.16	①	②	③	④
C	No.17	①	②	③	④
	No.18	①	②	③	④
D	No.19	①	②	③	④
	No.20	①	②	③	④
E	No.21	①	②	③	④
	No.22	①	②	③	④
F	No.23	①	②	③	④
	No.24	①	②	③	④
Part 3 G	No.25	①	②	③	④
H	No.26	①	②	③	④
I	No.27	①	②	③	④
J	No.28	①	②	③	④
K	No.29	①	②	③	④

※実際の解答用紙に似せていますが、デザイン・サイズは異なります。

・指示事項を守り、文字は、はっきり分かりやすく書いてください。
・太枠に囲まれた部分のみが採点の対象です。

4 English Composition

Write your English Composition in the space below.

5

10

15

20

2022年度第2回　英検準1級　解答用紙

【注意事項】

① 解答にはHBの黒鉛筆（シャープペンシルも可）を使用し、解答を訂正する場合には消しゴムで完全に消してください。

② 解答用紙は絶対に汚したり折り曲げたり、所定以外のところへの記入はしないでください。

③ マーク例

良い例	悪い例
●	◑ ✗ ◖

 これ以下の濃さのマークは読めません。

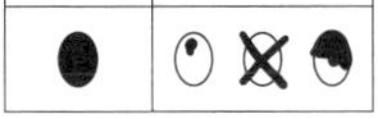

筆記解答欄

問題番号	1	2	3	4
(1)	①	②	③	④
(2)	①	②	③	④
(3)	①	②	③	④
(4)	①	②	③	④
(5)	①	②	③	④
(6)	①	②	③	④
(7)	①	②	③	④
(8)	①	②	③	④
(9)	①	②	③	④
(10)	①	②	③	④
(11)	①	②	③	④
(12)	①	②	③	④
(13)	①	②	③	④
(14)	①	②	③	④
(15)	①	②	③	④
(16)	①	②	③	④
(17)	①	②	③	④
(18)	①	②	③	④
(19)	①	②	③	④
(20)	①	②	③	④
(21)	①	②	③	④
(22)	①	②	③	④
(23)	①	②	③	④
(24)	①	②	③	④
(25)	①	②	③	④

（問題番号欄に「1」）

筆記解答欄

問題番号	1	2	3	4
(26)	①	②	③	④
(27)	①	②	③	④
(28)	①	②	③	④
(29)	①	②	③	④
(30)	①	②	③	④
(31)	①	②	③	④

（問題番号欄に「2」）

筆記解答欄

問題番号	1	2	3	4
(32)	①	②	③	④
(33)	①	②	③	④
(34)	①	②	③	④
(35)	①	②	③	④
(36)	①	②	③	④
(37)	①	②	③	④
(38)	①	②	③	④
(39)	①	②	③	④
(40)	①	②	③	④
(41)	①	②	③	④

（問題番号欄に「3」）

※筆記4の解答欄はこの裏にあります。

リスニング解答欄

	問題番号	1	2	3	4
	No.1	①	②	③	④
	No.2	①	②	③	④
	No.3	①	②	③	④
	No.4	①	②	③	④
	No.5	①	②	③	④
Part 1	No.6	①	②	③	④
	No.7	①	②	③	④
	No.8	①	②	③	④
	No.9	①	②	③	④
	No.10	①	②	③	④
	No.11	①	②	③	④
	No.12	①	②	③	④
A	No.13	①	②	③	④
	No.14	①	②	③	④
B	No.15	①	②	③	④
	No.16	①	②	③	④
C	No.17	①	②	③	④
	No.18	①	②	③	④
Part 2 D	No.19	①	②	③	④
	No.20	①	②	③	④
E	No.21	①	②	③	④
	No.22	①	②	③	④
F	No.23	①	②	③	④
	No.24	①	②	③	④
G	No.25	①	②	③	④
H	No.26	①	②	③	④
Part 3 I	No.27	①	②	③	④
J	No.28	①	②	③	④
K	No.29	①	②	③	④

※実際の解答用紙に似せていますが、デザイン・サイズは異なります。

・指示事項を守り、文字は、はっきり分かりやすく書いてください。
・太枠に囲まれた部分のみが採点の対象です。

4 English Composition

Write your English Composition in the space below.

5

10

15

20

2022年度第1回　英検準1級　解答用紙

【注意事項】

①解答にはHBの黒鉛筆(シャープペンシルも可)を使用し、解答を訂正する場合には消しゴムで完全に消してください。

②解答用紙は絶対に汚したり折り曲げたり、所定以外のところへの記入はしないでください。

③マーク例

良い例	悪い例
●	◑ ✖ ◉

 これ以下の濃さのマークは読めません。

筆記解答欄

問題番号	1	2	3	4
(1)	①	②	③	④
(2)	①	②	③	④
(3)	①	②	③	④
(4)	①	②	③	④
(5)	①	②	③	④
(6)	①	②	③	④
(7)	①	②	③	④
(8)	①	②	③	④
(9)	①	②	③	④
(10)	①	②	③	④
(11)	①	②	③	④
(12)	①	②	③	④
(13)	①	②	③	④
(14)	①	②	③	④
(15)	①	②	③	④
(16)	①	②	③	④
(17)	①	②	③	④
(18)	①	②	③	④
(19)	①	②	③	④
(20)	①	②	③	④
(21)	①	②	③	④
(22)	①	②	③	④
(23)	①	②	③	④
(24)	①	②	③	④
(25)	①	②	③	④

(筆記 1)

筆記解答欄

問題番号	1	2	3	4
(26)	①	②	③	④
(27)	①	②	③	④
(28)	①	②	③	④
(29)	①	②	③	④
(30)	①	②	③	④
(31)	①	②	③	④

(筆記 2)

筆記解答欄

問題番号	1	2	3	4
(32)	①	②	③	④
(33)	①	②	③	④
(34)	①	②	③	④
(35)	①	②	③	④
(36)	①	②	③	④
(37)	①	②	③	④
(38)	①	②	③	④
(39)	①	②	③	④
(40)	①	②	③	④
(41)	①	②	③	④

(筆記 3)

※筆記4の解答欄はこの裏にあります。

リスニング解答欄

問題番号			1	2	3	4
Part 1		No.1	①	②	③	④
		No.2	①	②	③	④
		No.3	①	②	③	④
		No.4	①	②	③	④
		No.5	①	②	③	④
		No.6	①	②	③	④
		No.7	①	②	③	④
		No.8	①	②	③	④
		No.9	①	②	③	④
		No.10	①	②	③	④
		No.11	①	②	③	④
		No.12	①	②	③	④
Part 2	A	No.13	①	②	③	④
		No.14	①	②	③	④
	B	No.15	①	②	③	④
		No.16	①	②	③	④
	C	No.17	①	②	③	④
		No.18	①	②	③	④
	D	No.19	①	②	③	④
		No.20	①	②	③	④
	E	No.21	①	②	③	④
		No.22	①	②	③	④
	F	No.23	①	②	③	④
		No.24	①	②	③	④
Part 3	G	No.25	①	②	③	④
	H	No.26	①	②	③	④
	I	No.27	①	②	③	④
	J	No.28	①	②	③	④
	K	No.29	①	②	③	④

※実際の解答用紙に似せていますが、デザイン・サイズは異なります。

・指示事項を守り、文字は、はっきり分かりやすく書いてください。
・太枠に囲まれた部分のみが採点の対象です。

4 English Composition

Write your English Composition in the space below.

5
10
15
20

2021年度第3回　英検準1級　解答用紙

筆記解答欄

問題番号	1	2	3	4
(1)	①	②	③	④
(2)	①	②	③	④
(3)	①	②	③	④
(4)	①	②	③	④
(5)	①	②	③	④
(6)	①	②	③	④
(7)	①	②	③	④
(8)	①	②	③	④
(9)	①	②	③	④
(10)	①	②	③	④
(11)	①	②	③	④
(12)	①	②	③	④
(13)	①	②	③	④
(14)	①	②	③	④
(15)	①	②	③	④
(16)	①	②	③	④
(17)	①	②	③	④
(18)	①	②	③	④
(19)	①	②	③	④
(20)	①	②	③	④
(21)	①	②	③	④
(22)	①	②	③	④
(23)	①	②	③	④
(24)	①	②	③	④
(25)	①	②	③	④

（欄1）

筆記解答欄

問題番号	1	2	3	4
(26)	①	②	③	④
(27)	①	②	③	④
(28)	①	②	③	④
(29)	①	②	③	④
(30)	①	②	③	④
(31)	①	②	③	④

（欄2）

筆記解答欄

問題番号	1	2	3	4
(32)	①	②	③	④
(33)	①	②	③	④
(34)	①	②	③	④
(35)	①	②	③	④
(36)	①	②	③	④
(37)	①	②	③	④
(38)	①	②	③	④
(39)	①	②	③	④
(40)	①	②	③	④
(41)	①	②	③	④

（欄3）

※筆記4の解答欄はこの裏にあります。

リスニング解答欄

	問題番号	1	2	3	4
Part 1	No.1	①	②	③	④
	No.2	①	②	③	④
	No.3	①	②	③	④
	No.4	①	②	③	④
	No.5	①	②	③	④
	No.6	①	②	③	④
	No.7	①	②	③	④
	No.8	①	②	③	④
	No.9	①	②	③	④
	No.10	①	②	③	④
	No.11	①	②	③	④
	No.12	①	②	③	④
Part 2 A	No.13	①	②	③	④
	No.14	①	②	③	④
B	No.15	①	②	③	④
	No.16	①	②	③	④
C	No.17	①	②	③	④
	No.18	①	②	③	④
D	No.19	①	②	③	④
	No.20	①	②	③	④
E	No.21	①	②	③	④
	No.22	①	②	③	④
F	No.23	①	②	③	④
	No.24	①	②	③	④
Part 3 G	No.25	①	②	③	④
H	No.26	①	②	③	④
I	No.27	①	②	③	④
J	No.28	①	②	③	④
K	No.29	①	②	③	④

※実際の解答用紙に似せていますが、デザイン・サイズは異なります。

切り取り線

・指示事項を守り、文字は、はっきり分かりやすく書いてください。
・太枠に囲まれた部分のみが採点の対象です。

4 English Composition

Write your English Composition in the space below.

5

10

15

20

Introduction

はじめに

実用英語技能検定（英検®）は，年間受験者数420万人（英検IBA，英検Jr.との総数）の小学生から社会人まで，幅広い層が受験する国内最大級の資格試験で，1963年の第1回検定からの累計では1億人を超える人々が受験しています。英検®は，コミュニケーションを行う上で重要となる思考力・判断力・表現力をはじめとして，今日求められている英語能力のあり方に基づいて，2024年度より1〜3級の試験形式の一部をリニューアルする予定です。

この『全問題集シリーズ』は，英語を学ぶ皆さまを応援する気持ちを込めて刊行しました。本書は，2023年度第2回検定を含む6回分の過去問を，皆さまの理解が深まるよう，日本語訳や詳しい解説を加えて収録しています。また，次のページにリニューアルについてまとめていますので，問題に挑戦する前にご確認ください。さらに，「新形式の要約問題ガイド」「新形式の二次試験・面接ガイド」も収録していますので，ぜひお役立てください。

本書が皆さまの英検合格の足がかりとなり，さらには国際社会で活躍できるような生きた英語を身につけるきっかけとなることを願っています。

最後に，本書を刊行するにあたり，多大なご尽力をいただきました入江 泉先生に深く感謝の意を表します。

2024年　春

2024年度から 英検 ㊟1級の 試験が変わります!

2024年度第1回検定より, 英検準1級の試験がリニューアルされます。新形式の英作文問題（ライティング）が追加されることが大きなポイントです。また, 二次試験（面接）の質問文が一部調整されます。リスニングは変更はありません。リニューアル前の試験形式と2024年度からの試験形式をまとめました。新試験の概要を把握し, 対策を始めましょう。

リニューアル前の試験				2024年度からの試験		

筆記（90分）　　　　　　　　　　　　　　**筆記（90分）**

大問1	短文の語句空所補充	25問	→	大問1	短文の語句空所補充	18問	問題数減
大問2	長文の語句空所補充	6問	→	大問2	長文の語句空所補充	6問	
大問3	長文の内容一致選択	10問	→	大問3	長文の内容一致選択	7問	問題数減
大問4	英作文（意見論述問題）	1問	↘	大問4	英作文（要約問題）	1問	1問追加
				大問5	英作文（意見論述問題）	1問	

二次試験・面接　　　　　　　　　　　　　**二次試験・面接**

ナレーション	→	ナレーション	
Questions No.1～4	→	Questions No.1～4	質問文調整

〈変更点〉

筆記	→ 短文の語句空所補充の問題数が18問に減ります。
	→ 長文の内容一致選択の問題数が7問に減ります。
	→ 英作文に要約問題が追加されます。
リスニング	→ 変更はありません。
面接	→ Question No.4に話題導入文が追加されます。答え方に変更はありません。

※2023年12月現在の情報を掲載しています。

新形式の要約問題ガイド

- **Instructions: Read the article below and summarize it in your own words as far as possible in English.**
- **Suggested length: 60-70 words**
- **Write your summary in the space provided on your answer sheet. <u>Any writing outside the space will not be graded.</u>**

From the 1980s to the early 2000s, many national museums in Britain were charging their visitors entrance fees. The newly elected government, however, was supportive of the arts. It introduced a landmark policy to provide financial aid to museums so that they would drop their entrance fees. As a result, entrance to many national museums, including the Natural History Museum, became free of charge.

Supporters of the policy said that as it would widen access to national museums, it would have significant benefits. People, regardless of their education or income, would have the opportunity to experience the large collections of artworks in museums and learn about the country's cultural history.

Although surveys indicated that visitors to national museums that became free increased by an average of 70 percent after the policy's introduction, critics claimed the policy was not completely successful. This increase, they say, mostly consisted of the same people visiting museums many times. Additionally, some independent museums with entrance fees said the policy negatively affected them. Their visitor numbers decreased because people were visiting national museums to avoid paying fees, causing the independent museums to struggle financially.

※英検公式サンプル問題は，公益財団法人 日本英語検定協会の発表によるものです。
　出典：英検ウェブサイト

1980年代から2000年代初頭まで，イギリスの多くの国立博物館・美術館は来館者から入館料を徴収していた。しかし，新しく選ばれた政府は芸術を支援した。政府は，博物館が入館料を引き下げられるよう，財政援助を提供するという画期的な政策を導入した。その結果，自然史博物館を含む，多くの国立博物館への入館が無料になった。

この政策の支持者たちは，国立博物館へのアクセスを広げるため，この政策には大きなメリットがあるだろうと述べた。学歴や収入に関係なく，人々は博物館にある膨大な芸術作品の収蔵物に触れ，国の文化史について学ぶ機会を持てるだろう。

調査によると，この政策の導入後，無料になった国立博物館への来館者数は平均70%増加したが，批判者たちはこの政策は完全に成功したわけではないと主張する。彼らによると，この増加は，主に同じ人が何度も博物館を訪れることによるものだという。さらに，入館料を徴収している一部の独立系博物館は，この政策が彼らに悪影響を及ぼしたと述べた。人々が入館料の支払いを避けようと国立博物館を訪れているために独立系博物館の来館者数は減少し，結果的に財政的に苦しくなった。

解答例

The British government implemented a policy that would help national museums lower their entrance fees. Supporters believed this policy would have the positive effect of making the museums more open to everyone. However, despite a significant increase in visitors, critics argued that this was the result of the same people visiting repeatedly. Also, there were independent museums with entrance fees that experienced financial difficulties due to a decline in visitors.

解答例の訳

イギリス政府は，国立博物館が入館料を引き下げるのを手助けする政策を実施した。支持者たちは，この政策が国立博物館を誰にでもより開かれたものにするというプラスの効果をもたらすと信じていた。しかし，来館者が大幅に増加したにもかかわらず，批判者たちは，これは同じ人々が繰り返し訪れた結果だと主張した。また，入館料を徴収する独立系博物館の中には来館者の減少が原因で財政難に陥った所もあった。

解説

STEP 1 記事を読み，段落ごとの要旨をつかむ

まず，段落ごとの要旨をつかみながら，記事全体をざっと読もう。第1段落には英文全体のトピック（第1段落の要旨）が含まれている。ここでは，イギリスの政策，博物館支

援，入館料の引き下げ［無料化］の3点を押さえよう。第2段落は政策のメリットについて，第3段落はAlthough A（プラス面），B（マイナス面）．の構造で話が展開する。

STEP 2 各要点を短くまとめ，論理マーカーを利用しながらつなげる

　解答例は，第1文「トピック導入（政策の概要）」，第2文「プラス面」，第3～4文「マイナス面」の4文構成（70語）。各段落の要点を1（～2）文で書いて全体を3～4文にまとめれば60-70語に収まるだろう。第2段落と第3段落は対照的な内容なので，HoweverやOn the other handなどの対比・逆接の論理マーカーでつなげよう。第3段落のAlthough A, Bの部分は，解答例では第3文でdespite A, Bに置き換えている。また，Additionally, ... の前後で書かれた2つのマイナス面は，～. Also, ... を用いて2文で表している。

ポイント 要点のまとめかた
●重要ではない情報や細かい情報は省く。
●具体的な情報を抽象化・一般化する。
●主語と動詞を含む「文」を「句」で表す。
●記事と同じ表現や解答内の表現の繰り返しを避ける。

　例えば，記事のFrom the 1980s to the early 2000sはあまり重要な情報ではないので解答に含めない。また，an average of 70 percentの部分も，具体的な数字の情報は重要ではないので抽象的にsignificantなどと短く表すことができる。同様に，regardless of their education or incomeもeveryoneと抽象化［一般化］して表せる。

　また，「文」を「句」に置き換えることもコツである。例えば，記事の最後のTheir visitor numbers decreasedという文は，a decline in visitorsという名詞句に置き換えられる。このようにして，表現を言い換えることで，語彙力・文法力があることをアピールしよう。

　そのほかの言い換えは，以下の記事→解答例を参考にしよう。
✓類義表現の利用：introduce→implement, drop→lower, benefits→positive effect, claim→argue, many times→repeatedly
✓派生語の利用：struggle financially→experience financial difficulties

書いた要約文を，次の観点からチェック！

□ 内容…英文の要点を適切に捉えているか。
□ 構成…論理的に文章を構築できているか。
□ 語彙・文法…適切な語彙・文法を用いているか。
□ 語彙・文法…文の構造や語句の言い換えなどに工夫があるか。

- **Instructions: Read the article below and summarize it in your own words as far as possible in English.**
- **Suggested length: 60-70 words**
- **Write your summary in the space provided on your answer sheet. <u>Any writing outside the space will not be graded.</u>**

In 2012, the Sustainable Development Solutions Network, a global initiative of the United Nations, began to publish the World Happiness Report. The report polls people from around the world in six categories such as social support, life expectancy, freedom, and corruption. Since the World Happiness Report was first published, one country has regularly topped the rankings: Finland.

What makes Finland the happiest place to live? For one thing, Finland boasts greater levels of equality than almost any other country, including gender and income balance. In addition, Finland's residents enjoy outstanding social services, including high-level education, low levels of corruption, and free, quality healthcare. They also have access to a natural environment excellent for exercise, which they use to keep fit through activities such as hiking, skiing, and swimming.

However, outstanding social services that support Finland's high standard of living are funded by some of the highest levels of income tax in the world. On top of that, many food and non-alcoholic drinks are costlier than the EU average. Also, there is the long, dark winter, which can cause depression. However, the Finns tend to be resilient and can often withstand temporary hardships in order to have long-term satisfaction.

解答欄

　2012年，国連の世界的イニシアチブである「持続可能な開発ソリューションネットワーク（SDSN）」は，『世界幸福度報告書』の発行を開始した。この報告書は，社会的支援，平均寿命，自由，汚職など6つのカテゴリーで世界中の人々に調査を行っている。『世界幸福度報告書』が初めて発行されて以来，ある1つの国がしばしばランキングのトップになっており，それはフィンランドである。

　何がフィンランドを住むのに最も幸福な場所にしているのだろうか。1つには，フィンランドは，ジェンダーや所得バランスを含め，ほかのほとんどの国よりも高いレベルの平等性を誇っている。加えて，フィンランドの住民は，高度な教育，汚職の少なさ，無料の質の高い医療などの優れた社会サービスを享受している。また，彼らは，体を動かすのに最適な自然環境にも恵まれており，ハイキング，スキー，水泳などのアクティビティを通して健康を維持するのにそれを利用している。

　しかし，フィンランドの高い生活水準を支える優れた社会サービスは，世界最高レベルの所得税によって賄われている。その上，多くの食品やノンアルコール飲料はEU平均よりも高価である。それに長く暗い冬があり，鬱の原因になることもある。しかし，フィンランド人は立ち直りの早い傾向にあり，たいていの場合，長期的な満足を得るために一時的な苦難に耐えることができる。

解答例

Finland is one of the happiest countries in the world. Reasons for this include the high-level equality, social welfare, and rich natural environment. On the other hand, the reality is that such a high quality of life for citizens is due to extremely high taxes and cost of living. Another negative aspect is the long, dark winter, which Finns seem to be able to endure for long-term happiness.

解答例の訳

　フィンランドは世界で最も幸せな国の1つである。その理由としては，高いレベルの平等性，社会福祉，豊かな自然環境などが挙げられる。一方で，それほど質の高い国民の生活は，極めて高い税金や生活費に起因しているのが現実である。もう1つのマイナス面は長く暗い冬だが，フィンランド人は長期的な幸福のために耐えることができるようだ。

解説

STEP 1 記事を読み，段落ごとの要旨をつかむ

　まず，段落ごとの要旨をつかみながら，記事全体をざっと読もう。第1段落には英文全

体のトピック（第1段落の要旨）が含まれている。ここでは，「世界一幸福なフィンランド」がトピックで，第2段落は幸福の理由＝プラス面，Howeverで始まる第3段落はマイナス面に展開する。

STEP 2 　各要点を短くまとめ，論理マーカーを利用しながらつなげる

　解答例は，第1文「トピック導入」，第2文「プラス面」，第3～4文「マイナス面」の4文構成（68語）。各段落の要点を1（～2）文で書いて全体を3～4文にまとめれば60-70語に収まるだろう。第2段落と第3段落は対照的な内容なので，On the other hand などの対比・逆接の論理マーカーでつなげよう。第2段落第1文の What makes ...? は理由を尋ねる表現で，解答例では Reasons for this include ...「その理由には…が挙げられる」で表している。include は具体例を表すのに便利な動詞だ。第3段落は，マイナス面の具体例を述べた後，On top of that, ... で情報が追加される。解答例では，the reality is that ...「…が現実だ」と，Another negative aspect is ... の2文でマイナス面をまとめている。

ポイント 　要点のまとめかた
●重要ではない情報や細かい情報は省く。
●具体的な情報を抽象化・一般化する。
●記事と同じ表現や解答内の表現の繰り返しを避ける。

　第1段落の大文字で始まる固有名詞などの詳しい情報は解答に含めず，フィンランドが世界一幸福な国の1つであるという事実のみを書けばよい。また，A, including B や A such as B の構造では A が重要な情報になる。natural environment excellent for ... → rich natural environment や，some of the highest levels ... in the world → extremely high, そして many food and non-alcoholic drinks are costlier → (extremely high) cost of living のように，具体的な情報を抽象化・一般化することで短くまとめることもポイント。

　そのほかの言い換えは，以下の記事→解答例を参考にしよう。
✓類義表現の利用：social support [services] → social welfare，residents → citizens，tend to *do* → seem to *do*（不確かさ・推量），can *do* → be able to *do*（能力），withstand → endure，in order to *do* → for（目的），satisfaction → happiness
✓派生語の利用：greater levels（名詞）→ high-level（形容詞・ハイフンでつないだ複合形容詞），costly（形容詞）→ cost（名詞）

書いた要約文を，次の観点からチェック！

☐ 内容…英文の要点を適切に捉えているか。
☐ 構成…論理的に文章を構築できているか。
☐ 語彙・文法…適切な語彙・文法を用いているか。
☐ 語彙・文法…文の構造や語句の言い換えなどに工夫があるか。

新形式の 二次試験・面接ガイド

旺文社オリジナル予想問題

- You have **one minute** to prepare.

- This is a story about a man who decided to move to the countryside with his family.
  You have **two minutes** to narrate the story.

- Your story should begin with the following sentence:
  One day, a man was walking down the street with his family.

（実際の問題カードはカラーです）

※『14日でできる！ 英検準1級 二次試験・面接 完全予想問題 改訂版』の「準備編（p.22〜）」に掲載されている問題のQuestion No.4に，話題導入文を追加して編集したものです。

Questions

No. 1   Please look at the fourth picture. If you were the man, what would you be thinking?

No. 2   Do people need to spend more money on raising children now than in the past?

No. 3   Do you think that it's important to have contact with nature in our daily lives?

No. 4   Animal species at risk of extinction often become a topic for discussion. Should the government do more to protect endangered animals around the country?

質問の訳

No. 1   4番目の絵を見てください。もしあなたがこの男性なら，どのようなことを考えているでしょうか。

No. 2   昔よりも，今の方が子供を育てるのに多くのお金を費やす必要がありますか。

No. 3   日々の生活で自然に触れることは大切だと思いますか。

No. 4   絶滅の危機にひんしている動物種がよく議論の話題になります。政府は国内の絶滅危惧動物を保護するためにもっと多くのことをすべきですか。

One day, a man was walking down the street with his family. There were a lot of people, cars, and buildings. He was telling his wife and his son how nice it would be to live in the countryside, where there was a lot of nature. They agreed with him. A week later, the man and his wife were looking at a magazine in their home. There was an advertisement for houses for sale in a village. His wife said to him, "Let's move there." He agreed with her suggestion. On the moving day, the family was having a picnic outside of their home in the countryside. They were eating sandwiches together. They were feeling happy. The next day, the man was waiting for the bus with his son. The man looked at the timetable and noticed there was only one bus per hour. The son was looking at his watch. He was worried about being late for school.

ナレーション例の訳

　ある日，男性が家族と道を歩いていました。たくさんの人，車そして建物であふれかえっていました。彼は妻と息子に自然に恵まれた田舎に住むことがどれほど素晴らしいことなのかを話していました。2人は彼に同意しました。1週間後，男性とその妻が家で雑誌を眺めていました。ある村で売り出し中の家の広告が載っていました。妻は彼に「そこへ移住しましょう」と言いました。彼は彼女の提案に同意しました。引っ越しの日，家族は田舎の家の外でピクニックをしていました。彼らは一緒にサンドウィッチを食べていました。彼らは幸せを感じていました。次の日，男性は息子とバスを待っていました。男性は時刻表を見て，1時間に1本しかバスがないと気付きました。息子は腕時計を見ていました。彼は学校に遅刻することを心配していました。

No.1 解答例

I'd be thinking how inconvenient life in the countryside is. There is only one bus per hour. Although the air is cleaner in the countryside, there are disadvantages, too.

No.1 解答例の訳

　田舎での生活はどんなに不便なのだろうと思っているでしょう。バスは1時間に1本しかありません。田舎の方が空気はいいけれど，欠点もあります。

No.2 解答例

Yes. Raising children has become much more expensive. Buying a home big enough for a family has become very expensive, and the cost of living has also gone up. Children also expect to have computers and smartphones these days.

　はい。子どもを育てるのにより多くのお金がかかるようになりました。家族が住むのに十分な大きさの家を買うことはとてもお金がかかるようになりましたし，生活費も値上がりしました。さらに最近では，子供はコンピューターやスマートフォンを持つのが当たり前にもなっています。

No.3 解答例

No. It's nice to go into nature from time to time, but living in a city is much more stimulating, because we can keep in touch with the latest developments in culture and technology.

No.3 解答例の訳

　いいえ。ときどき自然の中へ入っていくことはよいことですが，都心に住む方がはるかに刺激的です。なぜなら私たちは最新の文化的な発展や技術の発達に触れ続けることができるからです。

No.4 解答例

Yes, it should. There are fewer and fewer natural places where animals can live peacefully, so the government should provide safe areas for them. Many animals, like wild bears, are having difficulty finding food.

No.4 解答例の訳

　はい，そうすべきです。動物が無事に住むことができる自然の場所はだんだん少なくなっていますので，政府は安全な場所を提供すべきです。野生のクマなどの多くの動物は，食料を見つけることが困難になっています。

解説

　No. 4 は問題カードのトピックにやや関連した，社会性のある内容について，受験者自身の意見を問う形式である。新形式のQuestionには，話題導入文が加わる（p.11下線・青字部分）が，23年度までの問題と質問内容の本質は変わらない。23年度までの問題では，問題カードのトピックとかけ離れた内容について唐突に質問される印象があったが，話題導入文が加わることで，どんなテーマについて聞かれているのかが分かりやすくなるだろう。

　質問に解答するために，特定の分野についての深い知識は必要ない。日ごろからニュースなどに接する際，それに対してどのような意見・考え方があるのかを把握して自分なりに考えておくことが大切である。

もくじ

Contents

執　　筆：入江 泉, Richard Knobbs
編集協力：日本アイアール株式会社，株式会社鷗来堂，久島智津子，内藤 香
録　　音：ユニバ合同会社
デザイン：林 慎一郎（及川真咲デザイン事務所）
組版・データ作成協力：幸和印刷株式会社

本書の使い方

ここでは，本書の過去問および特典についての活用法の一例を紹介します。

過去問の取り組み方

1セット目

【実力把握モード】
本番の試験と同じように，制限時間を設けて取り組みましょう。どの問題形式に時間がかかりすぎているか，正答率が低いかなど，今のあなたの実力を把握し，学習に生かしましょう。
アプリ「学びの友」の自動採点機能を活用して，答え合わせをスムーズに行いましょう。

2～5セット目

【学習モード】
制限時間をなくし，解けるまで取り組みましょう。
リスニングは音声を繰り返し聞いて解答を導き出してもかまいません。すべての問題に正解できるまで見直します。

6セット目

【仕上げモード】
試験直前の仕上げに利用しましょう。時間を計って本番のつもりで取り組みます。
これまでに取り組んだ6セットの過去問で間違えた問題の解説を本番試験の前にもう一度見直しましょう。

※別冊の解答解説に付いている **正答率 ★75%以上** は，旺文社「英検®一次試験 解答速報サービス」において回答者の正答率が75%以上だった設問を示しています。ぜひ押さえておきたい問題なので，しっかり復習しておきましょう。

音声について

一次試験・リスニングと二次試験・面接の音声を聞くことができます。本書とともに使い，効果的なリスニング・面接対策をしましょう。

収録内容と特長

 一次試験・リスニング

本番の試験の音声を収録	➡	スピードをつかめる！
解答時間は本番通り10秒間	➡	解答時間に慣れる！
収録されている英文は，別冊解答に掲載	➡	聞き取れない箇所を確認できる！

 二次試験・面接（スピーキング）

実際の流れ通りに収録	➡	本番の雰囲気を味わえる！

・ナレーションの準備（本番と同じ1分間）
・ナレーション（ナレーション例を収録）
・質問（練習用に10秒の解答時間）

各質問のModel Answerも収録	➡	模範解答が確認できる！
Model Answerは，別冊解答に掲載	➡	聞き取れない箇所を確認できる！

2つの方法で音声が聞けます！

音声再生 サービス ご利用 可能期間	**2024年2月28日～2025年8月31日** ※ご利用期間内にアプリやPCにダウンロードしていただいた音声は，期間終了後も 引き続きお聞きいただけます。 ※これらのサービスは予告なく変更，終了することがあります。

 ① 公式アプリ「英語の友」 (iOS/Android) で **お手軽再生**

リスニング力を強化する機能満載

再生速度変換 （0.5～2.0倍速）　**お気に入り機能** （絞込み学習）　**オフライン再生**

バックグラウンド 再生　**試験日 カウントダウン**

［ご利用方法］　※画像はイメージです。

1 「英語の友」公式サイトより，アプリをインストール
   https://eigonotomo.com/ 英語の友 🔍
   （右の2次元コードから読み込めます）

2 アプリ内のライブラリよりご購入いただいた書籍を選び，
   「追加」ボタンを押してください

3 パスワードを入力すると，音声がダウンロードできます
   ［パスワード：hpnqbz］ ※すべて半角アルファベット小文字

※本アプリの機能の一部は有料ですが，本書の音声は無料でお聞きいただけます。
※詳しいご利用方法は「英語の友」公式サイト，あるいはアプリ内ヘルプをご参照ください。

② パソコンで音声データダウンロード（MP3）

［ご利用方法］

1 Web特典にアクセス　　詳細は，p.19をご覧ください。

2 「一次試験［二次試験］音声データダウンロード」から
　聞きたい検定の回を選択してダウンロード

※音声ファイルはzip形式にまとめられた形でダウンロードされます。
※音声の再生にはMP3を再生できる機器などが必要です。ご使用機器，音声再生ソフト等に関する技術
　的なご質問は，ハードメーカーもしくはソフトメーカーにお願いいたします。

> CDをご希望の方は，別売「2024年度版英検準1級過去6回全問題集CD」
> （本体価格2,400円＋税）をご利用ください。
>
> 持ち運びに便利な小冊子とCD4枚付き。　※本書では，収録箇所を**CD 1 1 ～ 14**のように表示。

Web特典について

購入者限定の「Web特典」を，みなさんの英検合格にお役立てください。

ご利用 可能期間	2024年2月28日～2025年8月31日 ※本サービスは予告なく変更，終了することがあります。	
アクセス 方法	スマートフォン タブレット	右の2次元コードを読み込むと， パスワードなしでアクセスできます！
	PC スマートフォン タブレット 共通	1. Web特典（以下のURL）にアクセスします。 https://eiken.obunsha.co.jp/p1q/ 2. 本書を選択し，以下のパスワードを入力します。 hpnqbz ※すべて半角アルファベット小文字

〈特典内容〉

(1)解答用紙

本番にそっくりの解答用紙が印刷できるので，何度でも過去問にチャレンジすることができます。

(2)音声データのダウンロード

一次試験リスニング・二次試験面接の音声データ（MP3）を無料でダウンロードできます。
※スマートフォン・タブレットの方は，アプリ「英語の友」（p.17）をご利用ください。

自動採点アプリ「学びの友」の利用方法

本書の問題は，採点・見直し学習アプリ「学びの友」でカンタンに自動採点することができます。

ご利用可能期間	**2024年2月28日～2025年8月31日** ※本サービスは予告なく変更，終了することがあります。 ※ご利用可能期間内にアプリ内で「追加」していた場合は，期間終了後も引き続きお使いいただけます。
アクセス方法	**「学びの友」公式サイトにアクセス** **https://manatomo.obunsha.co.jp/** （右の2次元コードからもアクセスできます）　学びの友 🔍

※iOS／Android端末，Webブラウザよりご利用いただけます。
※アプリの動作環境については，「学びの友」公式サイトをご参照ください。なお，本アプリは無料でご利用いただけます。
※詳しいご利用方法は「学びの友」公式サイト，あるいはアプリ内ヘルプをご参照ください。

［ご利用方法］

1 アプリを起動後，「旺文社まなびID」に会員登録してください
会員登録は無料です。

2 アプリ内の「書籍を追加する」より
ご購入いただいた書籍を選び，「追加」ボタンを押してください

3 パスワードを入力し，コンテンツをダウンロードしてください

パスワード：**hpnqbz**
※すべて半角アルファベット小文字

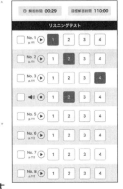

4 学習したい検定回を選択してマークシート
を開き，学習を開始します

マークシートを開くと同時にタイマーが動き出します。
問題番号の下には，書籍内掲載ページが表示されています。
問題番号の左側の□に「チェック」を入れることができます。

5 リスニングテストの音声は，
問題番号の横にある再生ボタンをタップ

一度再生ボタンを押したら，最後の問題まで自動的に進みます。

6 リスニングテストが終了したら，
画面右上「採点する」を押して答え合わせをします

※ライティング問題がある級は，「自己採点」ページで模範解答例を参照し，
観点別に自己採点を行ってください。

採点結果の見方

結果画面では，正答率や合格ラインとの距離，間違えた問題の確認ができます。

『問題ごとの正誤』では，プルダ
ウンメニューで，「チェック」し
た問題，「不正解」の問題，「チェ
ックと不正解」の問題を絞り込ん
で表示することができますので，
解き直しの際にご活用ください。

英検®Information

出典：英検ウェブサイト

英検準1級について

準1級では，「社会生活で求められる英語を十分理解し，また使用できる」ことが求められます。
転職や就職，単位認定，教員採用試験，海外留学や入試など，多方面で幅広く活用される資格です。
目安としては「大学中級程度」です。

試験内容

一次試験 筆記・リスニング

主な場面・状況	家庭・学校・職場・地域（各種店舗・公共施設を含む）・電話・アナウンス・講義など
主な話題	社会生活一般・芸術・文化・歴史・教育・科学・自然・環境・医療・テクノロジー・ビジネス・政治など

筆記試験 ⊘90分

問題	形式・課題詳細	問題数	満点スコア
1	文脈に合う適切な語句を補う。 問題数減	18問	
2	パッセージの空所に文脈に合う適切な語句を補う。	6問	750
3	パッセージの内容に関する質問に答える。 問題数減	7問	
4	与えられた英文の要約文を書く。（60〜70語） NEW	1問	750
5	指定されたトピックについての英作文を書く。（120〜150語）	1問	

リスニング ⊘約30分 放送回数／1回

問題	形式・課題詳細	問題数	満点スコア
Part 1	会話の内容に関する質問に答える。	12問	
Part 2	パッセージの内容に関する質問に答える。	12問	750
Part 3	Real-Life形式の放送内容に関する質問に答える。	5問	

変更ポイント

2024年度から英検準1級が変わる！

1 語彙問題・長文問題の問題数が削減されます。

大問1は25問から18問，大問3は10問から7問になります。

2 英作文問題が1問から2問に増えます。

既存の「意見論述」の問題に加え，「要約問題」が出題されます。与えられた英文を読み，その内容を英語で要約します。語数の目安は60〜70語です。

※要約問題の詳細は，「新形式の要約問題ガイド」（p.3〜）をご参照ください。

3 スピーキングNo.4の質問文に話題導入文が加わります。

受験者自身の意見を問う問題のうち，No.4の質問に話題導入文が追加されます。

※スピーキングの詳細は，「新形式の二次試験・面接ガイド」（p.10〜）をご参照ください。

二次試験 面接形式のスピーキングテスト

主な場面・題材	社会性の高い分野の話題
過去の出題例	在宅勤務・レストランでの喫煙・チャイルドシート・住民運動・キャッチセールス・護身術など

🗨 スピーキング ⏱ 約8分

面接の構成	形式・課題詳細	満点スコア
自由会話	面接委員と簡単な日常会話を行う。	
ナレーション	4コマのイラストの展開を説明する。（2分間）	
No.1	イラストに関連した質問に答える。	750
No.2／No.3	カードのトピックに関連した内容についての質問に答える。	
No.4	カードのトピックにやや関連した，社会性のある内容についての質問に答える。 質問文調整	

統計的に算出される英検CSEスコアに基づいて合否判定されます。Reading，Writing，Listening，Speakingの4技能が均等に評価され，合格基準スコアは固定されています。

≫ 技能別にスコアが算出される！

技能	試験形式	満点スコア	合格基準スコア
Reading（読む）	一次試験（筆記1〜3）	750	1792
Writing（書く）	一次試験（筆記4〜5）	750	
Listening（聞く）	一次試験（リスニング）	750	
Speaking（話す）	二次試験（面接）	750	512

● 一次試験の合否は，Reading，Writing，Listeningの技能別にスコアが算出され，それを合算して判定されます。
● 二次試験の合否は，Speakingのみで判定されます。

≫ 合格するためには，技能のバランスが重要！

英検CSEスコアでは，技能ごとに問題数は異なりますが，スコアを均等に配分しているため，各技能のバランスが重要となります。なお，正答数の目安を提示することはできませんが，2016年度第1回一次試験では，1級，準1級は各技能での正答率が7割程度，2級以下は各技能6割程度の正答率の受験者の多くが合格されています。

≫ 英検CSEスコアは国際標準規格CEFRにも対応している！

CEFRとは，Common European Framework of Reference for Languages の略。語学のコミュニケーション能力別のレベルを示す国際標準規格。欧米で幅広く導入され，6つのレベルが設定されています。
4技能の英検CSEスコアの合計「4技能総合スコア」と級ごとのCEFR算出範囲に基づいた「4技能総合CEFR」が成績表に表示されます。また，技能別の「CEFRレベル」も表示されます。

※ 4級・5級は4技能を測定していないため「4技能総合CEFR」の対象外。
※ 詳しくは英検ウェブサイトをご覧ください。

英検®の種類

英検には，実施方式の異なる複数の試験があります。従来型の英検とその他の英検の問題形式，難易度，級認定，合格証明書発行，英検CSEスコア取得等はすべて同じです。

英検®（従来型）

紙の問題冊子を見て解答用紙に解答。二次試験を受験するためには，一次試験に合格する必要があります。

英検 S-CBT

コンピュータを使って受験。1日で4技能を受験することができ，原則，毎週土日に実施されています（級や地域により毎週実施でない場合があります）。

英検 S-Interview

点字や吃音等，CBT方式では対応が難しい受験上の配慮が必要な方のみが受験可能。

※受験する級によって選択できる方式が異なります。各方式の詳細および最新情報は英検ウェブサイト（https://www.eiken.or.jp/eiken/）をご確認ください。

英検®（従来型）受験情報

※「従来型・本会場」以外の実施方式については，試験日程・申込方法が異なりますので，英検ウェブサイトをご覧ください。
※受験情報は変更になる場合があります。

◉ 2024年度 試験日程

	第1回	第2回	第3回
申込受付	3月15日▶5月8日	7月1日▶9月9日	11月1日▶12月16日
一次試験	6月2日（日）	10月6日（日）	2025年 1月26日（日）
二次試験	A 7月7日（日） B 7月14日（日）	A 11月10日（日） B 11月17日（日）	A 2025年 3月2日（日） B 2025年 3月9日（日）

※上記の申込期間はクレジット支払いの場合。支払い・申し込みの方法によって締切日が異なるのでご注意ください。
※一次試験は上記以外の日程でも準会場で受験できる可能性があります。
※二次試験にはA日程，B日程があり，年齢などの条件により指定されます。
※詳しくは英検ウェブサイトをご覧ください。

◉ 申込方法

団体受験 学校や塾などで申し込みをする団体受験もあります。詳しくは先生にお尋ねください。

個人受験 インターネット申込・コンビニ申込・英検特約書店申込のいずれかの方法で申し込みができます。詳しくは英検ウェブサイトをご覧ください。

お問い合わせ先

英検サービスセンター
TEL. 03-3266-8311
㊊〜㊎ 9：30〜17：00
（祝日・年末年始を除く）

英検ウェブサイト
www.eiken.or.jp/eiken/
詳しい試験情報を見たり，入試等で英検を活用している学校を検索したりすることができます。

2023年度の傾向と攻略ポイント

英検準1級は 2024 年度第1回検定から試験形式が一部変わります。ここでは，旧試験である 2023 年度第1回検定と第2回検定の分析をまとめています。あらかじめご了承ください。

一次試験　筆記（90 分）

1　短文の語句空所補充
文脈に合う適切な語句を補う。

問題数 **25問**
めやす **15分**

傾向 第1回・2回とも，例年通り 25 問のうち単語の意味を問うものが 21 問，句動詞の意味を問うものが4問出題された。出題される品詞のバランスは回により異なる。

攻略ポイント 語彙力を増やすには英字新聞などを通じて多くの英文に触れることが必要なのはもちろんだが，1つ新しい単語を覚えたら，同時にその単語の派生語（違う品詞の形）を調べて覚えるようにすると，語彙力を効率よく強化できる。

2　長文の語句空所補充
パッセージの空所に文脈に合う適切な語句を補う。

問題数 **6問**
めやす **15分**

傾向 約 250 語の2つの長文にそれぞれ空所が3つあり，適切な選択肢を選ぶという形式は例年と変わらない。今年度も，接続表現を問う問題が毎回出題された。

攻略ポイント 空所の前後を重点的に読み解くのが基本だが，それだけでは容易に正解が導けない場合もある。そのときは，長文全体の文脈の流れに視野を広げて読み解こう。

3　長文の内容一致選択
パッセージの内容に関する質問に答える。

問題数 **10問**
めやす **35分**

傾向 3つの長文は約 300 語，約 400 語，約 500 語の順で出題され，前半2つの長文に設問が3つ，最後の長文に設問が4つという形式は例年と変わらない。

攻略ポイント 設問の順序は長文の流れと基本的に一致しているので，解答につながる箇所を見つけるのは難しくはないが，設問を先に読んでから関連する情報を探しながら読む「スキャニング」と呼ばれる速読法が時間の節約に役立つ。

4　英作文
指定されたトピックについての英作文を書く。

問題数 **1問**
めやす **25分**

傾向 指定されたトピックについて，与えられた4つのポイントのうち2つを用いて，120〜150 語でエッセイを書くことが求められる。

攻略ポイント トピックの意味を正確に把握することを心がけよう。また，必ずしも自分の意見を正直に書く必要はなく，与えられたポイントから書きやすいものを選べばよい。過去問に挑戦することでパターンを身につけ，不安なく使える表現を増やそう。

一次試験　リスニング（約30分）

Part 1　会話の内容一致選択
会話の内容に関する質問に答える。

問題数 **12**問

傾向　100語前後の男女間の会話とそれに関する質問を聞き，問題用紙の選択肢の中から答えを選ぶという形式に変化はない。会話が行われる状況は，家庭，職場，学校，街中など多岐にわたっており，男女の人間関係もさまざまである。

攻略ポイント　それぞれの話者の意図，合意・決定したこと，一方がもう一方に提案していることなどに注意しながら聞くことが大切である。

Part 2　文の内容一致選択
パッセージの内容に関する質問に答える。

問題数 **12**問

傾向　150語前後のパッセージを聞き，続いて放送される2つの質問の答えを選択肢から選ぶ形式に変化はない。6つのパッセージのトピックは，環境，社会，健康，自然科学，文化など多岐にわたり，内容や使用される語彙も高度である。

攻略ポイント　2つの質問のうち，基本的に1つ目のものはパッセージの前半部分，2つ目は後半部分に関するものとなっている。しかし，中には「〜について何が分かるか」のように，全体の内容から判断しなければならないものもあるので，選択肢を先に読んで質問をある程度予測して聞くというテクニックも必要である。

Part 3　Real-Life形式の内容一致選択
Real-Life 形式の放送内容に関する質問に答える。

問題数 **5**問

傾向　問題用紙に印刷された状況と質問を10秒間で読んでから，電話の音声メッセージ，施設内アナウンスなど，日常生活で実際にあり得る100語前後のパッセージを聞き，選択肢の中から答えを選ぶ形式に変化はない。質問は基本的に全て「あなたは何をすべきか」などの適切な行動を問うものである。

攻略ポイント　あらかじめ状況設定と質問を理解してからリスニングを始めることができるので，必要な情報に注意を集中させて聞くことができる。しかしそのためには10秒で状況と質問（できれば選択肢まで）を読み切るだけの速読力も必要。

 二次試験　面接（約8分）

4コマのイラストがついたカードが渡される。1分の黙読の後，そのイラストのストーリーを2分間で説明するよう指示される。それから，4つの質問がされる。

最初の質問はイラストの4コマ目の特定の人物について「あなたがこの人物だったらどう思うか」というもの，残りの3つはイラストのトピックに関連した，あるいは一般的な社会問題について自分の意見を問うもの。意見には明快な理由や説明が伴わなければならない。

二次試験・面接の流れ

(1) 入室とあいさつ

係員の指示に従い，面接室に入ります。あいさつをしてから，面接委員に面接カードを手渡し，指示に従って，着席しましょう。

(2) 氏名と受験級の確認

面接委員があなたの氏名と受験する級の確認をします。その後，簡単な会話をしてから試験開始です。

(3) ナレーションの考慮時間

問題カードを手渡されます。指示文を黙読し，4コマのイラストについてナレーションの準備をします。時間は1分間です。

※問題カードには複数の種類があり，面接委員によっていずれか1枚が手渡されます。本書では英検協会から提供を受けたもののみ掲載しています。

(4) ナレーション

ナレーションをするよう指示されるので，問題カードで指定された言い出し部分から始めます。時間は2分間です。超過しないよう時間配分に注意しましょう。

(5) 4つの質問

面接委員の4つの質問に答えます。1つ目の質問に答える際には問題カードを見てもかまいませんが，2つ目以降は問題カードを裏返して答えます。また，自然な聞き返しであれば減点の対象になりません。積極的に自分の意見を話しましょう。

(6) カード返却と退室

試験が終了したら，問題カードを面接委員に返却し，あいさつをして退室しましょう。

2023-2

一次試験　2023.10.8実施
二次試験　A日程　2023.11.5実施
　　　　　C日程　2023.11.23実施

試験時間
筆記：90分
リスニング：約30分

Grade Pre-1

＊解答・解説は別冊p.5〜48にあります。
＊面接の流れは本書p.28にあります。

Pre 1

1 To complete each item, choose the best word or phrase from among the four choices. Then, on your answer sheet, find the number of the question and mark your answer.

(1) Layla found the workouts in the advanced class too (　　), so she decided to change to an easier class.
1 subtle　　**2** contrary　　**3** strenuous　　**4** cautious

(2) The tax accountant asked the woman to (　　) all her financial records over the past year. He needed to see them before he could begin preparing her tax forms.
1 punctuate　**2** compile　　**3** bleach　　**4** obsess

(3) Emilio discovered a small leak in one of the water pipes in his house. To be safe, he turned off the (　　) to stop the water until he knew exactly what the problem was.
1 depot　　**2** canal　　**3** valve　　**4** panel

(4) *A:* How long have you and Linda been (　　), Bill?
B: Oh, we've known each other for at least 10 years, maybe longer.
1 acquainted　**2** discharged　**3** emphasized　**4** subdued

(5) Our local community center usually has one main room, but when necessary, we can close the (　　) and create two smaller rooms.
1 estimation　**2** partition　　**3** assumption　**4** notion

(6) Tyler's father suggested that he get some foreign (　　) from his local bank before his vacation because changing money abroad is often more expensive.
1 tactic　　**2** bait　　**3** currency　　**4** menace

(7) Thanks to the country's (   ) natural resources, it is able to earn a great deal of money through exports such as metals, coal, and natural gas.

1 unjust   **2** insubstantial
3 elastic   **4** abundant

(8) At first, Enzo listed all six of his previous jobs on his résumé. He had to remove two of them, however, in order to (   ) the document into one page.

1 dispute   **2** mumble   **3** mistrust   **4** condense

(9) In most countries, foreigners working without a proper visa are (   ) if they are discovered. However, sending them home can cost a lot of money.

1 mended   **2** deported   **3** perceived   **4** distributed

(10) Tim is worried that he is spending too much time using his smartphone. He feels a strong (   ) to check his e-mail every few minutes.

1 suspension   **2** extension   **3** seclusion   **4** compulsion

(11) *A:* Did you make a New Year's (   ) this year, Serena?
   B: Yes, I decided to start eating healthy snacks instead of sweets between meals. It's been difficult to keep away from the chocolate and candy, though.

1 astonishment   **2** resolution
3 vulnerability   **4** repression

(12) Miranda noticed that the amount of money in her savings account was (   ), so she decided to start spending less every month.

1 grazing   **2** dwindling   **3** browsing   **4** rebounding

(13) The girl was scared of high places, so she (　　　) her father's hand. She held it tightly as they looked out the window from the top of the tower.

1 harassed　　**2** breached　　**3** drained　　**4** gripped

(14) Akiko could not help but be (　　　) when she saw her colleagues having a quiet conversation. She moved closer to them to hear what they were talking about.

1 obedient　　**2** flexible　　**3** sinful　　**4** nosy

(15) Due to the snowstorm, the climbers were unable to reach the mountain's (　　　). They had to turn around just a few hundred meters from the top.

1 subsidy　　**2** mirage　　**3** summit　　**4** crutch

(16) When Jonathan started at his company, he was often (　　　) all day. However, after a few months, he took on more tasks and now has little free time.

1 idle　　**2** agile　　**3** sane　　**4** needy

(17) *A:* Guess what? I've got an interview for that job as a TV announcer!

B: That's great, but don't be too (　　　) just yet. There'll be a lot of competition for that position.

1 courteous　　**2** optimistic　　**3** suspicious　　**4** flustered

(18) During her commute, Josie found the noise from the earphones of the train passenger next to her so (　　　) that she decided to move to another seat.

1 bothersome　　**2** compelling　　**3** flattering　　**4** daring

(19) *A:* I couldn't believe how crowded this year's summer parade was.

B: I know! There were so many (　　　) in the streets I could barely move.

1 patriots　　**2** spectators　　**3** mimics　　**4** executives

(20) Joseph was not sure if he could afford a taxi home from work, but after checking his wallet, he found that he had (　　) money for the ride.

1 ample　　　　**2** regal　　　　**3** vain　　　　**4** crafty

(21) (　　) involvement has been shown to enhance student performance in school. One example is helping children with schoolwork at home.

1 Obsolete　　**2** Numb　　　**3** Parental　　**4** Infamous

(22) Over the past few decades, many species have nearly been (　　) by pollution. However, recent conservation efforts are helping some of them to recover.

1 wiped out　　**2** broken up　　**3** fixed up　　**4** turned down

(23) Dave was happy when his neighbor gave him a basket of fresh vegetables, but when he got home, he realized he did not know how to (　　) cooking them.

1 go about　　**2** pull out　　**3** take in　　　**4** bring down

(24) *A:* Our company allows employees to wear comfortable clothes, as long as they don't look too unprofessional.
　　B: That's new for me. Wearing casual clothes was (　　) at my last job.

1 frowned upon　　　　　**2** carried on
3 entered into　　　　　**4** crossed off

(25) The regional manager visited the small branch office last week and (　　) a few meetings to observe how things were going there.

1 went back on　　　　　**2** sat in on
3 spoke down to　　　　　**4** looked up to

2 Read each passage and choose the best word or phrase from among the four choices for each blank. Then, on your answer sheet, find the number of the question and mark your answer.

The Documentary Boom

In recent years, the growth of TV streaming services has created a huge new market for documentaries. The number of documentaries being made has skyrocketed, providing welcome new opportunities for filmmakers, but there are also negative aspects. One issue is that many filmmakers feel they are (**26**). Some documentaries have attracted huge audiences and brought tremendous financial returns, so companies that operate streaming services have become more generous with their production budgets. With so much money involved, the intense pressure often makes filmmakers feel as though they have no choice but to alter the stories they tell to give them greater commercial appeal.

This has led to concerns regarding the (**27**) documentaries. While documentaries used to be considered a form of investigative journalism, there has been a noticeable shift in their subject matter. As the popularity of genres such as true crime has increased, the line between factual information and entertainment has become blurred. Documentaries, which were once devoted to informing viewers and raising awareness of problems in society, are too frequently becoming sensationalist entertainment designed primarily to shock or excite viewers.

Another worrying trend for filmmakers is the rise of celebrity documentaries. In the past, filmmakers generally followed the journalistic tradition of not paying ordinary subjects of documentaries for fear that doing so would encourage people to exaggerate or tell outright lies. Famous people, such as musicians, however, are now paid millions of dollars for their stories — often because such stars are guaranteed to attract viewers. (**28**), noncelebrities are also starting to demand compensation, which is creating a moral dilemma for filmmakers.

(26) **1** still being ignored
     2 not being paid enough
     3 losing control over content
     4 in need of large budgets

(27) **1** way people interpret
     2 people who appear in
     3 growing costs of creating
     4 decreasing social value of

(28) **1** Above all
     2 Understandably
     3 In contrast
     4 Nevertheless

Anting

The field of ethology involves studying animals in their natural habitats to understand their behavior. Drawing conclusions about the reasons behind what animals do, however, is not always easy. Certain birds, for example, display a behavior called "anting." This usually involves a bird picking up some ants with its beak and rubbing them on its feathers. (29   ), birds have even been observed sitting on anthills with their wings spread out and allowing ants to crawl all over their bodies. Despite extensive observation, ethologists remain unsure why birds engage in this behavior.

One popular theory is that (30   ). Ants naturally produce a substance called formic acid that protects them against bacteria and fungi, and which is also toxic to other insects. If this substance is rubbed onto a bird's feathers, it could help inhibit disease and deter harmful pests. While birds commonly use ants, some have been seen picking up certain beetles and millipedes instead. The fact that these organisms also produce chemicals that keep harmful pests away provides support for this theory.

Another proposed idea is that rubbing ants on a bird's feathers (31   ). In an experiment, scientists discovered that some birds were more likely to consume ants that had their formic acid removed by the scientists than ants that retained the chemical. The formic acid is stored in a sac located next to an ant's nutrient-rich abdomen. Anting, some scientists suspect, may cause ants to release their formic acid without birds having to try to remove the sacs with their beaks — a process that could damage the area of ants that makes them such an appealing snack.

(29) 1 In other words
2 For one thing
3 Similarly
4 Consequently

(30) 1 the ants eat organisms that harm the birds
2 the behavior contributes to birds' health
3 the behavior helps control ant populations
4 the birds are trying to attract other insects

(31) 1 helps remove damaged feathers
2 transfers nutrients to the ants
3 increases the bird's appetite
4 prepares the ants to be eaten

The Development of Colleges in the United States

Selling land is a common way to increase wealth, but for rural landowners in the United States during the nineteenth century, this was not always easy. Rural populations at the time were small, so landowners needed ways to attract buyers. One method was to keep prices low, but landowners also turned to another strategy: building colleges. Doing this made the land in their area more desirable, as colleges were centers of culture and learning. Colleges were built at an incredibly rapid pace, and by 1880, there were five times more colleges in the United States than there were in Europe.

With the exception of a few older, elite institutions, most US colleges only had a small number of students and instructors. Rather than being scholars, the faculty members were often religious men representing the different branches of Christianity that existed in the United States at the time. Administrators knew this would help to attract students from those religious organizations. Gaining admission to colleges was generally not difficult as long as students could pay the tuition, which, as a result of fierce competition to recruit students, was kept low. Unfortunately, low student numbers meant that many colleges were forced to close down, and those that survived could only continue operating through constant fundraising.

Demand for higher education, however, continued to increase along with the US population in the twentieth century. As the remaining colleges had well-established infrastructures, including land, buildings, and libraries, they were in a good position to accommodate this demand. Furthermore, they generally offered high-quality education and good sports and leisure facilities because one way they had survived was by being sensitive to students' needs. Another way the colleges ensured their futures was by maintaining close ties with their graduates, from whom they would receive generous donations. All of these factors have helped the US college system to transform itself into one of the most successful in the world.

(32) Why were so many colleges built in the United States in the nineteenth century?

1 Increasing levels of wealth in rural areas led to more families wanting their children to receive a college education.

2 Wealthy landowners built colleges as a way to improve their public image and ensure that they would be remembered after their death.

3 Europeans living in the United States wanted colleges that would provide the same level of education that was available in their home countries.

4 Building colleges was a way for people who owned land in rural areas to increase the value of their land and attract more buyers.

(33) What is true regarding many faculty members at US colleges in the nineteenth century?

1 They quit after a short time because of the poor conditions they were forced to work under.

2 Their salaries were usually paid by religious organizations rather than by the colleges themselves.

3 There was a high degree of competition among them to gain the best positions at the colleges.

4 Their religious backgrounds tended to be an effective way to get students to enroll at their colleges.

(34) One reason US colleges succeeded in the twentieth century was that they

1 formed partnerships with local sports teams to increase the quality of their physical education programs.

2 were able to increase their financial security by creating lasting relationships with their former students.

3 decreased the competition with other colleges by focusing on recruiting students mostly from their local areas.

4 kept their costs down by using facilities already available in the community instead of building their own.

Machine or Human?

In 2004, NASA's exploration rover Opportunity landed on Mars. The golf-cart-sized rover, which was nicknamed "Oppy," was sent to survey the planet and capture images of its surface. Oppy's mission was supposed to last 90 days, but the rover continued to beam pictures and data back to Earth for the next 15 years. During that time, it captured the public's imagination. In fact, people became so attached to Oppy that when it ceased to function, they sent messages of condolence over social media similar to those intended for a deceased person.

The act of giving human traits to nonhuman things, which is known as anthropomorphism, is something humans do naturally, even at a young age. It is not unusual, for example, for people of all ages to form emotional attachments to objects such as toys, cars, and homes. Even the engineers, who frequently referred to Oppy as "she" or thought of it as a child, were not immune to this tendency. One effect of projecting human qualities onto a nonliving object seems to be that this makes people feel protective of it and brings out concern for its well-being. NASA appears to have utilized this phenomenon to its advantage by deliberately making Oppy seem more human, designing it with eyelike camera lenses in a headlike structure that extended from its body. Prior to the Opportunity mission, well-publicized failures had weakened public confidence in NASA, and the agency's funding had been reduced. It has been suggested that giving Oppy human characteristics was an effective strategy to win over the public and perhaps even attract additional funding for NASA's mission.

While thinking of Oppy as a human may seem harmless, there can be unfortunate consequences to anthropomorphizing objects. Assuming AI works in the same way as the human brain, for example, may lead to unrealistic expectations of its capabilities, causing it to be used in situations where it is unable to provide significant benefits. Anthropomorphism can also make people apprehensive of nightmare scenarios, such as AI and machines rising up in rebellion against humans. This idea of machines as a threat arises from the misunderstanding that they reason in the same way as humans do. It appears, however, that people cannot help themselves from anthropomorphizing. As journalist Scott Simon writes, "if you spend a lot of time with a mechanism — talk to it, wait to hear from it and worry about it — even scientists begin to see personality in machinery."

(35) What do we learn about people's reactions to Oppy?

1 People immediately supported Oppy because they were interested in any new discoveries about Mars.

2 People found it difficult to relate to Oppy because little effort had been made to inform them about the significance of its mission.

3 People soon lost interest in Oppy's mission because the information Oppy sent back to Earth was too technical for nonscientists to understand.

4 People felt such an emotional connection to Oppy that they expressed sympathy for it when it stopped operating.

(36) According to the second paragraph, it seems likely that making Oppy appear more human was

1 a strategy designed to increase overall support for NASA's activities and to help it receive more money.

2 based on experiments in which children showed an increased interest in robots that looked like humans.

3 done because psychologists suggested that the strategy would make the engineers work harder to complete it on time.

4 the result of government pressure on NASA to make its designs more likely to be used in toys.

(37) According to the passage, what is a potential problem with anthropomorphism?

1 It can make people rely on machines to perform tasks that would be cheaper for humans to do themselves.

2 It can make people mistakenly assume that AI and machines do not need any guidance to perform tasks correctly.

3 The belief that AI and machines act in a similar way to humans can cause people to misunderstand what they are able to do.

4 The relationships scientists form with AI can cause them to prioritize its development over the needs of humans.

The Marian Reforms

Around the end of the second century BC, the Roman Republic faced the threat of an invasion by tribal peoples from Western Europe and experienced a series of humiliating defeats in Africa. Realizing that the Roman army was no longer able to meet the needs of the rapidly expanding republic, the Roman leader Gaius Marius set about implementing sweeping reforms. These became known as the Marian reforms, and they transformed the Roman army into a nearly unstoppable military machine that was arguably the most effective fighting force in ancient times. Traditionally, enlistment of soldiers into the Roman army had been on a temporary basis, which necessitated constant recruitment and inevitably led to new recruits often having no previous fighting experience. Furthermore, property ownership was required for entry into the army, and increasing poverty within the Roman Republic severely reduced the pool of potential recruits who could meet this requirement.

The Marian reforms consisted of several measures, including the removal of both property requirements and the need for recruits to prepare their own weapons and armor. This allowed even the poorest citizens to enlist and led to better-equipped soldiers because the army could standardize and improve the weapons and armor used. Soldiers in the army became known as "legionaries," and they were trained in military strategy. Perhaps most importantly, the reforms provided a crucial incentive for enlistment — any soldier who served for 16 years was compensated with a plot of farmland and full Roman citizenship. The rapid expansion of the Roman Republic meant there were many noncitizen inhabitants who lived in poverty and for whom an opportunity to escape their situation was hugely appealing.

The Roman army's better-trained and more highly motivated soldiers led to it achieving significant military triumphs that contributed to Rome's expansion. The land that former legionaries received was generally in newly conquered provinces, so these veterans were instrumental in spreading Roman culture. Their presence also made it easier to overcome local resistance to Roman rule and facilitated the process of integration into the Roman Republic. The mere presence of the veterans brought greater security to new territories, since they could assist in preventing rebellions and resisting invasions.

While the Marian reforms greatly improved the Roman army,

they also had an unexpected impact on Roman society that eventually led to the downfall of the republic. When the army was composed mostly of wealthy citizens enlisted on an as-needed basis, it had little influence on Roman politics. Following the Marian reforms, however, legionaries in the army became highly disciplined and developed an intense loyalty to their generals. In consequence, generals found it difficult to resist the temptation to use the forces under their command to gain political influence for themselves rather than to ensure the protection and expansion of the Roman Republic. This resulted in civil wars, and eventually, Julius Caesar successfully used the army to overthrow the elected government and declare himself the Roman leader. This marked the end of the relatively democratic Roman Republic and paved the way for the creation of a dictatorship ruled by all-powerful emperors.

(38) What was one reason for the Marian reforms?

    1 Financial problems within the Roman Republic meant a Roman leader had no choice but to reduce funding for the military.

    2 As the number of soldiers in the army increased, it became more difficult to transport them to Western Europe and Africa to defend the Roman Republic.

    3 Complaints arose among soldiers because they were forced to stay in the army for many years and received low pay for their service.

    4 A Roman leader was concerned that the army did not have the manpower or skills required to allow the Roman Republic to achieve its military goals.

(39) What was an important change that occurred because of the Marian reforms?

    1 A rule was introduced stating that only Roman citizens could join the Roman army, leading to more people trying to get Roman citizenship.

    2 Serving in the Roman army became more attractive because it was a way for people living in the Roman Republic to improve their lives.

3 The Roman army struggled to find enough recruits because it would only accept men who already had military experience.

4 The number of years that soldiers were required to spend in the Roman army was reduced, which lowered the average age of soldiers.

(40) According to the third paragraph, after the Roman army took over new territories,

1 the number of soldiers sent to those areas would be greatly increased to allow the army to attack neighboring regions and continue the expansion of the Roman Republic.

2 local people were invited to Rome's capital to learn the Roman language and culture so that they could quickly become accustomed to Roman society.

3 ex-soldiers were given land there, which made it much easier to control the local people and ensure that the areas could be defended from various threats.

4 the areas were often lost again quite quickly because it was impossible for the army to prevent the many rebellions that occurred.

(41) What effect did the Marian reforms have on Roman society?

1 The army was used as a political tool, creating a system in which a Roman leader gained his position by military power rather than by being chosen by the people.

2 The wealth and social standing of people who refused to serve in the army decreased, while former legionaries often obtained high government positions.

3 The Roman army became so large that the cost of maintaining it became a major cause of the fall of the Roman Republic.

4 The lack of discipline among the legionaries led to tension between Roman citizens and the army, which eventually resulted in civil wars.

4
- *Write an essay on the given TOPIC.*
- *Use TWO of the POINTS below to support your answer.*
- *Structure: introduction, main body, and conclusion*
- *Suggested length: 120–150 words*
- *Write your essay in the space provided on Side B of your answer sheet.*

Any writing outside the space will not be graded.

TOPIC

Should companies be required to produce goods that are easy to recycle?

POINTS

- Company profits
- Customer demand
- Pollution
- Product quality

リスニング

―――――――――― **Listening Test** ――――――――――

There are three parts to this listening test.

Part 1	Dialogues: 1 question each	Multiple-choice
Part 2	Passages: 2 questions each	Multiple-choice
Part 3	Real-Life: 1 question each	Multiple-choice

※**Listen carefully to the instructions.**

|||| Part 1 |||||||||||||||||||||||||||||||||||||||||||| ◀) ▶MP3 ▶アプリ ▶CD 1 **1**～**14**

No. 1
1 He cannot find his e-reader.
2 He does not want to buy e-books.
3 He has broken his e-reader.
4 He finds it hard to download e-books.

No. 2
1 Take private yoga classes.
2 Find a different activity.
3 Continue with his current class.
4 Join another yoga group.

No. 3
1 She has some new ideas for the division.
2 She knows little about publishing.
3 She was an excellent student.
4 She wants to increase staff salaries.

No. 4
1 She wants to help a family in need.
2 They no longer fit her well.
3 There is an event at her school.
4 She does not have storage space for them.

No. 5
1 It will help reduce his workload.
2 It will mean more work with independent agents.
3 It will make his company more successful.
4 It will lead to many staff being fired.

No. 6
1 They will become less expensive in the future.
2 They would not save the couple money.
3 They need to be replaced after a few years.
4 They do not have many environmental benefits.

No. 7
1 Miki has not completed her translation work.
2 The deadline is likely to change.
3 The client has made a number of mistakes.
4 Miki often does not work carefully enough.

No. 8
1 He found many online complaints.
2 The cost of the cruise has increased.
3 He cannot get time off from work.
4 He is unable to book another cruise.

No. 9
1 It has a lot of unique characters.
2 The show's writing has improved greatly.
3 The plot was hard to predict.
4 It may not be renewed for another season.

No. 10
1 He is busier than Yasuhiro.
2 He does not get along with Genevieve.
3 He often makes poor decisions.
4 He may not have enough experience.

No. 11
1 Her lectures tend to be long.
2 She gives too much homework.
3 Her political views are extreme.
4 She does not grade fairly.

No. 12
1 Search for solutions online.
2 Get help from a professional.
3 Ask their neighbors for advice.
4 Move to a quieter neighborhood.

(A)

No. 13

1 To improve the quality of their crops.
2 To give thanks for the food they grew.
3 To pray they could leave the desert.
4 To celebrate their time in Egypt.

No. 14

1 They have desert images on the walls.
2 They are covered to keep them cool.
3 Meals must be cooked in them.
4 People can see the sky from inside them.

(B)

No. 15

1 Vultures help stop them from affecting humans.
2 Vultures often spread them to other animals.
3 They can be deadly to vultures.
4 They survive in vultures' stomachs.

No. 16

1 Vultures' feeding habits help to reduce its effects.
2 It has increased vulture populations worldwide.
3 Vultures' food sources have changed because of it.
4 It has forced vultures to find new habitats.

(C)

No. 17

1 Workers often think they do not deserve praise.
2 Random praise can improve performance.
3 Too much praise can hurt performance.
4 Most bosses do not give enough praise.

No. 18

1 They tend to react negatively to praise.
2 They worry too much about their work.
3 They may benefit from having a growth mindset.
4 They affect the mindsets of workers around them.

(D)

No. 19
1 They believed an invasion would not happen.
2 They worried that the art would be destroyed.
3 They thought Canada was likely to be invaded.
4 They feared Germans would be able to steal the art.

No. 20
1 The importance of art during wartime.
2 A way to create larger mines.
3 The effects of low temperatures on paintings.
4 Ways of keeping art in good condition.

(E)

No. 21
1 To help warn about an attack.
2 To check the location of British soldiers.
3 To gather supplies for American troops.
4 To lead her father away from danger.

No. 22
1 There is evidence a different woman rode that night.
2 There are no records of an attack by the British army.
3 It was not officially documented.
4 A history book claims it did not happen.

(F)

No. 23
1 They had to relocate to more-populated areas.
2 They had to close due to unhappy customers.
3 They were not receiving enough snow.
4 They were opposed to using artificial snow.

No. 24
1 The use of artificial snow has hurt its business.
2 It makes use of the wind to help it operate.
3 It provides snow to other ski resorts in its local area.
4 Its slopes are at unusually high altitudes.

(G)

No. 25

Situation: You are staying at a hotel. It is 6:30 p.m. now, and you want to have dinner at a nearby restaurant around 7:00 p.m. The concierge tells you the following.

Question: Which restaurant should you choose?

1 Kingsley's.
2 Shrimp Lover.
3 Randy's.
4 Boca.

(H)

No. 26

Situation: You have decided to sell half of your collection of 500 music CDs. You call a shop that buys and sells used CDs and hear the following recorded message.

Question: What should you do?

1 Start the sales procedure online.
2 Begin packing your CDs into boxes.
3 Download a form from the website.
4 Make an appointment for an assessment.

(I)

No. 27

Situation: You are a college student. You want to learn about ancient Greeks and Romans and do not like group work. You are listening to an academic adviser's explanation.

Question: Which class should you take?

1 History 103.
2 Philosophy 105.
3 History 202.
4 Latin 102.

50

(J)

No. 28

Situation: The tablet computer you bought for your daughter two weeks ago has broken. It has a one-year warranty. You call the product manufacturer and hear the following recorded message.

Question: What should you do?

1 Press 1.
2 Press 2.
3 Press 3.
4 Press 4.

(K)

No. 29

Situation: You and your seven-year-old son are at a science museum. You want to take a tour. You must leave the museum in 45 minutes. You hear the following announcement.

Question: Which tour should you choose?

1 *Spark of Genius.*
2 *The Age of Dinos.*
3 *Deep into the Sea.*
4 *Museum after Dark.*

二次試験
面　接

問題カード（A日程）　◀》 ▶MP3 ▶アプリ ▶CD4 **1**～**5**

You have **one minute** to prepare.

This is a story about a couple who liked traveling.
You have **two minutes** to narrate the story.

Your story should begin with the following sentence:
One day, a couple was talking at a café.

Questions

No. 1   Please look at the fourth picture. If you were the woman, what would you be thinking?

No. 2   Will Japan continue to be a popular tourist destination in the future?

No. 3   Do you think employees in the service industry are treated well enough by their employers?

No. 4   Is people's quality of life these days better than it was in the past?

You have **one minute** to prepare.

This is a story about a couple whose son liked sports.
You have **two minutes** to narrate the story.

Your story should begin with the following sentence:
One day, a family was at home.

Questions

No. 1   Please look at the fourth picture. If you were the father, what would you be thinking?

No. 2   Should playing video games be considered a sport?

No. 3   Do you think parents should discuss important family issues with their children?

No. 4   Should the government provide more university scholarships for students?

2023-1

一次試験　2023.6.4実施
二次試験　A日程　2023.7.2実施
　　　　　C日程　2023.7.16実施

試験時間

筆記：90分
リスニング：約30分

Grade Pre-1

＊解答・解説は別冊p.49〜92にあります。
＊面接の流れは本書p.28にあります。

Pre 1

1 To complete each item, choose the best word or phrase from among the four choices. Then, on your answer sheet, find the number of the question and mark your answer.

(1) At first, Mick was (　　) by the idea of going to live abroad by himself. Once he did it, however, it was less difficult than he had feared.
1 pacified　　2 restored　　3 daunted　　4 tackled

(2) Students are advised to pace their studying throughout the semester instead of (　　) right before their exams.
1 cramming　　2 detaining　　3 swelling　　4 embracing

(3) The two candidates' tempers (　　) during the presidential debate. They angrily attacked each other's positions on issues throughout the night.
1 flared　　2 digested　　3 professed　　4 tumbled

(4) Many banks required government (　　) to stay in business after the stock market crash. The help mostly came in the form of large loans.
1 intervention　　　　　2 appreciation
3 accumulation　　　　　4 starvation

(5) Police must follow strict (　　) at a crime scene to make sure the evidence is not damaged or altered in any way.
1 tributes　　2 protocols　　3 reservoirs　　4 portions

(6) The umpire (　　) the two players for fighting. They were not allowed to play in the rest of the game.
1 slaughtered　　　　　2 administered
3 ejected　　　　　　　4 conceived

(7) Cats are known to be protective of their (　　　). They often attack other animals that they think could be a threat to their kittens.

1 prey **2** offspring **3** rituals **4** remains

(8) Fans of Greenville United were disappointed when the team's poor performance throughout the season led to its (　　) from the A-League to the B-League.

1 demotion **2** craving
3 aggravation **4** hassle

(9) Bibi loves hiking and playing sports, so she needs clothes that do not wear out too quickly. When she goes shopping, she generally buys clothing that is (　　　).

1 swift **2** aloof **3** shallow **4** durable

(10) Consumers should not (　　　) any personal information to callers claiming to be from the bank, as such calls are sometimes from criminals.

1 sway **2** detest
3 contemplate **4** disclose

(11) Because the tennis champion is unfriendly to other players and claims he is the greatest player who has ever lived, he is often criticized for his (　　　).

1 commodity **2** arrogance **3** neutrality **4** specimen

(12) Many readers found the author's novels (　　　). He was known for writing long, confusing sentences that had no clear meaning.

1 genuine **2** impending
3 subdued **4** incomprehensible

(13) "Class, I want you all to listen very (   )," the teacher said. "Much of what I will say is not in the textbook but will be on the test."

1 attentively   **2** consecutively
3 wearily   **4** eloquently

(14) The school is known for being at the (   ) of education. Its teachers use the newest teaching methods and the latest technology in the classroom.

1 forefront   **2** lapse   **3** doctrine   **4** myth

(15) The mayor used (   ) language in his speech because he thought it was extremely important that the citizens support his plan for public transportation.

1 forceful   **2** merciful   **3** futile   **4** tranquil

(16) When the pop singer died, she left her favorite charity a (   ) of over $10 million. "We are so grateful for her generosity," said a charity spokesperson.

1 rhyme   **2** justice   **3** legacy   **4** majority

(17) As they approached the top of the mountain, some of the hikers began to feel sick because of the low oxygen levels at the high (   ).

1 apparatus   **2** equation   **3** altitude   **4** mileage

(18) Ted lives on a (   ) income. He makes just enough to afford a small apartment, pay his bills, and occasionally go out for dinner.

1 blissful   **2** modest   **3** showy   **4** sturdy

(19) The carpenter was careful to choose a (　　　) piece of wood for the table. There would be problems if it did not have the same thickness throughout.

1 reckless　　**2** gaping　　**3** dreary　　**4** uniform

(20) Although Pieter was a private, quiet man who rarely showed his (　　　) for his children, they knew that he truly loved them.

1 affection　　**2** circulation　　**3** oppression　　**4** coalition

(21) Anton heard a strange (　　　) coming from his speakers, so he checked to make sure all the cables were properly connected.

1 buzz　　**2** peck　　**3** thorn　　**4** core

(22) Late last night, a man was caught trying to (　　　) a convenience store. The police forced him to drop his weapon and arrested him.

1 shrug off　　**2** sit out　　**3** run against　　**4** hold up

(23) Jill had always loved France, so when there was a chance to work in her company's Paris office, she (　　　) it. In fact, she was the first to apply.

1 plowed through　　　　**2** pulled on
3 threw off　　　　　　　**4** jumped at

(24) *A:* How's the class you signed up for going to (　　　) with your work schedule?

B: It's online, and I can study at my own pace. I can read the material when I get home from work, so it should be fine.

1 get over　　**2** fit in　　**3** hold onto　　**4** take after

(25) Before moving to her new section, Betty will (　　　) all of her current projects to the person who will be doing her job from now on.

1 beef up　　**2** bank on　　**3** hand over　　**4** slip by

Beyond Small Talk

Research indicates that the relationships people have can influence their well-being. Positive relationships not only lead to increased happiness but also have a beneficial effect on physical health. So far, most studies have focused on relationships with people we are close to, such as family members or friends. This makes sense, as when we have a problem or want to share our thoughts and opinions, we are most likely to talk to such people. (26), some recent studies have explored how we interact with strangers, and the results were rather surprising.

In one study, subjects were paired up with someone they had never met before, and each pair was asked to come up with a light discussion topic, such as the weather, and a more substantial one, such as their personal goals. At the beginning of the study, most subjects thought they would enjoy casual conversations more. After each conversation, the subjects were asked to rate it based on enjoyment and feeling of connection with their partners. The results showed that the (27). That is, most subjects reported having a more positive experience overall after discussing serious topics.

The study's results suggest that people would benefit from interacting on a deeper level with strangers. In fact, the subjects in the study generally expressed a desire to have meaningful conversations with people they did not know more often in their lives. However, they also thought that (28). The researchers believe that this assumption is incorrect, and that, for the most part, strangers are also interested in going beyond casual conversation.

(26) 1 In exchange
2 For instance
3 In contrast
4 In short

(27) 1 topics had made the subjects nervous
2 subjects' ratings did not always match
3 topic choices had been too varied
4 subjects' expectations had been wrong

(28) 1 communicating clearly would be difficult
2 other people did not share this desire
3 their family members would not approve
4 their privacy should come first

The Thing

After spending nearly a decade on a museum shelf in Chile, a mysterious fossil known as "The Thing" has finally been identified. Researchers now believe it is a 66-million-year-old soft-shelled egg and that it probably contained a mosasaur, a large aquatic reptile that existed around the same time as dinosaurs. Previous fossil evidence had suggested that mosasaurs (**29**   ). The researchers' findings challenge this idea, however, and the researchers say the fossil's size and the fact that it was discovered in an area where mosasaur fossils have been found support their conclusion.

Although the researchers are excited to have identified The Thing, it has opened a new debate. One theory suggests mosasaurs would have laid their eggs in open water, with the young hatching almost immediately. (**30**   ), some scientists believe the mosasaurs would have laid their eggs on the beach and buried them, much like some modern reptiles do. Further research, it is hoped, will reveal which of these is correct.

Another group of researchers from the United States has shed additional light on the eggs of prehistoric creatures after taking a closer look at previously discovered fossils of baby dinosaurs. It was believed that dinosaurs produced hard-shelled eggs, but the fossils on which this assumption was based represent a limited number of dinosaur species. Through their analysis, the US researchers discovered evidence that suggests the eggs of early dinosaurs were, in fact, soft-shelled. If true, this could explain why (**31**   ). Since softer materials break down easily, they are much less likely to be preserved in the fossil record.

(29) 1 were likely hunted by dinosaurs
2 relied on eggs for food
3 did not lay eggs
4 may not have existed with dinosaurs

(30) 1 Likewise
2 On the other hand
3 As a result
4 For example

(31) 1 few dinosaur eggs have been found
2 there are not more dinosaur species
3 some dinosaurs were unable to produce eggs
4 dinosaur babies often did not survive

The Chicken of Tomorrow

Before the 1940s, most chickens in the United States were raised on family farms, and the main emphasis was on egg production rather than obtaining meat. Poverty and food shortages were common at that time, so people wanted to maintain a regular source of protein without sacrificing their chickens. Additionally, there were a tremendous variety of chickens being raised, as farmers generally chose a breed based on how well it was adapted to the local conditions — whether it was suited to a dry or a humid climate, for example.

After World War II, however, the growing availability of meat such as pork and beef meant eggs could not compete as a source of protein. The US Department of Agriculture therefore set up an event called the Chicken of Tomorrow contest to find a type of chicken that could be raised economically and produced more meat. The overall winner, which was a combination of different breeds, grew faster and larger than other types, and it could adapt to various climates. Inspired by the contest, breeding companies began creating complicated mixtures of chicken varieties to guarantee a consistent supply of birds with these same desirable features. Since producing such genetic combinations was difficult, most farmers had no choice but to purchase young chickens from those companies rather than breeding them by themselves — a development that completely changed the industry.

The contest helped popularize the consumption of chicken meat, but this trend also had a dark side. It became more economical to raise massive numbers of chickens in large facilities where they were confined in small cages. Not only did this force numerous small farms out of business, but it also created conditions for the birds that, according to animal rights activists, caused the chickens stress and led to higher levels of sickness. While the contest made chicken a regular food item, some people questioned whether it was worth it.

(32) What is one thing that we learn about the US chicken industry before the 1940s?

1 The type of chicken raised on each farm usually depended on the climate in the area where the farm was located.

2 Each farm would raise more than one type of chicken in case there was a sudden change in environmental conditions.

3 Chickens were generally only eaten by very poor people or at times when there were food shortages.

4 Because there were so many chicken farms across the country, many of the eggs produced ended up being wasted.

(33) The US Department of Agriculture organized the Chicken of Tomorrow contest because

1 other types of meat, such as pork and beef, were becoming more expensive, so the American people wanted a cheaper alternative.

2 most chicken farms were focused on egg production, which led to a need to create a chicken that was more suitable for producing meat.

3 a large number of chicken farms in America went out of business, which severely decreased the availability of chicken meat.

4 the American people were tired of eating the same type of eggs for so long, so producers wanted a different type of chicken.

(34) What is one way that the contest affected the chicken industry?

1 Farmers learned that it was relatively easy to combine several types of chickens, which encouraged them to breed new varieties.

2 Although the number of small chicken farms increased across America, many of these were often poorly run and had cheap facilities.

3 It started a move toward keeping chickens in conditions that increased the birds' suffering and made them less healthy.

4 Farmers realized that improving their farming methods could help them to raise chickens that produced more and better-tasting meat.

Discipline in American Schools

For decades, methods of discipline used in American schools have been based on the theories of psychologist B. F. Skinner, who believed that systems of reward and punishment were the most effective methods of improving people's behavior. Commonly, students who break rules are given punishments, such as being prohibited from attending classes for a day or more or being made to stay in class after the school day ends. These are designed to teach the students to follow teachers' instructions and respect classmates. Recent psychological studies, however, have determined that as effective as punishment may be in bringing peace to the classroom temporarily, it can intensify the very behavior it is intended to correct when used continually over an extended period of time.

Many experts now believe that in order for children to learn to behave appropriately, it is essential that they develop self-control. When students are punished to make them obey the rules, they are being forced to adopt good behavior through external pressure. Self-control, on the other hand, comes from internal motivation, self-confidence, and the ability to be tolerant of others, and using punishment as a substitute for these things can actually delay or prevent their development. Similarly, the use of rewards such as stickers leads to students merely attempting to please the teacher rather than understanding the importance of gaining knowledge and social skills that will help them throughout their lives.

In recent years, an increasing amount of research has been backing up these ideas. A region of the brain known as the prefrontal cortex helps us to concentrate on tasks and is responsible for self-discipline and allowing us to consider the consequences of our actions. Research suggests that the prefrontal cortex may be less developed in students with behavioral problems. Fortunately, though, there is evidence that repeated experiences can alter the brain's structure, which suggests that it is also possible to influence the development of the prefrontal cortex. Child-behavior expert Ross

Greene believes that when educators change their attitudes so that they actually listen to students' feelings about their bad behavior and encourage them to come up with solutions to the issues they face, this can have a physical effect on the prefrontal cortex. Greene has designed a highly successful program that has greatly reduced behavioral problems at many schools, and as a result of the extensive media coverage his ideas have received in recent years, they are being adopted by more and more educators.

(35) What has psychological research shown about the use of punishment in schools?

1 It is only likely to be effective when it is used together with rewards in order to reduce its negative effects.
2 Though it may succeed in producing better behavior in the short term, it can actually be harmful in the long term.
3 There are various new types of punishment that are far more effective than physical punishment.
4 Using some form of punishment is necessary for forcing students to obey teachers and respect their classmates.

(36) According to the passage, what is one effect the use of rewards has on students?

1 It can teach them the advantages of hard work and make them better at focusing on their academic goals.
2 It causes them to want material things and makes them less aware of the need to behave in ways that are pleasing to other people.
3 It can prevent them from developing important skills that would be beneficial to them later in life.
4 It helps them to realize the importance of deciding their own goals rather than just doing what their teachers tell them to do.

(37) What does Ross Greene believe about children's brains?

1 Helping children solve their own problems can promote the

development of the part of the brain that controls behavior.

2 Since the brains of younger children function in a different way to those of older children, different methods of dealing with behavioral issues are necessary.

3 The region of the brain known as the prefrontal cortex may be less important in controlling children's behavior than some scientists believe it is.

4 Bad behavior does not only have a negative effect on children's academic performance but also permanently prevents the normal development of their brains.

Robert the Bruce and the Declaration of Arbroath

In 1286, the sudden death of King Alexander III of Scotland resulted in a power struggle among various nobles that nearly brought the country to civil war. To settle the matter, England's King Edward I was asked to select a new ruler from among the rivals. Edward, who himself had ambitions to ultimately rule Scotland, agreed only on the condition that the new leader pledged loyalty to him. He chose a noble named John Balliol as the new king, but resentment soon grew as England repeatedly exerted its authority over Scotland's affairs. The turning point came when Edward attempted to force Scotland to provide military assistance in England's conflict with France. When Balliol allied his nation with France instead, Edward invaded Scotland, defeated Balliol, and took the throne.

This was the situation faced by the Scottish noble Robert the Bruce as he attempted to free Scotland from English rule. Robert, whose father had been one of Balliol's rivals for the throne, gained political dominance and led a rebellion that drove English forces from Scotland. Robert was crowned king of Scotland in 1306, and although he enjoyed tremendous support domestically, he had angered the Pope, the leader of the Roman Catholic Church. Not only had he ignored the church's requests that he make peace with England, but he had also taken the life of his closest rival to the throne in a place of worship before being crowned king.

Scotland's leadership knew that the country would remain internationally isolated and vulnerable without the church's recognition. International acceptance of Scotland's independence would be especially important if the country were to exist in the shadow of a mighty nation like England, which still failed to officially acknowledge Robert as Scotland's king despite having retreated. In 1320, Scotland's most powerful nobles therefore gathered to create a document known today as the Declaration of Arbroath. It proclaimed Scotland's independence and requested the Pope recognize Robert as the country's ruler. The response the nobles received later in the year, however, indicated that the declaration initially had not been effective. The Pope not only refused Scotland's request but also failed to confirm its self-proclaimed independence, although he did urge England to pursue a peaceful resolution in its dealings with the nation. A few years later, however, the declaration's influence contributed to the Pope recognizing Robert and his kingdom after a peace treaty finally freed Scotland from England's threat.

Today, the Declaration of Arbroath is one of the most celebrated documents in Scottish history. Some historians even argue it inspired the US Declaration of Independence, although proof of this is lacking. Scholars generally agree, however, that what makes the Declaration of Arbroath so historic is the assertion that the king may rule only with the approval of the Scottish people; specifically, the nobles used the document to boldly insist on their right to remove any ruler who betrayed them. In this sense, the document was a pioneering example of a contract between a country's ruler and its people, in which the ruler was responsible for ensuring the people could live in a free society.

(38) What happened following the death of King Alexander III of Scotland?

1 Scotland was able to trick King Edward I into choosing John Balliol even though it was not in Edward's interest to do so.

2 King Edward I began to question the loyalty of the Scottish nobles who had not supported John Balliol's attempt to become king.

3 King Edward I attempted to use the situation to his advantage in order to increase his power over Scotland.

4 Scotland felt so threatened by France's military power that diplomatic relations between the countries worsened.

(39) What problem did Robert the Bruce face after he became king of Scotland?

    1 Although he was a great military leader, his lack of political skills led him to negotiate a poor agreement with England.

    2 The disagreements he had with his rivals about religion caused many Scottish people to stop supporting him.

    3 The religious differences between Scotland and England made it likely that Scotland would be attacked again.

    4 Because of the things he had done to gain power, Scotland could not get the support it needed to be safe from England.

(40) In the year the Declaration of Arbroath was written,

    1 it became clear that the Pope considered it a priority to recognize Scotland's independence as a nation.

    2 the Pope attempted to encourage peace between England and Scotland despite not acknowledging either Robert or his country.

    3 the promise of peace between England and Scotland was endangered by Scotland's attempt to get help from the Pope.

    4 Scotland was able to achieve enough international recognition to get the Pope to admit that Robert was the country's true king.

(41) What is one common interpretation of the Declaration of Arbroath?

    1 It demonstrates that Robert was actually a much better leader than people had originally thought him to be.

    2 It brought a new way of looking at the duty that a country's ruler had to the people he or she was governing.

    3 It reveals that there was much more conflict between Scottish rulers and nobles at the time than scholars once believed.

    4 It suggested that a beneficial system of government was not possible with a king or queen ruling a country.

4

- *Write an essay on the given TOPIC.*
- *Use TWO of the POINTS below to support your answer.*
- *Structure: introduction, main body, and conclusion*
- *Suggested length: 120–150 words*
- *Write your essay in the space provided on Side B of your answer sheet.*

Any writing outside the space will not be graded.

TOPIC

Should businesses provide more online services?

POINTS

- Convenience
- Cost
- Jobs
- The environment

リスニング

───── **Listening Test** ─────

There are three parts to this listening test.

Part 1	Dialogues: 1 question each	Multiple-choice
Part 2	Passages: 2 questions each	Multiple-choice
Part 3	Real-Life: 1 question each	Multiple-choice

※**Listen carefully to the instructions.**

▓▓▓▓ **Part 1** ▓▓▓▓▓▓▓▓▓▓▓▓▓▓▓▓▓▓▓▓▓▓ ◀» ▶MP3 ▶アプリ ▶CD 1 **28**～**41**

No. 1
1 Visit her brother in the hospital.
2 Submit her assignment.
3 Ask her brother for help.
4 Choose a new assignment topic.

No. 2
1 Too much money is spent on education.
2 The budget is likely to be decreased soon.
3 The government is wasting money.
4 The media is unfair to the government.

No. 3
1 The man will become much busier.
2 The woman will need to attend more meetings.
3 The woman dislikes the people on the fourth floor.
4 The man did not want his new position.

No. 4
1 To give her a massage.
2 To pick up some food.
3 To give her a gift certificate.
4 To do some housework.

No. 5
1 Ask the shop to replace the printer.
2 Get the old printer fixed.
3 Try to get money back from the shop.
4 Visit the shop to check other models.

No. 6	1 His client canceled the deal.
	2 The contract needed to be revised.
	3 The lawyer made a serious mistake.
	4 He arrived late for an important meeting.

No. 7	1 His boss does not trust him.
	2 He has very tight deadlines.
	3 He lacks the skills required.
	4 His boss is not well organized.

No. 8	1 Get a new sofa right away.
	2 Buy a sofa online.
	3 Look for a sofa on sale.
	4 Repair their current sofa.

No. 9	1 Checking the weather news.
	2 Taking a trip to their cabin this weekend.
	3 Preparing emergency supplies.
	4 Going out for ice cream.

No. 10	1 She lacks enthusiasm for her job.
	2 She is going to be dismissed.
	3 She is unpopular with the clients.
	4 She needs to improve her computer skills.

No. 11	1 The man should try to sell them for a profit.
	2 They should be hung in an art gallery.
	3 The man should find out what they are worth.
	4 They should be displayed properly.

No. 12	1 He forgot to fill the water bottles.
	2 He did not tell her the water would be turned off.
	3 He lost the notices about the water pipe inspection.
	4 He damaged the water pipes.

(A)

No. 13
1 When each of the crops is planted is important.
2 They only grow in a small region of North America.
3 They have difficulty competing with weeds.
4 There needs to be space between the plants.

No. 14
1 Use more-modern growing techniques.
2 Find new plants that can be grown in the desert.
3 Teach others how to grow the Three Sisters.
4 Recover forgotten growing methods.

(B)

No. 15
1 They do not give enough thought to their children's safety.
2 They are often forced to set strict rules for their children.
3 They should spend more time with their children.
4 They are giving their children a variety of experiences.

No. 16
1 Set times when streets are closed to cars.
2 Remove parking lots from playgrounds.
3 Build new roads outside the center of cities.
4 Make cars safer by changing their design.

(C)

No. 17
1 They explain how the rain forest formed.
2 They show what early humans looked like.
3 They include creatures that have died out.
4 They were used in religious ceremonies.

No. 18
1 They do not need to be preserved.
2 They were probably made by Europeans.
3 They used to be much more detailed.
4 They are not thousands of years old.

(D)

No. 19

1 It was based on a popular movie.
2 It gave away many luxury items.
3 It had weekly comedy competitions.
4 It led many people to buy TV sets.

No. 20

1 Starting a charity to support Black performers.
2 Fighting racism in the TV industry.
3 The unique advertisements he produced.
4 His amazing dancing ability.

(E)

No. 21

1 It occurs more often when people are younger.
2 Previous research on it had involved mainly male subjects.
3 It became more common after the nineteenth century.
4 People often mistake it for other feelings.

No. 22

1 Exploring large public locations.
2 Viewing spaces that had exactly the same furniture.
3 Performing the same activity in different spaces.
4 Entering a space with a familiar layout.

(F)

No. 23

1 They traveled faster than other arrows.
2 They were effective against armor.
3 They were the longest type of arrow.
4 They were commonly made with steel.

No. 24

1 He forced men to practice using longbows.
2 He was an expert at shooting a longbow.
3 He was badly injured in a longbow attack.
4 He sold longbows to foreign armies.

(G)

No. 25

Situation: You need a bag to use during your upcoming business trip. You will also go hiking using the bag on your days off. A shop employee tells you the following.

Question: Which bag should you buy?

1 The Western.
2 The Dangerfield.
3 The Spartan.
4 The Winfield.

(H)

No. 26

Situation: You need to park your car near the airport for 16 days. You want the best price but are worried about your car being damaged. A friend tells you about options.

Question: Which parking lot should you use?

1 SKM Budget Parking.
2 The Vanier Plaza Hotel.
3 Nelson Street Skypark.
4 The Econolodge.

(I)

No. 27

Situation: Your air conditioner suddenly stopped working, and its blue light is flashing. You call customer support and hear the following recorded message.

Question: What should you do first?

1 Remove the air conditioner filter.
2 Open up the air conditioner panel.
3 Disconnect the air conditioner.
4 Arrange a service appointment.

(J)

No. 28

Situation: You want to order a back issue of a monthly science magazine. You are interested in genetics. You call the magazine publisher and are told the following.

Question: Which issue should you order?

1 The July issue.
2 The August issue.
3 The October issue.
4 The November issue.

(K)

No. 29

Situation: You bought five cans of Bentham Foods tuna fish at the supermarket on May 30. You hear the following announcement on TV. You have not eaten any of the tuna.

Question: What should you do?

1 Take the cans to the store you bought them at.
2 Call the Bentham Foods recall hotline.
3 Arrange to have the cans picked up.
4 Visit the Bentham Foods website for instructions.

You have **one minute** to prepare.

This is a story about a university student who lived with his family.
You have **two minutes** to narrate the story.

Your story should begin with the following sentence:
One day, a university student was watching TV with his mother and grandfather.

Questions

No. 1   Please look at the fourth picture. If you were the university student, what would you be thinking?

No. 2   Do you think parents should be stricter with their children?

No. 3   Can people trust the news that they see on TV these days?

No. 4   Will more people choose to work past retirement age in the future?

23
年度第1回

面接

You have **one minute** to prepare.

This is a story about a woman who worked at a dentist's office.
You have **two minutes** to narrate the story.

Your story should begin with the following sentence:

One day, a woman was working at the reception desk of a dentist's office.

Questions

No. 1   Please look at the fourth picture. If you were the woman, what would you be thinking?

No. 2   Do you think it is harder to raise children now than it was in the past?

No. 3   Do you think companies focus too much on making their products cheaper?

No. 4   Will the government be able to meet the needs of Japan's aging society?

2022-3

一次試験　2023.1.22実施
二次試験　A日程　2023.2.19実施
　　　　　C日程　2023.3.5実施

Grade Pre-1

試験時間

筆記：90分
リスニング：約30分

＊解答・解説は別冊p.93～136にあります。
＊面接の流れは本書p.28にあります。

Pre

1 To complete each item, choose the best word or phrase from among the four choices. Then, on your answer sheet, find the number of the question and mark your answer.

(1) Fernando has been (   ) to the success of the company, so everyone is worried about what will happen after he quits next month.

1 desperate   2 philosophical

3 inadequate   4 instrumental

(2) Some people feel the film was (   ). Although it did not win any awards, there are those who believe it was a great work of art.

1 overtaken   2 overridden   3 underfed   4 underrated

(3) More than 50 million people (   ) during World War II. That is more deaths than in any other war in history.

1 worshiped   2 perished   3 haunted   4 jeered

(4) Walt's restaurant serves dishes that were traditionally eaten by poor people in the countryside. He says (   ) were skilled at creating delicious meals from cheap ingredients.

1 correspondents   2 janitors

3 captives   4 peasants

(5) The discovery of a serious (   ) in the design plans for the new building caused the construction to be delayed by several months.

1 clog   2 boom   3 flaw   4 dump

(6) When it came time to deliver her presentation, Rachel found herself (   ) with fear. She simply stood in front of everyone, unable to speak.

1 trimmed   **2** teased   **3** paralyzed   **4** acquired

(7) Despite the fact that the two countries had once fought each other in a war, they now enjoy an (   ) relationship and are, in fact, allies.

1 alleged   **2** amicable   **3** abusive   **4** adhesive

(8) Tina's new goal is to get healthy. In addition to including more vegetables in her diet, she has decided to (   ) an exercise program into her daily routine.

1 commemorate   **2** alienate
3 liberate   **4** incorporate

(9) Some historians believe the (   ) of dogs occurred over 10,000 years ago. They have been kept as pets and used to work on farms ever since.

1 elevation   **2** domestication
3 deception   **4** verification

(10) Oscar is well-known for his friendly personality and good manners. Every morning, he (   ) greets everyone in the office as he walks toward his desk.

1 scarcely   **2** courteously
3 tediously   **4** obnoxiously

(11) The plan for a new library was put on hold because of a lack of funds. A few years later, however, the plan was (   ), and construction work started.

1 deprived   **2** revived   **3** obstructed   **4** agitated

(12) Maggie's grandmother has recently become very (   ). She now needs help to walk and cannot climb stairs by herself.
1 poetic   2 savage   3 frail   4 rash

(13) The novelist likes to work in (   ). She says she can only write well when she is in her country house, which is located in an area with no people around.
1 solitude   2 corruption   3 excess   4 consent

(14) Archaeologists found many (   ), including pieces of jewelry and pottery, while digging at the ancient burial ground. These will be given to the local history museum.
1 setbacks   2 artifacts   3 pledges   4 salutes

(15) With faster Internet connections and better computers, more information can be (   ) at high speed than ever before.
1 transmitted   2 rejoiced   3 nauseated   4 offended

(16) Maria criticized her brother and called him (   ) after she learned that he had lost all of his money gambling.
1 pathetic   2 analytical   3 dedicated   4 ceaseless

(17) The architect was famous for designing buildings in a (   ) style. He wanted his designs to reflect current social and cultural trends.
1 preceding   2 simultaneous
3 plentiful   4 contemporary

(18) A lack of media (   ) left the town uninformed about the chemical leak. The media only started reporting about the incident once the leak was out of control.
1 enrollment   2 coverage   3 assortment   4 leverage

(19) After years of spending more money than taxes brought in, the government now has a (   ) of trillions of dollars.
1 fatigue   **2** petition   **3** deficit   **4** conspiracy

(20) The artist made a living by (   ) detailed figures out of stone. In order to cut such a hard substance, she used a number of special tools.
1 carving   **2** luring   **3** soothing   **4** ranking

(21) Ruth watched from the bench as her team ran up and down the court. Unfortunately, a shoulder injury had forced her to (   ) from the game.
1 withdraw   **2** bypass   **3** upgrade   **4** overload

(22) Jocelyn could see the storm (   ) from the west. The skies began to darken, and the wind gradually grew stronger.
1 rolling in   **2** adding up
3 holding out   **4** passing down

(23) The company suffered from five years of decreasing sales until it finally (   ). It closed its doors forever last week.
1 dialed up   **2** went under
3 came along   **4** pulled through

(24) The print on the contract was so small that Gus needed a magnifying glass to (   ) the words.
1 make out   **2** tune up   **3** draw up   **4** blow out

(25) The cat was (   ) her newborn kittens. She became nervous whenever anyone stepped too close to them.
1 packing up   **2** looking into
3 watching over   **4** showing up

Read each passage and choose the best word or phrase from among the four choices for each blank. Then, on your answer sheet, find the number of the question and mark your answer.

California Chinatown

In the late nineteenth century, Chinese immigrants to the United States faced significant discrimination from White Americans when looking for employment and accommodation. (26   ), they tended to live in neighborhoods known as Chinatowns, where there were better opportunities to find jobs and housing. One of the largest Chinatowns was in the city of San Jose, California, but because it was destroyed in a fire in 1887, little has been known about the lives of its inhabitants.

It was long assumed that the food items supplied to San Jose's Chinatown originated in Hong Kong and China. Recently, however, archaeologists' analysis of fish bones at a former trash pit has provided evidence that (27   ). These particular bones stood out because they belonged to a species known as the giant snakehead. Since the fish is native not to China or Hong Kong but rather to Southeast Asian nations, archaeologists believe it was transported to Hong Kong after being caught elsewhere, then shipped to the United States for consumption.

While the discovery offers insight into the complexity of the trade networks that supplied San Jose's Chinatown, other discoveries at the site have revealed information about the lifestyles of the neighborhood's immigrant residents. For example, it seems residents (28   ). While the presence of cow remains suggests residents had adopted the Western habit of eating beef, pig bones were the most common type of animal remains archaeologists discovered. As pork was a staple of the diets in their home country, the bones indicate the custom of raising and consuming pigs continued among the immigrants.

(26)　**1**　Consequently
　　　2　Despite this
　　　3　Similarly
　　　4　In contrast

(27)　**1**　has led to more mystery
　　　2　many foods were of poor quality
　　　3　this was not always the case
　　　4　not all shipments arrived safely

(28)　**1**　were more divided than previously thought
　　　2　often sent packages to China
　　　3　struggled to obtain enough food
　　　4　maintained some of their food traditions

Plant Plan

Most flowering plants rely on insects for pollination. When an insect makes contact with a flower, it gets pollen on its body. Then, when the insect moves around on the plant or visits another plant of the same species, this pollen comes into contact with the female part of that plant. This pollination process allows plant reproduction to occur. (29   ), the plants usually provide something the insect needs, such as a meal of nectar.

Flowering plants succeed in attracting pollinating insects in various ways. For example, some plants draw the attention of flies with the use of brightly colored petals. Researchers recently found that one plant, *Aristolochia microstoma*, attracts flies by smelling like the dead beetles that some flies lay eggs in. But the plant does more than simply (30   ). It temporarily traps them within its flowers; as a fly moves around inside, the pollen on its body spreads onto the plant. The plant also ensures its own pollen gets onto the fly's body so that the insect can pollinate another plant after being released.

The researchers found the plant actually releases the same chemical that gives dead beetles their smell. Because this chemical is rarely found in plants, the researchers believe the plant has evolved specifically to target flies that use dead beetles as egg-laying sites. They also say that (31   ). This comes from the fact that the plant's flowers are located among dead leaves and rocks on the ground — exactly where the flies usually search for dead beetles.

(29) 1 Rather
     2 In short
     3 Nonetheless
     4 In exchange

(30) 1 collect dead insects
     2 hide its smell from insects
     3 trick the flies with its smell
     4 provide a safe place for flies

(31) 1 there is further support for this theory
     2 the chemical has another purpose
     3 the plant is an important food source
     4 many insects see the plant as a danger

Fences and Ecosystems

Fences help to divide property and provide security, among other things. They can also affect ecosystems. A study in the journal *BioScience* concluded that fences create both "winners" and "losers" among animal species in the regions in which they are placed. According to the study, generalist species — those that can consume a variety of foods and can survive in multiple habitats — have little problem with physical boundaries. On the other hand, specialist species, which require unique conditions to survive, suffer from being cut off from a particular food source or geographical area. Because specialist species outnumber generalist species, the study found that for every winner, there are multiple losers.

The impact of fences is not limited to ecosystems. In the mid-twentieth century, Botswana in Southern Africa erected fences to address international regulations designed to prevent the spread of a disease affecting cattle. While the fences have helped protect cattle, they have prevented the seasonal movements of animals such as wildebeests and blocked their access to water. The resulting decline in wildebeest populations threatens not only the ecosystem but also the region's wildlife tourism. The government's continued reliance on fences has led to concerns that limiting animal migration will hurt wildlife tourism, which is valuable to Botswana's economy.

The negative ecological effects of fences can be limited by making changes to them to allow certain animals through. Nevertheless, the study's authors believe a more fundamental change is necessary. Eliminating all fences, they say, is not a realistic option; instead, fence planning should be carried out with an eye on the big picture. For example, fences are often constructed to obtain short-term results and then removed, but researchers have found that months — or even years — later, some animals continue to behave as if the fences are still there. Consideration should therefore be given to all aspects of fence design and location to ensure a minimal impact on ecosystems.

(32) The study introduced in the first paragraph showed that

1 fences that cross through more than one type of habitat benefit animals more than those built within a single habitat.

2 although fences create many problems, they have less of an effect on the ability of animal populations to survive than previously thought.

3 fences are effective at protecting some species from other harmful species that tend to use up the resources many animals need to survive.

4 although fences are not harmful to some species, they can have serious negative effects on a large number of animals.

(33) What is true with regard to the fences that were built in Botswana?

1 The changes that they caused in the migration patterns of animals resulted in the spread of disease among cattle.

2 They could be responsible for indirectly affecting an industry that is important to the country's economy.

3 They are considered necessary in order to increase the safety of tourists who visit the country to see wildlife.

4 The success they have had in reducing disease-spreading species has benefited ecosystems in unexpected ways.

(34) What is one reason that careful planning is necessary when constructing fences?

1 Changing the design of a fence after it has been built can actually cause more problems than building a new one.

2 It is possible that fences will continue to have an effect on animals in an area even after the fences have been removed.

3 Putting up multiple fences in a given area without a clear plan beforehand has not stopped animals from entering dangerous areas.

4 The number of animal species that make use of fences to protect themselves from predators has increased.

The Soccer War

In July 1969, there was a short yet intense war between the Central American countries of El Salvador and Honduras following a series of World Cup qualifying soccer matches they played against each other. Although the conflict is often called the "Soccer War," its causes went far beyond sports.

Honduras is much larger than El Salvador but is far less densely populated. Since the late 1800s, land in El Salvador had been controlled primarily by elite families, which meant there was little space for ordinary farmers. By the 1960s, around 300,000 Salvadorans had entered Honduras illegally to obtain cheap land or jobs. The Honduran government blamed the immigrants for its economic stresses and removed them from their lands, forcing them out of the country. Wealthy Salvadorans feared the negative economic effects of so many immigrants returning home and threatened to overthrow the Salvadoran president if military action was not taken against Honduras. This, combined with border disputes that had existed for many years, brought relations between the countries to a low point.

Tensions were raised further by the media of both countries, which made up or exaggerated stories that fueled their bitterness toward one another. The Salvadoran press accused the Honduran government of cruel and illegal treatment of Salvadoran immigrants, while the Honduran press reported that those same immigrants were committing serious crimes. Such reports were made at the request of the countries' governments: in El Salvador, the goal was to convince the public that military force against its neighbor was necessary, while in Honduras, the government wanted to gain public support for its decision to force Salvadoran immigrants out of the country.

The World Cup qualifying matches were happening at the same time as the migrant situation was intensifying. On the day of the last match, El Salvador accused Honduras of violence against Salvadorans and cut off relations, and within weeks, El Salvador's military attacked Honduras, beginning the war. Historians note that the term Soccer War was misleading. At the time, the United States was part of an alliance with Central American nations, but it chose to stay out of the war. In fact, according to an American diplomat, the inaccurate belief that a sporting event was behind the conflict led the US government to overlook its seriousness. Issues such as land ownership, which were the true origin of the conflict, remained unresolved. This led to continued political and social instability and, ultimately, a civil war in El Salvador in the following decades.

(35) According to the second paragraph, in what way were Salvadoran immigrants to Honduras a cause of the "Soccer War"?

    1 El Salvador's president believed the removal of the immigrants from their homes in Honduras was a sign that Honduras was going to attack.

    2 The Honduran government began sending poor Hondurans to seek land in El Salvador, causing upset Salvadoran farmers to move to Honduras in response.

    3 Rich Salvadorans pressured their government to make war against Honduras after the immigrants were forced out of their homes.

    4 The immigrants' constant movement back and forth between the countries created trouble for Honduran border officials.

(36) In the time before the start of the Soccer War, the media in each country

    1 attempted to pressure both governments to ensure that the Salvadoran immigrants received better treatment.

    2 were prevented by their governments from reporting on illegal acts that were being committed against citizens.

    3 put so much emphasis on the soccer rivalry that they failed to report more-important news about illegal acts.

    4 were asked by their governments to make up untrue or misleading news stories that made the other country look bad.

(37) What does the author of the passage suggest in the final paragraph?

    1 American diplomats still continue to worry that fighting will break out between Honduras and El Salvador again.

    2 The terrible effects of the Soccer War made Honduras and El Salvador realize that their actions leading up to the war were wrong.

3 A mistaken belief about the Soccer War meant that its real causes were not recognized, resulting in another conflict.

4 The US government's policies caused many Central American nations to cut off relations, making the conflict in the region worse.

Competing against Braille

Although Braille is the standard writing system for blind people today, this alphabet of raised dots representing letters was not always the only system. Another system, Boston Line Type, was created in the 1830s by Samuel Gridley Howe, a sighted instructor at a US school for blind people. Howe's system utilized the letters in the standard English alphabet used by sighted people, but they were raised so they could be felt by the fingers. Blind students, however, found it more challenging to distinguish one letter from another than they did with Braille. Nevertheless, Howe believed that the fact that reading materials could be shared by both blind and sighted readers outweighed this disadvantage. His system, he argued, would allow blind people to better integrate into society; he thought Braille encouraged isolation because it was unfamiliar to most sighted people.

It gradually became clear that a system using dots was not only easier for most blind people to read but also more practical, as the dots made writing relatively simple. Writing with Boston Line Type required a special printing press, but Braille required only simple, portable tools, and it could also be typed on a typewriter. Still, despite students' overwhelming preference for Braille, Boston Line Type remained in official use in schools for the blind because it allowed sighted instructors to teach without having to learn new sets of symbols. Even when Boston Line Type lost popularity, other systems continued to be introduced, leading to what became known as the "War of the Dots," a situation in which various writing systems competed to become the standard.

One of these, called New York Point, was similar to Braille in that it consisted of raised dots. Its main advantage was that typing it required only one hand. Braille, though, could more efficiently and clearly display capital letters and certain forms of punctuation. There were other candidates as well, and debates about which was superior soon became bitter. Blind people, meanwhile, were severely inconvenienced; books they could read were already in short supply, and the competing systems further limited their options, as learning a new system required great time and effort. At one national convention, a speaker reportedly summed up their frustrations by jokingly suggesting a violent response to the next person who invents a new system of printing for the blind.

The War of the Dots continued into the 1900s, with various groups battling for funding and recognition. In the end, the blind activist Helen Keller was extremely influential in ending the debate. She stated that New York Point's weaknesses in regard to capitalization and punctuation were extremely serious and that reading it was hard on her fingers. Braille won out, and other systems gradually disappeared. Although the War of the Dots interfered with blind people's education for a time, it had a silver lining: the intense battle stimulated the development of various technologies, such as new typewriters, that greatly enhanced blind people's literacy rates and ability to participate in modern society.

(38) What did Samuel Gridley Howe believe about Boston Line Type?

1 The time it saved blind people in reading made up for the fact that it took much longer to write than Braille.

2 The fact that it combined raised dots with other features made it easier for blind people to use it when communicating with one another.

3 Although it was difficult for students to learn, the fact that it could be read more quickly than Braille was a major advantage.

4 It was worth adopting because of the role it could play in helping blind people to better fit in with people who are able to see.

(39) In the second paragraph, what does the author of the passage suggest about Boston Line Type?

1 Its continued use was not in the best interests of blind people, whose opinions about which system should be used were seemingly not taken into account.

2 Teachers at schools for the blind convinced students not to use it because they thought systems with fewer dots would be easier for students to read.

3 Despite it causing the "War of the Dots," its popularity among students was a key factor in the development of other tools for blind people.

4 It was only successfully used in writing by students in schools for the blind after the introduction of the typewriter.

(40) The suggestion by the speaker at the national convention implies that blind people

1 felt that neither Braille nor the New York Point system could possibly meet the needs of blind readers.

2 were unhappy that the debates over which system to use were indirectly preventing them from accessing reading materials.

3 did not like that they were being forced to use a writing system that had not been developed by a blind person.

4 were starting to think that other types of education had become much more important than learning to read books.

(41) What conclusion does the author of the passage make about the War of the Dots?

1 It was so serious that it is still having a negative influence on the research and development of technology for the blind today.

2 It would have caused fewer bad feelings if Helen Keller had not decided that she should become involved in it.

3 It had some positive effects in the long term because the competition led to improvements in the lives of blind people.

4 It could have been avoided if people in those days had been more accepting of technologies like the typewriter.

4

- *Write an essay on the given TOPIC.*
- *Use TWO of the POINTS below to support your answer.*
- *Structure: introduction, main body, and conclusion*
- *Suggested length: 120–150 words*
- *Write your essay in the space provided on Side B of your answer sheet.*

Any writing outside the space will not be graded.

TOPIC

Agree or disagree: The government should do more to promote reusable products

POINTS

- Costs
- Effect on businesses
- Garbage
- Safety

22年度第3回

筆記

リスニング

―――――――― **Listening Test** ――――――――

There are three parts to this listening test.

Part 1	Dialogues: 1 question each	Multiple-choice
Part 2	Passages: 2 questions each	Multiple-choice
Part 3	Real-Life: 1 question each	Multiple-choice

※**Listen carefully to the instructions.**

‖‖‖‖ Part 1 ‖‖‖‖‖‖‖‖‖‖‖‖‖‖‖‖‖‖‖‖‖‖‖‖‖‖‖‖‖‖‖‖‖‖‖‖‖ ◀》 ▶MP3 ▶アプリ ▶CD 2 **1**～**14**

No. 1
1 Get the man to fill in for the receptionist.
2 Ask the man to fire the receptionist.
3 Do the receptionist's job herself.
4 Warn the receptionist about being late.

No. 2
1 He has to improve his class performance.
2 He cannot change his work schedule.
3 He will quit his part-time job.
4 He does not go to science class.

No. 3
1 He cannot pay his children's college fees.
2 He lives too far from his company.
3 He believes he is being underpaid.
4 He feels unable to leave his current job.

No. 4
1 She is frequently given new goals.
2 She is not paid enough for overtime work.
3 Her vacation request was denied.
4 Her report received negative feedback.

No. 5
1 She should complete her master's degree next year.
2 She should get some work experience.
3 She can rely on his help for one year.
4 She should save some money first.

No. 6	1 Review the website more carefully.
	2 Choose the same plan as the man.
	3 Request a meeting with personnel.
	4 Look for another insurance plan.

No. 7	1 He got stuck in heavy traffic.
	2 He had trouble with his car.
	3 He slept for too long.
	4 He got lost on the highway.

No. 8	1 Jason's teachers should make more effort.
	2 Jason should transfer to a private school.
	3 Jason's homework load has increased.
	4 Jason should be sent to a tutor.

No. 9	1 The man should return to his previous position.
	2 She will change her position soon.
	3 The man should spend more time at home.
	4 She would like to travel for work more.

No. 10	1 The station renovations are behind schedule.
	2 Her train was more crowded than usual.
	3 She had trouble changing trains.
	4 The station she always uses was closed.

No. 11	1 To keep her mind active.
	2 To improve her job skills.
	3 To take her mind off work.
	4 To get ideas for her fiction writing.

No. 12	1 He is an experienced mountain climber.
	2 He has not gotten much exercise recently.
	3 He wants to take a challenging trail.
	4 He dislikes riding in cable cars.

22年度第3回 リスニング

103

(A)

No. 13
1 To improve her failing health.
2 To show off her cycling technique.
3 To challenge a gender stereotype.
4 To test a new kind of bicycle.

No. 14
1 She helped companies to advertise their products.
2 She made and sold women's clothing.
3 She founded a spring water company.
4 She took jobs that were usually done by men.

(B)

No. 15
1 The images reminded them of Germany.
2 The images were made by professional artists.
3 The images were believed to bring good luck.
4 The images were painted on strips of fabric.

No. 16
1 More people have begun sewing as a hobby.
2 Tourism has increased in some areas.
3 Competition among farms has increased.
4 More barns have been built on farms.

(C)

No. 17
1 It lasted a little under a century.
2 It led to new discoveries about weather patterns.
3 It had the largest effect on people near volcanoes.
4 It had a global impact on farming.

No. 18
1 Europeans in North America started building large cities.
2 Forests expanded across the Americas.
3 The growing global population increased pollution.
4 Disease killed off many trees across Europe.

(D)

No. 19
1 The increase in noise caused by growing cities.
2 People's attempts to catch them.
3 The brightness of urban areas.
4 Growing competition with other insects.

No. 20
1 Locate fireflies that are not producing light.
2 Help them to get more funding for research.
3 Use a different type of light around their homes.
4 Make reports on any fireflies they see.

(E)

No. 21
1 To study dogs' understanding of words.
2 To study dogs' responses to different voices.
3 To study various ways of training dogs.
4 To study how dogs react to their owners' emotions.

No. 22
1 It was consistent with their owners' reports.
2 It varied depending on the breed of the dog.
3 It was opposite to that of human brains.
4 It increased in response to familiar commands.

(F)

No. 23
1 They help people to keep warm in winter.
2 They are useful for storing some vegetables.
3 Their name comes from their shape.
4 They are used to grow vegetables all year round.

No. 24
1 They help to support the local economy.
2 They provide a model for surrounding villages.
3 They help the fishing industry to survive.
4 They were found to contain valuable minerals.

(G)

No. 25

Situation: You have just landed at the airport. You need to get downtown as soon as possible. You are told the following at the information desk.

Question: How should you go downtown?

1 By bus.
2 By subway.
3 By taxi.
4 By light-rail.

(H)

No. 26

Situation: You speak some Italian but want to brush up before your vacation in Italy in three months. You are free on Mondays and Thursdays. A language-school representative tells you the following.

Question: Which course should you choose?

1 Martina's.
2 Giovanni's.
3 Teresa's.
4 Alfredo's.

(I)

No. 27

Situation: You have just arrived at a shopping mall to buy a new business suit. You want to save as much money as you can. You hear the following announcement.

Question: Which floor should you go to first?

1 The first floor.
2 The second floor.
3 The third floor.
4 The fourth floor.

(J)

Situation: You and your family are at a theme park. Your children are very interested in animals and nature. You hear the following announcement.

Question: Which attraction should you go to?

1 Lizard Encounter.
2 Discovery Drive.
3 Into the Sky.
4 Dream Fields.

(K)

Situation: You want your son to learn a new skill. He already takes swimming lessons after school on Wednesdays. A school administrator makes the following announcement.

Question: Who should you speak to?

1 Mr. Gilbert.
2 Ms. DeLuca.
3 Mr. Roth.
4 Ms. Santos.

22
年度第3回

リスニング

面 接

You have **one minute** to prepare.

This is a story about a president of a small company.
You have **two minutes** to narrate the story.

Your story should begin with the following sentence:
One day, a company president was walking around the office.

Questions

No. 1   Please look at the fourth picture. If you were the company
president, what would you be thinking?

No. 2   Do you think that salary is the most important factor when
choosing a career?

No. 3   Are people's opinions too easily influenced by the media?

No. 4   Should the government do more to protect workers' rights?

You have **one minute** to prepare.

This is a story about a girl who wanted to learn to skateboard.
You have **two minutes** to narrate the story.

Your story should begin with the following sentence:
One day, a girl was walking home from school.

110

Questions

No. 1 Please look at the fourth picture. If you were the girl, what would you be thinking?

No. 2 Is it important for parents to participate in their children's school life?

No. 3 Is playing sports a good way for young people to develop a strong character?

No. 4 Do you think international events such as the Olympics can improve relations between nations?

2022-2

一次試験　2022.10.9実施
二次試験　A日程　2022.11.6実施
　　　　　C日程　2022.11.23実施

Grade Pre-1

試験時間

筆記：90分
リスニング：約30分

＊解答・解説は別冊p.137〜180にありま
　す。
＊面接の流れは本書p.28にあります。

Pre
1

1 To complete each item, choose the best word or phrase from among the four choices. Then, on your answer sheet, find the number of the question and mark your answer.

(1) **A:** Mom, can you make hamburgers for dinner tonight?
B: Yes, but I'll have to take the meat out of the freezer and let it (   ) first.
1 reckon   **2** thaw   **3** stray   **4** shatter

(2) Jocelyn always reminded her son not to tell lies. She believed it was important to (   ) a strong sense of honesty in him.
1 remodel   **2** stumble   **3** overlap   **4** instill

(3) Zara was very angry with her boyfriend, but she forgave him after hearing his (   ) apology. She was sure that he really was sorry.
1 detectable   **2** earnest   **3** cumulative   **4** underlying

(4) At first, the Smiths enjoyed their backyard swimming pool, but keeping it clean became such a (   ) that they left it covered most of the time.
1 bureau   **2** nuisance   **3** sequel   **4** metaphor

(5) Throughout the course of history, many great thinkers were at first (   ) for their ideas before eventually being taken seriously.
1 saturated   **2** flattered   **3** ingested   **4** ridiculed

(6) At first, the little girl felt (   ) in front of the large audience at the speech contest, but after about a minute she began to feel more confident.
1 mortal   **2** bashful   **3** pious   **4** concise

(7) Typewriters are a ( ) of the past. They remind us how far technology has advanced since they were common in offices and homes.

1 jumble   **2** relic   **3** fraud   **4** treaty

(8) When the man approached the tiger's cage, the huge animal ( ) deeply. The man stepped back in fear at the terrifying sound.

1 sparkled   **2** leered   **3** disproved   **4** growled

(9) Police officers must promise to ( ) the law. This includes, of course, following the law themselves.

1 gravitate   **2** detach   **3** uphold   **4** eradicate

(10) All employees have a ( ) medical checkup every year. Companies are required by law to make sure all their workers do it.

1 gloomy   **2** compulsory   **3** reminiscent   **4** muddled

(11) Biology students must learn how cell ( ) works, as this process of a single cell splitting into two is commonly found in nature.

1 division   **2** appliance   **3** imposition   **4** longitude

(12) After the two companies ( ), several senior employees became unnecessary and lost their jobs.

1 merged   **2** posed   **3** conformed   **4** flocked

(13) In order to avoid becoming ( ) while exercising, one should always drink enough water. The longer the workout, the more water is necessary.

1 dehydrated   **2** eternal   **3** punctuated   **4** cautious

(14) Ken was always well behaved at home, so his mother was shocked when his teacher said he was one of the most ( ) students in his class.
1 momentary   **2** miniature   **3** disobedient   **4** invincible

(15) The police questioned ( ) at the scene of the crime, hoping someone who had been nearby had seen what happened.
1 bystanders   **2** reformers   **3** mourners   **4** pioneers

(16) Several generals attempted to ( ) the country's prime minister. However, they were unsuccessful, and he remains in power.
1 irrigate   **2** harmonize   **3** outpace   **4** overthrow

(17) Caleb finished a draft of his proposal, so he asked his manager to ( ) it. Unfortunately, she thought it still needed a lot of improvement.
1 scrub   **2** enchant   **3** prune   **4** evaluate

(18) American presidents Thomas Jefferson and John Adams exchanged letters with each other for over 50 years. This ( ) is an important part of American history.
1 matrimony   **2** federation
3 horizon   **4** correspondence

(19) During the riot, the town was in a state of ( ). People were out in the streets fighting and breaking windows, and many stores were robbed.
1 disclosure   **2** admittance   **3** attainment   **4** anarchy

(20) The flowers of some plants are actually ( ) and can be used to make salads both more delicious and more visually attractive.
1 stationary   **2** candid   **3** edible   **4** hideous

(21) No one was surprised when the famous scientist made many mistakes during his speech. He is (   ) for his poor speaking skills.

1 treacherous **2** momentous **3** flirtatious **4** notorious

(22) All of Brad's hard work and long hours (   ) when his boss gave him a promotion last month.

1 paid off **2** wrote back **3** chopped up **4** made over

(23) Since the CEO's speech was so vague, it took Gina a while to (   ) to the fact that the company was in serious financial trouble.

1 fill in **2** duck out **3** catch on **4** give up

(24) Each member of the team has a job to do for the new project, but the responsibility for coordinating all of their efforts (   ) the manager.

1 falls on   **2** squares with
3 drops by   **4** stacks up

(25) The employee tried to (   ) his theft from the company by destroying files and other evidence that proved his guilt.

1 tuck away **2** latch onto **3** cover up **4** doze off

2

Read each passage and choose the best word or phrase from among the four choices for each blank. Then, on your answer sheet, find the number of the question and mark your answer.

Nabta Playa's Stone Circle

Many prehistoric societies constructed stone circles. These were created for various reasons, such as tracking the sun's movement. The oldest such circle known to scientists can be found at Nabta Playa in Egypt. At around 7,000 years old, this circle predates England's Stonehenge — probably the world's best-known prehistoric stone circle — by more than 1,000 years. Nabta Playa's climate is extremely dry today, but this was not always the case. (26   ), heavy seasonal rainfall during the period when the circle was built led to the formation of temporary lakes, and these attracted cattle-grazing tribes to the area.

Nabta Playa's first settlers arrived around 10,000 years ago. Archaeologists have uncovered evidence that these settlers created a system of deep wells that gave them access to water year-round, and that they arranged their homes in straight rows and equipped them with storage spaces. They also practiced a religion that focused on the worship of cattle, which were central to their lives. These discoveries are evidence that the settlers (27   ).

Research findings show that some of the circle's stones would have lined up with the sun on the longest day of the year around 7,000 years ago. This suggests the circle was used as a calendar. One astrophysicist, however, believes the circle (28   ). He points out that the positions of other stones match those of stars in the constellation Orion at the time the circle was built. Because of this, he proposes that the circle was an astrological map showing the positions of stars in the night sky.

(26) **1** On the other hand
    2 In fact
    3 Despite this
    4 Similarly

(27) **1** questioned religious ideas
    2 lost interest in raising cattle
    3 experienced serious internal conflicts
    4 developed a sophisticated society

(28) **1** also had another purpose
    2 was created much earlier
    3 was originally built elsewhere
    4 caused people to avoid the area

The Good Roads Movement

Beginning in the late nineteenth century, the Good Roads Movement transformed America's landscape, helping to create the nation's system of roads and highways. This movement (29   ). While most people today assume that the road system was first developed in response to the needs of automobile drivers, this is a myth. Actually, the demand started mainly with cyclists. The invention of the modern bicycle led to a cycling craze in the 1890s, and millions of Americans wanted better, safer roads to cycle on.

Cyclists began pressuring local governments to improve the quality of roads, which were often poorly maintained and dangerous. At first, the movement was resisted by farmers, who did not want their tax dollars to be spent supporting the leisure activities of cyclists from cities. Gradually, however, farmers (30   ). One reason for this was an influential pamphlet called *The Gospel of Good Roads: A Letter to the American Farmer*. It convinced many farmers by emphasizing the benefits of roads, such as making it easier for them to transport their crops to markets.

As automobiles became common, the movement quickly gained momentum. (31   ), the invention of the Ford Model T in the early 1900s led to many new drivers, who were also eager for better roads. Millions of these affordable cars were sold, and the increase in drivers put pressure on governments to build more roads and improve the quality of existing ones.

(29) 1 was started by car manufacturers
2 had a surprising origin
3 created disagreement among drivers
4 angered many cyclists

(30) 1 increased their protests
2 started using different roads
3 began to change their minds
4 turned against cyclists

(31) 1 By contrast
2 In particular
3 Nonetheless
4 Therefore

22
年度第2回

筆記

Read each passage and choose the best answer from among the four choices for each question. Then, on your answer sheet, find the number of the question and mark your answer.

Recognizing Faces

Humans are generally very good at recognizing faces and quickly interpreting their expressions. This is achieved by having specific areas of the brain that specialize in processing facial features. The development of this ability makes sense in terms of evolution, since early humans would have needed to judge, for example, whether those around them were angry and therefore potentially dangerous. One unintended consequence, however, is that people often think they see faces on objects in their environment. People perceive these so-called false faces on a variety of objects, from clouds and tree trunks to pieces of food and electric sockets.

Researchers in Australia recently performed a study to learn more about how the brain processes false faces. Previous studies have revealed that for real faces, people's judgment of what emotion a face is expressing is affected by the faces they have just seen. Seeing a series of happy faces, for example, tends to make people assess the face they next see as expressing happiness. In the Australian study, the researchers showed participants a series of false faces that expressed a particular emotion. They found that, as with real faces, the participants' judgments of the emotions expressed by the false faces were affected by the ones they had just been shown. Based on this finding, the researchers concluded that the brain processes false faces in a way similar to how it processes real ones.

The researchers also noted that any object with features that even loosely resemble the layout of a human face — two eyes and a nose above a mouth — can trigger the brain to assess those features for emotional expression. In other words, the brain's criteria for recognizing a face are general rather than specific. The researchers say this is one reason the brain can assess facial expressions so quickly.

(32) In the first paragraph, why does the author of the passage mention objects such as clouds?

1 To support the idea that people's surroundings can affect how well they are able to judge the emotions of others.

2 To describe how people who cannot identify faces also have trouble identifying certain other objects.

3 To help explain that our reactions to everyday objects in our environment are controlled by different areas of the brain.

4 To provide examples of everyday things on which people imagine they can see faces.

(33) Previous studies have shown that

1 people's judgments about what emotions real faces are expressing are influenced by other real faces they have seen immediately before.

2 people attach emotional meaning to false faces more quickly than they do to real faces.

3 people tend to judge the emotions expressed by false faces as happier and more positive than those expressed by real faces.

4 people take longer to distinguish false faces when the faces are not expressing any emotions.

(34) What do the researchers in Australia say about the brain's ability to assess the emotions expressed by faces?

1 The ability will likely disappear over time as it no longer provides an advantage to humans in terms of survival.

2 The fact that the brain uses loose criteria to identify faces allows people to quickly judge the emotions faces express.

3 The brain is only able to accurately identify the emotions faces express if those faces have very specific features.

4 The evolution of this ability occurred even though it created disadvantages as well as benefits for humans in the past.

Durians and Giant Fruit Bats

The football-sized durian fruit is well known for its unpleasant smell and creamy, sweet flesh. Known as the "king of fruits," durians are believed to have originated in Borneo, but they are now cultivated more widely, with over half of all durians consumed worldwide being grown in Thailand. Durians have long been popular throughout Southeast Asia, but their popularity is now spreading to other parts of the world. There are hundreds of kinds of durians, but the Musang King variety, which is grown almost exclusively in Malaysia, is one of the most highly valued. Durians contain high levels of vitamins, so they are often promoted for their health benefits, which has led to rising exports. In fact, experts predict there will be a 50 percent increase in shipments from Malaysia to China alone during the next decade. In order to take advantage of this situation, many Malaysian farmers have stopped producing crops such as palm oil in favor of producing durians.

Durian trees are not easy to grow, however. They require regular watering and feeding with fertilizer, and they are highly sensitive to temperature. Furthermore, they do not naturally grow in groves, but rather thrive when grown among other trees and shrubs, so growing them in an orchard as a single crop presents a challenge. Ensuring sufficient pollination of the flowers for the trees to produce a good harvest of fruit is a further difficulty for farmers. One characteristic of durian trees is that their flowers only release pollen at night, so insects such as honeybees that feed during the day do not pollinate them. Animals that are active at night take over the role of pollination, but only about 25 percent of a durian tree's flowers ever get pollinated naturally. Because of this, many farmers resort to the labor-intensive practice of pollinating by hand.

Studies have shown that giant fruit bats are the main natural pollinators of durian flowers. However, these bats are chased away or killed by many farmers, who simply see them as pests because they cause damage and reduce profits by feeding on the fruit. The bats are also threatened as a result of being hunted and sold as food, since there is a belief in some Southeast Asian cultures that eating the bats' meat helps to cure breathing problems. Without educating people about the benefits of giant fruit bats, the bats' numbers may decline further, which could have serious consequences for durian farming.

(35) According to the first paragraph, what is true about durian production?

1 Durians are now mainly grown in Malaysia because there is no longer enough land available to cultivate them in other Southeast Asian countries.

2 Although durians have been selling well in places where they were traditionally grown, they have yet to gain popularity in other countries.

3 Premium varieties of durians have been criticized by consumers because they have no more nutritional value than cheaper varieties.

4 Because of the increasing demand for durians, Malaysian farmers are switching from growing other crops to growing durians.

(36) One factor that durian farmers need to consider is that

1 although durian trees can be grown in almost any warm climate, they do best in areas where there are few other plants growing.

2 the tendency of durian trees to push out other plants is causing a sharp decline in the number of native plants.

3 durian trees should be grown in a location where they can be easily found by honeybees and other daytime pollinators.

4 if durian trees are left alone to be pollinated naturally, the trees are unlikely to produce a large amount of fruit.

(37) What is one thing the author of the passage says regarding giant fruit bats?

1 Durian production might suffer if awareness is not raised about the important role giant fruit bats play in durian flower pollination.

2 Many people in Southeast Asia have become ill as a result of eating bat meat that was sold illegally at some markets.

3 Some durian farmers deliberately attract giant fruit bats to their orchards so that they can catch them and sell their meat.

4 There has been a significant drop in natural pollinators of durian flowers because many giant fruit bats have died from breathing problems.

The Long Range Desert Group

During World War II, the British fought against Germany and Italy in the deserts of North Africa. Desert warfare was characterized by small battles between troops that were widely spread out, and there was a need to move quickly and at night to avoid both detection and the dangerous daytime heat. The area's vast size and sandy terrain made transporting supplies difficult, and the lack of water severely limited operations.

However, for one British army officer, Major Ralph Bagnold, these harsh conditions presented a strategic opportunity. Having spent years exploring the North African desert before the war, Bagnold knew the terrain well, and he was convinced that a small, highly mobile motorized unit that could observe and track enemy forces would be invaluable. At first, British commanders rejected his proposal to form such a unit, believing airplanes were better suited for such long-range intelligence gathering. Bagnold insisted, however, that gathering information on the ground would be advantageous, and his persistence led to the formation of the Long Range Desert Group (LRDG), with Bagnold as commander, in June 1940.

The LRDG was an unconventional unit from the outset. Usual distinctions between ranks did not apply; officers and regular soldiers were on first-name terms, and they were all expected to perform the same tasks. Rather than seeking men who would fight bravely on the battlefield, Bagnold wanted individuals with great stamina, resourcefulness, and mental toughness — men who could, for example, remain motivated and alert for extended periods despite limited access to drinking water. With specialized trucks adapted to desert conditions, the LRDG's patrols were equipped to operate independently for around three weeks and over a range of more than 1,600 kilometers. All necessary items, such as fuel, ammunition, and food, were carried by the unit, so careful supply planning was extremely important.

The LRDG's work mainly involved traveling deep behind enemy lines to observe their movements. The unit had access to a range of weaponry, and while the men were primarily trained to gather intelligence, they also planted mines and launched attacks against enemy airfields and fuel depots. When the Special Air Service (SAS) — a British army unit formed in 1941 to conduct raids behind enemy lines — suffered heavy casualties after parachuting into enemy territory on its first mission, the LRDG was tasked with bringing back the survivors. The rescue mission was a success, and because of its men's extensive knowledge of the desert, the LRDG was given the responsibility of bringing the SAS to and from all future targets by land, providing both transportation and navigation. This almost certainly helped the SAS accomplish its raids with greater success and fewer casualties.

The LRDG's greatest achievement came in 1943, when the unit found a route that enabled British forces to get around heavily defended enemy lines without being detected, allowing them to attack at weaker points in the defenses. This was a crucial turning point in the campaign in North Africa and contributed greatly to the British victory there. The LRDG went on to make significant contributions to the war effort in Europe until 1945.

(38) Major Ralph Bagnold was able to convince British army commanders that

    1 their soldiers were having limited success on missions in the desert because they were not being supplied with the right resources.

    2 the airplanes being used to fly over enemy territory and make observations in the desert were in need of major improvements.

    3 he could lead a unit of men on missions in the desert despite the fact that he had little experience in such an environment.

    4 using a ground-based unit to gather information about enemy activities in the desert would be an effective strategy.

(39) What is true regarding the Long Range Desert Group (LRDG)?

    1 The characteristics of the men chosen for it and the way it operated were different from those of traditional military units.

    2 Because of its limited budget, it had to manage with fewer resources and older weapons than other units.

3 There were a large number of men in its patrols, so the officers had to have special training in management techniques.

4 The success of its missions was heavily dependent on the group having supplies sent to it behind enemy lines on a regular basis.

(40) Which of the following best describes the relationship between the LRDG and the Special Air Service (SAS)?

1 The two units were combined so that land and air raids could be performed at the same time.

2 The similar nature of their operations led to competition between the two units and their unwillingness to assist each other.

3 The LRDG used its knowledge of the desert to help the SAS improve both the effectiveness and safety of its missions.

4 The involvement of the SAS in LRDG missions made it more difficult for the LRDG to stay behind enemy lines for long periods of time.

(41) According to the author of the passage, what happened in 1943?

1 A mistake made by the LRDG allowed enemy forces to strengthen their hold on territory that the British hoped to gain.

2 The transfer of the LRDG to Europe meant the SAS had no choice but to attack enemy forces in a heavily defended area without LRDG support.

3 The activities of the LRDG made it possible for the British army to gain a significant advantage that led to it defeating enemy forces in the area.

4 British commanders decided the LRDG would be better put to use defending British-held territory than observing enemy activities.

4

- *Write an essay on the given TOPIC.*
- *Use TWO of the POINTS below to support your answer.*
- *Structure: introduction, main body, and conclusion*
- *Suggested length: 120–150 words*
- *Write your essay in the space provided on Side B of your answer sheet.*

Any writing outside the space will not be graded.

TOPIC

Should people trust information on the Internet?

POINTS

- Learning
- News
- Online shopping
- Social media

22
年度第2回
筆記

リスニング

―――――― **Listening Test** ――――――

There are three parts to this listening test.

Part 1	Dialogues: 1 question each	Multiple-choice
Part 2	Passages: 2 questions each	Multiple-choice
Part 3	Real-Life: 1 question each	Multiple-choice

※**Listen carefully to the instructions.**

░░░ Part 1 ░░░░░░░░░░░░░░░░░░ ◀» ▶MP3 ▶アプリ ▶CD 2 **28**〜**41**

No. 1
1 Get a blood test today.
2 Try to eat less for breakfast.
3 Go to lunch with Noah.
4 Have a medical checkup next week.

No. 2
1 She needs to take more time off.
2 She should be less concerned about money.
3 She is not ready for so much responsibility.
4 She deserves more pay.

No. 3
1 He needs to undergo further tests.
2 He will not be able to play in the game.
3 He needs to find a different form of exercise.
4 He has to stay at the hospital.

No. 4
1 Contact the new employee.
2 Speak to the manager.
3 Work the shift herself.
4 Change shifts with him.

No. 5
1 Contact the hotel about Internet access.
2 Confirm the meeting schedule.
3 Finish preparing the presentation.
4 Buy a ticket for the flight.

No. 6	1 Take a taxi home.
	2 Order more wine.
	3 Catch the last train home.
	4 Walk to the closest bus stop.
No. 7	1 Pick up the children from school.
	2 Cook dinner for his family.
	3 Buy the ingredients for tonight's dinner.
	4 Order food from a new restaurant.
No. 8	1 He has to pay an unexpected fee.
	2 He canceled his insurance policy.
	3 He is late for a meeting.
	4 The company cannot find his policy number.
No. 9	1 The man should not change his major.
	2 A career in communications might suit the man better.
	3 Graphic design is a good choice for the man.
	4 The man is not doing well in class.
No. 10	1 Find another online chat tool.
	2 Prepare a request for a software upgrade.
	3 Get more people to join online meetings.
	4 Ask to increase the company's budget.
No. 11	1 Go to the plant.
	2 Study Spanish.
	3 Meet with Barbara.
	4 Look for an interpreter.
No. 12	1 Radio for an ambulance.
	2 Move the woman's car for her.
	3 Give the woman a parking ticket.
	4 Wait in his police car.

(A)

No. 13
1 It could not fly high enough.
2 It was too small and light.
3 It could only fly short distances.
4 It used a rare kind of fuel.

No. 14
1 It was tougher than other planes.
2 It had a new kind of weapon.
3 It could land very quickly.
4 It could drop bombs accurately.

(B)

No. 15
1 Water supplies decreased.
2 The air became less polluted.
3 Many people had to leave the island.
4 The number of trees increased.

No. 16
1 How to classify the new ecosystem.
2 What to use the water supply for.
3 Whether native plants should be protected.
4 Where agriculture should be allowed.

(C)

No. 17
1 She carried her camera everywhere.
2 She made friends with emergency workers.
3 She lent her camera to the children she took care of.
4 She went to many places as a tourist.

No. 18
1 She became famous early in her career.
2 She mainly took photos at auctions.
3 She held very large exhibitions.
4 She did not show people her photos.

No. 19
1 It does not require the use of fresh water.
2 It can only be done in certain climates.
3 It produces a large amount of gas.
4 It uses less meat than it did in the past.

No. 20
1 The machines it uses are very expensive.
2 It is damaging to wide areas of land.
3 It releases chemicals into nearby farmland.
4 It is frequently dangerous for workers.

(E)

No. 21
1 Young people's changing interests.
2 Young people's increasing need for exercise.
3 Young people's economic situation.
4 Young people's passion for nature.

No. 22
1 They are unlikely to survive long.
2 They do not do well outside of cities.
3 They rarely employ local people.
4 They take up too much space.

(F)

No. 23
1 Alligators have efficient jaws.
2 Alligators are related to dinosaurs.
3 Alligators have muscles in unusual places.
4 Alligators evolved at the same time as *T. rex*.

No. 24
1 To help with food digestion.
2 To sense other animals.
3 To create new blood vessels.
4 To control their body temperature.

(G)

No. 25

Situation: You are on a plane that has just landed, and you need to catch your connecting flight. A flight attendant is making an announcement.

Question: What should you do first after getting off the plane?

1 Collect your luggage.
2 Take a bus to another terminal.
3 Find a gate agent.
4 Get a new boarding pass printed.

(H)

No. 26

Situation: You want to buy some stick-type incense to burn to help you relax. A store clerk tells you the following.

Question: Which incense brand should you buy?

1 Bouquet Himalaya.
2 Magnolia's Sanctuary.
3 Akebono.
4 Shirley's Gift.

(I)

No. 27

Situation: It is Monday, and you receive a voice mail from a representative at your new Internet provider. You have to work this Thursday from noon to 8 p.m.

Question: What should you do?

1 Reschedule for this weekend.
2 Reschedule for a weekday next week.
3 Reschedule for this Thursday morning.
4 Reschedule for this Friday after 6 p.m.

(J)

Situation: You are applying to a college to study psychology. An admissions officer is talking to you about your application.

Question: What should you do?

1 Pay your application fee.
2 Go to a campus event next week.
3 Get a letter of recommendation.
4 Submit your high school records.

(K)

Situation: You are on a trip abroad and want to take a free local tour. You get carsick easily. You are told the following at your hotel's information desk.

Question: Which tour is the best for you?

1 The one from 1 p.m.
2 The one from 2:30 p.m.
3 The one from 3 p.m.
4 The one from 5 p.m.

You have **one minute** to prepare.

This is a story about a couple that wanted to save money.
You have **two minutes** to narrate the story.

Your story should begin with the following sentence:
One day, a woman was talking with her husband.

Questions

No. 1   Please look at the fourth picture. If you were the woman, what would you be thinking?

No. 2   Do you think it is better to buy a home than to rent a place to live?

No. 3   Should Japan increase the amount of green space in its cities?

No. 4   Do people these days maintain a good balance between their private lives and their careers?

You have **one minute** to prepare.

This is a story about a couple who lived near the ocean.
You have **two minutes** to narrate the story.

Your story should begin with the following sentence:
One day, a couple was taking a walk by the beach.

Questions

No. 1   Please look at the fourth picture. If you were the husband, what would you be thinking?

No. 2   Do you think Japanese people should express their political opinions more?

No. 3   Do you think companies should do more to help society?

No. 4   Is it possible for the actions of individuals to help reduce global warming?

22
年度第2回

面接

2022-1

一次試験　2022.6.5実施
二次試験　A日程　2022.7.3実施
　　　　　C日程　2022.7.17実施

Grade Pre-1

試験時間

筆記：90分
リスニング：約30分

＊解答・解説は別冊p.181〜224にあります。
＊面接の流れは本書p.28にあります。

Pre

1 To complete each item, choose the best word or phrase from among the four choices. Then, on your answer sheet, find the number of the question and mark your answer.

---

(1) After considering the case, the judge decided to show (　　) and only gave the man a warning. She said that he was clearly very sorry for his crime.

1 disgrace　　**2** closure　　**3** mercy　　**4** seclusion

(2) Lisa looks exactly like her twin sister, but she has a completely different (　　). She is very calm and rarely gets angry, unlike her sister.

1 temperament　　　　**2** accumulation
3 veneer　　　　　　　**4** glossary

(3) *A:* Annabel, don't just (　　) your shoulders when I ask you if you've finished your homework. Give me a clear answer.
B: Sorry, Mom. I'm almost done with it.

1 echo　　**2** bow　　**3** dump　　**4** shrug

(4) When there is a big business convention in town, it is almost impossible to find a hotel with a (　　). Most hotels quickly get fully booked.

1 sprain　　**2** segment　　**3** transition　　**4** vacancy

(5) The detective (　　) the gang member for hours, but he would not say who had helped him commit the crime. Eventually, the detective stopped trying to get information from him.

1 discharged　　　　**2** converted
3 interrogated　　　　**4** affiliated

(6) To treat an injured ankle, doctors recommend (   ). This can be done by wrapping a bandage tightly around the injury.

1 depression   **2** progression   **3** compression   **4** suspicion

(7) *A:* It suddenly started raining heavily on my way home, and I got completely wet.

    B: You should have (   ) my advice and taken an umbrella with you.

1 molded   **2** heeded   **3** twisted   **4** yielded

(8) As a way of attracting more (   ) customers, the perfume company began advertising its products in magazines read mainly by wealthy people.

1 theatrical   **2** brutal   **3** frantic   **4** affluent

(9) The teacher said that, apart from a few (   ) errors, the student's essay was perfect. He gave it the highest score possible.

1 trivial   **2** conclusive   **3** palatial   **4** offensive

(10) The injured soccer player watched (   ) as his replacement played in the final game. He had really wanted to continue playing.

1 substantially **2** previously   **3** enviously   **4** relevantly

(11) The new hotel in front of Abraham's apartment building is not tall enough to (   ) his view of the mountains beyond the city. He can still see them clearly.

1 obstruct   **2** delegate   **3** entangle   **4** boost

(12) Having spilled red wine on the white carpet, Martha tried to remove the (   ) with soap and water. However, she could not remove it completely.

1 stain   **2** slit   **3** bump   **4** blaze

(13) The war continued for a year, but neither side could (   ). With victory seemingly impossible, the two countries agreed to stop fighting.

1 devise   **2** prevail   **3** evolve   **4** reconstruct

(14) The leader used the political instability in his country as a (   ) for introducing strict new laws aimed at preventing any opposition to his rule.

1 trance   **2** downfall   **3** rampage   **4** pretext

(15) The suspect continued to (   ) his innocence to the police. He told them repeatedly he had been nowhere near the place where the crime had occurred.

1 conceal   **2** counter   **3** expire   **4** assert

(16) Good writers make every effort to (   ) mistakes from their work, but occasionally they miss some errors and have to make corrections later.

1 eliminate   **2** expend   **3** stabilize   **4** oppress

(17) After the kidnappers returned the child to its parents in exchange for a large (   ), they tried to escape with the money. Police soon caught them, however, and returned the money to the couple.

1 ransom   **2** applause   **3** monopoly   **4** prank

(18) Gaspar applied to go to a (   ) university. Unfortunately, his grades were not good enough, so he had to go to a lesser-known one.

1 prestigious   **2** spontaneous   **3** cordial   **4** petty

(19) The spies (   ) themselves as army officers in an attempt to enter the military base without being noticed.

1 chronicled   **2** disguised   **3** rendered   **4** revitalized

(20) Timothy is a very ( ) employee. He is reliable and eager to help, and he always shows loyalty to his company and coworkers.

1 grotesque　　**2** defiant　　**3** devoted　　**4** feeble

(21) To help Paul lose weight, his doctor recommended that he ( ) his diet. Specifically, she suggested that he eat fewer fatty foods and more fiber.

1 modify　　**2** pluck　　**3** exclaim　　**4** distill

(22) *A:* I've been so busy at work, and now I have to ( ) training our newest employee.

　　B: That's too much. You should ask your boss if someone else can do it instead.

1 turn over　　　　　　　**2** contend with
3 prop up　　　　　　　　**4** count off

(23) The young boy tried to blame his dog for the broken vase. However, his mother did not ( ) the lie and sent him to his room.

1 fall for　　**2** hang on　　**3** see out　　**4** flag down

(24) In his speech, the CEO ( ) his plan for the company's development over the next five years. He hoped this would help guide everyone's work as the company grew.

1 mapped out　**2** leaped in　　**3** racked up　　**4** spaced out

(25) Last year, Harold spent all his money buying shares in various companies. He was ( ) the stock market performing well over the next few years.

1 casting away　　　　　　**2** putting down
3 stepping up　　　　　　　**4** betting on

Read each passage and choose the best word or phrase from among the four choices for each blank. Then, on your answer sheet, find the number of the question and mark your answer.

The Peter Principle

A theory known as the Peter Principle may explain why there are many people in managerial positions who (**26**). According to the theory, employees who perform well in lower-level positions will eventually rise to positions they are not prepared for. The reason for this is that employees generally get promoted based on how well they perform in their current positions. Although this kind of promotion policy may seem logical, failing to fully consider employees' strengths and weaknesses results in them eventually reaching positions for which their abilities are unsuited.

One study examined the careers of salespeople who were promoted to managerial positions. As expected, the study found that the best salespeople were the most likely to receive promotions, but it also found that they performed the worst in managerial roles. The study showed that promoting employees based solely on current performance (**27**). Not only do companies end up with poor managers but they also lose their best workers in lower-level positions.

The researchers who carried out the study say that one problem is that companies make the mistake of simply assuming that high-performing employees will naturally be good managers. In most companies, new employees receive specialized training in how to do their jobs. (**28**), new managers are often given little or no training. This seems to suggest that one way to lessen the effects of the Peter Principle is to provide proper training for new managers.

(26) 1 earn lower-than-average salaries
2 love their jobs
3 have worked for several companies
4 perform poorly

(27) 1 has two disadvantages
2 cannot be avoided
3 is a gamble worth taking
4 prevents creative thinking

(28) 1 Of course
2 On the other hand
3 What is more
4 For a similar reason

Nearsightedness

Nearsightedness has been increasing around the world at a rapid rate. People with this condition can see objects that are close to them clearly, but objects that are far away appear blurry. Many people blame this trend on the use of digital screens. They claim that using devices such as computers and smartphones leads to eyestrain, and that blue light, which is produced by digital screens, damages light-sensitive cells in the back of the eye. However, there is no clear evidence that digital screens (**29**   ).

In fact, the rise in nearsightedness began before digital screens became widely used. Some research suggests that the real issue is that people (**30**   ). This results in a lack of exposure to natural light. Nearsightedness is caused by the stretching of the lens in the eye, which reduces its ability to focus light. However, the release of dopamine, a chemical produced by the brain, can prevent this from occurring, and exposure to natural light leads to greater dopamine production.

Some experts say that being outdoors for about three hours a day can help prevent nearsightedness. For many people, however, doing this is impossible due to school and work schedules. (**31**   ), it may be more practical for people to change the kind of lighting they use in their homes. There is already lighting available that provides some of the benefits of natural light, and it is hoped that research will provide more alternatives in the future.

(29) 1 have long-term effects on eyesight
2 can help solve the problem
3 can be used on all devices
4 will improve in the future

(30) 1 sit too close to their screens
2 rely too much on vision
3 spend too much time indoors
4 fail to do enough physical exercise

(31) 1 In the same way
2 For example
3 Despite this
4 Instead

Honey Fungus

The largest living organism on Earth is not a whale or other large animal. Rather, it belongs to the group of organisms which includes mushrooms and toadstools. It is a type of fungus commonly known as honey fungus, and its rootlike filaments spread underground throughout a huge area of forest in the US state of Oregon. DNA testing has confirmed that all the honey fungus in the area is from the same organism, and, based on its annual rate of growth, scientists estimate it could be over 8,000 years old. They also calculate that it would weigh around 35,000 tons if it were all gathered together.

As impressive as this honey fungus is, it poses a problem for many trees in the forest. The fungus infects the trees and absorbs nutrients from their roots and trunks, often eventually killing them. Unfortunately, affected trees are usually difficult to spot, as the fungus hides under their bark, and its filaments are only visible if the bark is removed. In the late fall, the fruiting bodies of the fungus appear on the outside of the trees, but only for a few weeks before winter. Although the trees attempt to resist the fungus, they usually lose the battle in the end because the fungus damages their roots, preventing water and nutrients from reaching their upper parts.

Full removal of the honey fungus in Oregon has been considered, but it would prove to be too costly and time-consuming. Another solution currently being researched is the planting of tree species that can resist the fungus. Some experts have suggested, however, that a change of perspective may be necessary. Rather than viewing the effects of the honey fungus in a negative light, people should consider it an example of nature taking its course. Dead trees will ultimately be recycled back into the soil, benefiting the area's ecosystem.

(32) According to the passage, what is one thing that is true about the honey fungus in Oregon?

1 It is a combination of different mushroom species that started to grow together over time.

2 It grew slowly at first, but it has been expanding more rapidly in the last thousand years.

3 It shares the nutrients it collects with the trees and other types of plant life that it grows on.

4 It is a single organism that has spread throughout a wide area by growing and feeding on trees.

(33) Honey fungus is difficult to find because

1 the mushrooms it produces change color depending on the type of tree that it grows on.

2 it is generally not visible, except when it produces fruiting bodies for a short time each year.

3 not only does it grow underground, but it also has an appearance that is like that of tree roots.

4 it is only able to survive in areas that have the specific weather conditions it needs to grow.

(34) What do some experts think?

1 People should regard the honey fungus's effects on trees as a natural and beneficial process.

2 The only practical way to deal with the honey fungus is to invest more time and money in attempts to remove it.

3 Trees that have been infected by the honey fungus can be used to prevent it from spreading further.

4 The honey fungus can be harvested to provide people with an excellent source of nutrients.

Intentional Communities

For hundreds of years, people have formed self-sustaining communities, often referred to as intentional communities, which are characterized by shared ideals, collective ownership, and common use of property. The first known intentional community was established in the sixth century BC by a Greek philosopher. Over the following centuries, a number of such communities were created by religious groups wishing to live outside mainstream society. Some of these, such as Christian monasteries and the collective farms called kibbutzim in Israel, remained successful for generations, while others lasted only a few years.

In the twentieth century, philosophical idealism, as seen in the back-to-the-land movement of the 1960s and 1970s, also motivated people to form intentional communities. By the early 1970s, it has been estimated that there were thousands of such communities in the United States alone, though many of those later disbanded. The Foundation for Intentional Communities now lists fewer than 800 communities in the United States and just under 250 in the rest of the world. Intentional communities that failed generally faced a similar challenge. Some people who came to stay were committed to ideals of shared work, growing their own food, and living collectively, but others were less serious. A cofounder of one community recalled, "We had an impractical but noble vision that was constantly undermined by people who came just to play."

Not all intentional communities are destined to fall apart, however. The ongoing success of Damanhur, a spiritual and artistic collective near Turin, Italy, is attributed to open communication and a practical approach. Damanhur organizes its members into family-like groups of 15 to 20 people. The community has found that creating intimacy becomes difficult if a "family" has more than 25 people. In contrast, when there are too few people in the "family," there is not enough collective knowledge to allow for effective decision-making. Damanhur's ideals, which are outlined in its constitution, are upheld by elected leaders, and tensions in the community are handled by holding playful mock battles where people fight with paint-filled toy guns.

It seems that all successful intentional communities share a common trait: the ability to constantly think ahead. As one Damanhur member put it, "You should change things when they work — not when they don't work." This strategy of making changes before problems occur has worked well for Damanhur and other successful communities, which suggests it is an effective way for intentional communities to fulfill the needs of their members in the long term.

(35) A common issue faced by intentional communities that failed was that

1 a majority of the community was in favor of someone joining, but a small number of individuals opposed it.

2 people joined the community with genuine interest, but they lacked the skills or knowledge to contribute effectively.

3 some members worked hard to follow the community's ideals, while others took a more casual approach to communal living.

4 the community set out to complete an ambitious project, but it could not complete it because of a lack of knowledge and financial resources.

(36) What is true of the social structure at Damanhur?

1 "Families" are free to create their own rules and do not necessarily have to follow the rules contained in the community's constitution.

2 The number of people in a "family" is controlled to create the best conditions for resolving group issues and maintaining good relationships.

3 The mock battles that are intended to solve disagreements sometimes become serious and result in some members leaving their "families."

4 The community contains "families" of different sizes so that members can choose whether to live in a large or a small group setting.

(37) According to the passage, how is Damanhur similar to other successful intentional communities?

1 Members of the community are allowed to exchange their responsibilities from time to time to prevent them from becoming exhausted.

2 The type of work the community does to earn income changes periodically so that members can learn new skills.

3 Members of the community take turns carrying out maintenance on the buildings and equipment that are owned collectively.

4 The community continually finds ways to satisfy the needs of its members rather than simply reacting to problems when they arise.

The British in India

Established in 1600, the British-owned East India Company was one of the world's largest corporations for more than two centuries. By trading overseas with various countries, such as India and China, it was able to import luxury items from these countries into Britain. The British government received a portion of the company's vast profits, so it was more than willing to provide political support. Due to its size, power, and resources, which included a private army of hundreds of thousands of Indian soldiers, the company pressured India into accepting trade contracts that, in general, were only of benefit to the company. After winning a battle against a local ruler in the 1750s, the company seized control of one of the wealthiest provinces in India. As a result, the East India Company was no longer solely acting as a business but also as a political institution, and it began forcing Indian citizens to pay it taxes.

The East India Company gained a reputation among the countries it did business with for being untrustworthy. It also started to lose popularity within the British Parliament because the company's dishonest trading habits damaged foreign relations with China. Then, in the 1850s, angered by the way they were being treated, a group of soldiers in the East India Company's army rebelled. They marched to Delhi to restore the Indian emperor to power, and their actions caused rebellion against the British to spread to other parts of India. The rebellion was eventually brought under control after about two years, but it triggered the end of the East India Company. The British government, which blamed the East India Company for allowing the rebellion to happen, took control of India, and an era of direct British rule began. The British closed down the East India Company, removed the Indian emperor from power, and proceeded to rule India for almost a century.

While some claim that India benefited from British rule, typically using the construction of railways as an example, many historians argue that the country was negatively affected. In an effort to reinforce notions that British culture was superior, Indians were educated to have the same opinions, morals, and social preferences as the British. The British also implemented a policy known as "divide and rule," which turned Indians from different religious backgrounds against each other. The British government used this strategy to maintain its control over India, as members of these religions had joined forces during the earlier rebellion. However, nationalist feelings among Indians increased from the early 1900s, and India eventually gained its independence in the late 1940s.

Although the East India Company stopped operating more than a century ago, it has had a lasting influence. Some experts say it pioneered the concept of multinational corporations and ultimately led to the economic system of capitalism that is widespread today. Moreover, the connection between the British government and the East India Company set a precedent for using political power to help achieve business objectives.

22 年度第 1 回 筆記

(38) What was one result of India doing business with the East India Company?

1 India could afford to increase the size of its military because it was able to make trade deals with other countries.

2 India had little choice but to agree to business agreements that were unfavorable to it.

3 The Indian government needed to raise taxes in order to pay for losses from failed trade contracts.

4 The Indian government's relationship with China became worse, which almost resulted in a break in trade between the two countries.

(39) What led to the British government taking control of India?

1 The British government held the East India Company responsible for an uprising that occurred.

2 The Indian people voted for British rule after losing confidence in the Indian emperor's ability to rule the country effectively.

3 The Indian people asked for the help of the British in preventing a war between India and China.

4 The Indian emperor decided to join forces with the British as a political strategy to maintain control of India.

(40) One effect that British rule had on India was that

1 Indians were able to take part in the process of building a government that reflected their economic and social needs.

2 schools made an effort to educate their students to have an awareness of both Indian and British cultures.

3 divisions were created between different groups of Indians to prevent them from challenging British rule.

4 many of the railroads and other transportation systems built by the Indian government were destroyed.

(41) What does the author of the passage say about the East India Company?

1 The company prevented the British government from achieving its aim of expanding its rule to other countries in Asia.

2 While the company may have been successful during its time, its business model would not be effective in today's economy.

3 Although the company no longer exists, it has had a large impact on the present-day global economic landscape.

4 If the company had never been established, another one would likely have ended up having similar political and economic influence.

- *Write an essay on the given TOPIC.*
- *Use TWO of the POINTS below to support your answer.*
- *Structure: introduction, main body, and conclusion*
- *Suggested length: 120–150 words*
- *Write your essay in the space provided on Side B of your answer sheet.*

Any writing outside the space will not be graded.

TOPIC

Should people's salaries be based on their job performance?

POINTS

- Age
- Company profits
- Motivation
- Skills

一次試験
リスニング

———————— Listening Test ————————

There are three parts to this listening test.

Part 1	Dialogues: 1 question each	Multiple-choice
Part 2	Passages: 2 questions each	Multiple-choice
Part 3	Real-Life: 1 question each	Multiple-choice

※**Listen carefully to the instructions.**

‖‖‖ Part 1 ‖‖‖‖‖‖‖‖‖‖‖‖‖‖‖‖‖‖‖ ◀») ▶MP3 ▶アプリ ▶CD3 **1**～**14**

No. 1
1 He no longer drives to work.
2 His car is being repaired.
3 He cannot afford to buy gas.
4 His new bicycle was stolen.

No. 2
1 He wants to move out.
2 He likes to have parties.
3 He is not very open.
4 He is very messy.

No. 3
1 The other candidates were more qualified.
2 He forgot to call the manager yesterday.
3 The manager did not like him.
4 He missed the interview.

No. 4
1 The woman needs to pass it to graduate.
2 It does not match the woman's goals.
3 It is too advanced for the woman.
4 Passing it could help the woman find a job.

No. 5
1 The woman should take a break from school.
2 Working as a server is physically demanding.
3 Restaurant workers do not make much money.
4 Students should not get part-time jobs.

No. 6
1 Buy a gift from the list.
2 Decline the wedding invitation.
3 Speak to Carla and Antonio.
4 Return the silver dining set.

No. 7
1 It has large portions.
2 It is a short drive from home.
3 It is cheaper than other places.
4 It has a good reputation.

No. 8
1 Spend time hiking.
2 Go fishing at a lake.
3 Take a ski trip.
4 Go sightseeing.

No. 9
1 Some customers complained about it.
2 One of the posts needs to be revised.
3 Kenneth should not edit the latest post.
4 It should be updated more frequently.

No. 10
1 Her wallet is missing.
2 Her train pass expired.
3 She missed her train.
4 She wasted her money.

No. 11
1 She did not like the pianist's playing.
2 She arrived at the concert late.
3 She could not focus on the concert.
4 She was unable to find her ticket.

No. 12
1 Call him back in the evening.
2 Give him new delivery instructions.
3 Change her delivery option online.
4 Tell him what time she will be home.

(A)

No. 13
1 Water levels have decreased in many of them.
2 Laws to protect them need to be stricter.
3 Countries sharing them usually have the same usage rights.
4 They often make it difficult to protect borders.

No. 14
1 To suggest a solution to a border problem.
2 To suggest that poor nations need rivers for electricity.
3 To show that dams are often too costly.
4 To show how river usage rights can be complicated.

(B)

No. 15
1 It could be used as a poison.
2 It was tested on snakes.
3 It was difficult to make.
4 It was the first medical drug.

No. 16
1 It took many days to make.
2 Only small amounts could be made daily.
3 Production was very loosely regulated.
4 People there could watch it being made.

(C)

No. 17
1 They hunted only spirit bears with black fur.
2 They tried to keep spirit bears a secret.
3 They thought spirit bears were dangerous.
4 They believed spirit bears protected them.

No. 18
1 It is easier for them to catch food.
2 They are less sensitive to the sun.
3 It is harder for hunters to find them.
4 Their habitats are all well-protected.

No. 19

1 They generate power near where the power is used.
2 They are preferred by small businesses.
3 They do not use solar energy.
4 They are very expensive to maintain.

No. 20

1 Governments generally oppose its development.
2 Energy companies usually do not profit from it.
3 It can negatively affect property values.
4 It often pollutes community water sources.

(E)

No. 21

1 Caring for them costs too much money.
2 They are too difficult to capture.
3 They suffer from serious diseases.
4 They rarely live long after being caught.

No. 22

1 Zoos need to learn how to breed them.
2 Governments must make sure laws are followed.
3 They must be moved to new habitats.
4 Protecting them in the wild is not possible.

(F)

No. 23

1 They are more numerous than is typical.
2 They are similar to those of a distant area.
3 They are the largest in the region.
4 They include images of Europeans.

No. 24

1 To indicate certain times of the year.
2 To warn enemies to stay away.
3 To show the way to another settlement.
4 To provide a source of light.

22
年度第1回

リスニング

(G)

No. 25

Situation: You want to feed your parrot, Toby, but cannot find his pet food. You check your cell phone and find a voice mail from your wife.

Question: Where should you go to find Toby's food?

1 To the kitchen.
2 To the living room.
3 To the front door.
4 To the garage.

(H)

No. 26

Situation: You want to read a book written by the author Greta Bakken. You want to read her most popular book. A bookstore clerk tells you the following.

Question: Which book should you buy?

1 *The Moon in Budapest.*
2 *Along That Tree-Lined Road.*
3 *Mixed Metaphors.*
4 *Trishaws.*

(I)

No. 27

Situation: Your company's president is making an announcement about a change in office procedures. You want to take time off next week.

Question: What should you do?

1 Speak to your manager.
2 Submit a request on the new website.
3 E-mail the members of your department.
4 Contact ABC Resource Systems.

(J)

Situation: Your professor is showing your class a course website. You want to get extra credit to improve your grade.

Question: What should you do?

1 Submit an extra research paper through the website.
2 Complete additional reading assignments.
3 Create an online resource for the class.
4 Sign up for a lecture via the news section.

(K)

Situation: You are a writer for a newspaper. You arrive home at 8:30 p.m. and hear the following voice mail from your editor. You need two more days to finish your column.

Question: What should you do?

1 Send the file to Bill.
2 Send the file to Paula.
3 Call Bill's office phone.
4 Call Bill on his smartphone.

22
年度第1回 リスニング

問題カード（A日程）　　　▶MP3 ▶アプリ ▶CD 4 **37**〜**41**

You have **one minute** to prepare.

This is a story about a mayor who wanted to help her town.
You have **two minutes** to narrate the story.

Your story should begin with the following sentence:
One day, a mayor was having a meeting.

Questions

No. 1   Please look at the fourth picture. If you were the mayor, what would you be thinking?

No. 2   Do you think people should spend more time outdoors to learn about nature?

No. 3   Should companies provide workers with more vacation days?

No. 4   Should the government do more to protect endangered animals?

You have **one minute** to prepare.

This is a story about a woman who wanted to advance her career.
You have **two minutes** to narrate the story.

Your story should begin with the following sentence:
One day, a woman was talking with her company's CEO in the office.

Questions

No. 1   Please look at the fourth picture. If you were the woman, what would you be thinking?

No. 2   Are parents too protective of their children these days?

No. 3   Does the fast pace of modern life have a negative effect on people?

No. 4   Do you think the birth rate in Japan will stop decreasing in the future?

2021-3

一次試験　2022.1.23実施
二次試験　A日程　2022.2.20実施
　　　　　C日程　2022.3.6実施

試験時間

筆記：**90分**
リスニング：**約30分**

＊解答・解説は別冊p.225〜268にあります。
＊面接の流れは本書p.28にあります。

Grade Pre-1

Pre 1

1 To complete each item, choose the best word or phrase from among the four choices. Then, on your answer sheet, find the number of the question and mark your answer.

(1) Roberto was a true (　　　), so he immediately volunteered to join the army when his country was attacked by its neighbor.
1 villain　　　**2** patriot　　　**3** spectator　　　**4** beggar

(2) "Let's take a break now," said the chairperson. "We'll (　　　) the meeting in about 15 minutes to talk about the next item on the agenda."
1 parody　　　**2** resume　　　**3** impede　　　**4** erect

(3) The first time Dan tried skiing, he found it difficult, but on each (　　　) ski trip, he got better. Now he is an expert skier.
1 sufficient　　**2** arrogant　　**3** subsequent　　**4** prominent

(4) The professor is an expert in his field but his (　　　) behavior is a source of embarrassment to his colleagues. "He's always doing or saying strange things," said one.
1 secular　　　**2** eccentric　　　**3** vigilant　　　**4** apparent

(5) Because the vegetable stand was unable to (　　　) that the vegetables it sold were organic, Eddie refused to buy them. It was his strict policy to eat only organic foods.
1 diverge　　　**2** certify　　　**3** evade　　　**4** glorify

(6) As a school guidance counselor, Ms. Pereira specializes in helping students find their (　　　). She believes people should have careers that fit their personality and skills.
1 boredom　　　**2** vocation　　　**3** insult　　　**4** publicity

(7) The marathon runner was so thirsty after the race that she drank a large sports drink in just a few (   ) and then quickly asked for another one.

1 herds   **2** lumps   **3** gulps   **4** sacks

(8) The sleeping baby was (   ) by the loud music coming from her brother's room. She woke up crying, and it took a long time before she fell asleep again.

1 startled   **2** improvised   **3** prolonged   **4** tolerated

(9) *A:* I've been living in this apartment for a year now, and the (   ) is about to end. I have to decide if I should stay or move.

     B: If your rent will be the same, I recommend renewing your contract and staying.

1 token   **2** lease   **3** vicinity   **4** dialect

(10) The presidential candidate blamed the (   ) economy on the current president. He promised he would improve it if he were elected.

1 bulky   **2** functional   **3** ethnic   **4** sluggish

(11) *A:* Annie, how have you been? Did you enjoy your trip to Italy last year?

     B: I did, Pablo. Actually, I loved it so much that I've been (   ) moving there. I'd have to wait until my son graduates from high school, though.

1 contemplating   **2** emphasizing

3 vandalizing   **4** illustrating

(12) All the senators said they supported the new law, so it was no surprise when they voted for it (   ).

1 unanimously   **2** abnormally

3 mockingly   **4** savagely

(13) *A:* Did you go to Professor Markham's lecture?
B: I did, but it was so boring I could only (   ) it for 15 minutes. After that, I left and went to a café.

1 execute   **2** discern   **3** endure   **4** relay

(14) Houses built in cold regions can be surprisingly (   ) during the winter. Fireplaces, wood furniture, and nice carpets give the homes a warm, comfortable feeling.

1 rigid   **2** rash   **3** cozy   **4** clumsy

(15) Mrs. Wilson was angry when her son broke the window, but she was more disappointed that he tried to (   ) her by telling her that someone else had done it.

1 pinpoint   **2** suppress   **3** reroute   **4** deceive

(16) After Wanda was late for the third time in one month, her manager had a long talk with her about the importance of (   ).

1 congestion   **2** drainage   **3** optimism   **4** punctuality

(17) The young author decided not to follow (   ) storytelling rules and wrote his novel in a unique style.

1 vulnerable   **2** clueless   **3** conventional   **4** phonetic

(18) The items in the box were packaged carefully because they were (   ), but some of them were still damaged when they were being delivered.

1 coarse   **2** fragile   **3** immovable   **4** glossy

(19) The queen (   ) her adviser to the palace, but she became extremely angry when he took a long time to arrive.

1 summoned   **2** hammered   **3** mingled   **4** trembled

(20) The general knew his troops were losing the battle, so he ordered them to (　　　). Once they were safely away from the battlefield, he worked on a new plan to defeat the enemy.

1 entrust　　　**2** discard　　　**3** strangle　　　**4** retreat

(21) After Bill began university, he quickly realized that he did not have the (　　　) to study advanced math, so he changed his major to geography.

1 capacity　　　**2** novelty　　　**3** bait　　　**4** chunk

(22) The police officer was shocked when his partner suggested they (　　　) a suspect in order to force him to admit he had stolen money. Using violence in this way was not allowed.

1 rough up　　　**2** give out　　　**3** break up　　　**4** take over

(23) Julius was lucky to see a rare eagle on his first day of bird-watching. However, 20 years (　　　) before he saw another one.

1 held out　　　**2** went by　　　**3** laid off　　　**4** cut off

(24) *A:* Are you going to cancel your weekend beach trip? There's a typhoon coming.
B: We haven't (　　　) going yet. It depends on which direction the typhoon moves in.

1 ruled out　　　　　　　**2** stood down
3 dragged into　　　　　　**4** scooped up

(25) Jun always saved as much money as possible so he would have something to (　　　) if he lost his job.

1 look up to　　　　　　　**2** fall back on
3 come down with　　　　　**4** do away with

Read each passage and choose the best word or phrase from among the four choices for each blank. Then, on your answer sheet, find the number of the question and mark your answer.

Donor Premiums

In recent years, it has become common for charities to give donor premiums — small gifts such as coffee mugs — to people who donate money to them. Many charities offer them, and it is widely believed that people give more when they receive donor premiums. However, researchers say that donor premiums tend to (**26**). Most people initially give money because they want to make the world a better place or help those who are less fortunate. When they receive gifts, though, people can start to become motivated by selfishness and desire. In fact, they may become less likely to donate in the future.

There may, however, be ways to avoid this problem. Research has shown that telling people they will receive gifts after making donations is not the best way to ensure they will contribute in the future. In one study, donors responded better to receiving gifts when they did not expect them. (**27**), future donations from such people increased by up to 75 percent. On the other hand, donors who knew that they would receive a gift after their donation did not value the gift highly, regardless of what it was.

Donor premiums may also have indirect benefits. Experts say gifts can (**28**). Items such as fancy shopping bags with charity logos, for example, signal that a donor is part of an exclusive group. Such gifts not only keep donors satisfied but also increase the general public's awareness of charities.

(26) **1** use up charities' resources
     2 change donors' attitudes
     3 encourage people to donate more
     4 improve the public's image of charities

(27) **1** Instead
     2 Nevertheless
     3 In contrast
     4 Furthermore

(28) **1** help promote charities
     2 easily be copied
     3 have undesirable effects
     4 cause confusion among donors

Government Policy and Road Safety

Traffic-related deaths have declined in the United States due to the introduction of safety measures such as seat belts. Many critics of government policy claim, however, that fatalities could be further reduced with stricter government regulation. In fact, some say current government policies regarding speed limits may (29   ). This is because speed limits are often set using the "operating speed method." With this method, speed limits are decided based on the speeds at which vehicles that use the road actually travel, and little attention is paid to road features that could increase danger. Unfortunately, this means limits are sometimes set at unsafe levels.

Critics also point out that the United States is behind other nations when it comes to vehicle-safety regulations. In the United States, safety regulations are (30   ). Although some vehicles have become larger and their shape has changed, laws have not changed to reflect the increased danger they pose to pedestrians. Critics say that regulating only the safety of vehicle occupants is irresponsible, and that pedestrian deaths have increased even though there are simple measures that could be taken to help prevent them.

One measure for improving road safety is the use of cameras at traffic signals to detect drivers who fail to stop for red lights. Many such cameras were installed in the 1990s and have been shown to save lives. (31   ), the number of such cameras has declined in recent years. One reason for this is that there is often public opposition to them due to privacy concerns.

(29) **1** further support this trend
      2 reduce seat-belt use
      3 encourage dangerous driving
      4 provide an alternative solution

(30) **1** designed to protect those inside vehicles
      2 opposed by many drivers
      3 actually being decreased
      4 stricter for large vehicles

(31) **1** For instance
      2 Likewise
      3 Despite this
      4 Consequently

Caligula

The Roman emperor Caligula, also known as the "mad emperor," became so infamous that it is difficult to separate fact from legend regarding his life. During his reign, Caligula suffered what has been described as a "brain fever." It has often been said that this illness caused him to go insane, a claim that is supported by his seemingly irrational behavior following his illness. Today, however, some historians argue that his actions may have been a deliberate part of a clever, and horribly violent, political strategy.

After his illness, Caligula began torturing and putting to death huge numbers of citizens for even minor offenses. He also claimed to be a living god. These actions may suggest mental instability, but another explanation is that they were intended to secure his position. While Caligula was ill, plans were made to replace him, since he had not been expected to survive, and he likely felt betrayed and threatened as a result. Similarly, while claiming to be a god certainly sounds like a symptom of insanity, many Roman emperors were considered to become gods upon dying, and Caligula may have made the claim to discourage his enemies from assassinating him.

The story of how Caligula supposedly tried to appoint his horse Incitatus to a powerful government position is also sometimes given as evidence of his mental illness. However, Caligula is said to have frequently humiliated members of the Roman Senate, making them do things such as wearing uncomfortable clothing and running in front of his chariot. Elevating his horse to a position higher than theirs would have been another way to make the Senate members feel worthless. Eventually, though, Caligula's behavior went too far, and he was murdered. Efforts were made to erase him from history, leaving few reliable sources for modern historians to study. As a result, it may never be known whether he truly was the mad emperor.

(32) Some modern historians argue that

1 Caligula's seemingly crazy actions may actually have been part of a carefully thought-out plan.

2 the "brain fever" that Caligula suffered was more serious than it was originally believed to be.

3 Caligula should not be judged based on the period when he was suffering from a mental illness.

4 many of the violent acts that Caligula is reported to have carried out were performed by other Roman emperors.

(33) What may have been one result of Caligula's illness?

1 The fact that he almost died caused him to stop being interested in anything except gods and religion.

2 He felt that he could no longer trust anyone, leading him to change the way he governed.

3 Roman citizens thought he was still likely to die, so he attempted to show them that the gods would protect him.

4 He began to doubt old beliefs about Roman emperors, which led to serious conflicts with other members of the government.

(34) According to the passage, how did Caligula feel about the members of the Roman Senate?

1 He felt the people should respect them more, since they would do anything to protect him from his enemies.

2 He wanted to show his power over them, so he often found ways to make them feel they had no value.

3 He disliked them because he felt that they were physically weak and had poor fashion sense.

4 He was grateful for their support, so he held events such as chariot races in order to honor them.

The Friends of Eddie Coyle

In 1970, American writer George V. Higgins published his first novel, *The Friends of Eddie Coyle*. This crime novel was inspired by the time Higgins spent working as a lawyer, during which he examined hours of police surveillance tapes and transcripts in connection with the cases he was involved in. What he heard and read was the everyday speech of ordinary criminals, which sounded nothing like the scripted lines of TV crime dramas at the time. Higgins learned how real criminals spoke, and their unique, often messy patterns of language provided the basis for *The Friends of Eddie Coyle*. The novel's gritty realism was far removed from the polished crime stories that dominated the bestseller lists at the time. Higgins neither glamorized the lives of his criminal characters nor portrayed the police or federal agents in a heroic light.

One aspect that distinguishes *The Friends of Eddie Coyle* from other crime novels is that it is written almost entirely in dialogue. Given the crime genre's reliance on carefully plotted stories that build suspense, this was a highly original approach. Important events are not described directly, instead being introduced through conversations between characters in the novel. Thus, readers are given the sense that they are secretly listening in on Eddie Coyle and his criminal associates. Even action scenes are depicted in dialogue, and where narration is necessary, Higgins writes sparingly, providing only as much information as is required for readers to follow the plot. The focus is primarily on the characters, the world they inhabit, and the codes of conduct they follow.

Although Higgins's first novel was an immediate hit, not all readers liked the author's writing style, which he also used in his following books. Many complained that his later novels lacked clear plots and contained too little action. Yet Higgins remained committed to his belief that the most engaging way to tell a story is through the conversations of its characters, as this compels the reader to pay close attention to what is being said. Despite writing many novels, Higgins was never able to replicate the success of his debut work. Toward the end of his life, he became disappointed and frustrated by the lack of attention and appreciation his books received. Nevertheless, *The Friends of Eddie Coyle* is now considered by many to be one of the greatest crime novels ever written.

(35) According to the passage, George V. Higgins wrote *The Friends of Eddie Coyle*

   1 because he believed that the novel would become a bestseller and enable him to quit the law profession to write full time.

   2 after becoming frustrated about the lack of awareness among ordinary Americans regarding the extent of criminal activity in the United States.

   3 because he wanted to show readers how hard lawyers worked in order to protect the victims of crime.

   4 after being inspired by what he found during the investigations he carried out while he was a lawyer.

(36) In the second paragraph, what do we learn about *The Friends of Eddie Coyle*?

   1 Higgins wanted to produce a novel which proved that the traditional rules of crime fiction still held true in modern times.

   2 The novel is unusual because Higgins tells the story through interactions between the characters rather than by describing specific events in detail.

   3 Higgins relied heavily on dialogue throughout the novel because he lacked the confidence to write long passages of narration.

   4 Although the novel provides an authentic description of the criminal world, Higgins did not consider it to be a true crime novel.

(37) Which of the following statements would the author of the passage most likely agree with?

   1 Despite the possibility that Higgins could have attracted a wider readership by altering his writing style, he remained true to his creative vision.

   2 The first book Higgins produced was poorly written, but the quality of his work steadily increased in the years that followed.

3 It is inevitable that writers of crime novels will never gain the same level of prestige and acclaim as writers of other genres.

4 It is unrealistic for writers of crime novels to expect their work to appeal to readers decades after it was first published.

Mummy Brown

Thousands of years ago, ancient Egyptians began practicing mummification — the process of drying out the bodies of the dead, treating them with various substances, and wrapping them to preserve them. It was believed this helped the dead person's spirit enter the afterlife. Beginning in the twelfth century, however, many ancient mummies met a strange fate, as a market arose in Europe for medicines made using parts of mummies. People assumed the mummies' black color was because they had been treated with bitumen — a black, petroleum-based substance that occurs naturally in the Middle East and was used by ancient societies to treat illnesses. However, while ancient Egyptians did sometimes preserve mummies by coating them with bitumen, this method had not been used on many of the mummies that were taken to Europe. Furthermore, an incorrect translation of Arabic texts resulted in the mistaken belief that the bitumen used to treat mummies actually entered their bodies.

By the eighteenth century, advances in medical knowledge had led Europeans to stop using mummy-based medicines. Nevertheless, the European public's fascination with mummies reached new heights when French leader Napoleon Bonaparte led a military campaign in Egypt, which also included a major scientific expedition that resulted in significant archaeological discoveries and the documentation of ancient artifacts. Wealthy tourists even visited Egypt to obtain ancient artifacts for their private collections. In fact, the unwrapping and displaying of mummies at private parties became a popular activity. Mummies were also used in various other ways, such as being turned into crop fertilizer and fuel for railway engines.

One particularly unusual use of mummies was as a pigment for creating brown paint. Made using ground-up mummies, the pigment, which came to be known as mummy brown, was used as early as the sixteenth century, though demand for it grew around the time of

Napoleon's Egyptian campaign. Its color was praised by some European artists, who used it in artworks that can be seen in museums today. Still, the pigment had more critics than fans. Many artists complained about its poor drying ability and other negative qualities. Moreover, painting with a pigment made from deceased people increasingly came to be thought of as disrespectful — one well-known British painter who used mummy brown immediately buried his tube of the paint in the ground when he learned that real mummies had been used to produce it.

Even artists who had no objection to mummy brown could not always be certain its origin was genuine, as parts of dead animals were sometimes sold as mummy parts. Also, the fact that different manufacturers used different parts of mummies to produce the pigment meant there was little consistency among the various versions on the market. Additionally, the mummification process itself, including the substances used to preserve the bodies, underwent changes over time. These same factors make it almost impossible for researchers today to detect the presence of mummy brown in specific paintings. Given the pigment's controversial origins, however, perhaps art lovers would be shocked if they discovered that it was used in any of the paintings they admire.

(38) According to the author of the passage, why were ancient Egyptian mummies used to make medicines in Europe?

1 Disease was widespread in Europe at the time, so Europeans were willing to try anything to create effective medicines.
2 Because the mummies had not turned black in spite of their age, Europeans assumed they could provide health benefits.
3 Europeans mistakenly believed that a substance which was thought to have medical benefits was present in all mummies.
4 The fact that the mummies had religious significance to ancient Egyptians caused Europeans to believe they had special powers.

(39) What is one thing we learn about Napoleon Bonaparte's military campaign in Egypt?

1 A number of leaders saw it as a reason to also invade Egypt,

which led to the destruction of many ancient artifacts.

2 It revealed information about ancient Egyptian culture that led Europeans to change their opinion of medicines made from mummies.

3 It was opposed by wealthy Europeans, who thought it would result in their collections of ancient artifacts being destroyed.

4 It led to an increased interest in mummies and inspired Europeans to use them for a number of purposes.

(40) The author of the passage mentions the British painter in order to

1 provide an example of how the use of mummy brown was opposed by some people because it showed a lack of respect for the dead.

2 explain why mummy brown remained popular among well-known artists in spite of its poor technical performance.

3 give support for the theory that mummy brown was superior to other paint pigments because of its unique ingredients.

4 describe one reason why some artists developed a positive view of mummy brown after initially refusing to use it.

(41) What is one thing that makes it difficult to determine whether a painting contains mummy brown?

1 The substances that were added to the pigment to improve its color destroyed any biological evidence that tests could have detected.

2 The way that ancient Egyptians prepared mummies changed, so the contents of the pigment were not consistent.

3 Artists mixed the pigment with other types of paint before applying it to paintings, so it would only be present in very small amounts.

4 The art industry has tried to prevent researchers from conducting tests on paintings because of concerns that the results could affect their value.

4
- *Write an essay on the given TOPIC.*
- *Use TWO of the POINTS below to support your answer.*
- *Structure: introduction, main body, and conclusion*
- *Suggested length: 120–150 words*
- *Write your essay in the space provided on Side B of your answer sheet.*

Any writing outside the space will not be graded.

TOPIC
Should people stop using goods that are made from animals?

POINTS
- Animal rights
- Endangered species
- Product quality
- Tradition

リスニング

―――――――――――― **Listening Test** ――――――――――――

There are three parts to this listening test.

Part 1	Dialogues: 1 question each	Multiple-choice
Part 2	Passages: 2 questions each	Multiple-choice
Part 3	Real-Life: 1 question each	Multiple-choice

※**Listen carefully to the instructions.**

Part 1 ◀» ▶MP3 ▶アプリ ▶CD 3 **28**〜**41**

No. 1
1 His recent test scores.
2 Having to drop the class.
3 Finding a job.
4 Staying awake in class.

No. 2
1 The man could lose his job.
2 The man forgot his mother's birthday.
3 The man did not reply to her e-mail.
4 The man is not liked by the CEO.

No. 3
1 They take turns driving.
2 They were in a serious accident.
3 They work in a car repair shop.
4 Neither of them can drive next week.

No. 4
1 He cannot use his credit card.
2 He forgot to contact his card issuer.
3 He is short of cash today.
4 He lost his debit card.

No. 5
1 He is not suited to the call-center job.
2 He is learning the wrong interview techniques.
3 He should go to the interview he has been offered.
4 He should prioritize finding his dream job.

No. 6	1 Have the man take some tests.
	2 Encourage the man to exercise more.
	3 Give the man advice about work-related stress.
	4 Recommend the man to a specialist.

No. 7	1 He will take his vacation later in the year.
	2 He will meet with the personnel manager.
	3 He will do what his manager asks him to do.
	4 He will ask the woman to help him.

No. 8	1 It needs brighter colors.
	2 It fits the company's image.
	3 It is too similar to the current one.
	4 It needs to be redesigned.

No. 9	1 He has not read Alice's book yet.
	2 He cannot attend Alice's party.
	3 He is no longer friends with Alice.
	4 He was disappointed with Alice's book.

No. 10	1 Make sure she catches an earlier train.
	2 Use a different train line.
	3 Ride her bicycle to the office.
	4 Go into the office on weekends.

No. 11	1 Garbage collection has become less frequent.
	2 Garbage bags will become more expensive.
	3 Local taxes are likely to rise soon.
	4 The newspaper delivery schedule has changed.

No. 12	1 Try using some earplugs.
	2 Have Ranjit talk to her neighbors.
	3 Complain about her landlord.
	4 Write a message to her neighbors.

21年度第3回 リスニング

(A)

No. 13
1 There are too many food choices available.
2 Schools often prepare uninteresting food.
3 They copy their parents' eating habits.
4 They have a desire to lose weight.

No. 14
1 Getting children to help make their own meals.
2 Encouraging children to play more sports.
3 Sometimes letting children eat unhealthy foods.
4 Rewarding children for eating vegetables.

(B)

No. 15
1 Ching Shih's pirates gained a number of ships.
2 Many pirate commanders were captured.
3 Most of the pirates were killed.
4 Ching Shih agreed to help the Chinese navy.

No. 16
1 She left China to escape punishment.
2 She gave away her wealth.
3 She formed a new pirate organization.
4 She agreed to stop her pirate operations.

(C)

No. 17
1 Their numbers increase at certain times.
2 They are being hunted by humans.
3 Their habitats have become smaller recently.
4 They have been eating fewer snowshoe hares.

No. 18
1 They only travel when looking for food.
2 They sometimes travel long distances.
3 They live much longer than other wildcats.
4 They always return to their original territories.

(D)

No. 19
1 Modern burial places are based on their design.
2 They were used for religious purposes.
3 They were only used by non-Christians.
4 The entrances were only found recently.

No. 20
1 Women used to be priests long ago.
2 The tunnels were not used as churches.
3 Few early Christians were women.
4 Priests used to create paintings.

(E)

No. 21
1 They often have successful family members.
2 They often have low levels of stress.
3 They may miss chances to enjoy simple pleasures.
4 They may make people around them happy.

No. 22
1 They do not need family support to stay happy.
2 Their incomes are not likely to be high.
3 Their positive moods make them more active.
4 They are more intelligent than unhappy people.

(F)

No. 23
1 They are becoming better at fighting disease.
2 Their numbers are lower than they once were.
3 Many of them are not harvested for food.
4 The waters they live in are becoming cleaner.

No. 24
1 Native American harvesting practices helped oysters grow.
2 Native American harvesting methods included dredging.
3 Native Americans still harvest oysters.
4 Native Americans only harvested young oysters.

(G)

No. 25

Situation: You are about to take a tour bus around a town in Italy. You want to join the guided walking tour. You hear the following announcement.

Question: Which bus stop should you get off at?

1 Stop 4.
2 Stop 7.
3 Stop 9.
4 Stop 13.

(H)

No. 26

Situation: You are abroad on a working-holiday program. You call the immigration office about renewing your visa and are told the following.

Question: What should you do first?

1 Fill out an application online.
2 Request salary statements from your employer.
3 Show evidence of your savings.
4 Obtain a medical examination certificate.

(I)

No. 27

Situation: You are a supermarket manager. You want to reduce losses caused by theft. A security analyst tells you the following.

Question: What should you do first?

1 Give some staff members more training.
2 Install more security cameras.
3 Review customer receipts at the exit.
4 Clearly mark prices for fruit.

No. 28

Situation: You want a new washing machine. You currently own a Duplanne washing machine. You visit an electronics store in July and hear the following announcement.

Question: What should you do to save the most money?

1 Download the store's smartphone app.
2 Apply for the cash-back deal.
3 Exchange your washing machine this month.
4 Buy a new Duplanne washing machine in August.

(K)

No. 29

Situation: You see a suit you want in a local store, but it does not have one in your size. You do not want to travel out of town. A clerk tells you the following.

Question: What should you do?

1 Wait until the store gets some new stock.
2 Have the clerk check the other store.
3 Order the suit from the online store.
4 Have the suit delivered to your home.

You have **one minute** to prepare.

This is a story about a couple that wanted to be involved with their community.

You have **two minutes** to narrate the story.

Your story should begin with the following sentence:

One day, a husband and wife were going on a walk together.

Questions

No. 1   Please look at the fourth picture. If you were the wife, what would you be thinking?

No. 2   Do you think parents should participate in school events such as sports festivals?

No. 3   Do public libraries still play an important role in communities?

No. 4   Should more companies offer their employees flexible work schedules?

You have **one minute** to prepare.

This is a story about a woman who wanted to go on a trip.
You have **two minutes** to narrate the story.

Your story should begin with the following sentence:
One day, a woman was talking with her friend.

Questions

No. 1   Please look at the fourth picture. If you were the woman, what would you be thinking?

No. 2   Do you think it is good for university students to have part-time jobs?

No. 3   Do you think it is safe to give personal information to online businesses?

No. 4   Should the government do more to increase the employment rate in Japan?

旺文社の英検®書

☆ 一発合格したいなら「全問＋パス単」！

旺文社が自信を持っておすすめする王道の組み合わせです。

過去問集
過去問で出題傾向をしっかりつかむ！
☆ 英検®過去6回全問題集 1〜5級
[音声アプリ対応] [音声ダウンロード] [別売CDあり]

単熟語集
過去問を徹底分析した「でる順」！
☆ 英検®でる順パス単 1〜5級
[音声アプリ対応] [音声ダウンロード]

模試
本番形式の予想問題で総仕上げ！
7日間完成 英検®予想問題ドリル 1〜5級
[CD付] [音声アプリ対応]

参考書
申し込みから面接まで英検のすべてがわかる！
英検®総合対策教本 1〜5級
[CD付]

問題集
大問ごとに一次試験を集中攻略！
DAILY英検®集中ゼミ 1〜5級
[音声アプリ対応] [音声ダウンロード]

二次対策
動画で面接をリアルに体験！
英検®二次試験・面接完全予想問題 1〜3級
[DVD＋CD付] [音声アプリ対応]

このほかにも多数のラインナップを揃えております。

 旺文社の英検®合格ナビゲーター
https://eiken.obunsha.co.jp/
英検合格を目指す方のためのウェブサイト。
試験情報や級別学習法、おすすめの英検書を紹介しています。

※英検®は、公益財団法人 日本英語検定協会の登録商標です。

株式会社 旺文社　〒162-8680　東京都新宿区横寺町55
https://www.obunsha.co.jp/

2024年度版

文部科学省後援

英検®準1級

過去6回全問題集

別冊解答

旺文社

2024年度版

文部科学省後援

英検®
準1級
過去6回
全問題集

別冊解答

英検®は、公益財団法人 日本英語検定協会の登録商標です。　　旺文社

もくじ

Contents

正答率 ★75%以上 は，旺文社「英検®一次試験 解答速報サービス」において
回答者の正答率が 75%以上だった設問を示しています。

2023-2

解 答 一 覧

一次試験・筆記

1

(1)	3	(10)	4	(19)	2
(2)	2	(11)	2	(20)	1
(3)	3	(12)	2	(21)	3
(4)	1	(13)	4	(22)	1
(5)	2	(14)	4	(23)	1
(6)	3	(15)	3	(24)	1
(7)	4	(16)	1	(25)	2
(8)	4	(17)	2		
(9)	2	(18)	1		

2

(26)	3	(29)	3
(27)	4	(30)	2
(28)	2	(31)	4

3

(32)	4	(35)	4	(38)	4
(33)	4	(36)	1	(39)	2
(34)	2	(37)	3	(40)	3
				(41)	1

4　　解答例は本文参照

一次試験・リスニング

Part 1

No. 1	4	No. 5	3	No. 9	3
No. 2	3	No. 6	2	No.10	4
No. 3	1	No. 7	4	No.11	4
No. 4	1	No. 8	1	No.12	2

Part 2

No.13	2	No.17	2	No.21	1
No.14	4	No.18	3	No.22	3
No.15	1	No.19	2	No.23	3
No.16	1	No.20	4	No.24	2

Part 3

No.25	3	No.28	2
No.26	4	No.29	2
No.27	3		

(1) ─解答 ③
訳 レイラは，上級クラスのトレーニングが厳し過ぎると分かったので，より簡単なクラスに変更することにした。
解説 〈find＋O＋C〉「OがCと分かる」の用法。advanced → easier という変更から，上級クラスのトレーニングは厳しい（strenuous）と考えられる。subtle「（違いが）微妙な」，contrary「反対の」，cautious「慎重な」

(2) ─解答 ②
訳 税理士は，女性に過去1年間の全ての財務記録を収集するよう依頼した。彼は，彼女の納税申告書の作成を始める前にそれを確認する必要があった。
解説 〈ask＋O＋to *do*〉「Oに～するよう頼む」の形。目的語の all her financial records「全ての財務記録」に合う動詞は compile「（資料を）収集する」。punctuate「句読点を入れる」，bleach「漂白する」，obsess「（受動態で）取りつかれる」

(3) ─解答 ③
訳 エミリオは家の水道管の1本にわずかな水漏れを発見した。安全のため，彼は何が問題なのかが正確に分かるまで，水を止めるのにバルブを閉めた。
解説 水道管に水漏れ（leak）を発見した状況。水を止めるのに給水バルブ（valve）を閉めたと考えられる。turn off は「（栓をひねって）～（水）を止める」の意。depot「（鉄道・バスの）駅」，canal「運河」，panel「仕切り，羽目板」

(4) ─解答 ①
訳 A：あなたとリンダは知り合ってどれくらいになるの，ビル？
B：ああ，少なくとも10年，いやもっと長い付き合いかな。
解説 *be* acquainted (with each other) は「（互いに）知り合いである」の意味で，Bの know each other はその言い換え。それぞれ discharge「放出する，（人を）（義務などから）解放する」，emphasize「強調する」，subdue「制圧する」の過去分詞。

(5) ─解答 ② 正答率 ★75%以上
訳 私たちの地域公民館は，普段はメインルームが1つありますが，必要な際は，仕切りを閉めて，2つの小部屋を作ることができます。
解説 one main room を two smaller rooms にするのに何を閉めるかを考えると，partition「仕切り」である。estimation「評価，見積もり」，assumption「仮定」，notion「概念」

(6) ─解答 ③
訳 タイラーの父親は，海外で両替すると高くつくことが多いため，休暇の

前に地元の銀行で外貨をいくらか入手するよう彼に勧めた。

解説 get A from B に着目する。銀行から得られるのは foreign currency「外国通貨（外貨）」である。tactic「作戦」，bait「餌」，menace「脅し」

(7) ― 解答　④

訳 豊富な天然資源のおかげで，国は金属，石炭，天然ガスなどの輸出を通じて多額のお金を得ることができる。

解説 such as 以下は natural resources の具体例。it is able to ... はポジティブな内容なので，豊富な（abundant）天然資源があると分かる。unjust「不当な」，insubstantial「実体のない」，elastic「弾力性のある」

(8) ― 解答　④

訳 最初，エンゾは履歴書に6つの前職を全て記載した。しかし，その文書を1ページにまとめるのに，そのうちの2つを削除しなければならなかった。

解説 空所直後の the document は第1文の his résumé のこと。空所後に into があることと，6つの前職の記載から2つを削除するという状況を踏まえて，condense A into B「A を B に要約［短縮］する」で表す。dispute「議論する」，mumble「つぶやく」，mistrust「信頼しない」

(9) ― 解答　②

訳 ほとんどの国では，適切なビザなしで働いている外国人は，発見されると国外追放される。しかし，彼らを故郷に送り返すには多額のお金がかかり得る。

解説 第1文は主節も if 節も受動態で，if の後の they は空所前の foreigners ... visa「適切なビザなしで働いている外国人」を指している。deport「（外国人を）国外追放する」が文意に合う。それぞれ mend「修理する」，perceive「知覚する」，distribute「配布する」の過去分詞。

(10) ― 解答　④

訳 ティムはスマートフォンの使用に時間を費やし過ぎているのではないかと心配している。彼は数分ごとに E メールをチェックしなければならないという強い衝動を感じている。

解説 スマホの使用時間を心配する理由は，数分ごとに E メールをチェックしなければならないという衝動（compulsion）を感じているからである。suspension「一時的停止」，extension「延長」，seclusion「隔離」

(11) ― 解答　②

訳 A：今年の新年の抱負は立てた，セレナ？

B：うん，間食には甘い物の代わりに健康的なおやつを食べることを始めようと決めたわ。チョコレートやキャンディーを絶つのは難しいけど。

解説 B は間食に関する決意を述べているので，resolution「抱負」が適切。astonishment「驚き」，vulnerability「弱点」，repression「抑圧」

(12) – 解答 ②

訳　ミランダは，預金口座にあるお金の額が減っていることに気付いたので，毎月の出費を減らすことにした。

解説　出費を減らすことにした理由は，預金が減っているから。dwindle「縮まる，減少する」の過去進行形にする。それぞれ graze「擦りむく」，browse「（商品などを）見て歩く，ざっと目を通す」，rebound「跳ね返る」の -ing 形。

(13) – 解答 ④　　　　　　　　　　　　　　正答率 ★75%以上

訳　女の子は高い所が怖かったので，父親の手をしっかりつかんだ。彼らが塔のてっぺんから窓の外を見る間，彼女はその手をしっかりと握った。

解説　第 2 文の it は第 1 文の her father's hand を指し，この held it tightly と同義である grip「しっかりつかむ」の過去形 gripped が正解。それぞれ harass「困らせる」，breach「（法律などを）破る」，drain「（液体を）流出させる」の過去形。

(14) – 解答 ④

訳　アキコは，同僚たちが静かに会話をしているのを見て，詮索せずにはいられなかった。彼女は彼（女）らが何を話しているのか聞こうと彼（女）らに近寄った。

解説　アキコが静かに会話をしている同僚たちに近寄った理由を考えると，nosy「詮索好きな（≒ curious）」が文意に合う。obedient「従順な」，flexible「柔軟な」，sinful「罪深い」

(15) – 解答 ③

訳　吹雪で，登山者たちは山の頂上に到達できなかった。彼らは頂上からわずか数百メートルの所で引き返さなければならなかった。

解説　吹雪で登山者たちができなくなったのは，山の頂上（summit）に到達すること。subsidy「助成金」，mirage「蜃気楼（しんきろう）」，crutch「松葉づえ」

(16) – 解答 ①

訳　ジョナサンは会社に入社したころ，一日中何もしないことがよくあった。しかし，数カ月後，彼はより多くの業務を引き受け，今では暇な時間がほとんどない。

解説　However の前後に注意して読むと，入社当時は業務が少なく暇な（free）時間が多かったと予想できる。idle は「（仕事があるのに）怠惰な（≒ lazy）」と「何もしないでいる，暇な」の意味があり，ここでは後者の意味。agile「機敏な」，sane「正気な」，needy「非常に貧しい」

(17) – 解答 ②

訳　A：何だと思う？　例のテレビ局のアナウンサーの面接を受けることになったんだ！

　　B：それは素晴らしい，でもまだ楽観的になり過ぎないで。あのポジショ

ンは競争が激しいだろうから。

解説 Aが面接を受けるポジションについて，Bは a lot of competition「競争が激しい，競争率が高い」と言っているので，まだ楽観的（optimistic）にならないよう忠告していると考えられる。courteous「礼儀正しい」，suspicious「疑い深い」，flustered「どぎまぎした」

(18) – 解答

訳 通勤中，ジョシーは隣にいる列車の乗客のイヤホンから聞こえる音がうるさいと思ったので，別の席に移動することにした。

解説 〈so ～ that SV〉「とても～なので…」の構文。〈find＋O＋C〉「OがCと分かる」のOが the noise ... to her，空所に入る形容詞がCに当たる。別の席に移動したのは騒音がうるさい（bothersome）からである。compelling「説得力のある」，flattering「お世辞の」，daring「大胆な」

(19) – 解答 ・・・・・・・・・・ 正答率 ★75%以上

訳 A：今年の夏のパレードは信じられないほど混雑していたね。

　　B：ほんと！　通りにあまりにたくさんの観客がいたから，身動きするのがやっとだった。

解説 〈so ～ that SV〉「とても～なので…」の構文で，I could ... の前に that が省略されている。身動きするのがやっとだったのは，パレードが行われた通りに観客（spectators）が大勢いたからである。それぞれ patriot「愛国者」，mimic「模倣がうまい人［動物］」，executive「幹部」の複数形。

(20) – 解答 ・・・・・・・・・・・・・・・・・・・・・・・・・・・・・・・・・

訳 ジョセフは職場から家に帰るタクシー代を払う余裕があるかどうか確信がなかったが，財布を確認すると，乗車する十分なお金があると分かった。

解説 逆接を示す but に注意すると，タクシー代があるか分からなかったが，確認すると財布に十分な（ample）お金があった，とするのが自然。regal「威厳ある」，vain「無駄な」，crafty「悪賢い」

(21) – 解答 ③ ・・・

訳 親の関与は学校での生徒の成績を向上させることが明らかにされている。一例として，家庭で子供の宿題を手伝うことが挙げられる。

解説 第2文で示された「家庭で子供の宿題を手伝う」は親のすることと考えて，Parental involvement「親の関与」とする。obsolete「廃れた」，numb「無感覚な」，infamous「悪名高い」

(22) – 解答 ① ・・・

訳 過去数十年にわたり，多くの種が汚染によって絶滅しかけた。しかし，最近の保護活動により，その一部が回復しつつある。

解説 However に着目して，recover「回復する」と対比する wipe out「～を絶滅させる」の過去分詞が適切。第2文の them は「絶滅しかけた種」。

それぞれ break up「～を解散させる」, fix up「～を修復する」, turn down「～（音量など）を下げる，～を却下する」の過去分詞。

(23) –解答 **1** ••

> **訳** デイブは，隣人が籠1杯分の新鮮な野菜をくれたときうれしかったが，家に帰ると，それらを調理する方法が分からないことに気付いた。

> **解説** 空所後の them は隣人からもらった野菜のこと。but があるので，「うれしかったが，調理方法が分からない」という主旨の文だと推測できる。go about「～（仕事・問題など）に取りかかる」が適切。pull out「～を引き出す」, take in「～を取り込む」, bring down「～を降ろす」

(24) –解答 **1** ••

> **訳** A：わが社は，あまりにも職業にふさわしくないように見えない限り，社員が楽な服装をすることを許可しています。
> B：それは私にとって新鮮です。私の前職ではカジュアルな服を着るとひんしゅくを買いましたので。

> **解説** B の casual clothes は A の comfortable clothes の言い換えで，カジュアルな服装ができることは新鮮（new）と言っているので，前職ではそれができなかったと考える。*be* frown on [upon] で「ひんしゅくを買う」という意味。それぞれ carry on「～を続ける」, enter into「～に入る」, cross off「～を（リストなどから）線を引いて消す」の過去分詞。

(25) –解答 **2** ••

> **訳** 先週，地域責任者はその小さい支店を訪れ，幾つかの会議に同席してそこでの様子を観察した。

> **解説** 選択肢の中で meetings「会議」に合うのは sit in on「～に同席する」の過去形。それぞれ go back on「～（約束など）を破る」, speak down to「偉そうに～に話す」, look up to「～を尊敬する」の過去形。

一次試験・筆記 **2** | 問題編 p.34～37

全文訳 **ドキュメンタリー・ブーム**

　近年，テレビのストリーミングサービスの成長がドキュメンタリーの巨大な新しい市場を生み出している。制作されるドキュメンタリーの数は急増し，歓迎される新しい機会を映像作家たちに提供しているが，負の側面もある。問題の1つは，多くの映像作家が内容に対するコントロールを失いつつあると感じていることである。ドキュメンタリーの中には，多くの観客を引き付け，多大な金銭的リターンをもたらすものもあるため，ストリーミングサービスを運営する企業は制作予算を惜しまなくなってきている。それほど多くのお金が絡むため，強烈なプレッシャーによってしばしば映像作家たちはあたかも商業的により魅力的なものにするために話の内容を変えるしかないかのように感じ

ている。

　これは，ドキュメンタリーの社会的価値の低下に関する懸念を招いている。ドキュメンタリーは，以前は調査報道の一形態と考えられていたが，その主題には顕著な変化があった。犯罪ノンフィクションなどのジャンルの人気が高まるにつれて，事実情報とエンターテインメントとの間の線引きが曖昧になってきている。かつては社会の問題について視聴者に知らせたり，認識を高めたりすることを専門としていたドキュメンタリーは，あまりにも頻繁に，主に視聴者を驚かせ，刺激することを目的とした扇情的なエンターテインメントになっているのだ。

　映像作家たちにとってもう1つの心配な動向は，有名人のドキュメンタリーの台頭である。以前は，映像作家たちは通常，人々が大げさに言ったり，あからさまなうそをついたりするよう仕向けることになるのを恐れて，ドキュメンタリーの一般人の被写体には支払いをしないというジャーナリズムの慣例に従っていた。しかし今では，ミュージシャンなどの有名人は，自分の話に何百万ドルもの支払いを受けており，その理由は多くの場合，これらのスターはほぼ間違いなく視聴者を引き付けるからである。当然のことだが，有名人以外の人々も報酬を要求し始めており，これが映像作家たちに道徳的なジレンマを生み出している。

> 語句 skyrocket「急上昇する」，generous「物惜しみしない」，intense「強烈な」，have no choice but to *do*「～する以外に選択肢がない」，alter「変える」，investigative「調査の」，noticeable「顕著な」，factual「事実に基づく」，blur「曖昧にする」，sensationalist「扇情的［センセーショナル］な」，primarily「主に」，celebrity「有名人」，〈for fear that SV〉「～を恐れて」，exaggerate「誇張する」，outright「明白な」，compensation「報酬」，dilemma「ジレンマ，板挟み」

(26) － 解答 ③ ‥‥‥‥‥‥‥‥‥‥‥‥‥‥‥‥‥‥‥‥‥‥‥‥‥

> 解説 第1段落では，ドキュメンタリー市場の拡大について述べた後，「負の側面もある」と前置きをして，One issue is that ... から段落最後まで具体的な問題点が述べられる。最終文から，映像作家たちはドキュメンタリーをより魅力的なものにするために話の内容を変えるしかないと思っていることが分かる。下線部の内容を「内容に対するコントロールを失う」と表した **3** が適切。本文の stories を content に言い換えている。

(27) － 解答 ④ ‥‥‥‥‥‥‥‥‥‥‥‥‥‥‥‥‥‥‥‥‥‥‥‥‥

> 解説 空所のある文の主語 This は第1段落で述べた問題点のこと。どんな懸念をもたらしたかというと，続く説明から，ドキュメンタリーの「社会的価値の低下」である。used to be considered や過去時制の were once devoted と，there has been, has become blurred, are (too frequently) becoming などの現在にかかわる時制に着目して，以前と今の対比を読み取ろう。

(28) – 解答 ②

解説 文頭に入る論理マーカーの問題。空所前後は，有名人に大金を支払えば一般人（noncelebrities）も報酬を要求するのが当然→映像作家たちの道徳的ジレンマ，という流れで，Understandably「当然のことだが」が適切。

全文訳 蟻浴（ぎょく）

　動物行動学の分野は，動物の行動を理解するためにその自然生息地において動物を研究することである。しかし，動物がすることの理由について結論を導き出すのは必ずしも簡単ではない。例えば，ある鳥は「蟻浴」と呼ばれる行動を示す。これは通常，鳥がくちばしで何匹かアリを拾い上げてその羽根に擦り付ける行為である。同様に，鳥が翼を広げてアリ塚に座って，アリにその体中をはい回らせる様子も観察されている。広範な観察にもかかわらず，動物行動学者たちはなぜ鳥たちがこのような行動を取るのか，まだ確信を持てずにいる。

　有力な説の1つは，この行動は鳥の健康に寄与するというものである。アリは自らを細菌や真菌から保護する蟻酸という物質を自然分泌するが，これはほかの昆虫にとっては有毒でもある。この物質を鳥の羽根に擦り込むことにより，病気を防ぎ，有害な害虫を寄せ付けないようにできる。鳥は一般にアリを利用するが，代わりに特定の甲虫やヤスデを拾い上げているのを目撃されている鳥もいる。これらの生物も有害な害虫を近づかせない化学物質を分泌するという事実が，この説を裏付けている。

　別の提唱されている説は，鳥の羽根にアリを擦り付けることでアリに食べられる準備をさせるというものである。ある実験で，科学者たちは，一部の鳥は，蟻酸を保持したアリよりも，科学者によって蟻酸を除去されたアリを食べる可能性が高いことを発見した。蟻酸は，アリの栄養豊富な腹部の隣にある嚢（のう）の中に貯蔵されている。一部の科学者は，蟻浴は，鳥がくちばしでこの嚢を取り除くこと —— このプロセスはアリをこれほどの魅力的なおやつにしているアリの部位を傷つける可能性がある —— をしようとする必要なく，アリに蟻酸を放出させているのではないかと推測している。

語句 ethology「動物行動学」，beak「くちばし」，rub「擦り付ける」，anthill「アリ塚」，crawl「はう」，extensive「広範囲の」，ethologist「動物行動学者」，formic acid「蟻酸」，fungus「真菌（複数形は fungi）」，toxic「有毒な」，inhibit「抑制する」，deter「阻止する」，pest「害虫」，beetle「甲虫」，millipede「ヤスデ」，organism「生物」，retain「保持する」，sac「嚢」，nutrient-rich「栄養豊富な」，abdomen「腹部」

(29) – 解答 ③

解説 空所前は鳥がアリを羽に擦り付ける行為，空所後はアリに体中をはい回らせる行為についてなので，似たような内容を結び付ける Similarly が入る。タイトルの anting を知らなくても第1段落半ばで" "の形で登場し，詳しい説明があるので，文脈が理解できれば問題ない。

(30) – 解答 ②

解説 第2段落は anting の説の1つ目。空所後は，アリが分泌する物質である蟻酸（formic acid）が鳥を病気や害虫から守るという話なので，**2**「この行動（＝ anting）は鳥の健康に寄与する」が適切。文中に専門用語が多く出てくるが，知らない語があっても，「アリは formic acid という物質を出す」のように英語のまま読み進めればよい。また，bacteria and fungi や beetles and millipedes のように難語が and で結ばれている場合は，片方が分かれば他方はその同類だと思えばよい。

(31) – 解答 ④

解説 第3段落は anting の別の説。空所後は，鳥は formic acid のないアリを食べる傾向にあり，formic acid を貯蔵する sac をくちばしで取り除かずとも，anting をすることでアリに formic acid を放出させているのではないかという話。つまり，anting はアリを食べられる状態にしていると考えて，**4** が適切。最終文がやや難しいが，選択肢を順に空所に入れて，段落の要旨に合わないものを消去していけば **4** が残るだろう。

一次試験・筆記 **3** 問題編 p.38 ~ 44

全文訳 **アメリカ合衆国における大学の発展**

　土地の売却は富を増やすためのよくある方法であるが，19世紀のアメリカの農村の地主たちにとって，これは必ずしも簡単ではなかった。当時の農村人口は少なかったため，地主たちは買い手を引き付ける方法を必要としていた。1つの方法は価格を安く抑えることだったが，地主たちは別の戦略にも取り組んだ。それは大学を建てることであった。大学は文化や学びの中心地であったため，こうすることによって彼らの地域の土地がより望ましいものになった。驚くほど急速に大学が建設され，1880年までには，ヨーロッパの5倍の数の大学がアメリカに存在した。

　少数の古いエリート大学を例外として，ほとんどのアメリカの大学にはわずかな数の学生と講師しかいなかった。教員は学者というよりも，多くの場合，当時アメリカに存在したキリスト教のさまざまな宗派を代表する宗教家であった。大学経営者たちは，これがそういった宗教団体の学生を引き付けるのに役立つことを知っていた。大学への入学は一般的に，学生が学費を支払える限り，難しくはなかった。その学費は，学生募集の激しい競争の結果，低く抑えられていた。残念ながら，学生数が少ないことは多くの大学が閉鎖せざるを得なかったことを意味し，生き残った大学は常に資金集めをすることでしか経営を続けることができなかった。

　しかし，20世紀のアメリカの人口とともに，高等教育に対する需要も増え続けた。残った大学は，土地や建物，図書館など，しっかりと確立されたインフラがあったため，この需要に応えるのに有利な立場にあった。さらに，これらの大学はたいてい質の高い教

育や良いスポーツ・レジャー施設を提供していたが，それはこれらの大学が生き延びてきた方法の１つが学生のニーズに細やかに対応することだったからである。大学が自らの未来を確かなものにしたもう１つの方法は，寛大な寄付をしてくれる卒業生たちと密接なつながりを持ち続けたことであった。これら全ての要因が，アメリカの大学システムを世界で最も成功している大学システムの１つに変えるのに役立った。

語句 scholar「学者」，faculty「（大学）教員」，administrator「経営［管理］者」，admission「入学（許可）」，tuition「（大学の）授業料」，fierce「激しい」，recruit「募集する」，well-established「確立された」，infrastructure「インフラ」，accommodate「（要求などを）受け入れる」，graduate「卒業生」，transform A into B「A を B に変える」

(32) – 解答 **4** .... 正答率 ★75%以上

問題文の訳 なぜ 19 世紀にアメリカでそれほど多くの大学が建てられたのか。

選択肢の訳
1 農村地域の富裕度が高まったことで，子供たちに大学教育を受けさせたいと思う家庭が増えた。
2 裕福な地主たちが，自分たちの公的イメージを良くする手段，また死後も確実に記憶に残るようにする手段として大学を建設した。
3 アメリカに住むヨーロッパ人たちが，母国で受けられるのと同レベルの教育を提供してくれる大学を望んだ。
4 大学の建設は，農村地域に土地を所有する人々にとって，自分の土地の価値を高め，より多くの買い手を引き付ける方法だった。

解説 第１段落第２～３文から，大学建設は地主が土地の買い手を引き付ける方法だったことが分かる。また第４文から，大学は文化や学びの中心地だったため，大学建設で地域の土地がより望ましいものになる（more desirable = **4** の increase the value of their land）と考えたことが分かる。従って，**4** が正解。

(33) – 解答 **4** ....

問題文の訳 19 世紀のアメリカの大学の多くの教員について正しいものはどれか。

選択肢の訳
1 彼らは劣悪な条件下で勤務を強いられたために短期間で辞めた。
2 彼らの給与は通常，大学自体ではなく宗教団体から支払われた。
3 大学で最高の役職に就くために，彼らの間で激しい競争があった。
4 彼らの宗教的背景は，学生を自分の大学に入学させるのにしばしば効果的な方法となった。

解説 第２段落第２～３文から，大学経営者たちは，教員をキリスト教系の宗教家にすることで，それら宗教団体の学生を引き付けようと考えたことが分かる。第３文の this は前文の内容を受けている。

(34) – 解答 ....

問題文の訳 20 世紀にアメリカの大学が成功した理由の１つは，それらの大学が

選択肢の訳
1 体育プログラムの質を高めるために地元のスポーツチームとパート

　　ナーシップを結んだことである。

2　かつての学生と永続的な関係を築くことで，経済的な安定を高めることができたことである。

3　主に地元の学生を募集することに重点を置くことで，他大学との競争を軽減したことである。

4　独自の施設を建設する代わりに地域社会にすでにある施設を利用することで経費を抑えたことである。

> **解説**　20世紀に大学が成功した理由は，第3段落第2〜4文で幾つか書かれている。このうち，卒業生からの寄付について述べた第4文のAnother way ... と**2**が合う。それぞれ本文のgraduatesと**2**のformer students, maintaining close tiesとlasting relationshipsが言い換え。

全文訳　**機械か人間か？**

　2004年に，NASAの探査機オポチュニティーが火星に着陸した。「オッピー」という愛称を付けられた，ゴルフカートぐらいの大きさのこの探査機は，火星を調査し，その地表の画像を撮影するために送られた。オッピーのミッションは90日間続く予定であったが，この探査機はその後15年にわたり写真やデータを地球に送信し続けた。その間，オッピーは世間の想像力をかき立てた。実際，人々はあまりにもオッピーに愛着を持つようになったため，それが作動しなくなったときに，ソーシャルメディアを介して亡くなった人に向けるような哀悼のメッセージを送ったほどである。

　擬人化として知られている，人間以外のものに人間的特性を持たせるこの行為は，人間が幼いころからでも自然に行うものである。例えば，どの年齢の人にとっても，おもちゃや車，家などの物に情緒的愛着を形成することは，不自然ではない。エンジニアたちでさえ，オッピーのことを頻繁に「彼女」と言及したり，オッピーを子供のように思ったりしており，この傾向と無縁ではなかった。無生物の物に人間的性質を投影することの影響の1つは，これによって人はそれを守らないといけないという気持ちになり，それの健全性に対する気遣いを引き出すことだと思われる。NASAは，オッピーを体から伸びた頭のような構造物に目のようなカメラレンズを付けたデザインにして，オッピーを意図的により人間らしく見えるようにすることで，この現象をうまく利用したようである。オポチュニティーのミッション以前，広く報道された数々の失敗によってNASAに対する世間の信頼は弱まっており，NASAの資金は削減されていた。オッピーに人間的な特徴を持たせることは，世間の心をつかむこと，そしておそらくNASAのミッションのための追加資金を集めることにさえ有効な戦略であったと示唆されている。

　オッピーを人間と思うことは無害であるように思えるかもしれない一方で，物を擬人化することが不幸な結果を招くことがある。例えば，AIが人間の脳と同じように働くと想定することは，AIの能力に対する非現実的な期待につながる可能性があり，その結果，AIが大きな利益をもたらすことができない状況で使用されることになる。擬人化によって，AIや機械が人間に対して反乱を起こすといった悪夢のシナリオを人々が危惧するよ

うになることもあり得る。脅威としての機械というこの考えは，機械が人間と同じように論理的に思考するという誤解から生じている。しかし，人は擬人化せずにはいられないようである。ジャーナリストであるスコット・サイモンはこう書いている。「機械に話しかけたり，機械からの応答を待ったり，機械のことを心配したりなど，機械と長い時間を過ごせば，科学者たちでさえも機械に人格を見いだし始める」。

(35) – 解答

問題文の訳 オッピーに対する人々の反応について分かることは何か。

選択肢の訳
1 火星に関する新しい発見に興味があったため，人々はすぐにオッピーを応援した。
2 オッピーのミッションの重要性を人々に知らせる努力がほとんど行われていなかったため，人々はオッピーに親しみを感じるのが難しかった。
3 オッピーが地球に送り返した情報が専門的過ぎて科学者ではない人には理解できなかったため，人々は程なくしてオッピーのミッションへの興味を失った。
4 人々はオッピーに強い感情的なつながりを感じていたため，オッピーが作動しなくなったときはオッピーに哀悼の意を表した。

解説 第1段落から火星探査機オッピーのミッションを読み取る。当初の予定より長く運用されたというポジティブな内容の後，人々の反応について書かれた In fact, people ... の内容と **4** が一致する。それぞれ本文の〈so ~ that SV〉「とても～なので…」と **4** の〈such a [an] ~ that SV〉，ceased to function と stopped operating，condolence と sympathy が対応する。

(36) – 解答

問題文の訳 第2段落によると，オッピーをより人間らしく見せたことは，

選択肢の訳
1 NASA の活動に対する全体的な支持を増やすため，そしてより多くの資金を得られるようにするために計画された戦略だった，という可能性が高いようだ。
2 子供たちが人間に似たロボットへの興味の高まりを示した数々の実験に基づいていた，という可能性が高いようだ。
3 心理学者たちが，この戦略によりエンジニアたちが予定通りにそれを

完成させるためにより懸命に働くだろうと示唆したために行われた，という可能性が高いようだ。

4 NASAのデザインをおもちゃに使用しやすくするよう政府が圧力をかけた結果だった，という可能性が高いようだ。

解説 オッピーのデザインについては NASA appears to have utilized this phenomenon ... にある。この this phenomenon は前述から，擬人化によって人間が無生物の物に情緒的愛着を形成することを指す。この現象を利用してオッピーを人間のように見せたのである。この戦略の成果が書かれた最終文の an effective strategy to ... から，**1** が正解。それぞれ本文の win over the public と **1** の increase overall support, attract additional funding と receive more money が類義表現。

(37) – 解答 ③

問題文の訳 この文章によると，擬人化の潜在的な問題は何か。

選択肢の訳
1 人間が自分でやった方が安く済むであろう作業を行うのに機械を頼るようになる可能性がある。

2 AIや機械が作業を正しく行うのに何の指導も必要ないと人々が誤って思い込む可能性がある。

3 AIや機械が人間と同じように振る舞うという考えは，人々がそれらにできることを誤解する原因となり得る。

4 科学者たちがAIと築く関係は，彼らが人間の要求よりもAIの発展を優先させる原因になり得る。

解説 第3段落では，物を擬人化することの負の影響について話が展開する。「AIが人間の脳と同じよう働くと想定することは，AIの能力に対する非現実的な期待につながる可能性がある」という第2文の内容を言い換えている **3** が正解。**3** では，AIや機械の擬人化（The belief that AI and machines act in a similar way to humans）は，人々がそれらにできることを誤解する原因となり得る（cause people to misunderstand what they are able to do）と表している。

全文訳 **マリウスの改革**

　紀元前2世紀終わりごろ，ローマ共和国は西ヨーロッパの諸部族民による侵攻の脅威に直面し，アフリカにおいて数々の屈辱的な敗北を経験した。急激に拡大する共和国の要求にローマ軍はもはや応えることはできないと気付き，ローマの指導者ガイウス・マリウスは全面的な改革の実施に着手した。これらはマリウスの改革として知られるようになり，これらの改革はローマ軍を，古代においておそらく最も効果的な戦闘部隊であるほぼ無敵の軍事組織に変えた。伝統的に，ローマ軍への兵士の入隊は一時的なものであったため，継続的な募集を余儀なくされ，必然的に新兵は戦闘経験がないことが多かった。さらに，軍に入隊するには財産所有が必要とされたが，ローマ共和国内で拡大して

いた貧困によってこの要件を満たす潜在的な新兵の要員が大幅に減少した。

　マリウスの改革は，幾つかの施策から成り，財産要件と新兵が自分の武器や甲冑（かっちゅう）を用意する必要性の両方の撤廃が含まれていた。これによって最貧困層の市民までもが入隊することができるようになり，また軍は使用する武器や甲冑を標準化し改良することができたため，兵士たちの装備もより整うようになった。ローマ軍の兵士は「軍団兵」として知られるようになり，軍事戦略の訓練を受けた。おそらく最も重要であったのは，これらの改革が入隊への決定的な動機を与えていたことである。つまり，16年間兵役に服した兵士は誰でも，1区画の農地と完全なローマ市民権が報酬として与えられたのだ。ローマ共和国の急速な拡大は，貧困の中で暮らしている多くの非市民の住民がいることと，彼らにとってその状況から逃れられる機会は非常に魅力的だったことを意味していた。

　ローマ軍のよりよく訓練されより意欲的な兵士たちは，重要な軍事的勝利を収め，ローマの拡大に貢献した。元軍団兵が受け取った土地は通常，新規に占領した属州にあったため，これらの兵役経験者たちはローマの文化を広めるのに役立った。また彼らの存在は，ローマの支配に対する地元の抵抗に打ち勝つことを容易にし，ローマ共和国への統合の過程を促進した。兵役経験者がいるだけで，彼らは反乱を防いだり侵略に抵抗したりする手助けになったため，新しい領地により大きな安全をもたらした。

　マリウスの改革はローマ軍を大きく改善した反面，最終的にローマ共和国の崩壊につながる，ローマ社会への予期せぬ影響も与えた。軍が主に必要に応じて徴兵された裕福な市民で構成されているときは，軍はローマの政治にはほとんど影響力を持たなかった。しかしマリウスの改革後は，軍の軍団兵が非常に規律正しくなり，将軍たちに対する強い忠誠心を持つようになった。結果として，将軍たちは，ローマ共和国の保護や拡大を確実にするためよりも，自分たちが政治的な影響力を得るために自らの指揮下にある軍隊を利用したいという衝動を抑えるのが困難になった。これは内戦を結果的に生み，最終的にはユリウス・カエサルが軍を利用して，選出された政府を転覆させることに成功し，自分がローマの指導者だと宣言した。これは，比較的民主的だったローマ共和国の終焉（しゅうえん）を示し，全権力を持つ皇帝が統治する独裁政権の誕生への道を開いた。

（語句）humiliating「屈辱的な」，implement「実施する」，sweeping「全面的な」，unstoppable「止められない」，arguably「おそらく」，enlistment「入隊」，necessitate「必要とする」，inevitably「必然的に」，armor「甲冑」，enlist「入隊する，入隊させる」，legionary「（古代ローマの）軍団兵」，compensate A with B「AにBで報いる」，a plot of「1区画の〜」，triumph「勝利」，conquer「占領する」，province「（古代ローマの）属州」，veteran「兵役経験者，退役軍人」，instrumental「役に立つ」，facilitate「促進する」，integration「統合」，downfall「崩壊」，disciplined「規律正しい」，general「将軍」，temptation「衝動」，overthrow「転覆させる」，relatively「比較的」，pave the way for「〜への道を開く」，dictatorship「独裁政権」

(38) – 解答 **4**

問題文の訳 マリウスの改革の理由の1つは何だったか。

選択肢の訳
1 ローマ共和国内の財政問題は，ローマの指導者が軍への資金を削減せざるを得ないことを意味した。
2 軍の兵士の数が増加するにつれて，ローマ共和国を守るために彼らを西ヨーロッパやアフリカに輸送することがより困難になった。
3 兵士たちは何年間も軍にとどまることを強いられ，また軍務に対する賃金が低かったため，兵士たちの間で不満が生じた。
4 ローマの指導者は，軍にはローマ共和国が軍事目標を達成するのに必要な人員や技術がないことを懸念していた。

解説 第1段落の〈Traditionally, ＋過去完了〉はマリウスの改革以前の話で，この部分以降に改革の理由がある。「新兵に戦闘経験がない（＝ skills がない）」，「拡大する貧困によって潜在的な新兵が減少（＝ manpower がない）」の2点を含んだ**4**が正解。

(39) – 解答 **2**

問題文の訳 マリウスの改革によって起こった重要な変化は何だったか。

選択肢の訳
1 ローマ市民だけがローマ軍に入隊できるという規則が導入され，その結果，ローマ市民権を取得しようとする人が増えた。
2 ローマ軍で働くことは，ローマ共和国に住む人々が自分の生活を向上させる手段であったため，より魅力的なものになった。
3 ローマ軍は，すでに軍隊経験のある者しか受け入れなかったため，十分な新兵を見つけるのに苦労した。
4 兵士がローマ軍で過ごす必要のある年数が短縮され，兵士の平均年齢が下がった。

解説 第2段落参照。重要な話が続く目印 Perhaps most importantly, の後に手掛かりがある。改革によって，貧困層も入隊できるようになり，16年間兵役に服せば土地が与えられた。これを improve their lives と抽象的に表した**2**が正解。attractive は本文の appealing の言い換え。

(40) – 解答 **3**

問題文の訳 第3段落によると，ローマ軍が新しい領土を占領した後，

選択肢の訳
1 軍が近隣地域を攻撃し，ローマ共和国の拡大を継続できるようにするために，それらの地域に派遣される兵士の数が大幅に増えただろう。
2 地元の人々はローマの言語と文化を学ぶためにローマの首都に招かれたので，ローマ社会にすぐに慣れることができた。
3 元兵士たちはそこの土地が与えられ，それによって地元民を統制し，さまざまな脅威からその地域が確実に守られるようにすることがはるかに容易になった。
4 軍が多発する反乱を防ぐことは不可能だったため，それらの地域はし

ばしばすぐに再び失われた。

第3段落では元兵士が新たに占領した領土の土地を受け取った後の影響が書かれている。Their presence also ... と The mere presence ... の2文を適切にまとめた**3**が正解。それぞれ本文の overcome local resistance to Roman rule と**3**の control the local people, rebellions / invasions と various threats が対応している。

(41) –解答

問題文の訳 マリウスの改革がローマ社会に与えた影響は何か。

選択肢の訳
1 軍が政治的手段として利用され，ローマの指導者が市民に選ばれるのではなく軍事力によってその地位を獲得する仕組みを生み出した。

2 兵役を拒否した人々の富と社会的地位が低下したが，一方で元軍団兵はしばしば高い政治的地位を獲得した。

3 ローマ軍は非常に大規模になったため，その維持にかかる費用がローマ共和国崩壊の主な原因となった。

4 軍団兵内の規律の欠如がローマ市民と軍の間の緊張を生み出し，やがて内戦につながった。

解説 第4段落は負の影響に話が展開する。Following the Marian reforms, ... から，将軍たちは忠誠心ある軍団兵を利用して政治的影響力を得たいという衝動を抑えるのが困難だと感じていたこと，また This resulted in civil wars, ... から，これが内戦につながり，ユリウス・カエサル（＝正解**1**の a Roman leader）が軍を利用して（＝ by military power）選出された（＝ being chosen by the people）政府を転覆させ，全権力を持つ皇帝による独裁政権が誕生したことが分かる。

一次試験・筆記 **4** | 問題編 p.45

トピックの訳 企業はリサイクルしやすい製品を生産するよう求められるべきか。

ポイントの訳 ・企業の利益　・顧客の要望　・汚染　・製品の品質

解答例 Companies should be required to produce goods that are easy to recycle. This opinion is based on the following reasons: customer demand and pollution.

First, goods that are simple to recycle significantly reduce pollution. They not only lower the carbon footprint of factories but also lead to fewer products thrown away in landfills, where they often release harmful gases. Therefore, producing such goods is a key part of companies' environmental responsibility.

Second, customer demand for sustainable products has been

growing rapidly. Consumers are increasingly aware of the impact of their purchasing decisions, and many are actively seeking out eco-friendly products. If companies do not produce goods that are easily recyclable, they will fail to fulfill the needs of this growing market of environmentally conscious consumers.

In conclusion, producing goods that can be easily recycled should be required for companies, as this helps meet new consumer demands and protect the environment.

解説 序論：序論では，トピックに対する自分の意見を簡潔に書く。解答例ではまず，トピックの疑問文を肯定文に書き換えて Yes の立場を明確に示している。続いて This opinion is based on the following reasons:「この意見は次の理由に基づいている」という前置きの後，ポイントの Customer demand と Pollution を取り上げている。

本論：本論では，2つの観点に沿って，自分の意見を裏付ける理由・根拠を First, ..., Second, ... などの構成で書く。解答例の第2段落は Pollution の観点で，「リサイクルしやすい製品は汚染を大幅に削減する」と主張した後，汚染について掘り下げ，Therefore を用いて「従って，このような製品を生産することは企業の環境責任の重要な部分である」と意見を展開している。第2文の not only A but also B の構文や，関係詞節（ここでは where）を使って情報を追加する方法を確認しておこう。第3段落は Customer demand の観点で，「持続可能な製品に対する顧客の需要が急速に高まっている」という現状を述べた後，詳しい説明を続けている。should を含むトピックでは，第3文のように，if を用いて「もし～しなければ…だろう」という根拠の書き方も有効。

結論：最終段落では，序論で述べたトピックに対する意見を再主張する。解答例は In conclusion で始め，トピックの表現を言い換えて Yes の立場を示した後，その理由を as this helps ...「これは…につながるため」という表現でまとめている。問題用紙のポイントの語句はそのまま使う必要はない。例えば解答例の結論では Pollution の代わりに，protect the environment という表現を用いている。

そのほかの表現 reduce, lower, fewer, growing, rapidly, increasingly など，「増減・動向」を表す表現はさまざまなトピックで使える。動詞，形容詞，副詞を駆使してバリエーション豊かな文を書く練習をしておきたい。解答例では，「減」を表すのに，第2段落第1文では動詞 reduce を用い，続く第2文では動詞 lower，形容詞 fewer を用いている。また，トピックの「リサイクルしやすい製品」を意味する goods that are easy [simple] to recycle や goods that are easily recyclable などの関係詞節を用いた表現は，easily recyclable products や easy-to-recycle goods のように名詞句で表すと知的な印象を与える。

No.1－解答 **4** ・・・・・・・・・・・・・・・・・・・・・・・・・・・・ 正答率 ★**75%以上**

スクリプト ☆： Why are you reading that paperback book, Dad? I just gave you an e-reader for your birthday!

★： I already finished the book you downloaded for me.

☆： There's more where that came from. And there are a lot of free e-books on the Internet.

★： Yeah, I know. But downloading them is the problem.

☆： I'm always happy to help, Dad.

★： That would be great. And while you're at it, can you show me how to make the letters bigger on the reader?

☆： Of course.

Question: What is the man's problem?

全文訳 ☆： どうしてそんなペーパーバックの本を読んでるの，お父さん？　誕生日に電子書籍リーダーをあげたばかりじゃない！

★： 私のためにダウンロードしてくれた本はもう読み終わったよ。

☆： そこにはもっと本があるのよ。それにインターネット上には無料の電子書籍がたくさんあるわ。

★： うん，知ってる。でもダウンロードするのが問題なんだ。

☆： いつでも喜んで手伝うよ，お父さん。

★： それはとても助かるよ。ついでに，リーダーで文字を大きくする方法を教えてくれるかい？

☆： もちろん。

質問：男性の問題は何か。

選択肢の訳 **1** 電子書籍リーダーが見つからない。

2 電子書籍を買いたくない。

3 電子書籍リーダーを壊した。

4 電子書籍をダウンロードするのが難しいと思っている。

解説 冒頭のやりとりから，娘が父親の誕生日に電子書籍リーダーをあげたという状況をつかもう。父親の But downloading them is the problem. の them は e-books のことなので，**4** が正解。while you're at it は「事のついでに」という慣用表現。

No.2－解答 **3** ・・

スクリプト ☆： It's nice to see you coming to yoga class more regularly, José.

★： Yeah, I've been getting into it a little more lately. Still, the poses don't seem to get any easier.

22

☆： Be patient with yourself; change happens gradually.

★： Sometimes I feel embarrassed because the other students are so much more flexible.

☆： Don't worry about comparing yourself with anyone. Yoga is a holistic mind-and-body practice, not a competition.

★： I'll try to keep that in mind next time I fall over in class.

Question: What will the man probably do?

全文訳 ☆： あなたがより定期的にヨガ教室に来るのを見るのはうれしいわ，ホゼ。

★： ええ，最近ちょっとのめり込んじゃって。それでも，ポーズが簡単にできるようになるわけじゃないんですよ。

☆： 自分自身に我慢強くなることね，変化は徐々に起こるから。

★： ほかの生徒さんの体がずいぶん柔らかいから，ときどき僕は恥ずかしくなります。

☆： 誰かと自分を比べて気にする必要はないわ。ヨガは心身一体的な鍛錬であって，競争じゃないのよ。

★： 次にクラスで転倒したときにそれを思い出してみようと思います。

質問：男性はおそらく何をするか。

選択肢の訳 1 個人指導のヨガレッスンを受ける。

2 異なるアクティビティーを見つける。

3 今のクラスを続ける。

4 別のヨガグループに参加する。

解説 ヨガ教室での会話。未来の行動はたいてい会話の最後の方にある。男性は今後ヨガ教室で心掛ける（keep ～ in mind）ことを話しているので，今の教室に通い続けると考えて，**3** が正解。

No.3 – 解答

スクリプト ★： Have you met the new boss?

☆： I have. We discovered we're from the same hometown. We even went to the same high school, though she was a few years ahead of me.

★： Small world! What did you think of her?

☆： She's very knowledgeable about the publishing business. She has some interesting plans, and that's what our division needs.

★： Well, that's exciting. We need a supportive leader.

Question: What is one thing we learn about the new boss?

全文訳 ★： 新しい上司に会った？

☆： 会ったよ。私たち，故郷が同じことが分かったの。しかも同じ高校に通っていたのよ，彼女は私より数年先輩だけど。

★： 世間は狭いね！ 彼女のこと，どう思った？

☆： 出版業のことをとてもよく知っているね。面白い計画も幾つか持っているし，それはうちの部署が必要としているものだわ。

★： へえ，それは楽しみだ。僕たちには支えになるリーダーが必要だよね。

　　質問：新しい上司について分かることの1つは何か。

選択肢の訳　**1** 部署のための新しいアイデアを幾つか持っている。

　　2 出版業についてほとんど知らない。

　　3 素晴らしい学生だった。

　　4 従業員の給与を上げたいと思っている。

解説　話題は2人の新しい上司。女性の発言のうち，She has some interesting plans, and that's what our division needs. の部分と **1** が合う。会話中の plans を ideas に言い換えている。**2** は She's very knowledgeable about the publishing business. と合わない。

No.4 – 解答 ①

スクリプト　★： Why are all of your clothes piled up on the bed?

☆： I'm sorting through them to see which items I want to donate.

★： Didn't you do that about a month ago for a school fund-raiser? It's not like your size has changed since then.

☆： No, but the community center is gathering clothes for a family who just had a house fire. They lost everything.

★： That's terrible. Do they need men's clothes? I could part with a few items myself.

　　Question: Why is the woman giving away her clothes?

全文訳　★： どうして君の服が全部ベッドの上に山積みになっているの？

☆： どれを寄付したいか考えてみようと思ってそれらを整理しているの。

★： 学校の資金集めのイベントのために1カ月ほど前にそれをやってなかった？　あれから君のサイズが変わったわけじゃないだろう。

☆： うん，でもコミュニティーセンターが，家が火事になったばかりの家族のために服を集めているの。彼らは何もかも失ったのよ。

★： それはひどい。男性の服も必要かな？　僕も何点か手放せると思う。

　　質問：女性はなぜ自分の服を寄付しようとしているのか。

選択肢の訳　**1** 彼女は困っている家族を助けたい。

　　2 それらはもう自分のサイズに合わない。

　　3 学校で行事がある。

　　4 彼女はそれらを入れる収納スペースがない。

解説　女性の1番目と2番目の発言内容から，火事で何もかも失った家族に寄付するための服を選んでいることを理解しよう。**1** が正解で，その家族を in need「困っている」と表している。会話中の part with（〜を手放す）と質問の give away はいずれも女性の1番目の発言に出てくる

donate と同じ意味で使われている。

No.5 –解答 ③

スクリプト ★: Did you see the latest newsletter? It seems our merger with Evan's Real Estate is now official.

☆: I'm dreading moving our offices, but I admit it makes sense.

★: I agree. We've been working with their agents for years. This will just reduce our operating expenses and strengthen our market position.

☆: Yeah. But I've heard that some of our staff have decided to leave to work on their own.

★: I think the merger is just convenient timing for them. They've wanted to become independent for a while.

☆: Well, I'll still be sad to see them go.

Question: What is one thing the man says about the merger?

全文訳 ★: 最新のニューズレターを見た？ エバンズ・リアル・エステートとの合併が公式になったみたいだね。

☆: 私はオフィスを移転するのは嫌だけど，理にかなっていることは認めるわ。

★: 僕もそう思う。うちの会社は何年もあそこの代理店と一緒に仕事をしてきたからね。これでうちの運営費も削減されるだろうし，市場での地位も強化されるね。

☆: ええ。でも一部のスタッフは独立して働くために退職することを決めたって聞いたわ。

★: 彼らにとっては合併が単に都合のいいタイミングだっただけだと思うよ。ここしばらく独立したがっていたからね。

☆: へえ，それでも彼らが去るのを見るのは悲しくなるわ。

質問：男性が合併について言うことの1つは何か。

選択肢の訳 **1** それによって彼の作業量が減るだろう。

2 それによって自営の代理店との仕事が増えるだろう。

3 それによって彼の会社はより成功するだろう。

4 それによって多くのスタッフが解雇されるだろう。

解説 選択肢の主語 It は2人が話題にしている会社の合併（merger）。余裕があれば先に選択肢を見て主語の It が何かを推測してから放送を聞くとよい。男性の2番目の発言の This will just reduce ... がポイント。主語の This は合併のことで，「運営費を削減する」と「市場での地位を強化する」を正解の **3** では抽象的に more successful と表している。

No.6 –解答 ②

スクリプト ☆: What do you think about installing solar panels on our roof? The initial costs are a little high, but we'd save a lot on energy bills.

★： Well, panels *are* becoming more efficient, and they're eco-friendly. But I don't think they'd be a good match for us.

☆： Why not?

★： It would take something like 15 years to make our money back on the investment, but we won't be living in this house that long.

☆： But wouldn't solar panels make the place worth more when we sell it?

★： Not by much. By then, our panels would be outdated.

Question: What does the man say about solar panels?

全文訳 ☆： うちの屋根にソーラーパネルを設置するのをどう思う？　初期費用はちょっと高いけど，光熱費をかなり節約できるよ。

★： うーん，ソーラーパネルは確かにますます効率的になってきているし，環境にも優しい。だけど僕たちには合わないと思う。

☆： どうして？

★： 投資した分を取り戻そうとしたら15年ぐらいかかるだろうけど，僕たち，この家にそんなに長く住まないだろうね。

☆： でもソーラーパネルがあったら家を売るときに価値が上がるんじゃないの？

★： そんなに上がらないよ。そのころには，うちのソーラーパネルは時代遅れになっているだろう。

質問：男性はソーラーパネルについて何と言っているか。

選択肢の訳 1　将来，より安価になるだろう。

2　カップルのお金の節約にはならないだろう。

3　数年後に取り替える必要がある。

4　環境面でのメリットがあまりない。

解説 女性はソーラーパネルの設置について，光熱費が節約できると言うが，男性は，初期費用に投資したお金を取り戻せるほど長く今の家に住まないことと，売るときに家の価値は上がらないという点で反対する。つまりお金の節約にはならないという意見なので，**2** が正解。男性の panels *are* becoming ～. But ... について，*are* をやや強調することで「確かに～だが，…だ」という意味になり，But 以下に主張がくる展開。いったん相手の言うことを認めた上で反論する言い回しとして知っておこう。

No.**7** - 解答 ④

スクリプト ☆： Could you have a look at this translation, Jared?

★： Sure. Is it the one that Miki did for LTR Chemicals?

☆： Yes. Please give it extra attention because they're very particular about accuracy. We can't afford to lose them as a client.

★： OK. Is the deadline urgent?

☆： No, we're ahead of schedule and still have a few days until it's due. Miki has a tendency to rush to get things back to me quickly, even though I ask her to take her time.

★： OK, I'll give it a thorough check.

Question: What does the woman imply?

全文訳 ☆： この翻訳を見てくれるかしら，ジャレッド？

★： もちろん。ミキが LTR ケミカルズのためにやったものですか？

☆： そうよ。あの会社は正確さにはとても厳しいから，特に注意を払ってくださいね。クライアントとして失うわけにはいかないから。

★： 分かりました。締め切りは差し迫っていますか？

☆： いいえ，予定より早く進んでいて，期限までまだ数日あるわ。ミキは，時間をかけるように頼んでも，私に早く戻すために大急ぎでやってしまう傾向があるの。

★： 分かりました，徹底的に確認します。

質問：女性は何をほのめかしているか。

選択肢の訳 **1** ミキは翻訳作業を終えていない。

2 締め切りは変わる可能性が高い。

3 クライアントは多くの間違いをした。

4 ミキは十分ていねいに作業をしないことが多い。

解説 女性が男性にミキの翻訳を確認するよう頼んでいる場面。ミキは予定より早めに女性に提出したこと，女性の Miki has a tendency to ... から，ミキは作業を急いでやってしまう傾向があることが分かる。つまり，ミキはあまりていねいに作業（翻訳）しないと考えて，**4** が正解。会話中の has a tendency to *do*「～する傾向にある」を often で表している。女性の冒頭の Could you have a look at this translation, Jared? は典型的なイギリス英語のイントネーション（抑揚）で，その後の can't の発音が「キャント」ではなく「カント」である点も確認してみよう。

No.**8** -解答

スクリプト ☆： Honey, the travel agent just called. He said the cruise is nearly sold out, so we have to decide soon.

★： Actually, I've been having second thoughts. I was looking at reviews on several websites, and there seem to be a lot of dissatisfied customers.

☆： Really? A few of the ones I saw were very positive. Well, we don't have to go. I just think you should get some kind of reward for working so hard lately.

★： How about increasing our budget a bit and booking a cruise with a better reputation?

☆： OK. I'll talk to the agent.

Question: Why is the man worried about their holiday?

全文訳 ☆： あなた，さっき旅行会社から電話があったの。あのクルーズが売り切れ間近だから，早めに決めなきゃいけないって。

★： 実は，考え直していたところだったんだ。複数のウェブサイトでレビューを見ていたんだけど，不満を抱いている客が多いみたいで。

☆： そうなの？　私が見たものの幾つかはとても肯定的だったけどな。まあ，行かなくてもいいよ。最近あなたがすごく仕事をがんばっているから何かしらご褒美があってもいいと思ってるだけだから。

★： 少し予算を増やして，もっと評判のいいクルーズを予約するのはどう？

☆： 分かった。旅行会社と話してみる。

質問： 男性はなぜ2人の休暇について心配しているか。

選択肢の訳 **1**　彼はオンライン上で苦情を多く見つけた。

2　クルーズの料金が上がった。

3　彼は仕事を休めない。

4　彼は別のクルーズを予約できない。

解説 カップルが休暇のクルーズを計画している場面。男性が考え直している（have second thoughts）理由は，ウェブサイトで不満を示すレビューが多いから。**1** が正解で，それぞれ websites と online，dissatisfied「不満を持つ」と complaints「苦情」が類義表現。

No.**9** −解答

スクリプト ★： Did you watch the season finale of *Shield Force* last night?

☆： Of course! I thought that was the best episode of the entire season.

★： What did you think of the scene where Agent Martinez was revealed to be the traitor?

☆： That was such a shocker. I was so sure it was going to be Agent Turner, but the way they explained it made perfect sense.

★： Totally. The writing on that show is just fantastic.

☆： I can't wait to see what happens next season.

Question: What do the speakers imply about *Shield Force*?

全文訳 ★： 昨日の夜，『シールド・フォース』のシーズンの最終話を見た？

☆： もちろん！　シーズン全体の中で一番いい回だと思った。

★： マルティネス捜査官が裏切り者だと判明した場面はどう思った？

☆： あれは本当に衝撃的だった。私はターナー捜査官が裏切り者だろうと確信していたけど，彼らの説明の仕方ですっかり納得がいったわ。

★： 全くだね。あの番組の脚本はただただ素晴らしい。

☆： 次のシーズンはどうなるのか，見るのが待ちきれないわ。

質問： 話者たちは『シールド・フォース』について何をほのめかしてい

るか。

1 個性豊かな登場人物が多い。

2 番組の脚本がずいぶん良くなった。

3 筋書きが予測しにくいものだった。

4 次のシーズンに更新されないかもしれない。

選択肢の characters, show や, 会話冒頭の watch, season finale, episode などの語から, *Shield Force* はテレビ番組名だと推測できる。最終話について女性は衝撃的だったと言い, その理由は I was so sure it was going to be Agent Turner, but ... から, 裏切り者 (traitor) が予想と違っていた, つまり裏切り者は誰かという筋書き (plot) が予測しにくかったと推測できる。よって, **3** が正解。

No.**10** 解答 4

★: I've been thinking about assigning Mark to manage the new software project.

☆: Do you think he can handle it? I know he's bright, but he's only been with the firm for 18 months.

★: Well, I was originally considering Genevieve, but she's really got her hands full these days. That leaves either Mark or Yasuhiro.

☆: In that case, I guess we have no choice but to give it to Mark. The last time we put Yasuhiro in charge of a project, things quickly went off the rails.

Question: What does the woman imply about Mark?

★: 新しいソフトウエアのプロジェクトの管理にマークを任命しようと考えているんだけど。

☆: 彼にこなせると思う？ 彼が聡明なのは分かるけど, この会社に入ってまだ 18 カ月だよ。

★: うーん, 最初はジェネビーブを考えていたんだけど, 彼女は最近, 忙しくて手がいっぱいだ。だからマークかヤスヒロしかいない。

☆: それなら, マークにその仕事をさせるしかないのかな。前回ヤスヒロにプロジェクトを任せたとき, 早々に軌道から外れてしまったからね。

質問：女性はマークについて何をほのめかしているか。

1 ヤスヒロより忙しい。

2 ジェネビーブとうまくいっていない。

3 しばしば間違った判断を下す。

4 十分な経験がないかもしれない。

質問は放送の最後まで分からず, 会話中には 3 人の名前が出てくるため, 人名と特徴を整理しながら聞くことが求められる。プロジェクトの管理者にマークを考えていると述べる男性に対し, 女性は I know he's bright, but he's only been with the firm for 18 months. と言って不安な様子である。「入社してまだ 18 カ月」を抽象的に「経験が足りない」と言い換えた **4** が正解。それぞれ get *one's* hands full は「忙しくて手が離せない」，have no choice but to *do* は「〜する以外に選択肢がない」，go off the rails は「脱線する，道を踏み外す」という意味。

No.11 解答 ④

スクリプト ☆ : Hey, did you take Professor Ritter's Politics 302 class last semester?

★ : Yeah. Some of the lectures were interesting, but I wouldn't really recommend it.

☆ : Oh. I heard it involves a lot of reading. Was that the problem?

★ : Actually, the workload seemed reasonable to me. My issue was that when she was marking papers, Professor Ritter seemed to favor students who share her political views.

☆ : Oh, really?

★ : If I were you, I'd sign up for Professor Tamura's or Professor Wilson's class instead.

Question: What is the man's opinion of Professor Ritter?

全文訳 ☆ : ねえ，前学期のリッター教授の政治学 302 の授業を取ってた？

★ : うん。講義の幾つかは面白かったけど，あまりお勧めはしない。

☆ : あら。大量の読書が必要だって聞いたけど。それが問題だったの？

★ : 実のところ，僕にはその作業量は妥当に思えた。僕が言うところの問題点は，リッター教授が課題を採点しているとき，自分と同じ政治的見解を持っている学生をひいきしているように思えたことだ。

☆ : まあ，そうなの？

★ : 僕が君なら，代わりにタムラ教授かウィルソン教授の授業に登録するね。

質問：リッター教授についての男性の意見は何か。

選択肢の訳 **1** 彼女の講義は長い傾向にある。

2 彼女は課題を出し過ぎる。

3 彼女の政治的見解は極端である。

4 彼女は公平に点数を付けない。

解説 大学生同士の会話。男性は My issue was that ... の部分でリッター教授の問題点を話している。Professor Ritter seemed to favor students ... の favor は「（人を）えこひいき［特別扱い］する」という意味で，正解の **4** ではこれを not 〜 fairly「公平でなく」と表している。mark a paper は「答案［課題］を採点する」（この paper は可算名詞）で，選択肢 **4** の grade は mark と同義。**2** は，女性の言う a lot of reading を too much homework と言い換えているとも考えられるが，男性はこれを

reasonable「妥当な」と言って問題視していないので不適。

No.12 解答 ②

スクリプト
☆： We need to do something about the dogs. Their barking is becoming a real problem.

★： I don't know. Most dogs bark at strangers, no?

☆： Yes, but ours bark every time someone goes past the house. We'll get complaints from the neighbors if this keeps up.

★： Well, we've already tried every training method we could find online. I'm not sure what else we can do.

☆： I think we should hire a proper dog trainer. I know it'll be expensive, but it'll be worth it for some peace and quiet.

★： I guess you're right.

Question: What will the man and woman probably do?

全文訳
☆： 私たち，犬たちについて何か対策をしないといけないわ。犬が吠えるのが大きな問題になってきているの。

★： どうだろうね。ほとんどの犬は知らない人間に向かって吠えるよ，違うかい？

☆： そうね，でもうちの犬たちは誰かが家を通り過ぎるたびに吠えているよ。これが続けば近所から苦情を受けることになるわ。

★： うーん，オンラインで見つかった訓練方法はすでにどれも試したよね。ほかに何ができるか分からないな。

☆： ちゃんとしたドッグトレーナーを雇うべきだと思う。高くつくのは知っているけど，平穏のためにはやるだけの価値はあるわよ。

★： 君の言う通りかもね。

質問： 男性と女性はおそらく何をするか。

選択肢の訳
1 オンラインで解決策を調べる。
2 専門家からの助けを得る。
3 近所の人たちに助言を求める。
4 より閑静な地域に引っ越す。

解説 飼い犬が吠えるという問題について，男女が解決策を話し合っている。女性が最後に I think we should hire a proper dog trainer. と意見を述べ，男性は賛成している。正解は **2** で，放送文の a proper dog trainer を a professional に言い換えている。**1** はすでに試したことなので不適。放送文の peace and quiet は「平安と静寂，平穏」という意味の成句。

A

（スクリプト） **Sukkoth**

Sukkoth is a religious holiday celebrated by Jewish people around the world. It originated thousands of years ago as a harvest festival. During the festival, people demonstrated their appreciation to their god for the year's crops. Later, the holiday became connected with the time immediately after the ancient Jewish people had escaped from slavery in Egypt. According to tradition, the Jewish people wandered in the desert and had to live in fragile shelters called sukkahs that protected them from the heat of the sun.

Today, Jewish people celebrate the holiday by building a sukkah in their backyards or on balconies. Sukkahs generally have three walls, and the roof is made with leaves and has openings so that the stars are visible above. During the festival's seven days, people consume their meals in the sukkah, and if they live in a warm climate, they sleep in it as well.

Questions

No.13 Why did people originally celebrate Sukkoth?

No.14 What is one thing we learn about modern sukkah buildings?

（全文訳） **仮庵の祭り**

仮庵の祭りは，世界中のユダヤ人によって祝われる宗教的な祝日である。それは何千年も前に収穫祭として始まった。祭りの間，人々はその年の収穫物に対して神に感謝の気持ちを表した。その後，この祝日は，古代ユダヤ人がエジプトでの奴隷状態から脱出した直後の時期と結び付けられるようになった。伝承によると，ユダヤ人は荒野を放浪し，太陽の熱から身を守る仮庵と呼ばれる壊れやすい小屋で生活しなければならなかった。

今日，ユダヤ人は自宅の裏庭やバルコニーに仮庵を建ててこの祝日を祝う。仮庵は通常，壁が３面で，屋根は葉で作られており，隙間があるため，頭上に星が見える。祭りの７日間，人々は仮庵の中で食事をし，温暖な気候の中で暮らしている場合はその中で寝る。

No.13 解答 ② ・・

（質問の訳）　人々はもともと，なぜ仮庵の祭りを祝ったのか。

（選択肢の訳）　**1**　農作物の質を良くするため。
　　　　　2　自分たちが育てた食べ物に感謝するため。
　　　　　3　荒野を脱出できるよう祈るため。
　　　　　4　エジプトで過ごした時代を祝うため。

（解説）　タイトルが未知の固有名詞の場合，それが何なのかはたいてい冒頭で述

べられる。ここでは Sukkoth is a religious <u>holiday</u> から，Sukkoth は祝日だと分かる。祭りの起源を説明した中で，... demonstrated their appreciation to their god for the year's crops の部分から，**2** が正解。それぞれ demonstrate their appreciation を give thanks に，crops を the food they grew に言い換えている。

No.14 解答 ④

質問の訳 現代の仮庵の建物について分かることの1つは何か。

選択肢の訳 1 壁に荒野の絵が描かれている。
2 涼しく保つために覆われている。
3 食事はその中で調理しなければならない。
4 人々はその中から空を見ることができる。

解説 ユダヤ人が仮庵の祭りのときに建てる sukkah(s) の特徴を説明した中で，the roof ... has openings so that the stars are visible above から，屋根の開いた部分から星が見えることが分かる。〈so that SV〉「その結果 S が〜する，S が〜するように」の聞き取りを確認しよう。

B

スクリプト Vultures

Vultures are birds well-known for their diet, which consists of the remains of dead animals. This association has given many people a negative impression of the birds, but we in fact owe much gratitude to vultures. By eating dead animals, the birds prevent disease-causing germs from entering the environment, including water sources. And because the strong acid in their stomachs is so good at killing germs, vultures are unlikely to pass on diseases to humans.

The bodies of dead animals do more than spread disease — they also release CO_2 and other greenhouse gases as they decay on the ground. When vultures feed, they prevent this from happening. However, in many parts of the world today, vulture populations have declined significantly, resulting in millions of tons of extra greenhouse-gas emissions entering the atmosphere. Ensuring vulture populations remain healthy is therefore an important step in combating climate change.

Questions

No.15 What does the speaker say about disease-causing germs?

No.16 What is suggested about climate change?

全文訳 ハゲワシ

ハゲワシは，動物の死骸を主食とすることで有名な鳥である。この連想によって，多くの人はこの鳥に対して否定的な印象を持っているが，実は，私たちはハゲワシに大いに感謝しなければならない。動物の死骸を食べることで，この鳥は病気を引き起こす病原菌が水源を含む環境に侵入するのを防いでいるのだ。また，ハゲワシの胃の中の強酸

は病原菌を殺すのに非常に優れているため，ハゲワシが人間に病気をうつすことはまずない。

　動物の死骸は病気を蔓延させるだけでなく，地上で腐敗する際に二酸化炭素やそのほかの温室効果ガスも放出する。ハゲワシが餌（動物の死骸）を食べるとき，これが起こるのを防ぐ。しかし今日，世界の多くの地域でハゲワシの個体数が大幅に減少しており，その結果，何百万トンもの余分な温室効果ガスが大気中に排出されている。従って，ハゲワシの個体数を健全な状態に保つことは，気候変動と闘う上で重要な一歩である。

No.15 解答 ……………………………………………………

質問の訳 話者が病気を引き起こす病原菌について言っていることは何か。

選択肢の訳 1　ハゲワシはそれらが人間に影響を与えるのを防ぐのに役立つ。
2　ハゲワシはしばしばそれらをほかの動物に広める。
3　それらはハゲワシにとって致命的になり得る。
4　それらはハゲワシの胃の中で生き残る。

解説 but ... in fact の後には重要なことが話される。否定的な印象があるハゲワシだが，実は重要な役割を果たしているという展開。まず By eating dead animals, ... から，ハゲワシは死骸を食べることで，病気を引き起こす病原菌の蔓延を防いでいることが分かる。また，And because ... to humans. から，**1** が正解。

No.16 解答 ① ……………………………………………………

質問の訳 気候変動について示唆されていることは何か。

選択肢の訳 1　ハゲワシの食性がその影響を軽減するのに役立つ。
2　それは世界中でハゲワシの個体数を増やした。
3　それが理由でハゲワシの食料源が変化した。
4　それにより，ハゲワシは新たな生息地を見つけることを余儀なくされた。

解説 放送文の The bodies ... from happening. より，腐敗時に温室効果ガスを放出する動物の死骸をハゲワシが食べる（＝ **1** の feeding habits）と，大気中に排出される温室効果ガスが減る。よって個体数が減少しているハゲワシを守れば（＝放送文の Ensuring vulture populations remain healthy）気候変動への影響を軽減できる，という論理展開を理解しよう。

スクリプト **Praising Employees**

Everyone knows that praise is important for motivating employees and increasing their satisfaction. Surprisingly, however, according to researchers, praise can improve employee performance even when the employee does not earn the praise. When researchers gave praise to random workers, the quality of the workers' output increased dramatically compared to those who were not praised.

Another study suggests that some kinds of praise are more effective than others. The study identifies two kinds of mindsets. Those with a so-called fixed mindset think they are born with a certain level of ability and that they are unlikely to get better at things. On the other hand, those with a so-called growth mindset feel that they have the capability to acquire new skills and talents. It seems that praising *effort* rather than *results* may have a positive effect because it encourages a growth mindset in unhappy employees who would otherwise be frustrated with their jobs.

Questions

No.17 What is one thing research found about praising employees?

No.18 What does the speaker suggest about unhappy employees?

全文訳　**従業員を褒める**

　褒めることが従業員をやる気にさせ，満足度を高めるのに重要であることは誰もが知っている。しかし意外なことに，研究者たちによると，たとえその従業員が称賛に値しなくても，称賛は従業員の仕事ぶりを向上させ得るという。研究者たちが無作為に労働者を褒めたところ，褒められなかった労働者に比べて，その労働者の生産物の質が劇的に向上した。

　別の研究では，一部の種類の称賛がほかの称賛よりも効果的であることが示唆されている。この研究では，2種類の思考パターンを特定している。いわゆる固定型思考パターンを持つ人は，自分は生まれつき一定の能力を持っており，物事が上達する可能性は低いと考えている。一方で，いわゆる成長型思考パターンを持つ人は，自分には新しいスキルや才能を身に付ける能力があると感じている。「結果」ではなく「努力」を褒めることは，そうしないと仕事に失望しそうな不満を抱えた従業員に成長型思考パターンを促すので，プラス効果があるようだ。

No.17 解答 ·······

質問の訳　従業員を褒めることについて研究で分かったことの1つは何か。

選択肢の訳　**1**　労働者はしばしば自分は称賛されるに値しないと思っている。

　　2　無作為な称賛が仕事ぶりを向上させ得る。

　　3　褒め過ぎは仕事ぶりを損なう可能性がある。

　　4　ほとんどの上司が十分に褒めない。

解説　Surprisingly, however の後に重要な話が続く。称賛は従業員の仕事ぶりを向上させ得ると述べた後，具体的に説明した When researchers gave praise to random workers, ... に手掛かりがある。この文の the workers' output は無作為に選ばれて褒められた労働者の生産物のことなので，**2** が正解。それぞれ放送文の output と performance, increase と improve が同義。

質問の訳　話者は不満を抱えた従業員について何を示唆しているか。

選択肢の訳　**1** 称賛に否定的な反応を示す傾向がある。
2 自分の仕事について心配し過ぎている。
3 成長型思考パターンを持つことで恩恵を受けるかもしれない。
4 周囲の労働者の思考パターンに影響を与える。

解説　結果ではなく努力を褒めることにプラス効果がある理由は，そうしないと（＝努力を褒めないと）仕事に失望しそうな不満を抱えた従業員に成長型思考パターンを促すからである。成長型思考パターンを持つと仕事の満足度が高まる（＝ benefit）と考えて，**3** が正解。

D

スクリプト　**Manod Mine**

During World War II, there was great fear that Britain would be invaded by Nazi Germany. In this environment, it was decided that paintings from the National Gallery in London should be moved somewhere safer. At first, it was suggested that they be shipped to Canada, but British leaders worried about the threat from the German submarines that were sinking thousands of ships. Eventually, the art treasures were stored in an old mine in a remote area of Wales called Manod.

Transporting the art was extremely difficult as many of the works were large and had to be moved carefully through the small mine entrance. Furthermore, there was great concern that moisture and cold temperatures would damage the paintings, so special air-conditioned structures were built in the mine to contain them. Thanks to the project at Manod, the paintings survived the war, and much was learned about preserving art.

Questions

No.19 Why did British leaders reject the original plan?

No.20 What was learned from the experience at Manod?

全文訳　**マノド鉱山**

　第２次世界大戦中，イギリスはナチス・ドイツに侵略されるのではないかという大きな恐怖があった。こうした状況の下，ロンドンのナショナル・ギャラリーの絵画はより安全な場所に移されるべきだと決定された。当初は，それらの絵画を船でカナダに移送することが提案されたが，イギリスの指導者たちは何千隻もの船を沈めているドイツの潜水艦からの脅威を心配した。最終的に，その美術品の宝物はマノドと呼ばれるウェールズの辺境にある古い鉱山に保管された。

　美術品の多くは大きく，小さな鉱山の入り口を慎重に通す必要があったため，その美術品の運搬は極めて困難だった。さらに，湿気と低気温が絵画に損傷を与えるのではないかという大きな懸念があったため，鉱山内に絵画を収納する特別な空調装置を備えた

構造物が建設された。マノドでのプロジェクトのおかげで，絵画は戦争を生き延び，美術品の保存について多くのことが学ばれた。

No.19 解答 （2）

質問の訳　なぜイギリスの指導者らは当初の計画を拒否したのか。

選択肢の訳
1　侵略は起こらないだろうと信じていた。
2　美術品が破壊されるのではないかと心配した。
3　カナダは侵略されそうだと思った。
4　ドイツ人が美術品を盗むことができるのではないかと恐れた。

解説　At first, 〜. Eventually, ...「当初は〜だった。最終的には…」の展開をつかもう。質問の the original plan はカナダへの移送のことで，放送文の but British leaders worried ... から，イギリスの指導者らは，ドイツの潜水艦の脅威，つまり移送中の美術品の破壊を心配したのである。

No.20 解答 （4）

質問の訳　マノドでの経験から学ばれたことは何か。

選択肢の訳
1　戦時中の美術の重要性。
2　より大きい鉱山を作る方法。
3　絵画に対する低気温の影響。
4　美術品を良い状態に保つ方法。

解説　湿気と低気温で絵画が損傷を受ける可能性があったが，特別な構造物を作ることで絵画は無事に保管された。最後の Thanks to the project ... and much was learned about preserving art. から，この絵画の保存経験が学びにつながったので，**4** が適切。

E

スクリプト　**The Midnight Ride of Sybil Ludington**

On the night of April 26, 1777, during the American Revolution, a messenger arrived at American commander Henry Ludington's house. The messenger warned of a coming British attack, but Ludington's soldiers were scattered around the region. The commander's daughter, Sybil, bravely volunteered to alert them. Though just 16 years old, Sybil rode on horseback for over 65 kilometers in stormy weather. Thanks to her night ride, the troops assembled and drove away the British. After the war, however, Sybil was forgotten for many years.

Some historians question whether Sybil's ride ever really happened. While documents show that the British attack occurred, there are no official records of Sybil's journey. It appeared in a history book published in the 1800s, but the book failed to give sources to confirm it. Nevertheless, the story has been widely accepted, and Sybil has become a symbol of the role of women in the

American Revolution.

Questions

No.21 What was the purpose of Sybil Ludington's ride?

No.22 What is one reason some historians doubt Sybil's ride?

全文訳 シビル・ルディントンの夜中の乗馬

　アメリカ独立戦争中の 1777 年 4 月 26 日の夜，アメリカ軍司令官ヘンリー・ルディントンの家に 1 人の使者が到着した。その使者はイギリス軍の攻撃が来ると警告したが，ルディントンの兵士たちは各地に散らばっていた。司令官の娘シビルは，勇敢にも彼らに警告することを申し出た。シビルはわずか 16 歳だったが，荒天の中，馬に乗って 65 キロ以上の距離を走った。彼女の夜の乗馬のおかげで，軍隊は集結してイギリス軍を追い払った。しかし戦後，シビルは何年もの間忘れ去られていた。

　歴史家の中には，シビルの乗馬が本当にあったことなのかを疑問視する人もいる。文書にはイギリスによる攻撃があったことが示されているが，シビルの旅に関する公式記録は 1 つもない。それは 1800 年代に出版された歴史書に登場したが，この本はそれを裏付ける情報源を提供していなかった。それにもかかわらず，この話は広く受け入れられ，シビルはアメリカ独立戦争における女性の役割の象徴となった。

No.21 解答

質問の訳 シビル・ルディントンの乗馬の目的は何だったか。

選択肢の訳　**1**　攻撃に関して警告するのを手伝うため。
　　　　　　　2　イギリス兵たちの居場所を確認するため。
　　　　　　　3　アメリカ軍への物資を集めるため。
　　　　　　　4　自分の父親を危険から遠ざけるため。

解説　イギリス軍が攻撃してくるという使者の警告を受け，シビルは父親が率いる兵士たちにそれを伝えに行くと申し出た。bravely volunteered to alert them の them は Ludington's soldiers を指し，volunteer to *do* は「進んで～しようと申し出る」。その移動手段が乗馬（Sybil rode on horseback）だったので，**1** が正解。

No.22 解答

質問の訳 一部の歴史家がシビルの乗馬を疑う理由の 1 つは何か。

選択肢の訳　**1**　その夜は別の女性が馬に乗ったという証拠がある。
　　　　　　　2　イギリス軍による攻撃の記録が 1 つもない。
　　　　　　　3　公的に文書化されなかった。
　　　　　　　4　ある歴史書がそれは起こらなかったと主張している。

解説　質問の doubt は放送文の Some historians question whether ... の言い換え。While documents show that the British attack occurred, there are no official records of Sybil's journey. の下線部を言い換えた **3** が適切。While [Although] A, B.「A だが，B だ」では B に

重要な内容がくるので，主節（コンマ＝区切りの後）を意識して聞こう。**2** はこの While ... the British attack occurred の部分と合わない。**2** の no records という表現に引っかからないように。

F

(スクリプト) **Banff Sunshine Village**

During the economic boom of the 1950s in the US and Canada, interest in recreational activities increased dramatically. One activity that grew in popularity was skiing. However, many ski resorts found that they needed more snow on their mountains to meet customer demand. Machines were developed to create snow artificially using water and compressed air, enabling ski resorts to operate even without a lot of natural snowfall.

However, snowmaking requires significant energy consumption as well as water from reservoirs and lakes. A Canadian ski resort known as Banff Sunshine Village relies instead on a method called snow farming. The resort takes advantage of the area's windy conditions by putting up fences at high altitudes to catch snow that blows in from surrounding mountains. Later, the snow is transported down to slopes that need it. This allows the resort to maximize snow cover in an environmentally sustainable and energy-efficient way.

Questions

No.23 What does the speaker say about many ski resorts in the 1950s?

No.24 What is true about Banff Sunshine Village?

(全文訳) **バンフ・サンシャイン・ビレッジ**

1950 年代のアメリカやカナダの高度成長期に，レクリエーション活動への関心が飛躍的に高まった。人気が高まった活動の1つがスキーである。しかし，多くのスキー場は，客の需要を満たすには山にもっと多くの雪が必要であることに気付いた。水と圧縮空気を使って人工的に雪を作る機械が開発され，スキー場は天然の雪があまり降らなくても営業できるようになった。

しかし，人工雪の製造にはため池や湖の水だけでなく，多大なエネルギー消費も必要である。バンフ・サンシャイン・ビレッジとして知られるカナダのスキー場は，その代わりにスノー・ファーミングと呼ばれる手法に依存している。このスキー場は，周囲の山々から吹き込む雪を受け止める柵を高所に設置することで，この地域の風の強い条件をうまく利用している。その後，その雪は，雪を必要とするゲレンデに運び下ろされる。これにより，このスキー場は，環境的に持続可能でエネルギー効率の良い方法で積雪量を最大化することができる。

No.23 解答 ③

(質問の訳) 話者は 1950 年代の多くのスキー場について何と言っているか。

(選択肢の訳) **1** より人口の多い地域に場所を移さなければならなかった。

2 不満を持つ客たちが原因で閉業しなければならなかった。

3 十分な雪が降っていなかった。

4 人工雪を用いることに反対した。

解説 However, many ski resorts ... 以下に手掛かりがある。もっと多くの雪が必要（they needed more snow）ということはつまり，雪が十分になかったということなので，**3** が正解。

No.24 解答 ②

質問の訳 バンフ・サンシャイン・ビレッジについて何が正しいか。

選択肢の訳 **1** 人工雪の使用が商売に悪影響を与えている。

2 風を利用して運営の役に立てている。

3 地元のほかのスキー場に雪を提供している。

4 ゲレンデが異常に標高が高い所にある。

解説 バンフ・サンシャイン・ビレッジは snow farming（スノー・ファーミング）という手法を用いており，その説明を述べた The resort takes advantage of ... から，風を利用して周辺の山々から吹き込む雪を取り入れていることが分かる。takes advantage of を makes use of と表した **2** が正解。

一次試験・ リスニング	Part**3**	問題編 p.50〜51	🔊	▶MP3 ▶アプリ ▶CD 1 22〜27

G

スクリプト

You have 10 seconds to read the situation and Question No. 25.

We're near the harbor, so there are a lot of good seafood options. Kingsley's is a very popular lobster restaurant and bar, but it doesn't open until eight. Shrimp Lover is a seafood restaurant that just opened one month ago. It's about 45 minutes away by train. Randy's is a unique Mexican restaurant just a block away. They only have counter seats, but I'm sure you can be seated right away, even at dinner time. Then, there's Boca here in the hotel, but it's very difficult to get a table if you haven't booked at least a day in advance.

Now mark your answer on your answer sheet.

全文訳

　ここは港の近くなので，美味しい海鮮料理の選択肢がたくさんあります。キングスリーズは大人気のロブスターのレストラン兼バーですが，8 時まで開きません。シュリンプラバーは 1 カ月前にオープンしたばかりの海鮮料理店です。列車で 45 分ほどの距離です。ランディーズはわずか 1 ブロック先にあるユニークなメキシコ料理店です。カウンター席しかありませんが，夕食の時間帯でもすぐに席が取れると思います。そして，当

ホテル内にボカがありますが，少なくとも前日までに予約していないとテーブルを確保するのは非常に難しいです。

No.25 解答 3

状況の訳 あなたはホテルに泊まっている。今は午後6時30分で，午後7時ごろに近くのレストランで夕食を取りたいと思っている。コンシェルジュが次のように言う。

質問の訳 あなたはどのレストランを選ぶべきか。

選択肢の訳 1 キングスリーズ。 2 シュリンプラバー。
3 ランディーズ。 4 ボカ。

解説 10秒の間に問題用紙の*Situation*（状況）を読み，「午後7時ごろに」「ホテルの近くで」の2点を押さえよう。選択肢（ここではレストラン名）は通常，説明の順になっているので，聞きながら選択肢に○×を付けていくとよい。**1**は8時開店なので×。**2**はホテルの近くではないので×。**3**はjust a block awayからホテルに近いことが分かり，dinner time（＝7時ごろ）でも座れるので○。**4**は前日までの予約が必要なので×。

H

（スクリプト）

You have 10 seconds to read the situation and Question No. 26.

Welcome to CD Masters. This holiday season, don't miss out on our "CD Surprise" boxes with 30 random CDs inside. Additionally, to sell up to 99 CDs, any registered member can log into their account on our website and start the sales procedure. If you don't have an account, you can register today just by filling out the form on our website. If you would prefer to register over the phone, press 1. If you are looking to sell 100 or more CDs at once, press 2. A representative will speak with you to schedule a home visit to assess your CD collection.

Now mark your answer on your answer sheet.

（全文訳）

CDマスターズにようこそ。このホリデーシーズンは，30枚のCDがランダムに入った「CDサプライズ」セットをお見逃しなく。また，最大99枚のCDを売却するには，登録会員であればどなたでも，当社のウェブサイトでアカウントにログインし，売却手続きを開始することができます。アカウントをお持ちでない方は，ウェブサイトのフォームに記入するだけで今すぐご登録いただけます。お電話での登録をご希望の場合は，1を押してください。一度に100枚以上のCDを売りたい場合は，2を押してください。担当者がお客さまとお話しして，CDを査定するためにご自宅への訪問を予約いたします。

No.26 解答

状況の訳 あなたは 500 枚持っている音楽 CD の半分を売ることにした。中古 CD を売買している店に電話をすると，次のような録音メッセージが聞こえる。

質問の訳 あなたは何をすべきか。

選択肢の訳
1 オンラインで売却手続きを始める。
2 自分の CD を箱に詰め始める。
3 ウェブサイトからフォームをダウンロードする。
4 査定の予約をする。

解説 CD を 500 枚持っていて，その半分（250 枚）を売るので，to sell <u>up to 99 CDs</u>, ... の部分は軽く聞き流す。250 枚に関する情報を期待しながら聞き進めると，If you are looking to sell <u>100 or more CDs</u> at once, press 2. から，電話で 2 番を押せばよいことが分かる。さらに続きの A representative will speak ... to schedule a home visit to assess your CD collection. から，担当者と話して査定の予約を取る必要があると分かる。よって，**4** が正解。

I

スクリプト

You have 10 seconds to read the situation and Question No. 27.

In History 103, students can learn about European history in the eighteenth and nineteenth centuries. This class has no group projects, and there is an option available to take it online. Next, Philosophy 105 is for those who want to grasp the gist of Western philosophy, including that of ancient Greece and Rome. Students are expected to take part in spirited team debates in each class. History 202 is a lecture-based class and is non-interactive. It focuses primarily on ancient Egyptian, Greek, and Roman history. Finally, Latin 102 focuses exclusively on ancient Rome. In that class, you'll learn Latin by reading ancient Roman plays.

Now mark your answer on your answer sheet.

全文訳

歴史 103 では，学生は 18 世紀から 19 世紀にかけてのヨーロッパの歴史について学ぶことができます。このクラスにはグループ研究はなく，オンラインで受講する選択肢もあります。次に，哲学 105 は，古代ギリシャ・ローマを含む，西洋哲学の要点を把握したい人向けです。学生は各授業でチーム対抗の活発なディベートに参加することが求められます。歴史 202 は，講義中心のクラスで，非対話形式です。主に古代エジプト，ギリシャ，ローマの歴史に焦点を当てています。最後に，ラテン語 102 は古代ローマだけに焦点を絞っています。そちらのクラスでは，古代ローマの戯曲を読むことでラテン語を学びます。

No.**27** 解答 ③

状況の訳 あなたは大学生である。古代のギリシャ人とローマ人について学びたいと思っているが，グループワーク（共同作業）は好きではない。指導教官の説明を聞いている。

質問の訳 あなたはどのクラスを受講すべきか。

選択肢の訳
1 歴史103。
2 哲学105。
3 歴史202。
4 ラテン語102。

解説 状況から，「ancient Greeks and Romans について学びたい」「グループワーク（共同作業）は好きではない」の2つの条件を押さえよう。**1**は the eighteenth and nineteenth centuries が条件の ancient に合わない。**2**は team debates ＝共同作業と判断して×。**3**は講義中心で，古代ギリシャとローマの両方を学べるので○。**4**は古代ローマしか学べない。

J

スクリプト

You have 10 seconds to read the situation and Question No. 28.

Thank you for calling the TSS Electronics help desk. For corporate customers who have questions regarding the details of their contracts, press 1. For technical support or to request a replacement for any of our products currently under warranty, press 2. To arrange for a repair or check the repair status of a product outside of warranty, press 3. For information about the different tablet models and data plans that we provide, press 4. For all other inquiries, please remain on the line until a representative becomes available.

Now mark your answer on your answer sheet.

全文訳

TSS エレクトロニクスのヘルプデスクにお電話いただきありがとうございます。ご契約内容に関して質問のある法人のお客さまは，1を押してください。現在保証期間中の製品に対する技術サポートまたは交換のご依頼は，2を押してください。保証期間外の製品の修理手配または修理状況のご確認は，3を押してください。当社が提供するさまざまなタブレットの機種やデータプランについての情報は，4を押してください。そのほかの全てのお問い合わせは，担当者が対応できるまで電話を切らずにこのままお待ちください。

No.**28** 解答 ②

状況の訳 あなたが2週間前に娘のために買ったタブレットコンピューターが故障した。1年間の保証が付いている。製品メーカーに電話すると，次のような録音メッセージが聞こえる。

質問の訳 あなたは何をすべきか。

選択肢の訳
1 1を押す。
2 2を押す。

解説　状況から，2週間前に購入＋保証期間1年＝保証期間内ということと，選択肢が〈Press＋数字〉なので，数字がポイントになることを把握しよう。For technical support or to request a replacement for any of our products currently <u>under warranty</u>, press 2. から，**2** が正解。娘に買った製品なので **1** は For corporate customers が合わない。

K

You have 10 seconds to read the situation and Question No. 29.

Several tours will be starting shortly. First, *Spark of Genius* is an hour-long tour about electricity that includes an exciting 30-minute 3D movie. We also have *The Age of Dinos*, which is a tour that explores the fascinating period when dinosaurs ruled the earth. It takes half an hour. *Deep into the Sea* is a 40-minute tour that looks at amazing deep-sea creatures. It can be a little scary, so this tour is not recommended for children under the age of 10. Finally, don't forget you can make reservations for our *Museum after Dark* overnight tour to experience an unforgettable night among our amazing exhibits.

Now mark your answer on your answer sheet.

全文訳

　間もなく幾つかのツアーが始まります。まず，『天才の閃(ひらめ)き』は電気に関する1時間のツアーで，30分のわくわくする3D映画が含まれています。また『恐竜時代』というものもあり，恐竜が地球を支配していた魅力的な時代を探るツアーです。所要時間は30分です。『海の底へ』は，驚くべき深海生物を観察する40分のツアーです。少し怖いかもしれませんので，このツアーは10歳未満のお子さまにはお勧めしていません。最後に，当館の素晴らしい展示品に囲まれて忘れられない夜を体験できる夜間ツアー『夜の博物館』を予約できることをお忘れなく。

No.29 解答

状況の訳　あなたと7歳の息子は科学博物館にいる。ツアーに参加したいと思っている。45分後には博物館を出なければならない。次のようなアナウンスが聞こえる。

質問の訳　あなたはどのツアーを選ぶべきか。

選択肢の訳　**1** 『天才の閃き』。　　　**2** 『恐竜時代』。
　　　　　　3 『海の底へ』。　　　　**4** 『夜の博物館』。

解説　状況から，「息子は7歳」「45分後に出る」の2つの条件を押さえる。選択肢にツアーの名称が並んでいるが，各単語の意味を考えるのではなく，頭の中で発音を想像して準備をしよう。**1** は1時間のツアーなので時間的に×。**2** は，30分で，年齢制限もないので○。**3** は10歳未満に不向きなので×。**4** は夜間ツアーなので時間的に×。

解答例 **One day, a couple was talking at a café.** The man was telling the woman that he was able to take a week off for summer vacation, and she looked excited. That weekend, the couple was at home making plans for the holiday. The woman was showing him a "Guided Group Tours" brochure, but the man had no interest in it and told her that he would plan their trip himself. A few weeks later, the couple was visiting a tourist site with a traditional tower. There were many tourists. The man was looking at a popular restaurant on his phone and suggested that they go there next. One hour later, the couple arrived at the restaurant. A tour group had arrived before them and was going inside the restaurant. A waiter from the restaurant apologized and told them that the restaurant was fully booked.

解答例の訳 ある日，カップルがカフェで話をしていました。男性は女性に，夏休みとして1週間休みが取れると話しており，女性は興奮した様子でした。その週末，2人は家で休暇の計画を立てていました。女性は男性に「ガイド付き団体ツアー」のパンフレットを見せていましたが，彼はそれに興味がなく，自分で旅行を計画すると彼女に言いました。数週間後，2人は伝統的な塔のある観光地を訪れていました。観光客がたくさんいました。男性はスマートフォンで人気レストランを見ており，次はそこに行くことを提案しました。1時間後，2人はそのレストランに到着しました。2人の前にツアー客が到着しており，レストランに入っているところでした。レストランのウエーターが詫び，レストランは予約で満席だと2人に言いました。

解説 各コマの描写ポイントは，①男性の吹き出しに夏休みの日程を示すカレンダーがある，②その週末，女性が「ガイド付き団体ツアー」のパンフレットを見せ，男性は「僕が旅行を計画する」と言っている，③数週間後，2人は旅行中で，男性が「次はここ（＝レストラン）に行こう」と言っている，④1時間後，レストランの店員が「予約で満席です」と言っている。Let's 〜 のような提案は〈S＋suggested that＋S'＋動詞の原形〉で表すことができる。絵から分かる事実だけでなく人物の動作や表情をヒントに she looked excited, the man had no interest in it, A waiter from the restaurant apologized のような感覚的描写を加えると生き生きとした文章になる。

No. 1

解答例 I'd be thinking, "I had a feeling something like this would happen. Tour agencies reserve popular restaurants in advance. I should have insisted that we take the group tour."

解説 質問は「4番目の絵を見てください。もしあなたがこの女性なら，どのようなことを考えているでしょうか」。解答例は，2コマ目の状況を踏まえて，「こういうことが起こる予感がしていた」「団体ツアーに参加するよう主張するべきだった」という後悔を表している。後悔・非難を表す〈should (not) have＋過去分詞〉を使えるようにしておこう。

No. 2

解答例 Absolutely. Japan is known all over the world for its safety, hospitality, and good food. Thanks to social media, that information will continue to spread. The number of international visitors continues to increase yearly.

解説 質問は「日本は今後も人気の旅行先であり続けるでしょうか」。Absolutely は Yes の強意語。理由として安全性，もてなし，美食，ソーシャルメディアの影響を挙げた後，「海外からの観光客数は年々増え続けている」と締めくくっている。日本語の SNS は social media と表す。

No. 3

解答例 No. It's common for employees in the service industry to quit their jobs after a short period. This indicates they aren't satisfied with their working conditions. It's the employers' responsibility to keep their employees happy.

解説 質問は「サービス業の従業員は雇用主から十分な待遇を受けていると思いますか」。解答例は No の立場で，短期間での離職が一般的であることが労働条件への不満を示しているという根拠を述べた後，従業員を幸せにするのが雇用主の責任だと意見を展開している。It is ～ (for A) to *do*「(A が)…するのは～だ」を使いこなそう。

No. 4

解答例 Definitely. Advancements in technology have made people's lives more comfortable and convenient. For example, household appliances have reduced people's workload at home, so they have more time to do things they enjoy.

解説 質問は「最近の人々の生活の質は昔より良くなっていますか」。Definitely も Yes の強意語で，テクノロジーの進歩を根拠にして，For example で具体例を述べている。質問の better を more comfortable and convenient と具体化している点に着目。No の立場では，逆にテクノロジー進歩の欠点として情報過多や雇用減少を話すことができそうだ。

解答例　**One day, a family was at home.** The mother had been scolding their son, and the father came to see what was happening. The son seemed to have broken a vase by kicking a soccer ball in the house. He was crying as the mother explained to the father that their son's behavior was terrible. That weekend, the couple was out walking and saw a sign for a soccer school for kids in front of the ABC Culture Center. This gave the father an idea. A few months later, the son was proudly showing a trophy and a certificate for "best player" to his parents. They looked proud of him. At a parent-teacher meeting, the father and son were called in by the elementary school teacher. She was showing them the son's report card and said that he only did well in P.E. The son looked embarrassed.

解答例の訳　ある日，家族が家にいました。母親が息子を叱っていて，父親が様子を見に来ました。息子は家の中でサッカーボールを蹴って花瓶を割ってしまったようでした。母親が父親に息子の振る舞いがひどいと説明する間，息子は泣いていました。その週末，夫婦は散歩していて，ABCカルチャーセンターの前で子供向けのサッカースクールの看板を見ました。そこで父親はあるアイデアを思い付きました。数カ月後，息子は両親にトロフィーと「最優秀選手」の賞状を誇らしげに見せていました。夫婦は息子を誇りに思っているようでした。保護者会で，父親と息子は小学校の先生に呼び出されました。先生は2人に息子の成績表を見せていて，彼は体育だけは成績がいいと言いました。息子はきまりが悪そうでした。

解説　各コマの描写ポイントは，①息子が泣いていて，母親が「彼の振る舞いがひどい」と父親に言っている，②その週末，夫婦が子供向けのサッカースクールの看板を見ている，③数カ月後，息子が両親に「最優秀選手」の賞状を見せている，④保護者会で，先生が「彼は体育だけは成績がいい」と言っている。1コマ目は，息子が家の中でサッカーボールで遊んで花瓶を割った状況も説明しよう。2コマ目の父親の吹き出しはアイデアが浮かんだことを示す。状況や人物の表情をヒントに，scolding「叱って」，proudly「誇らしげに」，embarrassed「きまりが悪い」のような描写を適宜加え，自然な流れのストーリーにしよう。

No. 1

解答例 I'd be thinking, "My son is still young and full of energy. There's nothing wrong with only doing well in P.E. for now. Eventually, he'll settle down and start doing better in other subjects."

解説 質問は「4番目の絵を見てください。もしあなたがこの父親なら，どのようなことを考えているでしょうか」。解答例は，まだ若いので今は何も問題ない，そのうち他教科の成績も良くなるだろうという前向きな発言。逆に，〈should not have＋過去分詞〉などを使って「サッカースクールに入れるべきではなかった」という後悔を表すこともできるだろう。

No. 2

解答例 Definitely not. Sports are characterized by physical exercise that makes your body fit. Most video games involve just sitting. In fact, I think playing video games for a long time can be harmful to one's physical health.

解説 質問は「テレビゲームをすることはスポーツと見なされるべきですか」。Definitely (not). は強い賛成・反対を表す。解答例は No の立場で，ゲームはスポーツのような肉体運動を伴わず，それどころか（In fact）健康に悪影響を及ぼし得るという意見。Yes の立場では esports「e スポーツ」を取り上げることができそうだ。

No. 3

解答例 Yes. Important family decisions usually involve the children. They'll have an opinion on something that will affect their future. Furthermore, discussing issues will strengthen the relationships between family members.

解説 質問は「親は家族の重要な問題について子供と話し合うべきだと思いますか」。解答例は Yes の立場で，Furthermore を使って「子供は自分の将来にかかわることに意見がある」と「話し合いは家族間の関係を強化する」という2つの理由を述べている。No の立場では，家族の問題の責任や決定権は親にあるなどの意見も可能だろう。

No. 4

解答例 Yes. Education, including higher education, is a basic human right. Governments should provide equality to their citizens, so they should support more students from all economic backgrounds.

解説 質問は「政府は学生にもっと大学奨学金を提供すべきですか」。解答例は Yes の立場で，教育は基本的人権で，あらゆる経済的背景を持つ学生を平等に支援すべきという意見。「貧しい」「困難」などの否定的な表現の代わりに all economic backgrounds や regardless of their financial strength「経済力にかかわらず」と表すと知的な印象を与える。

2023-1

解答一覧

一次試験・筆記

1

(1)	3	(10)	4	(19)	4
(2)	1	(11)	2	(20)	1
(3)	1	(12)	4	(21)	1
(4)	1	(13)	1	(22)	4
(5)	2	(14)	1	(23)	4
(6)	3	(15)	1	(24)	2
(7)	2	(16)	3	(25)	3
(8)	1	(17)	3		
(9)	4	(18)	2		

2

(26)	3	(29)	3
(27)	4	(30)	2
(28)	2	(31)	1

3

(32)	1	(35)	2	(38)	3
(33)	2	(36)	3	(39)	4
(34)	3	(37)	1	(40)	2
				(41)	2

4　　解答例は本文参照

一次試験・リスニング

Part 1

No. 1	2	No. 5	3	No. 9	3
No. 2	3	No. 6	2	No.10	1
No. 3	1	No. 7	4	No.11	4
No. 4	4	No. 8	3	No.12	2

Part 2

No.13	1	No.17	3	No.21	1
No.14	4	No.18	4	No.22	4
No.15	2	No.19	4	No.23	2
No.16	1	No.20	2	No.24	1

Part 3

No.25	2	No.28	3
No.26	2	No.29	1
No.27	3		

(1) ―解答 ③

訳 最初，ミックは1人で海外に住むという考えにおじけづいていた。しかし，一度やってみると，恐れていたほど困難ではなかった。

解説 空所は受動態の過去分詞部分。At first → however の展開から，最初は恐れていたが実際はそうでもなかったという流れをつかもう。fear に似た意味の daunt「おじけづかせる」の過去分詞が適切。それぞれ pacify「なだめる」，restore「復活させる」，tackle「取り組む」の過去分詞。

(2) ―解答 ①

訳 学生には，試験の直前に詰め込むのではなく，学期を通して自分の勉強のペースを保つことが推奨される。

解説 instead of「～ではなく」に着目。「学期を通して自分の勉強のペースを保つ」の対比となる cram「詰め込む，詰め込み勉強をする」の -ing 形を入れるのが適切。それぞれ detain「留置する」，swell「腫れる」，embrace「抱擁する」の -ing 形。

(3) ―解答 ①

訳 大統領選の討論会の間に2人の候補者の怒りが爆発した。彼らは一晩中，諸問題に対する互いの立場を怒って攻撃し合った。

解説 第2文の angrily attacked「怒って攻撃した」へのつながりから，flare「(感情が)爆発する」の過去形が適切。それぞれ digest「(食物を)消化する」，profess「公言する」，tumble「転ぶ」の過去形。

(4) ―解答 ①

訳 株式市場の暴落の後，多くの銀行が事業を継続するために政府の介入を必要とした。その援助はほとんどが多額の融資の形で行われた。

解説 事業を継続するのに銀行が必要としたのは government intervention「政府の介入」である。to stay は目的を表す to 不定詞で，〈require＋O＋to *do*〉「O に～するよう要求する」ではないので注意。appreciation「感謝」，accumulation「蓄積」，starvation「飢餓」

(5) ―解答 ②

訳 警察は，犯罪現場では，証拠がいかなる形でも破損または改ざんされないことを確実にするため，厳格な手順に従わなければならない。

解説 警察が犯罪現場で従うものは strict protocols「厳格な手順［手続き］」。それぞれ tribute「賛辞」，reservoir「貯水池」，portion「部分」の複数形。

(6) ― 解答 3 ‥‥‥‥‥‥‥‥‥‥‥‥‥‥‥‥‥‥‥‥‥‥‥‥‥‥‥‥‥‥‥‥

訳 審判はけんかを理由に2人の選手を退場させた。彼らは試合の残り時間にプレーすることを許されなかった。

解説 umpire は「審判員」という意味だが，これを知らなくても for fighting や第2文の内容から，選手を退場させた（ejected）ことが想像できるだろう。それぞれ slaughter「虐殺する」，administer「管理する」，conceive「思い付く」の過去形。

(7) ― 解答 2 ‥‥‥‥‥‥‥‥‥‥‥‥‥‥‥‥‥‥‥‥‥‥‥‥‥‥‥‥‥‥‥‥

訳 猫は，自分の子を守ろうとすることで知られている。自分の子猫の脅威となり得ると思うほかの動物を攻撃することも多い。

解説 *be* protective of [toward] は「～を守ろうとする」という意味。第2文の their kittens を別の表現で表した offspring「子孫」が正解。prey「獲物」，ritual「儀式」の複数形，remain「（複数形で）残り，遺物」

(8) ― 解答 1 ‥‥‥‥‥‥‥‥‥‥‥‥‥‥‥‥‥‥‥‥‥‥‥‥‥‥‥‥‥‥‥‥

訳 グリーンビル・ユナイテッドのファンは，シーズンを通してのチームの成績不振がAリーグからBリーグへの降格につながったとき，失望した。

解説 when 以下にファンの失望の理由が書かれている。空所後の from A to B「AからBへ」とのつながりから，demotion「降格」が適切。craving「切望」，aggravation「悪化」，hassle「面倒，口論」

(9) ― 解答 4 ‥‥‥‥‥‥‥‥‥‥‥‥‥‥‥‥‥‥‥‥‥‥‥‥‥‥‥‥‥‥‥‥

訳 ビビはハイキングやスポーツが大好きなので，あまりすぐに傷まない服が必要である。買い物に行くとき，彼女はたいてい耐久性のある服を買う。

解説 clothing that is (   ) は第1文の clothes that ... quickly の言い換えで，durable「耐久性のある」が適切。wear out は「擦り切れて使えなくなる」。swift「迅速な」，aloof「冷淡な，離れた」，shallow「浅い」

(10) ‐ 解答 4 ‥‥‥‥‥‥‥‥‥‥‥‥‥‥‥‥‥‥‥‥‥‥‥‥‥‥‥‥‥‥

訳 消費者は，銀行からだと主張する電話の相手にいかなる個人情報も明かすべきではない。というのも，そのような電話は犯罪者からの場合もあるからだ。

解説 消費者の行為で，目的語 information に合う動詞は disclose「開示する」。〈dis-(反対)＋close(閉じる)〉＝秘密などを「公開する，暴露する」の意味。sway「動揺させる」，detest「憎む」，contemplate「熟考する」

(11) ‐ 解答 2 ‥‥‥‥‥‥‥‥‥‥‥‥‥‥‥‥‥‥‥‥‥‥‥‥‥‥‥‥‥‥

訳 そのテニスのチャンピオンはほかの選手たちに無愛想で，自分は史上最高の選手だと言い張るので，彼はその傲慢さでしばしば非難される。

解説 主節は criticize A for B「BのことでAを非難する」の受動態。前半に書かれている言動が非難の対象と考えて，arrogance「傲慢さ」を入れる。commodity「商品」，neutrality「中立」，specimen「標本」

(12) – 解答 ④

訳 多くの読者がその著者の小説を理解できないと感じた。彼は，明確な意味を持たない，長くて混乱させる文章を書くことで知られていた。

解説 第2文の long, confusing ... meaning で表された文章の特徴から，読者は小説を理解できない（incomprehensible）と感じたと判断できる。genuine「本物の」，impending「差し迫った」，subdued「控えめな」

(13) – 解答 ① ～～～～～～～～～～～～～～～～～～ 正答率 ★75%以上

訳 「クラスの皆さん，とても注意深く聞いてください」と先生が言った。「私が今から言うことの多くは教科書には載っていませんが，テストに出ます」。

解説 I want you all to ... は教室での先生から生徒への指示。先生は今から教科書には載っていないがテストに出ることを話すことから，注意深く（attentively）聞くよう指示するのが自然。consecutively「連続して」，wearily「疲れて，うんざりして」，eloquently「雄弁に」

(14) – 解答 ①

訳 その学校は教育の最前線にいることで知られている。教員たちは教室で最新の教育方法と最新技術を使用する。

解説 第2文の newest や latest から，学校は教育の最前線（forefront）にいると考えられる。at the forefront of で「～の最前線［最先端］に」の意味。lapse「過失」，doctrine「教義，学説」，myth「神話」

(15) – 解答 ①

訳 市長は，市民が公共交通機関に関する自分の計画を支持することが極めて重要だと考えたため，演説で力強い言葉を用いた。

解説 市民の支持を得るためにどんな演説をしたかを想像すると，力強い（forceful）言葉を用いたと考えられる。merciful「慈悲深い」，futile「無駄な」，tranquil「穏やかな」

(16) – 解答 ③

訳 そのポップ歌手が亡くなったとき，彼女は自分の大好きな慈善団体に1,000万ドルを超える遺産を残した。「私たちは彼女の寛大さにとても感謝しています」と慈善団体の広報担当者は述べた。

解説 leave A B「A に B を残す」の B が a（　　）of over $10 million に当たる。金額が続くことから，legacy「遺産」が適切。この行為が第2文では generosity「寛大さ」と表されている。rhyme「韻」，justice「正義」，majority「多数派」

(17) – 解答 ③

訳 山の頂上に近づくにつれ，標高が高い所で酸素濃度が低いために気分が悪くなり始めたハイカーもいた。

解説 山頂に近づくにつれて高くなるのは標高（altitude）。また，気分が悪く

なるのは標高が高い所で酸素濃度が低くなるため。apparatus「器具一式」，equation「方程式」，mileage「総マイル数」

(18) – 解答 **2** ....

訳 テッドはささやかな収入で暮らしている。彼は狭いアパートに住み，請求書を払い，ときどき外食する程度の稼ぎしかない。

解説 第2文の makes (money) はテッドの稼ぎのこと。just enough to afford は「〜を払うのにやっとの金額」という意味で，これを modest income と表すのが適切。modest は「（数量・金額が）あまり多くない」。blissful「至福の」，showy「派手な」，sturdy「頑丈な」

(19) – 解答 **4** ....

訳 大工はテーブル用に均一な木材を選ぶように気を配った。全体的に同じ厚みでないと問題が発生するからだ。

解説 第2文が第1文の理由になっており，the same thickness「同じ厚み」を「均一な木材」と表すのが適切。uniform は形容詞で「（外観や性質が）均一の，同形の」。reckless「無謀な」，gaping「（口が）大きく開いた」，dreary「物寂しい」

(20) – 解答 **1** ....

訳 ピーターは滅多に子供たちに愛情を示さない，非社交的で物静かな男だったが，子供たちは彼が自分たちを心から愛していることを知っていた。

解説 主節の they と them はピーターの子供たちのこと。Although A, B.「A だが，B」の構造から，truly loved them に対比する内容を考えると，子供たちに滅多に見せなかったのは愛情（affection）である。circulation「循環」，oppression「抑圧」，coalition「（政党などの）連立」

(21) – 解答 **1** ....

訳 アントンはスピーカーから奇妙な低いうなりが聞こえたので，全てのケーブルが正しく接続されていることを確認した。

解説 heard a strange（　　）coming from his speakers から，スピーカーから奇妙な音が聞こえたことが推測できる。buzz「低いうなり，（ハチや機械の）ブーンという音」，peck「つつくこと，コツコツつつく音」のうち，スピーカーから聞こえる音として buzz が適切。thorn「とげ」，core「芯」

(22) – 解答 **4** ....

訳 昨夜遅く，ある男がコンビニで強盗しようとして捕まった。警察は彼に武器を捨てさせ，彼を逮捕した。

解説 逮捕の理由はコンビニで強盗しようとしたから。hold up は「〜（銀行・店など）を襲って強奪する」の意味。shrug off「〜を無視する，〜を振り払う」，sit out「〜に参加しない」，run against「〜に不利になる」

(23) – 解答 **4** •

訳 ジルはずっとフランスが大好きだったので，会社のパリ事務所で働く機会があったとき，それに飛びついた。実際，彼女が応募した最初の人物だった。

解説 空所後の it は「会社のパリ事務所で働く機会」のこと。好きな国で働く機会を得たいと思うのが自然なので，jumped at「～に飛びついた」が適切。それぞれ plow through「～をかき分けるようにして（苦労して）進む」，pull on「～を身に着ける，～（ロープなど）を引き寄せる」，throw off「～を払いのける」の過去形。

(24) – 解答 **2** •

訳 A：あなたが申し込んだ講座は仕事のスケジュールにどう適合しますか。
B：オンラインなので，自分のペースで勉強できます。資料は仕事から帰宅したら読めますので，大丈夫でしょう。

解説 主語の the class に対する句動詞が問われている。B の返事の内容から，勉強と仕事の両立について尋ねていると考えて，fit in with「～に適合する，～にうまく溶け込む」が適切。get over「～を乗り越える」，hold onto「～にしっかりつかまる」，take after「～に似ている」

(25) – 解答 **3** • ★**正答率 75%以上**

訳 新しい部署へ移る前に，ベティは今後彼女の仕事をする人に，今抱えているプロジェクトの全てを引き継ぐつもりだ。

解説 新しい部署へ移る前にベティがすることは，仕事の引き継ぎである。hand over A to B で「A を B に引き継ぐ」の意味。beef up「～を増強する」，bank on「～を当てにする」，slip by「（時・機会が）いつの間にか過ぎる」

一次試験・筆記 **2** 問題編 p.62～65

全文訳 **世間話を超える**

　人が持つ関係が人の健康を左右し得ることが研究によって示されている。良好な関係は幸福の増加につながるだけではなく，身体的な健康にも有益な効果がある。これまでのところ，ほとんどの研究が家族や友人などの親しい人たちとの関係に注目してきた。これは当然のことで，というのも，私たちは問題を抱えていたり，考えや意見を共有したいと思ったりしたときには，そういった人たちに話すことが多いからである。その一方で，最近の研究の中には私たちが知らない人とどのように交流するのかを調査したものもあり，その結果はやや意外なものだった。

　ある研究では，被験者たちがこれまで会ったことのない人とペアを組まされ，各ペアは天気などの軽い話題と，個人的な目標などのもっと実質的な話題を考え出すよう求め

54

られた。この研究を開始したときは，ほとんどの被験者たちが，自分たちは気軽な会話の方をより楽しむだろうと考えていた。各会話の後，被験者たちはその会話を，楽しさと，会話の相手とつながっているという感覚に基づいて評価するよう求められた。結果は，被験者たちの予想が間違っていたことを示した。つまり，ほとんどの被験者たちは，真剣な話題を話し合った後に，全体的により有意義な体験をしたと報告したのである。

　この研究結果は，人は，知らない人とより深いレベルで交流することで利益を得るかもしれないことを示唆している。実際，この研究の被験者たちは，概して，自分の生活の中で知らない人と意味のある会話をもっとしたいという願望を示した。しかし，彼らはまた，ほかの人たちはこの願望を持っていないとも思っていた。研究者たちは，この思い込みは間違っており，多くの場合，知らない人も気軽な会話を超えることに興味を持っていると信じている。

　語句 beneficial「有益な」，interact with「～と交流する」，subject「被験者」，substantial「実質的な」，rate「評価する」，that is「つまり」，overall「全体的に」，benefit from「～から利益を得る」，desire「願望」，meaningful「意味のある」，assumption「思い込み」

(26) – 解答 ③

　解説　文頭に適切な論理マーカーを補う問題。空所前は「これまでは（So far）ほとんどの研究が親しい人たちとの関係に注目してきた」，空所後は「最近の研究（recent studies）は知らない人との交流を調査している」と，対照的な内容になっている。よって，In contrast「その一方で，対照的に」が適切。

(27) – 解答 ④

　解説　空所には研究結果が入る。当初被験者たちは，自分たちが（真剣な話題よりも）気軽な会話の方を楽しむだろうと考えていた。しかし，空所後の That is「つまり」の後の内容から，実際は，真剣な話題の方が有意義な体験をしたと報告した。つまり，結果は「被験者たちの予想（＝気軽な会話をより楽しむ）が間違っていた」と言える。

(28) – 解答 ②

　解説　However があるので，空所には前述と対照的な内容が入る。また，空所後の this assumption は空所に入る内容を受けている。この2点を満たすのは2で，「被験者たちは知らない人と意味のある会話をもっとしたいと思っている」→「しかし，ほかの人たちはこの願望を持っていないとも思っている（＝ this assumption）」→「この思い込みは間違っている」という流れ。

　全文訳　**ザ・シング**

　チリの博物館の棚で10年近く過ごした後，「ザ・シング（物体）」として知られる謎の化石の正体がついに判明した。研究者たちは，今ではこれが6,600万年前の軟卵であ

り，この中身はおそらく，恐竜とほぼ同時期に存在した大型の水生爬虫類であるモササウルスだと考えている。以前の化石証拠は，モササウルスは卵を産まないと示唆していた。しかし，研究者たちによるこの発見はこの考えに疑問を投げかけるものであり，研究者たちは，この化石の大きさや，それがモササウルスの化石が見つかった場所で発見されたという事実が，彼らの結論を裏付けていると言う。

研究者たちは「ザ・シング」の正体を特定できたことに喜んでいるが，それは新たな議論の口火を切った。一説には，モササウルスは開水域で卵を産み，子供はほぼ直後に孵化しただろうとも言われている。その一方で，科学者の中には，モササウルスは，一部の現代の爬虫類のように，浜辺で卵を産み，それを埋めたのだろうと信じている人もいる。さらなる研究によって，これらのどれが正しいかが判明することが期待されている。

アメリカの別の研究者チームは，以前に発見された恐竜の赤ちゃんの化石をさらに詳しく調べた後，この先史時代の生物の卵にさらなる光明を投じた。恐竜は殻の硬い卵を産むと考えられていたが，この仮説の基となった化石は限られた恐竜種のものであった。解析を通じて，アメリカの研究者たちは，初期の恐竜の卵は実は軟殻であったことを示唆する証拠を発見した。もしこれが本当なら，恐竜の卵がほとんど見つかっていない理由をこれで説明できるかもしれない。軟らかい成分は分解されやすいため，化石の記録に残る可能性が極めて低いからだ。

> 語句　identify「(動植物の) 分類学上の属・種を決定する」，aquatic「水生の」，reptile「爬虫類」，challenge「異議を唱える」，theory「学説」，hatch「(卵が) かえる，孵化する」，reveal「明らかにする」，shed light on「〜に光明を投じる」，prehistoric「先史時代の」，assumption「仮説」，break down「分解される」

(29) – 解答 ③

解説　謎の化石「ザ・シング」の正体が明らかになった話。それは 6,600 万年前の軟卵であり，中身はモササウルスだと考えられている。Previous → however に着目して，「以前の化石証拠は〜と示唆していた。しかし，…」の展開をつかむ。また，「しかし，この発見はこの考えに疑問を投げかける」の this idea は前の mosasaurs （　　）を受けている。この 2 点を満たすには，「モササウルスは卵を産まない」とするのが適切。

(30) – 解答 ②

解説　空所前は「モササウルスが開水域で卵を産み，子供はほぼ直後に孵化した」という説，空所後は「浜辺で卵を産み，それを埋めた」という別の説。これらを結ぶのは，On the other hand「その一方で」である。

(31) – 解答 ①

解説　空所前の If true は「初期の恐竜の卵が軟殻なら」という意味。空所後の Since softer materials ... the fossil record. は this could explain why （　　）の根拠になっており，空所前後は，「もし初期の恐竜の卵が軟殻なら，化石の記録に残りにくいため，これが恐竜の卵がほとんど見

つかっていない理由となる」という主旨である。

一次試験・筆記 **3** │ 問題編 p.66 ～ 72

全文訳 **明日の鶏**

　1940 年代以前，アメリカではほとんどの鶏が家族経営の農場で飼育されており，肉を得るより，主に卵の生産に重点が置かれていた。当時は貧困と食料不足が一般的であったため，人々は鶏を犠牲にすることなく安定したタンパク源を維持したかったのである。加えて，農家は通常，鶏がその地の条件にどの程度適応しているか —— 例えば乾いた気候または湿潤な気候に適しているか —— に基づいて品種を選んだため，飼育されている鶏の種類も非常に多かった。

　しかし，第 2 次世界大戦後に豚肉や牛肉などの食肉が普及すると，鶏卵はタンパク源として張り合えなくなった。従って，米国農務省は経済的に飼育でき，より多くの食肉を生み出す鶏の品種を見つけるために「明日の鶏」コンテストと呼ばれるイベントを立ち上げた。総合優勝した鶏は，異なる品種のかけ合わせであったが，ほかの品種よりも速く，大きく育ち，さまざまな気候に適応することができた。このコンテストに着想を得て，これらと同じ望ましい特長を持った鶏の安定した供給を保証するために，育種の会社は複雑な組み合わせの鶏の品種を作り始めた。この遺伝子の組み合わせを作り出すことは難しかったため，ほとんどの農家は自ら品種改良するより，これらの会社から若鶏を購入するほかなく，この開発はこの産業を完全に変えてしまった。

　このコンテストは，鶏肉の消費普及に貢献したが，この傾向には負の側面もあった。鶏が狭いケージに閉じ込められる大きな施設で，大量の鶏を飼育する方がより経済的になったのだ。これは多くの小規模農場を廃業に追いやっただけではなく，動物愛護活動家らによると，鶏にとって，ストレスを引き起こし，より病気になりやすい環境を生み出したという。このコンテストは鶏を一般的な食品にしたが，その価値はあったのかを疑問視する人もいた。

　　語句 emphasis「重要視」，protein「タンパク質」，sacrifice「犠牲にする」，tremendous「（大きさ・数量などが）途方もない」，consistent「安定した」，genetic「遺伝子の」，have no choice but to *do*「～するしかない」，popularize「普及させる」，massive「極めて多い」，confine「閉じ込める」，numerous「数多くの」，out of business「廃業して」，activist「活動家」

(32) – 解答 •••

問題文の訳 1940 年代以前のアメリカの養鶏産業について分かることの 1 つは何か。

選択肢の訳　**1**　各農場で飼育される鶏の品種は通常，その農場が位置する地域の気候に左右された。

　　2　各農場は，環境条件の急激な変化に備えて，複数の品種の鶏を飼育し

ていた。

3 鶏は一般的に，非常に貧しい人々によって，または食糧不足のときにのみ食された。

4 全国に非常に多くの養鶏場があったため，生産された卵の多くが無駄になっていた。

解説 まず，第1段落第1文から，当時，養鶏では肉よりも卵の生産が重要視されていたことを押さえよう。その後の Additionally, ... の長い1文がポイント。要約すると，農家はその土地の気候への順応性に基づいて鶏の品種を選んでいたという話なので，**1** が適切。

(33) – 解答 ②

問題文の訳 米国農務省が「明日の鶏」コンテストを開催した理由は

選択肢の訳 **1** 豚肉や牛肉といったほかの種類の肉がより高価になりつつあったため，アメリカ国民がより安価な代替品を求めていたからであった。

2 ほとんどの養鶏場が卵の生産に重点を置いており，そのため食肉の生産により適した鶏を作り出す必要が生じたからであった。

3 アメリカの多くの養鶏場が廃業し，鶏肉の入手可能性が大幅に低下したからであった。

4 アメリカ国民が長い間同じ種類の卵を食べることに飽きていたため，生産者たちが異なる品種の鶏を求めていたからであった。

解説 「明日の鶏」コンテスト開催の目的は，第2段落第2文の「より多くの食肉を生み出す鶏の品種を見つけるため」（＝食肉の生産により適した鶏を作り出す必要が生じた）である。またこの文には therefore があるので，開催の理由はその前の「鶏卵では豚肉や牛肉に張り合えなくなった」（＝卵の生産に重点を置いていられなくなった）だと分かる。よって，**2** が正解。

(34) – 解答 ③ ‥‥‥‥‥‥‥‥‥‥‥ 正答率 ★75%以上

問題文の訳 コンテストが養鶏産業に与えた影響の1つは何か。

選択肢の訳 **1** 農家は，数品種の鶏をかけ合わせることが比較的簡単であると知り，新品種を育成する気になった。

2 アメリカ全土で小規模養鶏場の数が増加したものの，その多くは経営状態が悪く，設備も安っぽいものだった。

3 鶏の苦痛を増大させ，その健康を損なわせるような環境で鶏を飼育する動きが始まった。

4 農家は，飼育方法を改善することで，より多くの，そしてより味の良い肉を生み出す鶏を育てることができることに気付いた。

解説 第3段落第1文で鶏肉の普及には負の側面（a dark side）もあったと前置きし，詳しい説明が続く。その負の側面を要約した **3** が正解。本文の were confined in small cages / caused the chickens stress と **3**

の the birds' suffering, 同様に higher levels of sickness と less healthy がそれぞれ対応している。

全文訳 **アメリカの学校におけるしつけ**

　何十年もの間，アメリカの学校で用いられたしつけの方法は，賞罰を与える方式が人の行動を改善するのに最も効果的な方法だと信じていた心理学者 B. F. スキナーの説に基づくものだった。一般的に，ルールを破る生徒は，1日以上授業に出席することを禁じられたり，放課後に居残りさせられたりするなどの罰を与えられる。これらの罰は，生徒たちに教師の指示に従ったり，クラスメートを尊重したりすることを教えることを意図している。しかし，最近の心理学研究によると，罰は教室に一時的に平和をもたらすのに効果的であるかもしれないが，長期的に継続して使用されるとその罰が矯正しようとしている対象である行動そのものを強化する可能性があることが明らかになった。

　多くの専門家は今では，子供たちが適切に行動できるようになるには，自制心を養うことが必須であると信じている。生徒たちは，ルールを守るよう罰せられるとき，外圧によって良い行動を取ることを強要されている。一方で，自制は内的なモチベーション，自信，他者への寛容さからきており，これらの代わりに罰を使うことは実際にはそれらの発達を遅らせたり阻害したりしかねない。同様に，シールなどの褒美の利用も，生徒たちが自分の人生を通して自分の役に立つであろう知識や社会的技能を獲得する大切さを理解するよりも，ただ教師を喜ばせようとすることにつながる。

　近年，こうした考えを裏付ける研究が増えている。前頭葉前部皮質として知られる脳の領域は，私たちが仕事に集中することを助け，自律をつかさどり，自分の行動の結果を考えることができるようにする役割を担っている。研究は，行動に問題のある生徒たちは前頭葉前部皮質があまり発達していない可能性があることを示唆している。しかし幸運なことに，繰り返しの経験によって脳の構造を変えることができる証拠があり，これは前頭葉前部皮質の発達に影響を及ぼすことも可能であることを示唆している。児童行動の専門家であるロス・グリーンは，教育者が態度を変えて，生徒たちの悪い行動についての彼らの気持ちに実際に耳を傾け，彼らが直面している問題に対する解決策を考え付くように促せば，これは前頭葉前部皮質に物理的な影響を与える可能性があると考えている。グリーンは，多くの学校で問題行動を著しく減少させた極めて効果の大きいプログラムを作り，近年彼のアイデアがメディアで広く取り上げられた結果，それはますます多くの教育者によって採用されている。

語句 discipline「しつけ」，psychologist「心理学者」，reward「褒美」，punishment「罰」，〈prohibit＋O＋from -ing〉「Oが〜するのを禁じる」，intensify「増強させる」，*be* intended to *do*「〜することを目的とする」，continually「継続的に」，an extended period of time「長期間」，appropriately「適切に」，self-control「自制（心）」，obey「従う」，external「外部（から）の」，internal「内部の，内面的な」，self-confidence「自信」，tolerant「寛容な」，substitute「代替」，sticker

「シール」，merely「ただ単に」，attempt to *do*「～しようと試みる［努める］」，back up「～を裏付ける」，prefrontal cortex「前頭葉前部皮質」，self-discipline「自律」，consequence「結果」，behavioral「行動に関する」，alter「変える」，educator「教育者」，extensive「広範囲の」，media coverage「マスコミ報道」

(35) – 解答 ②

問題文の訳 心理学の研究は，学校における罰の使用について何を示したか。

選択肢の訳
1 その負の効果を軽減するために褒美と一緒に使用された場合にのみ効果を発揮する可能性が高い。
2 短期的にはより良い行動を生み出すことに成功するかもしれないが，長期的には実際に有害になる可能性がある。
3 体罰よりもはるかに効果的なさまざまな新しい種類の罰がある。
4 何らかの罰を使用することは，生徒たちに，教師に従いクラスメートを尊重するよう強いるのに必要である。

解説 第 1 段落参照。For decades → Recent / however の展開から，長らくしつけの方法は賞罰［アメとムチ］が効果的と信じられていたが，最近の研究では違う，という流れ。Recent psychological studies, however, ... から，罰は一時的にはプラスだが長期的にはマイナスという話なので，**2** が正解。それぞれ本文の temporarily と **2** の in the short term，同じく over an extended period of time と in the long term が対応している。

(36) – 解答 ③

問題文の訳 この文章によると，褒美の使用が生徒に与える影響の 1 つは何か。

選択肢の訳
1 それは，生徒に勤勉であることの利点を教え，生徒は学業の目標によりうまく集中できるようになる。
2 そのせいで生徒は物質的な物を欲しがるようになり，他人を喜ばせるように振る舞う必要性をあまり意識しなくなる。
3 それは，生徒が後の人生で自分の役に立つであろう重要な技能を伸ばすことを妨げる可能性がある。
4 それは，生徒が教師に言われたことをただこなすのではなく，自分自身の目標を決めることの重要性を理解するのに役立つ。

解説 第 2 段落は罰の悪影響の後，褒美の悪影響に話が展開する。褒美について書かれた Similarly, ... を参照。understanding the importance of ... their lives と **3** の developing important skills ... later in life が類義表現。rather than「～よりも」の後の内容を，**3** では否定表現〈prevent ＋O＋ from -ing〉「O が～するのを妨げる」で表している。

(37) – 解答 ①

問題文の訳 ロス・グリーンが子供の脳について信じていることは何か。

選択肢の訳　**1**　子供が自分自身の問題を解決するのを手助けすることで，行動を制御する脳の部分の発達を促すことができる。

　　　　　2　年齢の低い子供の脳は年齢の高い子供の脳と働きが異なるため，問題行動への対処も異なる方法が必要である。

　　　　　3　前頭葉前部皮質として知られる脳の領域は，子供の行動を制御する上で，一部の科学者が信じているほど重要ではないかもしれない。

　　　　　4　悪い行動は子供の学業成績に悪影響を与えるだけでなく，脳の正常な発達を永久に妨げる。

解説　ロス・グリーンの見解は第3段落の Child-behavior expert Ross Greene believes ... にある。「教育者が生徒に，問題に対する解決策を考え付くように促せば，前頭葉前部皮質（prefrontal cortex）に物理的な影響を与える」とあり，この prefrontal cortex は同段落第2文から，**1** の the part of the brain that controls behavior「行動を制御する脳の部分」と言える。よって，**1** が正解。

全文訳　**ロバート・ザ・ブルースとアーブロース宣言**

　1286年，スコットランド王アレクサンダー3世の突然の死がさまざまな貴族たちの間の権力争いにつながり，危うく国に内戦をもたらすところだった。事態を収拾するため，イングランド王エドワード1世は競争者の中から新しい統治者を選ぶように求められた。自身も最終的にはスコットランドを統治する野望を抱いていたエドワード王は，新しい指導者が彼に忠誠を誓うことを条件に承諾した。彼はジョン・ベイリャルという貴族を新しい王に選んだが，スコットランドの問題にイングランドが繰り返しその権力を振るうにつれ，ほどなく反感が募っていった。転機はエドワード王がイングランドのフランスとの対立に軍事援助を提供するよう，スコットランドに強硬に求めたときに訪れた。ベイリャル王がそれどころか自国とフランスの間で同盟を結んだとき，エドワード王はスコットランドに攻め入り，ベイリャル王を打ち負かして王座に就いた。

　これがスコットランド貴族であるロバート・ザ・ブルースがスコットランドをイングランドの支配から解放しようとしていたときに直面していた状況であった。父親が王位争いにおけるベイリャル王の競争相手の1人だったロバートは，政治的優位に立ち，スコットランドからイングランド軍を追い出す反乱を率いた。ロバートは1306年にスコットランド王に即位し，国内からは絶大な支持を得たが，ローマカトリック教会の指導者であるローマ教皇を怒らせた。彼はイングランドと和解してほしいという教会の要望を無視しただけではなく，王に即位する前に王座への最も有力な競争相手を礼拝所で殺しもしたのだ。

　スコットランドの指導者たちは，教会の承認がないと国が国際的に孤立し脆弱（ぜいじゃく）になることを知っていた。スコットランドの独立が国際的に受け入れられることは，国がイングランドのような強国の陰に存在するのであれば特に重要となるが，イングランドは撤退したにもかかわらず，まだロバートを正式にスコットランドの王と認めていなかった。

そこで，1320年，スコットランドの有力貴族たちが集まり，現在では「アーブロース宣言」として知られる文書を作成した。それはスコットランドの独立を宣言し，ロバートを国の統治者として認めることをローマ教皇に求めるものであった。しかし，その年の後になって貴族たちが受けた反応は，当初この宣言に効果がなかったことを示していた。ローマ教皇は，スコットランドとの関係において平和的な解決を追求するようイングランドに強く要請したが，スコットランドの要求を拒絶しただけではなく，スコットランド自ら主張した独立も追認しなかった。しかし数年後，この宣言の影響力は，平和条約がついにスコットランドをイングランドの脅威から解放した後，ローマ教皇がロバートと彼の王国を承認するのに貢献した。

　現在では「アーブロース宣言」はスコットランド史上最も有名な文書の1つとなっている。歴史家の中には，その証拠はないが，それがアメリカ独立宣言に着想を与えたと主張する者さえいる。しかし，学者たちは，「アーブロース宣言」をこれほど歴史的なものにしているのは，国王はスコットランド国民の承認がないと統治できないという主張である，という点で概ね意見が一致している。具体的に言うと，貴族たちはこの文書を使って，自分たちを裏切ったどんな統治者も排除する権利があることを大胆に主張したのである。この意味では，この文書は国の統治者とその国民との間の契約の先駆的な例であり，その契約では，統治者は国民が自由社会で生きられるようにする責任があった。

　語句　declaration「宣言」，noble「貴族」，ambition「野望」，ultimately「最終的には」，pledge「誓う」，loyalty「忠誠心」，resentment「恨み，反感」，exert「(権力を) 行使する」，authority「権力」，affair「問題，出来事」，turning point「転機」，ally「同盟する」，throne「王座」，dominance「優勢」，rebellion「反乱」，crown「王 [女王] にする」，domestically「国内で」，place of warship「礼拝所，教会」，vulnerable「脆弱な」，mighty「強力な」，retreat「撤退する」，proclaim「宣言する」，self-proclaimed「自ら主張した」，〈urge＋O＋to *do*〉「Oに～するよう強く要請する」，pursue「追求する」，resolution「解決 (策)」，treaty「条約」，assertion「主張」，specifically「具体的には」，boldly「大胆に」，betray「裏切る」，pioneering「先駆的な」

(38) − 解答

問題文の訳　スコットランド王のアレクサンダー3世の死後，何が起こったか。

選択肢の訳　1　スコットランドは，そうすることはエドワード1世の利益にならないにもかかわらず，エドワード1世をだましてジョン・ベイリャルを選ばせることができた。

2　エドワード1世は，王になるというジョン・ベイリャルの試みを支持しないスコットランドの貴族たちの忠誠心に疑問を持ち始めた。

3　エドワード1世は，スコットランドに対する権力を増大させるために，自分に有利になるよう状況をうまく利用しようとした。

4 スコットランドはフランスの軍事力に非常に脅威を感じたため，両国間の外交関係が悪化した。

解説 第1段落参照。スコットランド支配を狙っていたイングランド王のエドワード1世は，スコットランド王アレクサンダー3世の死後に起きた貴族たちの間の権力争いに乗じて（＝ use the situation to his advantage），自分に忠誠を誓うことを条件に（＝ increase his power over Scotland）ベイリャルをスコットランドの新しい王に選んだ。よって，**3** が正解。

(39) – 解答 ④ ••••••••••••••••••••••••••••••••••

問題文の訳 ロバート・ザ・ブルースはスコットランド王になった後，どんな問題に直面したか。

選択肢の訳
1 彼は偉大な軍事指導者だったが，彼の政治的能力の欠如が，イングランドと不利な協定を取り決めることにつながった。
2 彼は競争者たちと宗教に関する意見の相違があったため，多くのスコットランド国民が彼を支持しなくなった。
3 スコットランドとイングランドの間の宗教的な違いにより，スコットランドが再び攻撃される可能性が高くなった。
4 彼が権力を握るために行ったことが理由で，スコットランドはイングランドから安全でいるために必要な支援が得られなかった。

解説 第2段落は過去形と過去完了形に着目して，出来事の前後関係を理解しよう。ロバートは王に即位する前，最も有力な競争相手を礼拝所で殺すなどして（＝権力を握るために行ったこと），ローマ教皇を怒らせた。そして第3段落から，ローマ教皇はロバートを統治者として認めてほしいというスコットランドの要求を拒絶し，スコットランドの独立も認めなかった（＝支援が得られなかった）ことが分かる。よって，**4** が正解。

(40) – 解答 ② ••••••••••••••••••••••••••••••••••

問題文の訳 「アーブロース宣言」が書かれた年，

選択肢の訳
1 ローマ教皇が，スコットランドの国家としての独立を認めることが優先事項だと考えていることが明らかになった。
2 ローマ教皇は，ロバートも彼の国も認めなかったにもかかわらず，イングランドとスコットランドの間の平和を促進しようとした。
3 イングランドとスコットランドの間の講和の約束は，スコットランドがローマ教皇から助けを得ようとしたことで危険にさらされた。
4 スコットランドは，ロバートが国の真の王であることをローマ教皇に認めてもらうのに十分な国際的認知を得ることができた。

解説 第3段落参照。「アーブロース宣言」は1320年で，同年の出来事は later in the year, however, ... 以下にある。ローマ教皇は，スコットランドとの関係において平和的な解決を追求するようイングランドに強く要請した（＝平和を促進しようとした）が，ロバートも彼の国も認め

なかった。正解は **2** で，本文の The Pope not only ... の A, although B「Bだが，A」を B despite A「Aにもかかわらず，B」と言い換えている。

(41) − 解答 ②

問題文の訳 「アーブロース宣言」の一般的な解釈の１つは何か。

選択肢の訳 1 ロバートは実際，国民が当初考えていたよりもはるかに優れた指導者だったことを示している。

2 国の統治者が統治する国民に対して負う義務について，新しい見方をもたらした。

3 当時のスコットランドの統治者たちと貴族たちの間には，学者がかつて考えていたよりもはるかに多くの対立があったことを明らかにしている。

4 王や女王が国を統治していては有益な政治体制が成り立たないことを示唆した。

解説 第４段落参照。「アーブロース宣言」の解釈が複数書かれている中で，最終文の In this sense, ... と **2** が合う。本文の a pioneering example「先駆的な例」を **2** では a new way of looking「新しい見方」と表している。

一次試験・筆記 **4** | 問題編 p.73

トピックの訳 企業はもっとオンラインサービスを提供すべきか。

ポイントの訳 ・利便性　・コスト　・仕事　・環境

解答例　In today's fast-paced digital world, I believe businesses should provide more online services. The benefits of doing so are related to convenience and cost.

　Firstly, providing more online services leads to increased convenience. For instance, online customer support provides people with the means to contact businesses whenever they have queries. This can be particularly beneficial for busy people or international customers who live in different time zones.

　Additionally, online services can be cost-effective for businesses. With the rise of e-commerce, moving to online digital platforms can reduce expenses and streamline operations. Selling products online, for example, can help businesses cut utility bills. Companies can also reach a wider audience and increase profits without constructing more physical stores.

In conclusion, businesses should provide more online services, as this will not only allow them to enhance customers' experiences but also reduce operating costs.

解説 序論：序論（第1段落）では，トピックに対する自分の意見を簡潔に書く。解答例では，In today's fast-paced digital world「今日のペースの速いデジタル世界では」で始め，I believe の後にトピックの表現を続けて賛成の立場を明らかにしている。そして The benefits of doing so are related to「そうすることのメリットは～に関連している」の表現で，ポイントの Convenience と Cost を取り上げている。

本論：本論では，2つの観点に沿って，自分の主張を裏付ける理由・根拠を Firstly, ... Secondly [Additionally], ... などの構成で書く。解答例の第2段落は Convenience の観点で，「より多くのオンラインサービスを提供することは利便性の向上につながる」と述べた後，For instance を用いて具体的にオンラインのカスタマーサポートを挙げ，顧客側の利便性を説明している。形容詞 convenient の代わりに beneficial を用いている点に着目。第3段落は Cost の観点で，「企業にとって費用対効果が高い」と述べた後，「e コマースの台頭により，デジタルプラットフォームに移行することで，経費を削減し業務を合理化できる」という企業側の利点を述べ，for example を用いて具体的な説明を続けている。ポイントの Cost を cost-effective や expenses などの語を用いて工夫して表している点に着目。オンラインショップに対する「実店舗」は physical store [shop] と表す。このように，本論となる第2，3段落では，第1文目で明確な主張（トピックセンテンス＝その段落の主張の要約文）を書き，その後 for example などを用いて具体的な説明を2～3文書くと適切な語数になるだろう。

結論：結論（最終段落）では，序論で述べたトピックに対する意見を再主張する。解答例は In conclusion「結論として」で始め，トピックの表現を用いて賛成の立場を示した後，理由を表す as に続いて not only A but also B「A だけでなく B も」を用いて2つの観点を再確認している。

そのほかの表現 第3段落の With the rise of「～の台頭により」はほかのトピックでも使えるだろう。この文の moving to の意味上の主語は businesses なので，businesses can reduce expenses and streamline operations by moving to (online) digital platforms「企業は～に移行することで…できる」と表すこともできる。ほかに Instead of more physical stores, ...「実店舗を増やす代わりに，…」など，〈主語＋動詞〉ばかりではなく副詞句や分詞構文で文を始めるとバリエーションが豊かな文章になる。

No.1 – 解答 ② .... 正答率 ★75%以上

スクリプト
☆: Hi, Professor. Can I talk to you about my assignment?

★: Sure. I was surprised when you didn't turn it in at the start of class. That's never happened before.

☆: My brother was in an accident, and I was at the hospital with him.

★: I'm sorry to hear that. Is he OK?

☆: Yes, he's home now, but I didn't have time to get my assignment done.

★: Well, I can let you turn it in tomorrow. How would that be?

☆: Great. Thank you!

Question: What will the woman probably do tomorrow?

全文訳
☆: こんにちは，教授。私の課題についてお話しできますか？

★: もちろん。あなたが授業の始めに提出しなかったときには驚きました。これまでそういうことはなかったので。

☆: 私の兄［弟］が事故に遭って，病院で彼に付き添っていたんです。

★: それは気の毒に。彼は大丈夫なのですか？

☆: はい，彼はもう帰宅していますが，私は課題を済ませる時間がありませんでした。

★: そうですか，明日提出してもいいことにできますよ。それでどうですか？

☆: 助かります。ありがとうございます！

質問：女性は明日，おそらく何をするか。

選択肢の訳
1　入院中の兄［弟］を見舞いに行く。
2　彼女の課題を提出する。
3　彼女の兄［弟］に助けを求める。
4　新しい課題のトピックを選ぶ。

解説 教授と女子学生の会話で，話題は女性の課題（assignment）。今日提出できなかった事情を聞いた教授は，I can let you turn it in tomorrow と言う。これに対して女性はお礼を述べているので，明日課題を提出すると考えられる。よって，**2**が正解。turn ～ in「～を提出する」を submit で表している。

No.2 – 解答 ③ .... 正答率 ★75%以上

スクリプト
☆: I can't believe the government wants to raise taxes again.

★: They say it's necessary to pay for the new education plan.

☆: Well, it seems like there are a lot of areas in the budget that could be reduced instead. Spending on highways, for one.

★： That's for sure. I read a news report just yesterday saying that few drivers are using the new highways, even though they cost billions.

☆： Right. I'd write a letter to the government if I thought it'd do any good.

Question: What do these people think?

全文訳 ☆： 政府がまた税金を引き上げたいなんて信じられない。

★： 彼らは新しい教育計画の費用を賄うために必要と言っているね。

☆： うーん，代わりに減らせる予算の分野はたくさんありそうだけど。高速道路に使っている分とか，例を1つ挙げると。

★： 確かにその通りだね。ちょうど昨日，何十億もかかったにもかかわらず，新しい高速道路を使っている運転手はほとんどいないという報道を読んだばかりだよ。

☆： その通り。もし政府に手紙を書いてどうにかなるならそうしているよ。

質問： この人たちはどう思っているか。

選択肢の訳 1 教育に費やされているお金が多過ぎる。
2 間もなく予算が減りそうである。
3 政府はお金を無駄にしている。
4 メディアが政府に対して不公平である。

解説 話題は税金の引き上げ。男性が，税金の引き上げは新しい教育計画の費用を賄うのに必要だと政府は言っている，と述べると，女性は（税金を引き上げる）代わりに減らせる予算の分野があると返答する。その後，2人は具体的に高速道路の費用への不満で意見が一致する。つまり2人は「政府はお金を無駄にしている」と思っていると判断できる。

No.3 – 解答 ① ･････････････････････････････････････ 正答率 ★75%以上

スクリプト ★： Thanks for inviting me to lunch.

☆： Sure. I wanted to celebrate your promotion. It's too bad I won't see you as often, though, since you'll be moving to the fourth floor.

★： Well, we'll still have meetings together. And maybe we could have a weekly lunch or something.

☆： Great idea. But you'll probably be eating at your desk a lot more often.

★： That's true. I guess my workload is going to be pretty heavy.

☆： Yes, at least until you get used to your new position.

Question: What is one thing we learn from the conversation?

全文訳 ★： ランチに招待してくれてありがとう。

☆： どういたしまして。あなたの昇進をお祝いしたかったの。あなたは4階に移動するから，あまり会えなくなるのは残念だけど。

★： でも，まだ会議は一緒にするよ。それに週に1回はランチか何かできる
　　かもしれない。

☆： とてもいいアイデアね。でも，あなたはこれから自分のデスクで食べる
　　ことがもっと増えるでしょうね。

★： 確かにね。仕事量が結構多くなるんだろうな。

☆： ええ，少なくとも，あなたが新しい役職に慣れるまでは。
　　質問：この会話から分かることの1つは何か。

選択肢の訳 **1**　男性は（今より）ずっと忙しくなる。

　　　　　2　女性はもっと多くの会議に出席する必要が出てくる。

　　　　　3　女性は4階にいる人たちが好きではない。

　　　　　4　男性は自分の新しい役職を望んでいなかった。

解説　男性の I guess my workload is going to be pretty heavy. が決め手。
正解 **1** では「仕事量が結構多くなる」を become much busier で表し
ている。男性の発言直前にある女性の you'll probably be eating at
your desk a lot more often もヒントになる。

No.**4** – 解答　④　•••

スクリプト ☆： I'm going next door to see Carol. I'll be back in an hour.

★： Sure. By the way, how is she doing after her surgery?

☆： She's doing much better, but she still has trouble moving around.
　　Today, I'm going to do a little cleaning and prepare some food
　　for her that she can just heat up.

★： I'm sure she appreciates your help.

☆： I think she does. The other day, she got me a gift certificate to a
　　spa so I can get a massage.

Question: Why is the woman visiting her neighbor?

全文訳 ☆： 隣に行ってキャロルに会ってくるわ。1時間で帰るね。

★： 分かった。ところで，手術の後の彼女の様子はどう？

☆： だいぶ良くなっているけど，動き回るのはまだ難しいわね。今日は少し
　　掃除をして，温めるだけでいい食事を彼女に作ってあげるつもりよ。

★： 君の助けを彼女は喜んでいるに違いないね。

☆： そう思うわ。先日，私がマッサージを受けられるようにスパのギフト券
　　をくれたの。
　　質問：女性はなぜ隣人を訪問しているのか。

選択肢の訳 **1**　彼女にマッサージをするため。

　　　　　2　食べ物を受け取るため。

　　　　　3　彼女にギフト券を渡すため。

　　　　　4　家事をするため。

解説　最初のやりとりから，隣人のキャロルは手術したばかりだと推測できる。

女性がキャロルの家に行く理由は，Today, I'm going to do ... から，術後のキャロルを世話するため。「掃除をする」「食事を作る」という具体的な行為を抽象的に housework と表した **4** が正解。

No.**5**－解答　③

(スクリプト)　☆：Alan, the printer is giving me that error message again.

★：Are you sure the paper is the right size?

☆：Of course. I've checked it several times.

★：This is ridiculous. We just bought that printer two weeks ago. I'll call the computer shop and ask them to replace it.

☆：I think we should try to get a refund instead. I've seen reviews saying this brand's printers frequently need to be repaired.

★：OK, I'll look into it. We can use our old one until we decide which model we want to buy.

Question: What will the man probably do first?

(全文訳)　☆：アラン，プリンターがまたあのエラーメッセージを表示しているの。

★：用紙のサイズは本当に合っているの？

☆：もちろんよ。何度か確認したわ。

★：ばかげているよ。あのプリンターは2週間前に買ったばかりなんだ。パソコンショップに電話して交換してもらうように頼むよ。

☆：それよりも返金してもらうようにした方がいいと思う。このメーカーのプリンターは頻繁に修理してもらう必要があるというレビューを見たの。

★：分かった，調べてみる。どのモデルを買うか決めるまで古いのを使ったらいいしね。

質問：男性はおそらく，まず何をするか。

(選択肢の訳)　**1**　店にプリンターを交換するよう頼む。

2　古いプリンターを修理してもらう。

3　店からお金を返してもらうようにする。

4　ほかのモデルを見るために店に行く。

(解説)　do first を含む未来の行動を問う問題では，会話中で話される複数の行動のうち，会話の後で最初に取る行動を理解する必要がある。ここでは，店に電話して交換してもらうよ→（反論）それよりも（instead）返金してもらった方がいい→ OK，という流れから，交換の **1** は誤り，返金の **3** が正解。get a refund を **3** では get money back と表している。

No.**6**－解答　②

(スクリプト)　☆：How was your business trip to Tokyo last week?

★：It was a disaster.

☆：What happened? Did the client back out of the deal?

★：No, but their lawyer objected to the wording of the contract, and there was a big delay while we modified the text. Then, before we could finalize the deal, we had an emergency at headquarters, and I had to return immediately.

☆: That's awful.

★: Yes. I'm going to have to go back to Tokyo in a couple of weeks.

Question: What was one problem the man had during his trip?

全文訳 ☆: 先週の東京出張はどうだった？

★: 最悪だったよ。

☆: 何があったの？　クライアントが取引から手を引いたの？

★: いや，でも彼らの弁護士が契約書の文言に反対して，文章を修正したらものすごく遅れてしまったんだ。それから，取引をまとめられる前に，うちの本部で緊急事態があって，すぐに戻ってこなければならなかったんだよ。

☆: それはひどいわね。

★: うん。また数週間のうちに東京に戻らないといけないんだ。

質問：男性が出張の間に抱えた問題の1つは何だったか。

選択肢の訳 **1** 彼のクライアントが取引を中止した。

2 契約書を修正する必要があった。

3 弁護士が深刻な間違いを犯した。

4 彼は重要な会議に遅れて到着した。

解説 男性は，東京出張の感想を disaster「大惨事，最悪の事態」と表現した後，問題について詳しく話す。幾つかある問題の中で，their lawyer objected ... we modified the text「文章を修正したことでかなり遅れた」の部分と **2** が合う。**2** の revised は modified の言い換え。Did the client back out of the deal? に No と答えているので **1** は誤り。

No.**7** －解答 ④ ･････････････････････････････････････

スクリプト ☆: Hi, Nick. How's your new job going?

★: Well, it's taking me a while to adjust.

☆: Are your responsibilities very different from your last job?

★: No, but my boss is. She always says she's going to do things but then forgets about them! I'm constantly having to remind her about deadlines.

☆: That sounds frustrating.

★: It sure is. Still, at least she isn't bothering me about my work.

☆: I guess things could be worse.

Question: What does the man say about his new job?

全文訳 ☆: こんにちは，ニック。新しい仕事はどう？

★: そうだね，慣れるのに時間がかかっているよ。

☆： 職務が前職とだいぶ違うの？

★： いや，でも，上司がね。彼女はいつも何かすると言っているんだけど，その後それについて忘れてしまうんだ！　僕は常に締め切りについて彼女にリマインドしないといけなくて。

☆： それはいらいらしそうね。

★： 本当にそうなんだ。それでも，少なくとも彼女は僕の仕事に干渉してこないけど。

☆： まだいい方かもしれないね。

質問： 男性は新しい仕事について何と言っているか。

選択肢の訳
1　上司が彼を信じていない。
2　締め切りが非常に厳しい。
3　彼は必要とされる技能に欠けている。
4　上司の要領が良くない。

解説　男性は新しい仕事で上司に不満がある様子。No, but my boss is. は女性の質問を受けて「前職の上司とは違う」という意味。その上司について説明した She always says ... の部分を not well organized と表した **4** が正解。形容詞 organized は人について使うとき，「（物事に系統的に対応して）きちんとしている，まめな」という意味。things could be worse は「もっと悪い状況もあり得る＝（それと比べると）まだいい方だ」という慣用表現。否定文 things couldn't be worse だと「それ以上悪いことはない＝最悪だ」の意味になる。

No.8 － 解答　**3**　・・・・・・・・・・・・・・・・・・・・・・・・・・・・・・・　正答率 ★**75%以上**

スクリプト ★： I'm thinking we should replace the sofa soon. It's getting pretty worn out.

☆： Do you want to check out that new furniture store down the road?

★： Nah, I was thinking of just getting one online. That's usually much cheaper.

☆： Really? I'd rather we try a sofa out before actually buying it.

★： I suppose you're right. Our budget isn't very large, though, so we'll probably have to put off the purchase until the store offers some discounts.

☆： Let's look around some other stores, too. They might have some good deals on.

Question: What will the couple probably do?

全文訳 ★： そろそろソファを買い替えた方がいいと思っているんだ。結構くたびれてきているよね。

☆： この先にある，あの新しい家具店を見に行く？

★： いや，とりあえずオンラインで買おうかと思ってた。その方がたいてい

ずっと安いし。

☆： そうなの？ 私はどちらかというと実際に買う前にソファを試してみたいわ。

★： 君の言う通りかもしれないね。でも僕たちの予算はそんなにないから，店が割引を始めるまで買うのは先送りしなければならないだろうね。

☆： ほかの店も幾つか見てみましょう。お得なものがあるかもしれないし。

質問：カップルはおそらく何をするか。

選択肢の訳 **1** すぐに新しいソファを手に入れる。

2 オンラインでソファを買う。

3 特価のソファを探す。

4 今あるソファを修繕する。

解説 話題はソファの買い替え。家具店を見に行くか→オンラインで安いものを買うつもりだった→（反論）店で試したい→（納得）でも予算が少ない→ほかの店も見よう，という流れ。offers some discounts や have some good deals on の表現から，2人はお得な値段の（= on sale）ソファを買うことで意見が一致しているので，**3** が正解。

No.**9** – 解答 ③ ･････････････････････････ 正答率 ★**75%以上**

スクリプト ☆： It's so warm today! Hard to believe it's February. I could even go for some ice cream.

★： Today is lovely, but the weather report says we may get a big snowstorm this weekend.

☆： Are you kidding? That would be a temperature drop of nearly 20 degrees.

★： We'd better check how much food and water we have and go to the grocery store if necessary.

☆： Good idea. After getting snowed in at our cabin last year, I want to make sure we're stocked up just in case.

Question: What does the man suggest?

全文訳 ☆： 今日は本当に暖かいね！ 2月だなんて信じられない。アイスクリームを食べに行きたいぐらいよ。

★： 今日はいい天気だけど，天気予報によると今週末に激しい吹雪が来るかもしれないんだって。

☆： 冗談でしょう？ それって20度近く気温が下がるってことよ。

★： 食料と水がどれぐらいあるか確認して，必要なら食料雑貨店に行かないと。

☆： いいね。去年，大雪で山小屋に閉じ込められたから，念のためしっかりと備蓄しておきたいわ。

質問：男性は何を提案しているか。

選択肢の訳 **1** 天気ニュースを確認すること。

2 今週末に山小屋へ出かけること。

3 防災用品を備えておくこと。

4 アイスクリームを食べに行くこと。

解説 会話前半から，今日は暖かいが，今週末は吹雪が来るという展開を押さえよう。男性の提案は We'd better check how much food and water we have and go to the grocery store if necessary. にあり，food and water を emergency supplies と表した **3** が正解。had better は主語によって意味合いが異なる。we なら提案，you なら忠告・命令となる。

No.**10** 解答

スクリプト ★: Good morning, Ms. Redfield. I just got a call from Irene. She says she needs to take a half day off this morning.

☆: Again? That's the second time this week.

★: Yes. I'm a bit worried. She's also been late quite a few times in the last couple of months.

☆: She's quite skilled with computers, though, and the clients seem very satisfied with her. I *am* concerned about her motivation, however. It might be best to have a talk with her, in case she's considering leaving the company.

★: I'll set up a meeting.

Question: What does the woman imply about Irene?

全文訳 ★: おはようございます，レッドフィールドさん。先ほどアイリーンから電話がありました。彼女は今日の午前中，半休を取らなければいけないそうです。

☆: また？　今週2回目よ。

★: ええ。少し心配です。彼女はここ数カ月，何度も遅刻しています。

☆: 彼女はコンピューターにかなり強いんだけどね。それに，クライアントたちも彼女にとても満足しているようだし。でも私が心配しているのは彼女のやる気だわ。退職を考えている場合もあるから，彼女と話してみるのが一番いいかもしれない。

★: 面談を設定しますね。

質問：女性はアイリーンについて何をほのめかしているか。

選択肢の訳 **1** 仕事への情熱に欠ける。

2 解雇される予定だ。

3 クライアントたちに不人気である。

4 コンピューターの技能を伸ばす必要がある。

解説 部下と上司が第3者のアイリーンについて話している。女性（上司）は I *am* concerned about her motivation と言っており，「やる気（のなさ）が心配」を「仕事への情熱に欠ける」と捉えて，**1** が正解。強調し

たいときは I'm ではなく I *am* と省略せずに言う。

No.11 解答 ④

スクリプト
☆: Hey, Jack! How was your trip to the Yucatán?
★: Great. Check out these paintings I picked up.
☆: Wow! They're gorgeous! Did you find them at a local gallery?
★: No, I got them from artists at local markets, and they were unbelievably cheap.
☆: Well, you should get better frames for them before you put them on the wall.
★: Actually, I looked into that today. They cost 10 times what the paintings did, so I'm hesitant.
☆: I really think they deserve better than these cheap frames, don't you?

Question: What does the woman say about the paintings?

全文訳
☆: あら，ジャック！　ユカタン旅行はどうだった？
★: すごく良かったよ。僕が買ってきたこれらの絵画を見てよ。
☆: わあ！　見事ね！　現地の画廊で見つけたの？
★: いや，現地の市場で画家から買ったんだ。信じられないぐらい安かったよ。
☆: ねえ，壁に掛ける前にもっと良い額縁を買った方がいいわね。
★: 実のところ，今日見てきたんだ。絵の値段の10倍するから，ためらってる。
☆: 私は絶対これらの絵画はこんな安っぽい額縁よりもっと良いものがふさわしいと思うけど，そう思わない？

質問：女性は絵画について何と言っているか。

選択肢の訳
1　男性は利益を得るためにそれらを売ろうとするべきだ。
2　それらは画廊に飾られるべきだ。
3　男性はそれらにどれだけの価値があるかを調べるべきだ。
4　それらは適切に飾られるべきだ。

解説
話題は男性が旅行で買ってきた絵画。女性は you should get better ... と I really think they deserve ... の部分で，壁に掛ける前にもっと良い額縁を買うべきだと提案している。「適切に飾られるべき」と表した **4** が正解。会話中の put ～ on the wall と選択肢 **2** の be hung，**4** の be displayed はどれも「飾る」の類義表現。

No.12 解答 ②

スクリプト
☆: Hey, Joseph? There's no water coming from the faucet.
★: Oh, right, they're inspecting the pipes down the street.
☆: What? That's news to me.
★: Sorry, I forgot to tell you. There won't be any water until 7 p.m.

We got a couple of notices about it while you were out of town.

☆ : Why didn't you tell me earlier? I wanted to wash some clothes tonight for work tomorrow.

★ : I'm sorry. I did prepare some bottles of water, so we have enough for cooking and drinking.

☆ : That's something, at least.

Question: Why does the man apologize to the woman?

全文訳 ☆ : ねえ，ジョセフ。蛇口から水が出てこないの。

★ : ああ，そうそう，この道路の先で水道管を点検しているんだよ。

☆ : 何ですって？　そんなの知らなかったわ。

★ : ごめん，君に言うのを忘れていたよ。午後7時まで水が出ないんだ。君が町を出ていた間に何度か通知が来たんだ。

☆ : なんでもっと早く教えてくれなかったの？　明日の仕事のために今夜，服を洗いたかったのに。

★ : ごめんね。でも僕がボトルの水を何本か用意しておいたから，料理用と飲む用は十分にあるよ。

☆ : 少なくとも，何もないよりいいわね。

質問：男性はなぜ女性に謝っているのか。

選択肢の訳 1　彼はボトルに水を入れるのを忘れた。

2　彼は水が止められることを彼女に言わなかった。

3　彼は水道管点検に関する通知を紛失した。

4　彼は水道管に損傷を与えた。

解説 女性は，水が出ないのは水道管を点検しているからだと知ると，What? と驚いた様子。That's news to me.「それは初耳だ，知らなかった」と言う女性に対し，男性は，Sorry, I forgot to tell you. と言って女性に伝え忘れたことを謝っているので，**2**が正解。続く女性の Why didn't you tell me earlier? →男性の I'm sorry. ... の流れもヒントになる。

一次試験・リスニング **Part2** | 問題編 p.76〜77 | 🔊 ▶MP3 ▶アプリ ▶CD 1 **42**〜**48**

A

スクリプト **The Three Sisters**

For centuries, Native Americans all over North America grew corn, beans, and squash, which were often called the Three Sisters. The Three Sisters were planted together because of the strong benefits that the combination brings. When beans are grown with corn, the corn provides support for the beans as they climb up to get more sunlight. Additionally, squash keeps weeds away, and beans increase the amount of the beneficial chemical nitrogen in the soil. To make the combination work, however, planting each crop at the time when it will most help the others is essential.

In the distant past, Native American farmers were even able to grow the Three Sisters in the desert areas of the American southwest, but, unfortunately, most of this knowledge has been lost. Some Native Americans are currently working to rediscover the techniques that would allow them to grow the vegetables in very dry conditions.

Questions

No.13 What is one thing that we learn about growing the Three Sisters?

No.14 What are some Native Americans trying to do now?

全文訳 **スリーシスターズ**

何世紀にもわたり，北アメリカ各地のネイティブアメリカンは，しばしばスリーシスターズと呼ばれる，トウモロコシ，豆，カボチャを栽培していた。スリーシスターズが一緒に植えられたのは，その組み合わせがもたらす強力な利点のためである。豆がトウモロコシと一緒に栽培されると，豆がより多くの日光を浴びようと伸びる間にトウモロコシは豆の支えとなる。また，カボチャは雑草を寄せ付けず，豆は土壌中に有益な化学物質である窒素の量を増やす。しかし，この組み合わせをうまく機能させるには，それぞれの作物をほかの作物に最も役立つ時期に植えることが不可欠である。

遠い昔，ネイティブアメリカンの農民たちは，アメリカ南西部の砂漠地帯でさえスリーシスターズを栽培することができた。しかし残念なことに，この知識のほとんどは失われてしまった。現在，一部のネイティブアメリカンは，非常に乾燥した条件下でこれらの野菜を栽培できる技術を再発見しようと取り組んでいる。

No.13 解答

質問の訳 スリーシスターズの栽培について分かることの1つは何か。

選択肢の訳 **1** それぞれの作物をいつ植えるかが重要である。

2 北アメリカの狭い地域でのみ育つ。

3 雑草との競合で苦戦している。

4 植物と植物の間に空間が必要である。

解説 まず冒頭から，タイトルの The Three Sisters が3つの作物（トウモロコシ，豆，カボチャ）のことだと理解しよう。この3つの作物を一緒に植える利点を説明した中で，planting each crop at the time when it will most help the others is essential の部分と **1** が合う。essential を important に言い換えている。

No.14 解答

質問の訳 今，一部のネイティブアメリカンがしようとしていることは何か。

選択肢の訳 **1** より近代的な栽培技術を用いる。

2 砂漠で栽培できる新たな植物を見つける。

3 スリーシスターズの栽培方法をほかの人たちに教える。

4 忘れ去られた栽培方法を取り戻す。

解説 後半は In the distant past, ... で昔のこと，Some Native Americans are currently working to ... で今のことを述べている。質問は now「今」のことで，知識のほとんどは失われてしまった→現在，栽培技術の再発見に取り組んでいるという流れから，**4** が正解。それぞれ放送文の rediscover と **4** の recover，techniques と methods が類義。

B

スクリプト **Children in Cities**

In previous generations, children generally had more freedom to explore their surroundings. These days, parents commonly prohibit children from taking walks, crossing streets, or even playing at playgrounds unsupervised. Author Tim Gill argues children today would benefit from being allowed to do things on their own. However, he acknowledges that since modern cities have become increasingly dangerous places, it is difficult for parents to avoid setting strict rules for children.

Gill believes design is the key to making cities child friendly. Cities are currently designed to allow people to travel easily by car, but cars are one of the greatest threats to children's safety. Rather than simply building more playground spaces, Gill wants to make cities safer for children to move through. While completely rebuilding cities is not realistic in the short term, Gill suggests that easier measures such as turning streets into car-free zones for a short time each week could have immediate benefits.

Questions

No.15 What does Tim Gill imply about modern parents?

No.16 What is one thing Gill suggests that cities do?

全文訳 **都市の子供たち**

以前の世代では，一般的に，子供には周囲を探検する自由がもっとあった。最近では，親は，監視がないところで子供が散歩したり，道路を横断したり，遊び場で遊んだりすることさえ禁じるのが一般的である。作家のティム・ギルは，現代の子供は自分で物事を行うことを許されることで得るものがあると主張する。しかし彼は，現代の都市はますます危険な場所になっているため，親が子供に厳しい規則を設けないようにするのは難しいことを認めている。

ギルは，デザインこそが都市を子供に優しいものにする鍵だと考えている。現在，都市は人々が車で簡単に移動できるように設計されているが，車は子供の安全にとって最大の脅威の１つである。ギルは，単に遊び場を増やすのではなく，都市を子供が移動するのにより安全な場所にしたいと思っている。都市を完全に作り直すことは短期的には

現実的ではないが，毎週短時間，道路を自動車乗り入れ禁止区域にするなどのより簡単な対策ですぐに効果が得られるだろう，とギルは提案している。

No.15 解答 2

質問の訳 ティム・ギルは現代の親について何をほのめかしているか。

選択肢の訳 1 子供の安全を十分に考えていない。

2 しばしば子供に厳しい規則を設けることを余儀なくされる。

3 もっと多くの時間を子供と過ごすべきだ。

4 子供にさまざまな経験をさせている。

解説 ティム・ギルは，Author Tim Gill argues ... 以下で現代の子供はもっと自分で行動できる環境にあるべきだとしつつも，However 以下で，現代の都市の危険性から，「親が子供に厳しい規則を設けないようにするのは難しい」(it is difficult for parents to avoid setting strict rules for children) ことも認めている。この部分と **2** が合う。

No.16 解答 1

質問の訳 ギルが都市に行うよう提案していることの 1 つは何か。

選択肢の訳 1 道路を自動車通行禁止にする時間を設ける。

2 遊び場から駐車場をなくす。

3 都市中心部の外に新しい道路を建設する。

4 設計を変えることで自動車をより安全なものにする。

解説 ギルの提案は Gill suggests that ... にある。turning streets into car-free zones for a short time から，**1** が正解。car-free「自動車乗り入れ禁止の」を **1** では closed to cars と表している。-free は「〜のない」を表し，closed は「(道路が) 閉ざされた」。

スクリプト **Art in the Amazon**

An enormous collection of primitive paintings discovered in the Amazon jungle is causing debate among scientists. Thousands of images have been discovered on rock walls, and the team of researchers who discovered them believe that they include representations of extinct creatures that disappeared after the Ice Age ended. If so, the artists may have been the first humans ever to reach the Amazon region, arriving before it was covered in rain forest. Many of the larger animals appear to be surrounded by men with their hands raised in the air, and it is suspected the animals were being worshipped.

Other scientists, however, have expressed doubts regarding the age of the paintings. Since the images are extremely well-preserved, these critics believe it is likely they were painted centuries rather than millennia ago. Furthermore, since the images lack detail, the scientists argue that they might represent creatures brought to the Americas by Europeans.

Questions

No.17 What does the team of researchers believe about the paintings?

No.18 What do some other scientists think about the paintings?

全文訳　**アマゾンの芸術**

　アマゾンのジャングルで発見された原始絵画の膨大なコレクションが科学者たちの間で議論を呼んでいる。岩壁に描かれた何千もの絵が発見され，発見した研究者チームは，その中には氷河期が終わった後に姿を消した絶滅生物の描写が含まれていると信じている。もしそうなら，描いた人たちはアマゾン地域に到達した最初の人類であり，熱帯雨林に覆われる前に到着した可能性がある。大型の動物の多くは両手を宙に上げた人間に囲まれているように見え，その動物たちが崇拝されていたのではないかと思われている。

　しかし，ほかの科学者たちはその絵画の年代に関して懐疑的な見解を示している。それらの絵は極めてよく保存されているため，これらの批判者たちは，何千年も前ではなく数世紀前に描かれた可能性が高いと考えている。さらに，絵は細部を欠いているため，その科学者たちは，ヨーロッパ人によってアメリカ大陸に持ち込まれた生物を表しているのではないかと主張している。

No.17 解答

質問の訳　研究者チームがこの絵画について信じていることは何か。

選択肢の訳　**1** 熱帯雨林が形成された経緯を説明している。

　　2 初期の人類の外見を示している。

　　3 絶滅した生物を含んでいる。

　　4 宗教儀式で使われた。

解説　アマゾンで発見された岩壁画の話。放送文の the team of researchers ... believe that they include representations of extinct creatures that disappeared ... から，**3** が正解。extinct「絶滅した」は形容詞で，正解 **3** では動詞 died out（≒ disappeared）と表している。

No.18 解答 ④

質問の訳　一部のほかの科学者たちはこの絵画についてどう思っているか。

選択肢の訳　**1** 保存される必要はない。

　　2 おそらくヨーロッパ人によって制作された。

　　3 以前はもっと細部が描かれていた。

　　4 何千年も前のものではない。

解説　ほかの科学者たちについては Other scientists, however, ... 以下で述べられる。these critics believe ... の these critics は Other scientists のことで，壁画はアマゾン地域に到達した最初の人類が描いたという考えに批判的な人たちのこと。彼らは壁画が何千年も前（放送文の millennia ago ＝選択肢 **4** の thousands of years old）ではなく数世紀前に描かれ

たと考えているので，**4** が正解。A rather than B は「A だ→ B ではなく」と聞こえた順に理解しよう。

D

（スクリプト）**Milton Berle**

Milton Berle was one of America's most famous comedians. He was successful on stage and in films, and in the 1940s, he began hosting one of the world's first television programs. Berle's variety show was known for its silly comedy and wide range of guest performers. Televisions were rare luxury items when it began, but the program was such an incredible hit that it became a driving reason behind the huge increase in TV ownership.

As well as his pioneering work as an entertainer, Berle also fought for civil rights, famously helping to break down barriers against Black performers appearing on TV. When an advertiser tried to prevent a Black dance group from appearing on his show, Berle refused to perform until the advertiser gave in and the dancers were allowed on. Berle also set a record for appearing in more charity performances than any other performer.

Questions

No.19 What is one thing that we learn about Milton Berle's TV show?

No.20 What is one thing Berle was known for?

（全文訳）**ミルトン・バール**

ミルトン・バールはアメリカの最も有名なコメディアンの1人だ。彼は舞台や映画で成功を収め，1940年代には世界初のテレビ番組の1つの司会を始めた。バールのバラエティー番組は，おばかなコメディーと幅広いゲスト出演者で知られていた。番組が始まった当時，テレビは希少な贅沢品だったが，番組が驚異的にヒットしたため，テレビの所有者数が激増する起爆剤となった。

エンターテイナーとしての先駆的な活動だけでなく，バールは公民権のためにも闘い，有名な話としては黒人パフォーマーのテレビ出演に対する障壁を打ち破る手助けをした。黒人ダンスグループが自分の番組に出演するのを広告主が阻止しようとしたとき，バールは，広告主が折れてダンサーたちの出演が許可されるまで出演を拒否した。バールはまた，ほかのどのパフォーマーよりも多くの慈善興行に出演したという記録も作った。

No.19 解答 **4**

（質問の訳）ミルトン・バールのテレビ番組について分かることの1つは何か。

（選択肢の訳）　**1**　ある人気映画に基づいていた。

　　　　　　　2　多くの贅沢品を配った。

　　　　　　　3　コメディーコンテストを毎週開催した。

　　　　　　　4　多くの人がテレビを購入するきっかけになった。

（解説）手掛かりは Televisions were ..., but the program was such an

incredible hit that it became a driving reason behind the huge increase in TV ownership. にある。長い1文だが，but が聞こえたらその後をよく聞こう。driving reason がよく分からなくても such ～ that ... の展開（原因→結果）を捉え，番組がヒットした結果テレビの ownership が increase したという大意がつかめたら，**4** が選べるだろう。

No.20 解答 **②** ....

質問の訳 バールが知られていたことの1つは何か。

選択肢の訳 **1** 黒人パフォーマーを支援するために慈善団体を設立したこと。
2 テレビ業界での人種差別に立ち向かったこと。
3 彼が制作したユニークな広告。
4 彼の驚くべきダンス能力。

解説 As well as ～, ... の構造では，重要なことが話される「...」の部分（ポーズの後）に耳を傾けよう。Berle also fought for civil rights, famously helping ... から，バールは黒人のテレビ出演に貢献したことで有名だと分かる。これを正解の **2** では fighting racism と表している。

E

スクリプト **Déjà Vu**

The term "déjà vu" refers to a person's feeling that they have already experienced the situation they are currently in. While causes for déjà vu have been proposed since the nineteenth century, little research was done on it until the 2000s, when the scientist Alan Brown studied the phenomenon. He found that people experience it less as they age and that it is usually triggered by a location or setting.

More recently, researchers used virtual reality to study déjà vu. They had subjects enter virtual environments, such as bowling alleys or subway stations. Some of these spaces were laid out similarly — for example, pieces of furniture with similar shapes but different appearances were arranged in the same positions. The researchers found subjects were more likely to feel déjà vu when entering new spaces that were organized like spaces they had previously entered. Still, they say this is likely just one of many factors that cause déjà vu.

Questions

No.21 What was one of Alan Brown's findings about déjà vu?

No.22 In the virtual reality study, what led some subjects to experience déjà vu?

全文訳 **デジャビュ**

「デジャビュ（既視感）」という言葉は，現在自分が置かれている状況をすでに経験し

たことがあるかのように感じることを指す。デジャビュの原因は 19 世紀からずっと提唱されてきたが，2000 年代に科学者のアラン・ブラウンがこの現象を研究するまで，ほとんど研究は行われていなかった。彼は，人は年齢を重ねるにつれてデジャビュ体験が減ること，そしてデジャビュは通常，場所や場面によって引き起こされることを発見した。

　最近では，研究者たちがデジャビュを研究するために仮想現実を用いた。彼らは被験者たちに，ボウリング場や地下鉄の駅などの仮想環境に入ってもらった。これらの空間の幾つかは同じような配置になっていた。例えば，似たような形だが見た目が異なる家具が同じ位置に配置された。研究者たちは，被験者たちは，以前入った空間と同じように配置された新しい空間に入ると，デジャビュを感じる可能性が高いことを発見した。それでも，これはデジャビュを引き起こす多くの要因の 1 つに過ぎない可能性が高い，と彼らは言う。

No.21 解答　①

質問の訳　デジャビュに関するアラン・ブラウンの発見の 1 つは何か。
選択肢の訳　**1**　人が若いほど頻繁に起こる。
　　　　　　　2　それ以前の研究では被験者は主に男性だった。
　　　　　　　3　19 世紀以降によりありふれたものになった。
　　　　　　　4　人はそれをほかの感情と勘違いすることが多い。

解説　タイトルは英語ではないが（déjà vu はフランス語），音声から「デジャビュ（既視感）」と分かるだろう。ブラウンの発見について述べた He found that people experience it less as they age がポイント。it は déjà vu を指し，「人は年齢を重ねるにつれてデジャビュ体験が減る」を「若いほど頻繁に起こる」と表した **1** が正解。

No.22 解答　④

質問の訳　仮想現実の研究において，一部の被験者にデジャビュ体験をもたらしたものは何か。
選択肢の訳　**1**　広い公共の場所を探検すること。
　　　　　　　2　全く同じ家具を備えた空間を見ること。
　　　　　　　3　さまざまな空間で同じ活動を行うこと。
　　　　　　　4　見覚えのある配置の空間に入ること。

解説　The researchers found subjects were ... から，被験者たちは以前入った空間と同じような配置になっている新しい空間に入るとデジャビュを感じる可能性が高いことが分かった。were organized like spaces they had previously entered「以前入った空間と同じように配置された」を，正解の **4** では a familiar layout「見覚えのある配置」と表している。

スクリプト　**The English Longbow**

During medieval times, one of the deadliest weapons used by English armies was the longbow. About two meters in length, this powerful weapon allowed an archer to fire extremely rapidly, shooting up to six arrows per minute. A variety of arrows were used, such as the bodkin and the broadhead. The bodkin arrow was the most common, and its narrow tip could pass through most kinds of armor. The larger broadheads, on the other hand, caused more-devastating wounds to lightly armored enemies.

Though highly effective, the longbow required years of practice to master. Since it was an essential tool for English armies, King Henry VIII even passed a law requiring that all healthy males train regularly in its use. Examinations of the skeletons of longbowmen have found that this training actually altered them physically. Bones in their arms became thickened, and their spines became twisted through constant use of the bow.

Questions

No.23 What is one thing that we learn about bodkin arrows?

No.24 What does the speaker say about King Henry VIII?

全文訳 **イングランドのロングボウ**

中世の間，イングランド軍によって使用された最も破壊的な武器の１つがロングボウである。長さが約２メートルあるこの強力な武器により，射手は極めて速く射ることができ，１分間に最大６本の矢を放った。ボドキンやブロードヘッドなど，さまざまな矢が使用された。ボドキン矢が最も一般的で，その細い先端はほとんどの甲冑を貫通することができた。一方，（ボドキン）より大きなブロードヘッド矢は，軽装甲の敵にさらに致命的な傷を負わせた。

ロングボウは非常に効果的ではあったが，習得するのに何年もの練習を要した。ロングボウはイングランド軍にとって不可欠な道具だったため，ヘンリー８世は，健康な男性全員にその使い方を定期的に訓練することを義務付ける法律までも制定した。ロングボウ弓兵の骨格を調べたところ，この訓練によって実際，彼らは肉体的に変化したことが分かった。弓を使い続けることで，彼らの腕の骨は太くなり，背骨はねじれていた。

No.23 解答 ②

質問の訳 ボドキン矢について分かることの１つは何か。

選択肢の訳
1 ほかの矢よりも速く飛んだ。
2 甲冑に対して効果的だった。
3 最も長い部類の矢だった。
4 一般的に鋼鉄でできていた。

解説 タイトルの longbow の bow は「弓」だが，冒頭から，昔イングランド軍が使った weapon「武器」としての弓矢の話と分かる。矢（arrow）の種類には bodkin や broadhead があり，それぞれの特徴が述べられる。

質問は bodkin についてで，The bodkin arrow ... could pass through most kinds of armor. から，**2** が正解だと判断できる。

No.24 解答 ①

質問の訳 話者はヘンリー8世について何と言っているか。

選択肢の訳 **1** 男性にロングボウを使う練習を強制した。
2 ロングボウを射る名手だった。
3 ロングボウの攻撃で重傷を負った。
4 外国軍にロングボウを売った。

解説 ヘンリー8世について述べた King Henry VIII even passed a law requiring that all healthy males train regularly in its use. と **1** が合う。放送文の passed a law requiring「〜を義務付ける法律を制定した」を〈force＋O＋to *do*〉「O に〜することを強制する」で表している。

| 一次試験・リスニング | Part**3** | 問題編 p.78 〜 79 | 🔊 | ▶MP3 ▶アプリ ▶CD 1 49〜54 |

G

スクリプト

You have 10 seconds to read the situation and Question No. 25.

OK, the Western is an all-leather backpack. It converts to a briefcase, so it's great for business environments. It's a bit heavy, though, so I wouldn't use it on long walks. The Dangerfield is a waxed canvas backpack that's water-resistant, so it's great for outdoor activities. It's also handsome enough for the office. The Spartan is also made of waxed canvas. It's very functional but a bit too sporty for professional contexts. The Winfield is a similar bag, but it's made of water-resistant leather. The thin strap can make it uncomfortable to carry for extended periods of time, though.

Now mark your answer on your answer sheet.

全文訳

まず，ウエスタンは総革のバックパックです。ブリーフケースにもなるのでビジネスシーンに最適です。ただ，少し重いので，私なら長時間歩くには使わないと思います。デンジャーフィールドは，耐水性のあるワックス加工された帆布生地のバックパックなので，アウトドア活動に最適です。オフィス用としても十分見栄えが良いです。スパルタンもワックス加工の帆布生地製です。非常に機能的ですが，仕事用としてはややスポーティー過ぎます。ウインフィールドも似たようなバッグですが，耐水性のある革でできています。ただ，ストラップが細いので，長時間持ち歩くのは苦痛かもしれません。

No.25 解答 ②　　　　　　　　　　　　　　　正答率 ★75%以上

状況の訳 あなたは次の出張で使うバッグを必要としている。休みの日にはそのバッグを使ってハイキングにも行く予定である。店員が次のように言う。

質問の訳 あなたはどのバッグを買うべきか。

選択肢の訳 1　ウエスタン。　　　　　　2　デンジャーフィールド。
3　スパルタン。　　　　　　4　ウインフィールド。

解説 問題用紙に書かれた ***Situation***（状況）から，仕事にもハイキングにも使えるバッグが必要であることを押さえよう。放送では選択肢の4種のバッグが順に説明される。ウエスタンは長時間歩くのに不向き。デンジャーフィールドはアウトドアにもオフィスにもよいので**2**が正解。スパルタンは仕事用として too sporty（too はネガティブな意味）で，ウインフィールドも長時間の持ち歩きに不向き。

H

スクリプト

You have 10 seconds to read the situation and Question No. 26.

Nearest to the airport are SKM Budget Parking and the Vanier Plaza Hotel. They both offer covered parking lots that feature security patrols. SKM Budget Parking is the better deal at $13 per day. It only offers short-term parking, though, for up to a week max. If your trip is longer than that, you could pay a $17 rate at the Vanier Plaza Hotel. If an open, non-patrolled parking lot is acceptable, then Nelson Street Skypark offers parking for $9 per day. Another option would be the Econolodge, which is $19 per day. It's indoors and quite safe, though it's a little far.

Now mark your answer on your answer sheet.

全文訳

空港にごく近いのはSKMバジェット・パーキングとバニエ・プラザ・ホテル。どちらもセキュリティーパトロールのある屋根付き駐車場だ。SKMバジェット・パーキングの方が1日当たり13ドルでお得。でも最大1週間までの短期駐車しかできない。旅行がそれより長いなら，バニエ・プラザ・ホテルで17ドル払う手もあるだろう。パトロールのない屋根なし駐車場でもいいなら，ネルソン・ストリート・スカイパークが1日当たり9ドルで駐車できる。また別の選択肢はエコノロッジかな。そこは1日当たり19ドル。屋内でとても安全，少し遠いけどね。

No.26 解答 ②　　　　　　　　　　　　　　　

状況の訳 あなたは16日間空港近くに車を駐車する必要がある。最安値を望んでいるが，車が破損しないか心配である。友人があなたに選択肢を伝える。

質問の訳 あなたはどの駐車場を利用すべきか。

選択肢の訳 1　SKMバジェット・パーキング。

2 バニエ・プラザ・ホテル。

3 ネルソン・ストリート・スカイパーク。

4 エコノロッジ。

解説 空港近くで 16 日間，安くて安全に駐車できるのはどこか。SKM とバニエはどちらも安全面は OK。SKM は 16 日間駐車できないので消去。バニエは 17 ドル（→保留）。ネルソンは open, non-patrolled「屋根なしでパトロールなし」＝安全性が低いので消去。エコノロッジは少し遠いが安全で 19 ドル。バニエの 17 ドルの方が安いので，**2** のバニエが条件に最も合う。

スクリプト

You have 10 seconds to read the situation and Question No. 27.

Please look at the display. If the green light is blinking, this means it needs to be cleaned. To do this, simply remove the filter and clean it carefully. You can find a tutorial video on our website. If the blue light is flashing, the air conditioner may be overheating. In such a case, you can speed up cooling by leaving the panel open. Be sure to unplug the air conditioner before touching the unit. If this does not solve the problem, and you would like to schedule a service call by a technician, press 1.

Now mark your answer on your answer sheet.

全文訳

ディスプレイを見てください。緑色のライトが点滅している場合は，洗浄が必要であることを意味します。これを行うには，フィルターを取り外し，ていねいに洗浄するだけです。弊社のウェブサイトで説明動画をご覧いただけます。青色のライトが点滅している場合は，エアコンが過熱している可能性があります。このような場合は，パネルを開けたままにしておくことで冷却を早めることができます。本体に触れる前に必ず電源を抜いてください。これでも問題が解決せず，技術者による修理サービスを予定に入れたい場合は，1 を押してください。

No.27 解答 ③ ....

状況の訳 あなたのエアコンが突然作動しなくなり，青色のライトが点滅している。カスタマーサポートに電話をして，次のような録音メッセージを聞く。

質問の訳 あなたはまず何をすべきか。

選択肢の訳 **1** エアコンのフィルターを取り外す。

2 エアコンのパネルを開ける。

3 エアコンの電源を切る。

4 （修理）サービスの予約をする。

解説 問題用紙の状況から，点滅しているライトは青色なので，If the <u>blue</u>

light is flashing, ... 以下をよく聞く。問題はエアコンの過熱で，解決法は by leaving the panel open から，パネルを開けること（＝選択肢 **2**）だが，続く Be sure to unplug the air conditioner before touching the unit. より，その前に電源を抜く必要がある。よって，**3** が正解。unplug → disconnect の言い換え。

（スクリプト）

You have 10 seconds to read the situation and Question No. 28.

I understand you've only read the September issue. I'll explain the others briefly. The July issue has an overview of the latest advancements in physics, centering on last year's breakthrough in the field of particle physics. The next issue focuses on recent genetic discoveries and various ongoing experiments with DNA and RNA, but unfortunately, this one is out of print. The October issue is also centered around research in genetics, especially its potential medical applications. Finally, if you'd like to deepen your understanding of modern geology, the November issue would be perfect. It thoroughly explains the current mainstream theories on volcano formation.

Now mark your answer on your answer sheet.

全文訳

　9月号しか読んでいないとうことですね。ほかの号を簡単に説明しましょう。7月号は，素粒子物理学の分野における昨年の躍進を中心に，物理学の最新の進歩を概説しています。その次の号は，最近の遺伝子発見と，DNA と RNA を使った進行中のさまざまな実験に焦点を当てていますが，残念ながら，この号は絶版です。10月号も遺伝学の研究，特にその医療への応用の可能性に焦点を当てています。最後に，現代地質学の理解を深めたい場合，11月号が最適でしょう。火山形成に関する現在の主流の理論を徹底的に解説しています。

No.28解答 **③**

状況の訳　あなたは月刊科学雑誌のバックナンバーを注文したいと思っている。あなたは遺伝学に興味がある。雑誌の出版社に電話をすると，次のように言われる。

質問の訳　あなたはどの号を注文すべきか。

選択肢の訳　**1** 7月号。　　　　　　**2** 8月号。
　　　　　　3 10月号。　　　　　　**4** 11月号。

解説　放送文中には多くの専門用語が出てくるが，状況にある genetics「遺伝学」に関する号はどれか？　という点に絞って聞けばよい。The next issue ...「（7月号の）次の号＝8月号」のテーマは遺伝子だが絶版（out of print）で手に入らないので **2** は消去。続く The October issue is also centered around research in <u>genetics</u>, ... から，**3** が正解。

スクリプト

You have 10 seconds to read the situation and Question No. 29.

Bentham Foods is recalling all cans of its tuna sold from May 15 to July 1 because of suspected health risks. Customers who have consumed tuna from these cans are advised to call our recall hotline. For unopened cans, if you have one or more cases of 24 cans, please visit our website for instructions on how to arrange a pickup and a full refund. Customers with less than one case may exchange the cans or return them for a full refund at the store where they were purchased. The cans don't pose any risk while unopened, but please avoid consuming tuna from any cans bought during the affected dates.

Now mark your answer on your answer sheet.

全文訳

ベンサム・フーズは，健康上のリスクの疑いがあるため，5月15日から7月1日までに販売された全てのツナ缶を回収しています。これらの缶のツナを召し上がったお客さまは，弊社のリコールホットラインにお電話ください。未開封の缶については，24缶入りケースを1つでもお持ちのお客さまは，弊社ウェブサイトにアクセスして，引き取りおよび全額返金を手配する方法についての指示をご確認ください。お持ちの缶が1ケースに満たないお客さまは，購入された店で缶を交換されるか，返品して全額返金をお受けください。缶は未開封のうちは何の危険性もありませんが，対象期間中に購入された缶のツナは召し上がらないようにしてください。

No.29 解答

状況の訳 あなたは5月30日にスーパーマーケットでベンサム・フーズのツナ缶を5缶購入した。テレビで次のような告知を聞く。あなたはそのツナ缶を全く食べていない。

質問の訳 あなたは何をすべきか。

選択肢の訳
1　購入した店に缶を持って行く。
2　ベンサム・フーズのリコールホットラインに電話をする。
3　缶を引き取りに来てもらうよう手配する。
4　ベンサム・フーズのウェブサイトにアクセスして指示を確認する。

解説 問題用紙の状況から，話題はツナ缶のリコールだと推測しよう。買ったのは5缶で，食べていないので，Customers with less than one case may ... の条件に該当する。less than one case は「1ケース（24缶）より少ない」。「買った店で交換または返品」と言っているので，**1** が正解。**2** はツナを食べた人，**3** と **4** は1ケース以上購入した人の場合。

解答例 **One day, a university student was watching TV with his mother and grandfather.** The TV program was explaining that many elderly drivers were involved in traffic accidents. The grandfather looked concerned by this news and said that he should stop driving. The other family members agreed. The next week, the student was walking outside of ABC Driving School. He was holding a registration form for the school as he had decided to get a driver's license. A few months later, the grandfather and the mother were sitting at home. The student was proudly holding his driver's license and said to his grandfather that now he could drive him anytime. The grandfather seemed delighted to hear this. That weekend, the grandfather was looking at his calendar. He seemed pleased to have made many plans. The mother told her son that his grandfather had plans every weekend.

解答例の訳 ある日，大学生が母親と祖父と一緒にテレビを見ていました。そのテレビ番組では，多くの高齢ドライバーが交通事故にかかわっていると解説していました。祖父はこのニュースに心配した様子で，自分は運転をやめた方がいいと言いました。ほかの家族も同意しました。翌週，その学生は ABC 自動車教習所の外を歩いていました。彼は運転免許証を取得することに決めたので，教習所の登録用紙を手に持っていました。数カ月後，祖父と母親は自宅で座っていました。学生は運転免許証を誇らしげに持ち，これでいつでも車で連れて行ってあげられるよと祖父に言いました。祖父はそれを聞いて喜んでいるようでした。その週末，祖父はカレンダーを見ていました。彼はたくさんの予定を入れたことに満足している様子でした。母親は息子に，祖父は毎週末予定があると言いました。

解説 各コマの描写ポイントは，①3人が「高齢ドライバーにかかわる事故」に関する番組を見て，祖父が「運転をやめた方がいい」と言っている，②翌週，大学生が自動車教習所にいる，③数カ月後，学生が祖父に「いつでも車で連れて行けるよ」と言っている，④その週末，祖父がカレンダーを見ていて母親が「彼は毎週末予定がある」と言っている。1コマ目はグラフに着目して The number of traffic accidents involving elderly drivers is increasing.「高齢ドライバーにかかわる交通事故が増えている」，3コマ目の大学生は The student seemed to have gotten his driver's license「運転免許を取得したようだ」と表すこともできる。

No. 1

解答例 I'd be thinking that I'll need to talk to my grandfather about his plans. I want to help him get around and enjoy himself, but I also need to be able to make my own plans on the weekends sometimes.

解説 質問は「4番目の絵を見てください。もしあなたがこの大学生なら，どのようなことを考えているでしょうか」。解答例は，毎週末祖父に付き添うのは難しいという方向性の答え。but を用いて，祖父を楽しませたい気持ちと自分自身の予定を大事にしたい気持ちを含めている。

No. 2

解答例 I don't think so. Children need to have some freedom in their lives. Having too many rules prevents children from expressing themselves. Also, children need to learn how to make their own decisions.

解説 質問は「親はもっと自分の子供に厳しくするべきだと思いますか」。解答例は No の立場で，Also を用いて2つの理由（子供は自由であるべき，自分で意志決定をすべき）を述べている。〈prevent＋O＋from -ing〉「（主語のせいで）O は～できない」のような無生物主語（解答例は動名詞主語）の文を使えると好印象になる。Yes の立場では，しつけの重要性について述べることができるだろう。

No. 3

解答例 I don't think so. There is tough competition between TV stations to get more viewers. This means that they often exaggerate news stories. Unfortunately, this is also true for many newspapers and news websites these days.

解説 質問は「人々は最近テレビで見るニュースを信頼できますか」。解答例は No の立場で，根拠としてテレビ局間の熾烈（しれつ）な競争，記事の誇張を挙げ，Unfortunately を用いて「多くの新聞やニュースウェブサイトにも当てはまる」と締めくくっている。

No. 4

解答例 Yes. People will receive less money from the national pension system in the future, so they'll have to continue working for several years. Otherwise, they'll be unable to live comfortably after they retire.

解説 質問は「今後，定年を過ぎても働くことを選ぶ人は増えるでしょうか」。解答例は Yes の立場で，将来的に国民年金の受給額が減るので数年は働き続けなければならないだろう，というネガティブな視点の意見。同じ Yes の立場でも，収入面や，経験・知識を社会のために役立てる，健康維持などの点で，働き続けるメリットを根拠にすることもできるだろう。

解答例 **One day, a woman was working at the reception desk of a dentist's office.** There were many patients in the waiting room, including children. The children looked very unhappy to be at the dentist and were crying. The woman was concerned to see this. A few days later, the woman was speaking with the dentist. She suggested that the dentist's office should provide toys for children to play with while they wait. The dentist thought it would be a good idea and agreed. The next week, there was a play area with some toys in the waiting room. Some children were playing with the toys, and they looked happy to be at the dentist. The woman was glad to see this. Later that day, the woman was looking at the toys with the dentist. The toys seemed to be badly damaged, and the dentist said that they already needed new toys.

解答例の訳 ある日，女性が歯科医院の受付で働いていました。待合室には子供を含む多くの患者がいました。子供たちは歯医者にいるのがとても嫌そうで，泣いていました。女性はそれを見て心配していました。数日後，女性は歯科医と話をしていました。彼女は，歯科医院は，子供が待ち時間に遊べるおもちゃを用意すべきだと提案しました。歯科医は良い考えだと思い，同意しました。翌週，待合室にはおもちゃがある遊び場ができていました。何人かの子供がおもちゃで遊んでいて，歯医者にいることがうれしそうでした。女性はそれを見て喜びました。その日の後ほど，女性は歯科医と一緒におもちゃを見ていました。おもちゃはひどく破損している様子で，歯科医はもう新しいおもちゃが必要だと言いました。

解説 各コマの描写ポイントは，①女性が歯医者の受付にいて，子供たちが泣いている，②数日後，女性が子供用のおもちゃを用意することを提案し，歯科医がうなずいている，③翌週，おもちゃの遊び場があり，子供が満足そう，④その日の後ほど，破損したおもちゃを見て，歯科医が「もう新しいおもちゃが必要だ」と言っている。「歯科医院」は dental clinic でもよい。dentist は「歯科医」（人）を表すが，at the dentist のように場所としても使える。1コマ目と3コマ目は，unhappy → happy のように，子供の変化を明確に表現したい。4コマ目は，The toys were broken and stuffed animals were torn.「おもちゃは壊れ，ぬいぐるみは破れていた」など，おもちゃを詳しく描写することもできるだろう。

No. 1

解答例 I'd be thinking that we should buy more durable toys this time. Many children play with the toys every day, so it's not surprising that the first ones got damaged quickly.

解説 質問は「4番目の絵を見てください。もしあなたがこの女性なら，どのようなことを考えているでしょうか」。解答例は「もっと丈夫なおもちゃを買うべき」とおもちゃに焦点を当てた意見。ほかには，おもちゃを置くという考えは良くなかったという方向で，おもちゃで遊ぶ代わりに本を読む，テレビを見るなど，別の対策を提案する手もあるだろう。

No. 2

解答例 I don't think so. Technology makes it easy for parents to keep their children safe, as parents can use smartphones to contact their children easily or check their locations. Also, there's a lot of free advice for parents available online.

解説 質問は「子育ては昔と比べて今の方が大変だと思いますか」。解答例はNoの立場で，Alsoを用いてテクノロジーがもたらす恩恵を2つ述べている。Yesの立場では，助けが少ない核家族で共働きの家庭のケースや，教育費の高騰，競争激化などの観点を根拠にできるだろう。

No. 3

解答例 Not at all. These days, saving money is the first priority for most people. That means people will prefer to buy cheaper products, and companies that make cheap products will survive in the long run.

解説 質問は「企業は製品を安くすることに焦点を置き過ぎていると思いますか」。激しい同意はDefinitely.，反対はNot at all.と表せる。解答例は質問のtoo muchを受けて，「安価な製品に焦点を置き過ぎている（＝控えるべき）ということは全くない」という意見。多くの人にとって節約が最優先事項で，安価な製品を好むからという理由を述べている。

No. 4

解答例 Yes. Recently, there have been major advancements in medical technology. This includes robots that can take care of elderly patients. Also, the government is working to increase the number of medical facilities.

解説 質問は「政府は日本の高齢化社会のニーズに応えることができるでしょうか」。解答例はYesの立場で，理由は医療技術の進歩と，政府の取り組み（医療機関の増設）の2点。具体例・代表例を述べたいとき，文（S＋V）ならFor example，物（名詞）ならThis includes ...やsuch asを使うとよい。ここでは医療技術の進歩の代表例としてrobotsを挙げている。

2022-3

解 答 一 覧

一次試験・筆記

1

(1)	4	(10)	2	(19)	3
(2)	4	(11)	2	(20)	1
(3)	2	(12)	3	(21)	1
(4)	4	(13)	1	(22)	1
(5)	3	(14)	2	(23)	2
(6)	3	(15)	1	(24)	1
(7)	2	(16)	1	(25)	3
(8)	4	(17)	4		
(9)	2	(18)	2		

2

(26)	1	(29)	4
(27)	3	(30)	3
(28)	4	(31)	1

3

(32)	4	(35)	3	(38)	4
(33)	2	(36)	4	(39)	1
(34)	2	(37)	3	(40)	2
				(41)	3

4　解答例は本文参照

一次試験・リスニング

Part 1	No. 1	4	No. 5	2	No. 9	4
	No. 2	1	No. 6	3	No.10	3
	No. 3	4	No. 7	3	No.11	1
	No. 4	1	No. 8	1	No.12	2

Part 2	No.13	3	No.17	4	No.21	1
	No.14	1	No.18	2	No.22	3
	No.15	3	No.19	3	No.23	2
	No.16	2	No.20	4	No.24	1

Part 3	No.25	2	No.28	2
	No.26	4	No.29	1
	No.27	4		

(1) ― 解答 ④

訳 フェルナンドはずっと会社の成功に貢献してきたため，彼が来月辞めた後どうなるのか，誰もが心配している。

解説 心配の理由は，会社の成功にかかわった人が辞めるからだと推測できる。*be* instrumental to「〜に役立つ，貢献する」が適切。desperate「絶望的な」，philosophical「哲学（上）の」，inadequate「不適切な」

(2) ― 解答 ④

訳 その映画は過小評価されたと感じる人もいる。それは１つも賞を取らなかったが，素晴らしい芸術作品だったと考える人もいる。

解説 those who believe ... より，映画を好意的に捉えた人がいたことが分かる。従って，受賞しなかったことで，その映画が過小評価された（underrated）と感じる人がいたと推測できる。それぞれ overtake「追い越す」，override「（提案などを）無効にする」，underfeed「十分に食べ物を与えない」の過去分詞。

(3) ― 解答 ②

訳 第２次世界大戦中，５千万人を超える人が亡くなった。それは，歴史上のほかのどの戦争よりも多い死者数である。

解説 第２文の deaths を手掛かりに，perished を入れる。perish「死ぬ」は die や *be* killed の婉曲語。それぞれ worship「礼拝する」，haunt「（幽霊などが）出没する」，jeer「あざける」の過去形。

(4) ― 解答 ④

訳 ウォルトのレストランは，田舎の貧しい人々が伝統的に食べていた料理を提供している。彼は，農民たちは安い材料でおいしい食事を作ることに長けていたと言う。

解説 空所後の *be* skilled at -ing は「〜するのに長けている」。第１文から，田舎の人々を表す peasants「農民，小作人」が適切。それぞれ correspondent「特派員」，janitor「管理人」，captive「捕虜」の複数形。

(5) ― 解答 ③

訳 新しい建物の設計図に重大な欠陥が発見されたため，建設が数カ月遅れた。

解説 〈cause ＋ O ＋ to *do*〉「O に〜させる（原因となる）」は主語（原因）→ to 不定詞（結果）の関係。建設が遅れた原因は，重大な欠陥（flaw）の発見である。clog「詰まり，障害物」，boom「（経済の）急成長，（人気などの）急上昇」，dump「ごみ捨て場」

(6) ― 解答 ③

訳 プレゼンテーションを行う時間になったとき，レイチェルは自分が恐怖

で身がすくんでいることに気付いた。彼女は話すことができず，ただみんなの前で立ち尽くした。

解説 〈find *oneself*＋C〉は「自分が～だと気付く」。後の「恐怖で」や「話すことができない」から，paralyze「まひさせる，動けなくする」の過去分詞が合う。be paralyzed with fear で「恐怖で身がすくむ」。それぞれ trim「刈り込む」，tease「からかう」，acquire「得る」の過去分詞。

(7) ― 解答 ②

訳 両国はかつて戦争で戦ったという事実にもかかわらず，現在は友好的な関係を享受しており，実のところ，同盟国である。

解説 despite「～にもかかわらず」による論理展開と，enjoy「享受する」，allies「同盟国」から，両国は良い関係だと判断し，amicable「友好的な」が適切。alleged「～と申し立てられている」，abusive「虐待的な」，adhesive「粘着性の」

(8) ― 解答 ④

訳 ティナの新しい目標は健康になることである。食事にもっと野菜を含めることに加え，彼女は日課に運動プログラムを組み込むことにした。

解説 健康になるためにすることとして，including more vegetables in her diet と（　）an exercise ... の２つが述べられている。incorporate A into B で「A を B に取り入れる［組み込む］」。commemorate「祝う」，alienate「疎外する」，liberate「解放する」

(9) ― 解答 ②

訳 犬の家畜化は１万年以上前に起こったと考える歴史家もいる。それ以来ずっと，犬はペットとして飼われ，農作業で使われてきた。

解説 第２文の They は dogs を指し，第２文全体の内容を名詞で表すと domestication「家畜化」である。elevation「高度，上昇」，deception「ごまかし」，verification「検証」

(10) ― 解答 ②

訳 オスカーは人懐っこい性格と礼儀正しいことで有名だ。毎朝，彼は自分の机に向かって歩きながら，オフィスのみんなにていねいにあいさつをする。

解説 礼儀正しい人がすることは，ていねいに（courteously）あいさつすることである。scarcely「ほとんど～ない」，tediously「うんざりするほど」，obnoxiously「不愉快なほど」

(11) ― 解答 ②

訳 新図書館の計画は，資金不足のために保留になった。しかし，数年後，その計画は復活し，建設工事が始まった。

解説 however による論理展開と，後の「建設工事が始まった」へのつながりから，保留になった計画が再開したと推測できる。revive「復活させる」の過去分詞が適切。put ～ on hold は「～を保留する」。それぞれ

deprive「奪う」，obstruct「邪魔する」，agitate「扇動する」の過去分詞。

(12) − 解答 ③

訳 マギーの祖母は最近，体がとても弱くなってきた。彼女は今，歩くのに助けが必要で，階段を1人で上ることができない。

解説 第2文で表された祖母の様子を形容する語として frail「弱い，病弱な」が適切。poetic「詩的な」，savage「どう猛な」，rash「軽率な」

(13) − 解答 ①

訳 その小説家は独りで仕事をするのが好きだ。彼女は，自分の田舎の家にいるときしかうまく書けないと言っていて，それは周りに人がいない場所にある。

解説 第2文の an area with no people around と似た意味になるよう，in solitude「独りで」とする。solitude は寂しさだけでなく誰にもわずらわされない自由さも意味する。corruption「堕落」，excess「過剰」，consent「承諾」

(14) − 解答 ② ⸱⸱⸱⸱⸱⸱⸱⸱⸱⸱⸱⸱⸱⸱⸱⸱⸱⸱⸱⸱⸱ 正答率 ★75%以上

訳 考古学者たちは，古代の埋葬地で発掘を行っている最中に，宝石や陶器の破片などの多くの人工遺物を発見した。これらは地元の歴史博物館に寄贈される予定だ。

解説 考古学者が発見し，博物館に寄贈されるものは artifacts「人工遺物」。直後の pieces of jewelry and pottery はその具体物である。それぞれ setback「つまずき，逆行」，pledge「誓約」，salute「敬礼」の複数形。

(15) − 解答 ① ⸱⸱⸱⸱⸱⸱⸱⸱⸱⸱⸱⸱⸱⸱⸱⸱⸱⸱⸱⸱⸱ 正答率 ★75%以上

訳 インターネット接続の高速化とコンピューターの改良により，かつてないほど多くの情報を高速で送信することができる。

解説 主語 more information に対する動詞として，*be* transmitted「送信される」が適切。それぞれ rejoice「喜ぶ」，nauseate「吐き気を起こさせる」，offend「気分を害する」の過去分詞。

(16) − 解答 ①

訳 マリアは兄［弟］がギャンブルで全財産を失ったことを知った後，彼を批判し，彼を哀れだと言った。

解説 after 以下の内容から，兄［弟］を形容する語として pathetic「哀れな」が適切。call A B は「A を B と言う［考える］」の意味。analytical「分析的な」，dedicated「献身的な」，ceaseless「絶え間ない」

(17) − 解答 ④

訳 その建築家は現代的なやり方で建物を設計することで有名だった。彼は自分の設計に現在の社会的・文化的傾向を反映させたいと思った。

解説 第2文は第1文の補足説明で，current「現在の」と似た意味の contemporary「現代の，現代的な」が適切。preceding「先行する，

前述の」，simultaneous「同時に起こる」，plentiful「豊富な」

(18) – 解答 **2** ....

訳 マスコミによる報道不足のため，町はその化学物質の漏えいについて知らされていなかった。マスコミが事件について報道し始めたのは，漏えいが制御不能になってからだった。

解説 coverage は「（新聞・テレビなどの）報道，取材」という意味があり，media coverage で「マスコミ報道」。空所後の〈leave + O + C〉は「（結果として）O を C の状態に至らせる」の意味。enrollment「登録」，assortment「詰め合わせ」，leverage「てこの作用，影響力」

(19) – 解答 **3** ....

訳 税収を上回るお金を何年も費やした結果，政府は現在，何兆ドルもの赤字を抱えている。

解説 after は結果を表し，spending more money ... の結果，生じるのは deficit「赤字」である。a deficit of ～ dollars は「～ドルの赤字」の意味。fatigue「疲労」，petition「請願（書）」，conspiracy「陰謀」

(20) – 解答 **1** .... 正答率 ★75%以上

訳 その芸術家は石から細部までこだわった肖像を彫り上げることで生計を立てた。そのような硬い物質を削るために，彼女は多くの特別な道具を使った。

解説 make a living by -ing で「～して生計を立てる」。第 2 文の a hard substance は第 1 文の stone の言い換えで，cut と類義の carve「彫る」が適切。carve A out of B で「B から A を彫って作る」。それぞれ lure「誘惑する」，soothe「なだめる」，rank「等級付けする」の -ing 形。

(21) – 解答 **1** ....

訳 ルースはチームのみんながコート内を走って行き来する様子をベンチから見守った。不運にも，肩のけがにより，彼女は試合から退くことを余儀なくされていたのだ。

解説 〈force + O + to do〉「O に～するよう強いる」は主語（原因）→ to 不定詞（結果）の関係。けがで試合に出られない状況を想像し，withdraw from「～への出場を取り消す」とする。bypass「（手続きなどを）無視する」，upgrade「性能を高める」，overload「過剰な負担をかける」

(22) – 解答 **1** ....

訳 ジョスリンは嵐が西から押し寄せてくるのが見えた。空が暗くなり始め，風が次第に強くなってきた。

解説 〈see + O + -ing〉「O が～しているのが見える」の構文で，the storm is rolling in「嵐が押し寄せてくる」の意味関係。それぞれ add up「合計する」，hold out「耐える，～（手など）を差し出す」，pass down「～を（後世に）伝える」の -ing 形。

(23) −解答 ②

訳 その会社は，最終的に倒産するまで，5年間売り上げの減少に苦しんだ。先週，同社は永久に店を閉めた。

解説 正解の go under と第2文の close *one's* doors は「倒産する」の婉曲表現。それぞれ dial up「電話回線でネットワークに接続する」，come along「やって来る」，pull through「苦境を乗り切る」の過去形。

(24) −解答 ①

訳 契約書の活字があまりに小さかったので，ガスは文字を判読するのに虫眼鏡が必要だった。

解説 主語の The print は small と形容されていることから，「印刷された活字」の意味で，空所後の the words はその言い換えである。「～を判読する」という意味の make out が適切。tune up「～を調律する」，draw up「～（文書）を作成する」，blow out「～を吹き消す」

(25) −解答 ③

訳 その猫は，生まれたばかりの子猫たちを見守っていた。誰かが子猫に近づき過ぎるたびに神経質になった。

解説 第2文の She は The cat（親猫）のことで，その様子から，親猫は子猫を見守っていた（was watching over）と分かる。それぞれ pack up「～を荷造りする」，look into「～を調べる」，show up「現れる，～を目立たせる」の -ing 形。

一次試験・筆記 **2** 問題編 p.90～93

全文訳 カリフォルニアの中華街

19世紀後半，アメリカ合衆国の中国人移民は，職や住む場所を探している際に白人のアメリカ人からの深刻な差別に直面していた。その結果，彼らは仕事や住居が見つかりやすい，中華街として知られる地域に住みがちだった。最大の中華街の1つは，カリフォルニアのサンノゼ市にあったが，1887年の火災で破壊されたため，その住民たちの暮らしについてはほとんど分かっていない。

サンノゼの中華街に供給されていた食品は，香港と中国からのものだと長らく考えられていた。しかし最近，考古学者たちが，かつてのごみ捨て穴にあった魚の骨を分析したことで，必ずしもそうではなかったという証拠が得られた。これらの特定の骨はジャイアントスネークヘッドとして知られる種のものだったため，注目を浴びた。この魚は中国や香港原産ではなく，東南アジア諸国原産であるため，考古学者たちはそれが別の所で漁獲されたのちに香港に輸送され，その後消費向けにアメリカ合衆国に出荷されたと考えている。

この発見がサンノゼの中華街に供給した貿易網の複雑さについての知見をもたらす一

方で，その場所でほかに発見されたものによって，この地域の移民の住民たちの暮らしぶりに関する情報が明らかにされた。例えば，住民たちは食の伝統をある程度維持していたようである。牛の残存物の存在が，牛肉を食す西洋の習慣を住民たちが身に付けていたことを示唆する一方で，考古学者たちが発見した動物の残存物で最も多かったのは豚の骨であった。豚肉は彼らの母国の主食だったので，これらの骨は移民の間で豚の飼養および消費の慣習が続いていたことを示している。

significant「著しい」，discrimination「差別」，inhabitant「住民」，originate「由来する」，archaeologist「考古学者」，pit「（地面の）大きな穴」，stand out「目立つ」，snakehead「スネークヘッド（東南アジアに生息する巨大な雷魚）」，elsewhere「別の場所で」，reveal「明らかにする」，remain「（複数形で）残存物」，staple of the diets「主食」

(26) — 解答 **1**

解説 文頭に適切な論理マーカーを補う問題。空所前は，中国人の移民が差別を受け，職や住む場所に苦労していたという主旨。その結果（Consequently），「仕事や住居が見つかりやすい中華街に住んでいた」という流れが適切。

(27) — 解答 **3**

解説 It was long assumed that A. Recently, however, archaeologists' analysis ... has provided evidence that B.「長らく A と考えられていたが，最近考古学者たちの分析で B という証拠が得られた」という展開。これに合うのは **3** で，この後詳しい説明が続く。this is not the case は「この場合はそうではない」という意味の慣用句で，これに not always「必ずしも～とは限らない」が混じった表現。

(28) — 解答 **4**

解説 空所後の「母国（中国）の主食である豚の骨が多く見つかった→移民の住民の間で豚の飼養および消費の慣習が続いていたことを示す」という内容から，**4**「（母国の）食の伝統をある程度維持していた」が合う。the custom of raising and consuming pigs が some of their food traditions に，continued が maintained に言い換えられている。

全文訳 **植物の計画**

　ほとんどの顕花植物（花を咲かせる植物）は受粉を昆虫に頼る。昆虫が花に接触すると，その体に花粉が付着する。そしてその昆虫が植物上を動き回ったり，同種の別の植物に行ったりすると，この花粉がその植物のめしべに触れる。この受粉のプロセスによって，植物の繁殖が起こる。引き換えに，植物は，例えば食事としての花蜜のような，昆虫が必要とするものを通常提供する。

　顕花植物は，さまざまな方法で受粉する昆虫をうまく引き寄せる。例えば，一部の植物は，鮮やかな色の花弁を使ってハエの注意を引く。研究者たちは最近，アリストロキア・

ミクロストマ（*Aristolochia microstoma*）という植物が，一部のハエが卵を産み付ける死んだ甲虫のようなにおいを出すことでハエをおびき寄せることを発見した。しかしこの植物はただ単にそのにおいでハエをだますだけではない。その花の中に一時的にハエを閉じ込めるのだ。中でハエが動き回るにつれ，その体についた花粉が植物上に広がる。さらにこの植物は，ハエが解き放たれた後に別の植物に受粉できるよう，自らの花粉が確実にハエの体に付くようにする。

　研究者たちは，死んだ甲虫のにおいの元となる化学物質と同じものをこの植物が実際に放出していることを突き止めた。この化学物質は植物には珍しいため，この植物は死んだ甲虫を産卵場所として使うハエを標的にするよう，とりわけ進化したと研究者たちは考えている。彼らはまた，この説にはさらなる裏付けがあると言う。これは，この植物の花が地面の枯葉や石にまぎれた場所 —— まさにハエが通常死んだ甲虫を探す場所 —— にあるという事実に由来する。

> 語句 pollination「受粉」，pollen「花粉」，reproduction「繁殖」，nectar「花蜜」，pollinate「受粉する」，fly「ハエ」，petal「花弁」，beetle「甲虫」，ensure「確実に～するようにする」，specifically「特に」，target「標的にする」，egg-laying「産卵」

(29) – 解答 ④

> 解説 第1段落は植物と昆虫の共生関係の説明。空所前は「植物は昆虫の受粉によって繁殖する」＝植物が受ける恩恵，空所後は「植物は昆虫が必要なもの（花蜜など）を提供する」＝昆虫が受ける恩恵の話で，これらを結ぶのは，**4** の In exchange「引き換えに」である。

(30) – 解答 ③

> 解説 第2段落の前半部分から，死んだ甲虫のようなにおいを出すことでハエをおびき寄せるというアリストロキア・ミクロストマの特徴をつかもう。空所前の more than simply は「ただ単に～だけでなく」の意味。But の展開に注意して読み進めると，ハエをおびき寄せるだけでなく，花の中に一時的に閉じ込めることが分かるので，**3** が正解。

(31) – 解答 ①

> 解説 空所前では研究者たちのアリストロキア・ミクロストマの進化に関する仮説が述べられている。この内容を **1** の this theory で受け，空所後の This が **1** の further support for this theory「この説のさらなる裏付け」を受けていると捉えると文脈が通る。come from the fact that は「～という事実に由来する」の意味で，ここでは that 以下が「この説のさらなる裏付け」の詳しい説明となる。

一次試験・筆記 **3** 問題編 p.94 ～ 100

全文訳 **柵と生態系**

　柵は，とりわけ，土地を仕切ったり，安全を提供したりするのに役立つ。柵はまた，生態系に影響を及ぼすこともある。『バイオサイエンス』誌に掲載の研究では，柵は，それらが設置されている地域の動物種の間で「勝者」と「敗者」を生み出していると結論付けた。この研究によると，多種の食べ物を摂取し，多様な生息地で生存できるゼネラリスト（万能型）の種にとって，物理的な境界はほとんど問題にならない。その一方で，生存に独特の環境を要するスペシャリスト（特化型）の種は，特定の食料源や地理的範囲から切り離されることによって困難な状況に陥る。スペシャリストの種は，ゼネラリストの種より数が多いため，この研究では，それぞれの勝者に対して複数の敗者が出ることが判明した。

　柵の影響は，生態系に限定されるものではない。20世紀半ば，アフリカ南部にあるボツワナは，畜牛を冒す病気のまん延を防止する目的で設けられた国際規則に対処するために柵を設置した。柵は畜牛の保護には役立った反面，ヌーなどの動物の季節的移動を妨げ，これらの動物の水へのアクセスを阻んだ。その結果としてのヌーの個体数減少は，生態系のみならずその地域の野生動物を対象とした観光事業も脅かす。政府の継続的な柵への依存は，動物の移動を制限することが，ボツワナの経済にとって貴重である野生動物を対象とした観光事業に悪影響を与えるのではないかという懸念につながった。

　柵による生態学的な悪影響は，特定の動物が通過できるように柵を変えることによって抑制することができる。それでもなお，この研究の筆者たちは，もっと根本的な変化が必要だと考えている。彼らは柵の全撤去は現実的な選択肢ではないとし，その代わりに全体に目を向けて柵の設置計画を実施するべきだとしている。例えば，柵は短期的な結果を得るために建設され，その後撤去されることが多いが，研究者たちは，動物の中には何カ月，時に何年経っても，まだそこに柵があるかのように振舞い続けるものがいることを発見した。従って，確実に生態系への影響を最小限にするために，柵の設計や場所のあらゆる側面が考慮されるべきである。

　　語句　generalist「多方面の能力・才能を持つ人，万能家」, multiple「多様な」, boundary「境界」, geographical「地理的な」, outnumber「数で勝る」, erect「設置する」, address「対処する」, continued「継続する」, reliance on「～への依存」, migration「（動物の）移動」, *be* valuable to「～にとって貴重である」, fundamental「根本的な」, eliminate「取り除く」, aspect「側面」, minimal「最小限の」

(32) – 解答

　問題文の訳　第1段落で紹介された研究が示したことは

　選択肢の訳　**1**　複数の種類の生息地をまたぐ柵は，単一の生息地内に建設された柵よりも多くの利益を動物にもたらす。

　　　　　　2　柵は，多くの問題を引き起こすが，動物個体群の生存能力への影響は以前考えられていたよりも少ない。

　　　　　　3　柵は，多くの動物が生存に必要とする資源を使い果たす傾向にあるほ

かの有害な種から一部の種を守るのに効果的である。

4 柵は，一部の種には害がないものの，多くの動物に深刻な悪影響を与える可能性がある。

解説 第1段落冒頭で柵の利点に触れた後，第2文で「生態系に影響を及ぼす」という欠点を述べ，詳しい説明を続けている。対比を表す On the other hand の前後の内容を表した**4**が正解。柵は，ゼネラリスト（some species）には害がないがスペシャリスト（ゼネラリストより数が多い = a large number of animals）には深刻な悪影響があるという主旨。

(33) – 解答 ②

問題文の訳 ボツワナに建設された柵に関して正しいのはどれか。

選択肢の訳
1 柵が動物の移動パターンに変化をもたらした結果，畜牛の間で病気がまん延した。

2 柵は，国の経済にとって重要な産業に間接的に影響を与える原因になり得る。

3 柵は，野生動物を見るために国を訪れる観光客の安全を高めるために必要だと考えられている。

4 柵が病気をまん延させる種の減少に成功したことで，予期せぬ形で生態系が恩恵を受けた。

解説 ボツワナの柵について書かれた第2段落からの出題。第4～5文によると，柵を設置した結果，ヌーの個体数が減り，生態系のみならず，ボツワナの経済にとって貴重な野生動物を対象とした観光事業に（間接的に）悪影響を与える可能性がある。正解は**2**で，an industry that is important to the country's economy が第5文の wildlife tourism, which is valuable to Botswana's economy と同じような意味である。

(34) – 解答 ②　　　　　　　　　　　　　　　正答率 ★75%以上

問題文の訳 柵を建設する際に慎重な計画が必要な理由の1つは何か。

選択肢の訳
1 柵を建設した後に設計を変更すると，実際には新しい柵を建設するよりも多くの問題が生じる可能性がある。

2 柵が撤去された後でさえも，柵は地域内の動物に影響を与え続ける可能性がある。

3 事前に明確な計画を立てずに特定の地域に複数の柵を設置することは，動物が危険な地域に侵入するのを防いでいない。

4 捕食者から身を守るために柵を利用する動物種の数が増えた。

解説 第3段落参照。柵は，全体に目を向けた計画的な設置が必要で，その理由の1つが For example 以下にある。... and then removed, but ... as if the fences are still there より，柵が撤去された後も，まだそこに柵があるかのように振る舞い続ける動物がいることを continue to have an effect on animals と表している**2**が正解。

全文訳　**サッカー戦争**

　1969年7月に，中央アメリカの国であるエルサルバドルとホンジュラスとの間で，一連のワールドカップ予選の同2国間のサッカーの試合に続いて短くも激しい戦争があった。この争いはしばしば「サッカー戦争」と呼ばれるが，その原因はスポーツをはるかに超えていた。

　ホンジュラスはエルサルバドルよりずっと国土が広いが，人口密度は圧倒的に低い。1800年代後半以来，エルサルバドルの土地は主に上流階級によって支配されていたが，これはつまり，一般の農家にはほとんど場所がなかったことを意味した。1960年代までには，およそ30万人のエルサルバドル人が安い土地や仕事を得ようとホンジュラスに不法入国していた。ホンジュラス政府は，自国の経済的な苦境の原因が移民にあるとして，彼らをその土地から立ち退かせて国から追い出した。裕福なエルサルバドル人は，それほど多くの移民が帰国することによる経済への悪影響を恐れて，ホンジュラスに対して軍事行動を起こさないとエルサルバドルの大統領を打倒すると脅した。この状況と，何年も続いていた国境紛争とが相まって，両国の関係は最悪となった。

　両国のメディアによって，お互いの国に対する敵意をあおる話がでっち上げられたり，誇張されたりしたため，さらに緊張が高まった。エルサルバドルのマスコミは，ホンジュラス政府のエルサルバドル人移民に対する残酷かつ不法な扱いを非難する一方で，ホンジュラスのマスコミはその同じ移民が重大な罪を犯していると報道した。このような報道は，これらの国の政府の要請によって行われた。エルサルバドルでは，目標は，隣国に対する軍事力が必要だと一般市民に納得させることで，一方ホンジュラスでは，政府は，エルサルバドル人移民を自国から追い出すという決定に対する一般市民の支持を得ることを望んだ。

　ワールドカップ予選の試合は，移民状況が緊迫してきていたときと同じ時期に行われていた。最終試合の日，エルサルバドルは，ホンジュラスのエルサルバドル人に対する暴力を非難し，関係を断ち切り，数週間のうちに，エルサルバドルの軍隊がホンジュラスを攻撃し，開戦した。歴史学者たちは，「サッカー戦争」は誤解を招く表現だったと指摘する。当時，アメリカ合衆国は，中央アメリカ諸国と同盟関係にあったが，この戦争にかかわらないことを選んだ。実際，あるアメリカ人外交官によると，スポーツイベントが紛争の背後にあるという不正確な思い込みが，アメリカ政府がその深刻さを見過ごすことにつながった。争いの真の発端だった土地の所有権などの問題は，未解決のままとなった。この結果，政治的・社会的に不安定な状態が続き，最終的にはその後数十年にわたるエルサルバドルの内戦につながった。

　　語句　intense「激しい」，qualifying match「予選試合」，conflict「紛争」，*be* densely populated「人口密度が高い」，primarily「主に」，overthrow「打倒する」，dispute「紛争」，tension「緊張」，make up「〜（話）をでっち上げる」，exaggerate「誇張する」，fuel「（感情を）あおる」，bitterness「敵意」，cruel「残酷な」，intensify「増す，激化する」，alliance「同盟」，diplomat「外交官」，inaccurate「不正確な」，

overlook「見過ごす」，instability「不安定（な状態）」，ultimately「最終的には」

(35) – 解答 **3** ⋯⋯⋯⋯⋯⋯⋯⋯⋯⋯⋯⋯⋯⋯⋯⋯⋯⋯⋯

問題文の訳 第2段落によると，どのようにしてホンジュラスへのエルサルバドル人移民が「サッカー戦争」の原因になったのか。

選択肢の訳
1 エルサルバドルの大統領は，移民をホンジュラスの家から退去させたことは，ホンジュラスが攻撃しようとしている兆候だと思った。
2 ホンジュラス政府は，貧しいホンジュラス人をエルサバドルに土地を求めに行かせ，その結果，動揺したエルサルバドルの農民たちがそれに対抗してホンジュラスに移住した。
3 裕福なエルサルバドル人は，移民が家から退去させられた後，ホンジュラスに戦争を仕掛けるよう政府に圧力をかけた。
4 両国間を行き来する絶え間ない移民の移動が，ホンジュラスの国境管理員にとって面倒を引き起こした。

解説 第2段落はエルサルバドル人のホンジュラスへの不法入国や国から追い出された経緯について。Wealthy Salvadorans ... から，裕福なエルサルバドル人はホンジュラスに対して軍事行動を起こさないとエルサルバドルの大統領を打倒すると脅したことが分かる。「軍事行動を起こす」を make war と表した **3** が正解。

(36) – 解答 **4** ⋯⋯⋯⋯⋯⋯⋯⋯⋯⋯⋯⋯⋯⋯⋯⋯⋯⋯⋯

問題文の訳 サッカー戦争が始まる前の時期，それぞれの国のメディアは

選択肢の訳
1 エルサルバドル人移民が確実により良い待遇を受けられるよう，両国政府に圧力をかけようとした。
2 国民に対して犯されている違法行為を報道することを政府によって妨げられた。
3 サッカーのライバル関係を強調し過ぎたため，違法行為に関するもっと重要なニュースを報じ損ねた。
4 相手国を悪者にするような，真実でない，あるいは誤解を招くニュース記事をでっち上げるよう，政府から求められた。

解説 第3段落第1文から，両国のメディアが相手国に対する敵意をあおるような話をでっち上げたりして，関係が悪化したことが分かる。続く第2文 The Salvadoran press ..., while the Honduran press ...（対比表現）で各国の報道について具体的な説明があり，第3文で「このような報道は，これらの国の政府の要請によって行われた」とある。

(37) – 解答 **3** ⋯⋯⋯⋯⋯⋯⋯⋯⋯⋯⋯⋯⋯⋯⋯⋯⋯⋯⋯

問題文の訳 この文章の筆者は最終段落で何を示唆しているか。

選択肢の訳
1 アメリカの外交官たちは，ホンジュラスとエルサルバドルの間で再び戦闘が勃発するのではないかとまだ心配し続けている。

2 サッカー戦争の悲惨な影響により，ホンジュラスとエルサルバドルは，戦争に至るまでの自分たちの行動が間違っていたことに気付いた。

3 サッカー戦争に対する誤った思い込みにより，真の原因が認識されず，結果として別の紛争をもたらした。

4 アメリカ政府の政策により，多くの中米諸国が関係を断ち，その地域の紛争がいっそう悪化した。

解説 最終段落の In fact, ... から最終文までを参照。スポーツイベントが紛争の背後にあるという不正確な思い込みにより，アメリカ政府は争いの深刻さを見過ごし，最終的にエルサルバドル内戦につながったという主旨で，**3** が正解。本文の inaccurate belief と **3** の mistaken belief，true origin と real causes，overlook と were not recognized，a civil war in El Salvador と another conflict がそれぞれ対応する。

全文訳 **ブライユ点字と張り合う**

　ブライユ点字法は，今日における目が不自由な人のための標準文字体系であるが，文字を表現するこの盛り上がった点のアルファベットだけが常に唯一の文字体系だったわけではなかった。1830年代に，アメリカの盲学校の目の見える講師であるサミュエル・グリッドリー・ハウによって，ボストンラインタイプという別の文字体系が作成された。ハウの文字体系は，目の見える人々が使う標準英語アルファベットの文字を使用していたが，指で触って感じ取れるように盛り上がっていた。しかし，目が不自由な生徒たちは，ブライユ点字よりも1つ1つの文字を区別するのに苦労していた。それにもかかわらず，ハウは目の見えない読者と見える読者のどちらもが読み物を共有できるということがこの短所より重要であると考えていた。彼はこの文字体系によって目が不自由な人が社会により溶け込めるようになると主張した。彼は，ほとんどの目の見える人にとってなじみがないという理由から，ブライユ点字は孤立を助長すると思っていた。

　点を使う文字体系は，ほとんどの目が不自由な人にとって読みやすいだけではなく，点字は書くことが比較的簡単なため，より実用的でもあることが次第に明らかになった。ボストンラインタイプによる筆記は，特殊な印刷機を必要としたが，ブライユ点字は単純で持ち運び可能な道具しか必要とせず，タイプライターで打ち込むこともできた。それでも，生徒たちはブライユ点字を圧倒的に好んでいたにもかかわらず，ボストンラインタイプが盲学校で公式利用され続けていたのは，目の見える講師たちが新しい記号一式を覚える必要なく教えることができたからだった。ボストンラインタイプが人気を失っても，ほかの文字体系が導入され続け，「点字戦争」として知られることになる，さまざまな文字体系が標準になるために競い合う状況に発展した。

　そういった文字体系の1つにニューヨークポイントと呼ばれるものがあり，盛り上がった点から成るという点においてブライユ点字と似ていた。その主な利点は，それを打ち込むのに片手しか必要としないことであった。しかし，ブライユ点字は，より効率的かつ明確に大文字や一定の句読点を表示することができた。ほかにも候補はあり，ど

れが勝っているかについての議論もじきに激しくなった。その間，目が不自由な人は非常に不便な思いをさせられていた。読める本はすでに供給不足だった上，新しい文字体系を覚えるには膨大な時間と労力を要するため，文字体系の競合が彼らの選択肢をさらに狭めた。ある全国会議で，1人の演説者が，目が不自由な人向けの新しい活字体系を次に発明した人には暴力をもって対応すると冗談めかしてほのめかすことで，彼らの不満をまとめて代弁したという話もあった。

　点字戦争は1900年代に入っても続き，さまざまな団体が資金援助や認知を求めて争っていた。最終的に，視覚障がいのある活動家のヘレン・ケラーがこの議論に終止符を打つのに極めて強い影響を与えた。彼女は，ニューヨークポイントの大文字使用と句読法に関する短所は非常に深刻で，それを読むことは彼女の指の負担となると述べた。ブライユ点字が勝ち抜き，ほかの文字体系は次第に消えていった。点字戦争は一時期には目が不自由な人の教育の妨げとなったが，一筋の光明もあった。激しい競争が，新しいタイプライターなど，目が不自由な人の識字率と近代社会に参加する能力を著しく向上させるさまざまな技術の開発を促した。

> 語句 　sighted「目の見える」，utilize「利用する」，distinguish A from B「A を B と区別する」，outweigh「(重要性が)勝る」，integrate into「～に溶け込む」，isolation「孤独」，printing press「印刷機」，overwhelming「圧倒的な」，capital letter「大文字」，punctuation「句読(法)，句読点」，bitter「(言動が)激しい」，reportedly「伝えられるところによると」，sum up「～を要約する」，jokingly「冗談めかして」，activist「活動家」，influential「影響力の強い」，in regard to「～に関して」，capitalization「大文字で書くこと」，silver lining「一筋の光明，希望の兆し」〈比喩表現〉，enhance「高める」，literacy「識字能力」

(38) –解答 ④

> 問題文の訳 　サミュエル・グリッドリー・ハウはボストンラインタイプについて何を信じていたか。

> 選択肢の訳 　**1**　目が不自由な人の読む時間を節約したことは，ブライユ点字よりも書くのにはるかに時間がかかったという事実の埋め合わせをした。
> 　**2**　盛り上がった点をほかの特性と組み合わせたという事実により，目が不自由な人が互いに意思疎通を図るときに使いやすくなった。
> 　**3**　生徒にとって習得が難しかったが，ブライユ点字よりも速く読めるという事実は大きな利点であった。
> 　**4**　目の見えない人が見える人にもっとうまく溶け込むのを助けるという役割を担うことができるため，採用する価値があった。

> 解説 　第1段落参照。ボストンラインタイプの文字の区別に生徒たちは苦労していたが，ハウは目の見えない人と見える人が読み物を共有できる点で優れていると信じていた。ハウの主張が書かれた His system, he argued, ... と **4** が合う。better integrate into society を better fit in

106

with people who are able to see と表している。

(39) – 解答

問題文の訳　第2段落で，この文章の筆者はボストンラインタイプについて何を示唆しているか。

選択肢の訳
1　その継続的な使用は，目が不自由な人の利益を最優先に考えていなかった。どの文字体系を使用すべきかについての彼らの意見は考慮されていないように思われた（からだ）。
2　盲学校の講師たちは点が少ない文字体系の方が生徒たちにとって読みやすいと考えていたため，それを使用しないよう生徒たちを説得した。
3　「点字戦争」を引き起こしたにもかかわらず，それが生徒たちの間で人気があったことは目が不自由な人向けのほかの道具を開発する上で重要な要素だった。
4　それが筆記において盲学校の生徒にうまく使われるようになったのは，タイプライターが導入された後のことであった。

解説　盲学校の生徒たちはブライユ点字を圧倒的に好んでいたにもかかわらず，目の見える講師の利点からボストンラインタイプが盲学校で公式利用され続けていた。つまり，生徒たちの意見が反映されなかったと言えるので，**1** が正解。in the best interests of は「～の利益を最優先に考える」という意味。remained in official use と Its continued use が類義表現。

(40) – 解答

問題文の訳　全国会議での演説者の発言でほのめかされていることは，目が不自由な人は

選択肢の訳
1　ブライユ点字もニューヨークポイントも，目が不自由な読者のニーズを満たすことはできないだろうと感じていた。
2　どの文字体系を使用すべきかをめぐる議論が，間接的に彼らの読み物へのアクセスを妨げていることに不満だった。
3　目が不自由な人によって開発されたものではない文字体系の使用を強制されることを嫌がった。
4　本が読めるようになることよりもほかのタイプの教育の方がはるかに重要になったと思い始めていた。

解説　第3段落参照。読める本はすでに供給不足だった上，文字体系の競合のせいでさらに選択肢が狭まるなど，目の不自由な人は不便な思いをしていた。At one national convention, ... 部分の演説者の発言は，このような目が不自由な人の不満を冗談混じりに表したものである。the competing systems further limited their options「文字体系の競合が彼らの選択肢をさらに狭めた」などを参考にして，**2** が正解。

(41) – 解答 ③

問題文の訳　この文章の筆者は点字戦争についてどのような結論を出しているか。

1 非常に深刻であったため，今日も依然として目が不自由な人のための技術の研究開発に悪影響を及ぼしている。

2 もしヘレン・ケラーが関与すべきだと判断していなかったら，さほど悪い感情を引き起こさなかっただろう。

3 競合が，目が不自由な人の生活改善につながったため，長期的には幾つかのプラスの影響をもたらした。

4 もし当時の人々がタイプライターのような技術をもっと受け入れていたなら，避けることができたかもしれない。

解説 最終段落参照。点字戦争はヘレン・ケラーの発言によって終わりを迎え，ブライユ点字が勝ち残った。一時期には（for a time）目が不自由な人の教育の妨げとなったが，長期的には（in the long term），silver lining の後に書かれているようなプラスの影響ももたらした。**3**が正解で，本文最終文の the development of various technologies, ... participate in modern society を抽象的に improvements in the lives of blind people と表している。

一次試験・筆記 **4** 問題編 p.101

トピックの訳 賛成か反対か：政府は再利用可能な製品の促進にもっと力を入れるべきだ。

ポイントの訳 ・コスト ・企業への影響 ・ごみ ・安全性

解答例 I agree that the government should do more to promote reusable products, particularly in relation to garbage and costs.

Firstly, increasing the adoption of reusable products will directly impact the amount of garbage that humans produce. Throwing away items after a single use, for example, is a significant factor in the buildup of waste in landfills all over the world. By encouraging greater awareness of reusable products, governments can actively help the environment.

Secondly, reusable products can be cost-effective for both consumers and businesses. People still buy plastic bags at supermarkets, and many restaurants purchase single-use chopsticks. Government promotion of reusable alternatives, however, would save money for shoppers and reduce overhead costs for businesses, which could have a wider positive economic impact.

In conclusion, I feel that promoting reusable products should be a priority for the government because the environmental and cost benefits are too important to ignore.

解説　序論：トピックが *Agree or disagree:* で始まる場合，第 1 段落で賛成または反対の立場を明らかにする。I agree [disagree] (that) の後，トピックの内容を続けるとよい。解答例は，particularly in relation to「特に〜に関して」を用いてポイントの Garbage と Costs を取り上げている。

本論：本論では，First(ly), ...，Second(ly), ... などを使って，賛成・反対の根拠・理由を，2 つの観点に沿って説明する。解答例の第 2 段落は Garbage の観点で，再利用可能な製品採用の増加は人間が出すごみの量に直接影響すると述べた後，for example を用いて具体的に説明している。そして garbage「ごみ」を the environment「環境」に結び付け，再利用可能な製品の認知度を高めることで政府は積極的に環境保護に貢献できるとしている。第 3 段落は Costs の観点で，再利用可能な製品は消費者と企業の両方にとって費用対効果が高いと述べた後，レジ袋や箸を例に説明を続けている。

結論：最終段落は，In conclusion「結論として」などを使って，賛成・反対の立場を再主張する。解答例は，トピックの表現を言い換えて，再利用可能な製品の促進は政府にとって優先事項であるべきだと賛成の立場を主張した後，the environmental and cost benefits の部分で 2 つの観点を根拠として再び取り上げている。too important to ignore「無視できないほど重要な」のような主張を強める表現が使えると説得力が増す。なお，解答例ではトピックの「再利用可能な製品 [代替品] の促進」に対応する表現が何度か出てくるが，increasing the adoption of reusable products, encouraging greater awareness of reusable products, Government promotion of reusable alternatives のように，表現を少しずつ変えている点に注目したい。

そのほかの表現　第 2 段落の impact the amount of garbage の impact「影響を与える」は，ここではごみが減ることを意味しているので，more reusable products will <u>reduce</u> the amount of garbage「再利用可能な製品が増えるとごみの量が減る」や the promotion of reusable products will lead to a <u>reduction</u> of waste「再利用可能な製品の推進はごみの削減につながる」のように表すこともできる。ポイントの Effect on businesses は，賛成の立場で用い，Eco-friendly efforts can improve the company's image.「環境に配慮した取り組みは企業のイメージアップにつながる」などの意見が可能だろう。

No.**1** – 解答 **4**

スクリプト ☆： Hi, Ron. Why are you sitting there? Where's the new receptionist?

★： She called to say she'll be late.

☆： Again? That's the third time since she started. What's her excuse now?

★： She said her babysitter hasn't turned up yet.

☆： I know she has her problems, but it can't go on like this. I'll have to have a talk with her.

★： Please do. I'm tired of filling in.

Question: What is the woman going to do?

全文訳 ☆： こんにちは，ロン。なぜあなたがそこに座っているの？ 新しい受付係はどこ？

★： 彼女は遅れるって電話してきました。

☆： また？ 仕事を始めてからこれで3度目じゃない。今度はどんな理由で？

★： ベビーシッターがまだ来ていないそうです。

☆： 彼女が問題を抱えているのは知っているけど，こんな状態が続くのは良くないわ。彼女と話をしないと。

★： そうしてください。代わりを務めるのはうんざりですよ。

質問：女性は何をするか。

選択肢の訳 **1** 男性に受付係の代わりをさせる。

2 男性に受付係を解雇するよう頼む。

3 受付係の仕事を自分でする。

4 遅刻について受付係に警告する。

解説 オフィス内の会話。最初のやりとりから，受付係の遅刻のため男性が受付に座っていることが想像できる。女性は I'll have to have a talk with her. と言っており，have a talk を warn と表した **4** が正解。話者のこの後の行動は，たいてい会話の後半に手掛かりがある。

No.**2** – 解答 **1**

スクリプト ☆： Tim, I'm concerned about your performance in my science class.

★： Didn't I pass the test yesterday?

☆： No, and you've missed several assignments.

★： I'm sorry. I've had to work late every night this month at my part-time job.

☆： Well, we need to solve this problem.

★： OK. I'll talk to my boss about cutting back my hours.

☆： And how about coming in for extra work before or after school?

★： Thanks, Mrs. Roberts. I'll be here early tomorrow morning.

Question: What conclusion can be made about the student?

全文訳 ☆： ティム，科学の授業のあなたの成績が気掛かりです。

★： 昨日のテストには合格しませんでしたか？

☆： はい，それから幾つか課題も未提出です。

★： すみません。今月はアルバイトで毎晩遅くまで働かなければならなかったので。

☆： うーん，この問題を解決しなければならないわね。

★： 分かりました。勤務時間を減らすことについて上司に話します。

☆： それと，学校が始まる前か終わった後に補習しにくるのはどうかしら？

★： ありがとうございます，ロバーツ先生。明日の朝早くここに来ます。

質問：生徒についてどんな結論を出すことができるか。

選択肢の訳 **1** 彼は授業の成績を上げなければならない。

2 彼は仕事のスケジュールを変更できない。

3 彼はアルバイトを辞めるだろう。

4 彼は科学の授業に出ない。

解説 先生は，科学の成績が思わしくない生徒を心配し，we need to solve this problem と言って一緒に問題を解決しようとしている。how about coming ...? で学校が始まる前か終わった後に補習しにくるよう提案しているのは成績を上げるためなので，**1** が正解。この文の extra work はバイトの仕事ではなく勉強である点に注意。生徒はバイト先の上司に相談して勤務時間を調整しようとしているので，**2** と **3** は不適。

No.3 – 解答 ④

スクリプト ☆： Hey, Dave. You look down. What's wrong?

★： Well, mostly, it's just that I'm not enjoying my job.

☆： Have you thought about doing something else?

★： Yes, but I haven't been able to find anything that pays as well. With the kids almost in college and the house payments, I can't really just quit.

☆： I hear you. Well, I hope things work out for you.

★： Thanks, but right now I'm not very optimistic.

Question: What is the man's problem?

全文訳 ☆： あら，デイヴ。落ち込んでいるようね。どうしたの？

★： まあ，ほとんど，仕事が楽しくないだけなんだけどね。

☆： 何かほかのことをしようと考えたことはないの？

★： あるよ，でも同じくらい稼げる仕事を見つけることができていないんだ。うちの子供たちがもうすぐ大学生で，家の支払いもあるから，ただ辞め

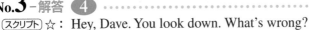

るっていう訳にもいかないし。

☆： 言いたいことは分かるわ。まあ，うまくいくといいわね。

★： ありがとう，でも今はあまり楽観的にはなれないな。

　　質問：男性の問題は何か。

選択肢の訳　**1** 彼は子供たちの大学の学費を払えない。

　　　　　　2 彼の住まいが会社から遠過ぎる。

　　　　　　3 彼は十分な給料をもらっていないと思っている。

　　　　　　4 彼は今の仕事を離れることはできないと感じている。

解説　男性の発言から，仕事が楽しくなく，転職も検討しているが，良い仕事は見つかっていないことが分かる。I can't really just quit を言い換えた **4** が正解。転職は子供の学費や家の支払いのため給与がネックになっているが，学費を払えないとは言っていないので，**1** は不適。

No.**4** – 解答

スクリプト　★： Morning, Fiona. Coffee?

☆： Make it a big one! I was working on a project report until midnight last night. I can't believe I'm here so late every day.

★： Didn't they warn you about the overtime when you interviewed?

☆： Well, they sort of did. What really bothers me, though, is that every time I think I've achieved my targets, my manager changes them.

★： That's corporate life. At least you have summer vacation to look forward to.

☆： Yeah. I hope they actually let me take it!

　　Question: What is the woman's main complaint?

全文訳　★： おはよう，フィオナ。コーヒーはどう？

☆： たっぷり頼むわ！　昨夜は真夜中までプロジェクトの報告書に取り組んでいたの。毎日こんなに遅くまでここにいるなんて信じられないわ。

★： 面接のときに残業のことは予告されなかった？

☆： まあ，それらしいことは言っていたわね。でも何が本当の悩みかというと，目標を達成したと思うたびに部長がそれを変更してくることよ。

★： それが会社人生ってやつさ。少なくとも楽しみにできる夏休みがある。

☆： そうね。夏休みを本当に取らせてくれるといいのだけど！

　　質問：女性の主な不満は何か。

選択肢の訳　**1** 彼女は頻繁に新しい目標を与えられる。

　　　　　　2 彼女は残業代が十分に支払われていない。

　　　　　　3 彼女の休暇届が却下された。

　　　　　　4 彼女の報告書が否定的な意見を受けた。

解説　最初のやりとりから，女性は残業に不満がある様子。質問の main complaint は，What really bothers me, ... I've achieved my

112

targets, my manager changes them. の発言から，**1** が正解。them は my targets を指し，**1** では goals と表されている。女性は夏休みが取れるか不安に思っているが，休暇届が却下されたわけではないので **3** は不適。

No.5 -解答 ②

スクリプト ☆： Dad, I want to go to grad school straight after university. Maybe I'll do a master's in psychology.

★： That's a big commitment, and it doesn't sound like you have a clear plan. How about working for a few years first?

☆： I'm afraid if I don't do this soon, I never will. I'm worried about the cost, though.

★： I've told you I'd help with that. But I really think a year or two in the real world would give you valuable experience.

☆： OK. Let me think about it a bit more.

Question: What does the man tell his daughter?

全文訳 ☆： お父さん，大学卒業後はそのまま大学院に行きたいのだけど。心理学の修士課程に進もうかなって。

★： それは大きな覚悟がいるね。それに明確な計画があるわけでもなさそうだな。先に数年働いてみるのはどうだい？

☆： あいにく，すぐにこれをしなかったら，一生しないと思うの。費用については心配してるけど。

★： それについては助けてあげると言ったよね。でも実社会で1，2年過ごすのも貴重な経験になると本当に思うんだ。

☆： 分かった。もう少し考えさせて。

質問：男性は娘に何と言っているか。

選択肢の訳 1 彼女は来年，修士号を取得するべきだ。

2 彼女は実務経験をするべきだ。

3 彼女は1年間彼の支援に頼ることができる。

4 彼女はまず，多少のお金を貯めるべきだ。

解説 大学院に進みたいと娘に相談された父親は，How about working for a few years first? や But I really think ... valuable experience. から，その前に実社会で働くことを勧めている。よって，**2** が正解。父親の I've told you I'd help with that. の that は学費のことだが，1年間とは言っておらず，また，大学院に行く前に働くことを勧めているので，**3** は不適。働くのは貯金のためではなく経験のためなので **4** も不適。

No.6 -解答 ③

スクリプト ★： Shelly, personnel asked me to remind you the deadline for enrolling in an insurance plan is tomorrow.

☆： I know, but I have no idea which one's best for me.

★： They're all described on the company website. Why don't you look there?

☆： I have, but it wasn't very helpful. I find all the different options so confusing.

★： Maybe you should have someone in personnel explain the choices again.

☆： I guess I have no choice.

Question: What will the woman probably do next?

全文訳 ★： シェリー，保険の申し込み期限は明日だって君に念のため言っておくよう，人事部に言われたよ。

☆： 知ってるけど，どれが一番私に合っているのか分からないの。

★： 全部，会社のウェブサイトで説明されているよ。そこを見てみたら？

☆： 見たけど，あまり役に立たなかった。ありとあらゆるオプションがあって本当にややこしいのよ。

★： 人事部の誰かにもう一度選択肢を説明してもらった方がいいんじゃない。

☆： そうするしかなさそうね。

質問： 女性はおそらく次に何をするか。

選択肢の訳 1　ウェブサイトをもっとていねいに見直す。

2　男性と同じプランを選ぶ。

3　人事部との面談を申請する。

4　別の保険プランを探す。

解説　最初のやりとりから，女性は明日が申し込み期限の保険が選べない様子である。男性の Maybe you should have someone in personnel explain the choices again. という提案に同意しているので，**3** が正解。〈have＋人＋動詞の原形〉で「（人）に〜してもらう」という意味。

No.7 −解答 ③ ･･･････････････････････････

スクリプト ★： Happy birthday, Kimiko!

☆： Farouk, there you are! I was getting worried you wouldn't make it to the party. Did you get lost?

★： Sorry to be so late. No, your house was easy to find. Actually, I felt a little drowsy, so I pulled off the highway for a short nap. The next thing I knew, an hour had passed.

☆： Well, I'm just glad you made it here safely. How was the traffic?

★： Not as heavy as I'd feared. Is it all right if I sit down?

☆： Of course.

Question: Why did the man arrive late?

全文訳 ★： 誕生日おめでとう，キミコ！

☆： ファルーク，そこにいたのね！ あなたがパーティーに間に合わないかもって心配になっていたところよ。迷ったの？

★： こんなに遅れてごめん。違うんだ，君の家は簡単に見つかったよ。実のところ，少し眠かったから，ちょっと仮眠を取ろうとハイウェイを降りたんだ。次に気が付いたら，1時間経ってたんだ。

☆： まあ，ここに無事にたどり着いてよかったわ。道はどうだった？

★： 心配していたほど混んでいなかった。座ってもいい？

☆： もちろんよ。

質問：男性はなぜ到着が遅れたのか。

選択肢の訳
1 彼は渋滞に巻き込まれた。
2 彼の車が故障した。
3 彼は長く寝過ぎた。
4 彼はハイウェイで道に迷った。

解説 男性がパーティーに遅れてきた理由は，Actually, ... 以降にある。ちょっと仮眠を取るつもりが気付いたら1時間経っていたという状況を，パーティーに遅れるほど「長く寝過ぎた」と表した **3** が正解。drowsy「眠い」が分からなくても後の for a short nap で状況をつかもう。

No.8 – 解答

スクリプト
☆： Honey, look at Jason's report card. He's still struggling in math.

★： I guess I should start helping him with his homework again.

☆： I think it's past that point now. We need to seriously consider getting him a tutor.

★： We're already paying so much for his private schooling. Shouldn't his teachers be doing something about it?

☆： I understand your frustration, but I think some one-on-one time in another environment would really help him.

★： I just hate to think of spending even more money right now.

Question: What does the man think?

全文訳
☆： あなた，ジェイソンの成績表を見て。まだ数学で苦労しているよ。

★： またあの子の宿題を手伝い始めた方がいいのかな。

☆： もうその段階は過ぎていると思う。個人教師をつけることを真剣に考えないと。

★： すでに私立校の授業料にかなりのお金を払ってるよ。先生たちがそれについて何とかするべきじゃないの？

☆： あなたの不満は分かるけど，違う環境で一対一の時間を持つことが本当にあの子のためになると思うわ。

★： 今はただこれ以上お金を使うことは考えたくないな。

質問：男性はどう思っているか。

1 ジェイソンの先生たちはもっと努力すべきだ。

2 ジェイソンは私立学校に転校すべきだ。

3 ジェイソンの宿題の量が増えた。

4 ジェイソンは個人教師のところに行かせるべきだ。

解説 夫婦の会話で，話題は息子ジェイソンの数学の成績不振について。女性は個人教師を雇うべきと思っているが，男性は Shouldn't his teachers be doing something about it? と反対する。**1** が正解で，do something を make more effort と表している。男性は宿題の手伝いをほのめかしているが，量［負担］(load) が増えたとは言っていないので **3** は不適。

No.9 – 解答 ④

スクリプト ☆ : Hello, Michael. How are you liking your new position? I hear it's been keeping you on the road quite a bit.

★ : Yes, I've spent more time abroad recently than I have at home.

☆ : I envy you. I'm tired of going to the office every single day.

★ : Well, even though I'm traveling, mostly all I get to see is the inside of hotels and factories.

☆ : I hope you're not regretting changing positions.

★ : No, things should settle down soon.

Question: What does the woman imply?

全文訳 ☆ : こんにちは，マイケル。新しいポジションはどう？　結構出張が多いって聞いているけど。

★ : うん，最近は自宅にいるより海外で過ごす時間の方が長いよ。

☆ : うらやましいな。私は毎日毎日，出社するのに飽きちゃって。

★ : まあ，旅行しているとは言え，たいていの場合，見ることができるものと言えばホテルや工場の中くらいだよ。

☆ : あなたが異動したことを後悔していないといいのだけど。

★ : していないよ，状況はすぐに落ち着くはずさ。

質問：女性は何をほのめかしているか。

選択肢の訳 1 男性は前のポジションに戻るべきだ。

2 彼女はもうすぐ異動する。

3 男性は自宅でもっと時間を過ごすべきだ。

4 彼女はもっと出張をしたい。

解説 女性の最初の発言の on the road「出張中で」や，後の男性の発言の more time abroad と I'm traveling などから，男性が新しいポジションに就き海外出張が多いことが分かる。これに対し女性は I envy you.「うらやましい」と言っているので，続く「毎日出社するのに飽きている」は「もっと出張をしたい」という意図があると考えて，**4** が正解。

No.10 解答

スクリプト ★： Morning, Deborah. Hey, are you OK?

☆： What? Oh, sorry, Stan. I'm just in a bad mood.

★： What happened?

☆： I got confused while transferring at Baxter Station and almost missed my usual train. It's like a maze now because of the construction.

★： They're doing major renovations, right?

☆： Yes, and the directions for passengers were unclear. I never thought I'd get lost in the train station I use every morning.

★： How long will the work continue?

☆： Until the end of the year. I guess I'll have to get used to it.

Question: Why is the woman in a bad mood?

全文訳 ★： おはよう，デボラ。ねえ，大丈夫？

☆： 何？　あら，ごめんなさい，スタン。ちょっと機嫌が悪くて。

★： 何があったの？

☆： バクスター駅で乗り換えるときに混乱して，もう少しでいつもの列車に乗り遅れるところだったの。工事のせいで今は迷路みたいになっているから。

★： 大掛かりな改修をしているんだって？

☆： そう，それに乗客に対する案内が不明確だったの。毎朝利用している列車の駅で迷うなんて思いもしなかったわ。

★： 工事はいつまで続くの？

☆： 年末まで。慣れるしかなさそうね。

質問：女性はなぜ機嫌が悪いのか。

選択肢の訳 **1** 駅の改修工事が予定より遅れている。

2 彼女が乗った列車がいつもより混んでいた。

3 彼女は列車の乗り換えに苦労した。

4 彼女がいつも利用する駅が閉鎖されていた。

解説 女性は I'm just in a bad mood. と言って機嫌が悪い様子。その理由を説明した I got confused ... because of the construction. と次の発言の I'd get lost in the train station などから，駅が改修工事をしていて「乗り換えに苦労した」ことが分かる。よって，**3** が正解。

No.11 解答

スクリプト ★： Have you finished that book already?

☆： Yes. Since I turned 50, I've been trying to read more for mental stimulation. I want to stay sharp and alert.

★： That's great. Lately, all I ever read are boring work-related documents and manuals.

☆： That does sound dull. These days, I'm mostly reading historical fiction, although sometimes I try to read science books for general audiences.

★： Maybe I should start reading some fiction as well, before I forget how to enjoy a book.

Question: Why is the woman reading books?

全文訳 ★： その本，もう読み終わったの？

☆： うん。50歳になって以来，頭を刺激するためにもっと読書をしようとしているの。頭の働きを良く保って，きびきびしていたいからね。

★： それはいいね。最近僕は，つまらない仕事関連の文書やマニュアルしか読んでいないよ。

☆： それは退屈そうね。最近私は，歴史小説を読むことがほとんどだけど，ときどき一般読者向けの科学本も読むようにしているわ。

★： 僕も小説を読み始めようかな，本の楽しみ方を忘れないうちに。

質問：女性はなぜ読書をしているのか。

選択肢の訳 1 頭を活発に保つため。
2 仕事のスキルを向上させるため。
3 気持ちを仕事からそらすため。
4 自分の小説執筆のためのアイデアを得るため。

解説 女性は最初の発言で，読書の理由として，..., I've been trying to read more for mental stimulation. I want to stay sharp and alert. と言っている。stay (mentally) sharp は「頭の働きを良く保つ」，alert は「機敏な，きびきびした」という意味で，**1** が正解。

No.12 解答 ② ··

スクリプト ☆： Which trail should we take, Jack?

★： Trail A looks like the easiest one. The cable car carries us halfway up the mountain, and then we hike for about an hour to the peak.

☆： How about something more challenging? I think we could handle climbing the whole way.

★： I don't know. All the overtime I've been working recently has really cut into my workouts. I'm not sure my legs will carry me all the way up.

☆： All right. Trail A it is, then.

Question: What do we learn about the man?

全文訳 ☆： どのコースを進むべきかしら，ジャック？

★： Aコースが一番簡単そうだね。ケーブルカーが山の中腹まで運んでくれて，そこから山頂まで1時間ほどハイキングするよ。

☆：　もっとやりがいのあるのはどう？　全行程を歩いていけると思うよ。

★：　どうかな。僕は最近ずっと残業で，運動できていなかったんだ。頂上に行きつくまで脚が持つか分からない。

☆：　分かった。じゃあ，Aコースにしましょう。

質問：男性について何が分かるか。

選択肢の訳 **1**　彼は熟練した登山家である。

2　彼は最近，あまり運動をしていない。

3　彼はやりがいのあるコースを選びたい。

4　彼はケーブルカーで登るのが好きではない。

解説　登山コース（trail）を選んでいる場面。男性は簡単なAコースがいいと思っているようで，その理由は，彼の2番目の発言から，運動不足で脚に自信がないから。**2**が正解で，All the overtime ... has really cut into my workouts.「残業が運動に食い込んだ」はつまり，残業のせいで運動不足だということ。workoutsと正解の選択肢のexerciseが同義。How about something more challenging? と言っているのは女性なので**3**は不適。

一次試験・リスニング **Part 2** 問題編 p.104〜105　▶MP3 ▶アプリ ▶CD 2 **15**〜**21**

A

スクリプト **Annie Londonderry**

Annie Cohen Kopchovsky — commonly known as Annie Londonderry — was the first woman to ride a bicycle around the world. Some people say she did this in response to a bet that a woman could not make such a journey, though the truth of that story is debated. When she began her journey in 1894, she had only ridden a bicycle a few times. Still, she wanted to prove women had the mental and physical strength to meet such a challenge.

Londonderry believed women should be less restricted in their family and work lives and encouraged women to wear whatever clothing they wanted. In fact, she wore men's clothing for much of her journey. Along the way, Londonderry made money in various ways, including telling stories of her adventures and displaying companies' advertising posters on her bicycles. In fact, the nickname "Londonderry" comes from the name of a spring water company whose product she promoted.

Questions

No.13 What is one reason Annie Londonderry began her trip?

No.14 What is one way Londonderry earned money on her trip?

アニー・ロンドンデリー

　アニー・コーエン・コプチョフスキー（通称アニー・ロンドンデリー）は，自転車で世界一周した初めての女性である。彼女は，女性はそのような旅ができないという考えを受けてそれをしたと言う人もいるが，この話の真相は議論が交わされている。1894年に旅を始めたとき，彼女は数回しか自転車に乗ったことがなかった。それでも彼女は，女性にはそのような挑戦に立ち向かう精神的・肉体的強さがあると証明したいと思った。

　ロンドンデリーは，女性は家庭生活や仕事生活においてもっと制約が緩和されるべきだと思っており，女性が自分の着たい服を着ることを奨励した。実際，彼女は，旅の大部分で男性用の服を着ていた。道中，ロンドンデリーは，自分の冒険談を語ったり，自転車に企業の広告ポスターを貼ったりするなど，さまざまな方法でお金を稼いだ。実のところ，「ロンドンデリー」という愛称は，彼女が製品を宣伝した湧き水会社の名前に由来している。

No.**13**解答 ③

　　質問の訳　アニー・ロンドンデリーが旅を始めた理由の1つは何か。
　　選択肢の訳　**1**　衰えつつある健康を改善するため。
　　　　　　　2　自転車の技術を見せびらかすため。
　　　　　　　3　性別に関する固定観念に挑むため。
　　　　　　　4　新しい種類の自転車を試走するため。
　　解説　in response to a bet that a woman could not make such a journey や she wanted to prove women had ... から，ロンドンデリーは女性にはできないと思われていた旅に挑戦したことが想像できる。これを challenge a gender stereotype と表した **3** が正解。後の believed women should be less restricted ... や encouraged women to ... なども手掛かりになる。

No.**14**解答 ①

　　質問の訳　ロンドンデリーが旅の途中でお金を稼いだ方法の1つは何か。
　　選択肢の訳　**1**　彼女は企業が自社製品を宣伝するのを手伝った。
　　　　　　　2　彼女は女性用の服を制作して販売した。
　　　　　　　3　彼女は湧き水会社を設立した。
　　　　　　　4　彼女は通常は男性が行う仕事に就いた。
　　解説　旅の途中でお金を稼いだ方法については，Along the way, Londonderry made money in various ways の後に including A and B が続き，お金を稼いださまざまな方法（various ways）の具体例が2つ述べられている。この後者 displaying companies' advertising posters on her bicycles と **1** が合う。

B

　スクリプト　**Barn Quilts**

Quilting involves sewing layers of fabric into patterns to create a warm, attractive blanket known as a quilt. On farms in some parts of the US, however, quilt patterns are also used for a different purpose: to create artwork on the side of barns. The practice of painting symbols on barns was first brought to the US in the 1800s by German immigrants, who believed the images would bring good fortune to their farms.

In 2001, one American woman decided to paint a quilt design on her barn to honor her mother, who had been a quilt maker. She encouraged other barn owners to decorate their barns with similar designs, now known as "barn quilts." This led to the creation of a "barn quilt trail" — a series of local barn quilts that visitors could view. Many communities now have such trails, and the boost to tourism has improved local economies.

Questions

No.15 What does the speaker say about the paintings made by German immigrants?

No.16 What has been one effect of "barn quilts" in the US?

全文訳 **バーンキルト**

キルティングとは，キルトとして知られる暖かくて魅力的な毛布を作るために布を何枚も重ねて模様に縫い合わせることである。しかし，アメリカの一部の地域の農場では，キルト模様は別の用途にも使われている。それは，納屋の側面に芸術品を生み出すことである。納屋に象徴を描くこの習慣は，1800年代に，それらの絵は農場に幸運をもたらすと信じていたドイツからの移民によって最初にアメリカに持ち込まれた。

2001年，あるアメリカ人女性が，キルト職人だった母親をしのんで，自分の納屋にキルトのデザインを描くことにした。彼女はほかの納屋の所有者にも，現在「バーンキルト」として知られる同様のデザインで納屋を装飾するよう呼びかけた。これが「バーンキルト・トレイル」──訪問者たちが見ることのできる一連の地域のバーンキルト──の誕生につながった。現在では，多くの地域社会に同様のトレイルがあり，観光事業への後押しが地域経済を活性化させている。

No.**15** 解答 ・・

質問の訳　話者はドイツからの移民が描いた絵について何と言っているか。

選択肢の訳　**1** その絵は彼らにドイツを思い起こさせた。

2 その絵はプロの芸術家によって作られた。

3 その絵は幸運をもたらすと信じられていた。

4 その絵は細長い布切れに描かれた。

解説　質問の German immigrants を含む箇所に手掛かりがある。German immigrants, who believed the images would bring good fortune to their farms から，**3**が正解。fortune を luck と表している。

No.**16** 解答 ②

質問の訳 アメリカの「バーンキルト」の影響の1つは何であるか。

選択肢の訳 1 より多くの人が趣味として裁縫を始めた。
2 一部の地域で観光事業が成長した。
3 農場間の競争が激化した。
4 より多くの納屋が農場に建てられた。

解説 "barn quilts" という語句が出てくる部分（..., now known as "barn quilts."）に続く説明に手掛かりがある。Many communities now ... the boost to tourism has improved local economies. から，**2** が正解。boost，improve，increase はどれもプラス（増）の意味を表す。

スクリプト **The Little Ice Age**

An era known as the Little Ice Age began in the fourteenth century and continued for around 500 years. Carbon dioxide levels in the atmosphere dropped considerably, which lowered air temperatures around the world. This resulted in reduced agricultural harvests worldwide. The traditional explanation is that this ice age came about due to erupting volcanoes and decreased solar activity.

However, according to more-recent research, farmland returning to forest may have been a major factor in the cooling of the planet. The native populations of North, Central, and South America had cleared large areas of forest for farming. When European colonists arrived in the late fifteenth century, they brought terrible illnesses. This caused the native populations to drop dramatically and left them unable to maintain the land. Researchers claim this resulted in a large increase in forest growth, which meant less carbon dioxide and a cooler planet.

Questions

No.17 What is true about the Little Ice Age?

No.18 According to more-recent research, what happened that led to the Little Ice Age?

全文訳 **小氷河期**

小氷河期として知られる時代は，14世紀に始まり，約500年間続いた。大気中の二酸化炭素濃度が大幅に低下し，それによって世界中の気温が下がった。この結果，世界的に農作物の収穫量が減少した。従来の説によると，この氷河期は，火山の噴火や太陽活動の低下によって生じたという。

しかし，最近の研究によると，農地が森林に戻ったことが，地球を寒冷化した大きな要因だった可能性がある。北アメリカ，中央アメリカ，南アメリカの先住民たちは，農業のために広大な面積の森林を伐採していた。ヨーロッパの入植者が15世紀後半に到

着したとき，彼らはひどい病気を持ち込んだ。これにより，先住民の人口は劇的に減少し，彼らは土地を維持できなくなった。この結果，森林が大きく成長し，二酸化炭素の減少と地球の寒冷化をもたらしたと研究者たちは主張している。

No.17 解答

質問の訳 小氷河期について何が正しいか。

選択肢の訳 1　1世紀弱続いた。
2　気象パターンに関する新たな発見につながった。
3　火山近くの人々に最も大きな影響を与えた。
4　農業に世界的な影響を与えた。

解説 小氷河期の説明部分で，世界中の気温が下がった結果として reduced agricultural harvests worldwide「世界的に農作物の収穫量が減少した」と言っている。これを had a global impact on farming「農業に世界的な影響を与えた」と表した **4** が正解。

No.18 解答 ②

質問の訳 最近の研究によると，小氷期は何が原因で起こったのか。

選択肢の訳 1　北アメリカのヨーロッパ人が大都市の建設を始めた。
2　森林がアメリカ大陸全体で拡大した。
3　世界人口の増加が汚染を増大させた。
4　病気がヨーロッパ全土で多くの木々を枯らした。

解説 従来の説ではなく最近の研究について問われている。小氷河期（地球の寒冷化）は農地が森林に戻ったことが要因だと述べ，その説明が続く。北アメリカ，中央アメリカ，南アメリカのアメリカ大陸全体（＝ across the Americas）で先住民が森林を伐採して農地にしていたが，入植者が持ち込んだ病気が原因で人口が激減し農地を維持できなくなり，森林が大きく成長した。よって，**2** が適切。a large increase in forest growth を Forests expanded と表している。

D

スクリプト **Disappearing Fireflies**

Fireflies are one of the most beloved insects because of their ability to create light, but firefly populations seem to be declining. The expansion of urban areas is a problem, not only because it destroys fireflies' habitats but also because of the constant artificial light in cities and suburbs. Fireflies attract mates by flashing their lights, so when these flashes become difficult to see, fireflies have trouble reproducing successfully.

Unfortunately, there have not been many studies of fireflies, in part because they are difficult to locate when they are not creating light. Scientists largely depend on information from amateurs, who report seeing fewer fireflies recently.

Fireflies' light-flashing patterns vary by species, and scientists are requesting that more people count firefly flashes and report their observations. In this way, scientists will be able to better track the various species.

Questions

No.19 What is one thing the speaker says is putting fireflies in danger?

No.20 What have scientists asked people to do?

全文訳　**消えゆくホタル**

　ホタルは，光を発する能力のため，最も愛されている昆虫の１つだが，ホタルの個体数は減少しているようだ。都市部の拡大が１つの問題で，それがホタルの生息地を破壊するからだけでなく，都市や郊外で常に人工的な光があることも理由である。ホタルは光を点滅させることで相手を引き寄せるため，これらの光が見えにくくなると，ホタルはうまく繁殖できなくなる。

　残念ながら，ホタルの研究はあまり行われていない。その理由の１つは，ホタルは光を発していないときに居場所を特定するのが難しいからだ。科学者たちは，最近ホタルを見かけなくなったと報告するアマチュアからの情報に大きく頼っている。ホタルの発光パターンは種によって異なるため，科学者たちは，より多くの人がホタルの発光を数え，その観察結果を報告するよう求めている。これにより，科学者たちはさまざまな種をより正確に追うことができるようになる。

No.19 解答 ③

質問の訳　話者は，ホタルを危険にさらしているものの１つは何だと言っているか。

選択肢の訳
1　成長している都市によって生じる騒音の増加。
2　ホタルを捕まえようとする人間の試み。
3　都市部の明るさ。
4　ほかの昆虫との高まる競争。

解説　質問の put ~ in danger はホタルの個体数減少の危機を指している。その要因として The expansion of <u>urban areas</u> と述べた後，さらに not only because ~ but also because of ... で理由が２つ続く。この後者 the constant artificial light in cities and suburbs「都市や郊外で常にある人工的な光」から，**3** が正解。

No.20 解答 ④

質問の訳　科学者たちは人々に何をするように求めているか。

選択肢の訳
1　光を発していないホタルの居場所を特定する。
2　科学者たちがより多くの研究資金を得るのを助ける。
3　家の周りで別の種類の明かりを使う。
4　人々が目にするどんなホタルについても報告する。

解説　scientists are requesting that more people ... に手掛かりがある。〈request that SV〉が質問では〈ask＋O＋to *do*〉で表されている。

people に続く count firefly flashes and report their observations から，**4** が正解。その前の科学者たちがアマチュアの情報に大きく頼っているという話も参考になる。**1** は，光を発していないホタルの居場所を特定するのは難しく，人々に求めていることではないので不適。

E

（スクリプト）**Smart Dogs**

Dogs can be taught to respond to many words. For example, they can obey commands to sit or roll over. But do dogs actually process and understand words in the same way humans do? One team of researchers attempted to investigate this question. The researchers wanted to gather data directly from dogs themselves rather than from their owners' reports, so they used an imaging machine to scan dogs' brains while the dogs heard different words.

Before the scan, the dogs, which were of various breeds, were taught certain words. While the dogs were in the machine, the words they had been taught and words they did not know were both spoken to them. Surprisingly, the dogs' brains showed more activity after they heard the unfamiliar words. This is the reverse of a human response — our brains are more active in response to words we know.

Questions

No.21 What was the purpose of the research?

No.22 What did the researchers discover about the dogs' brain activity?

（全文訳）**賢い犬**

犬は多くの言葉に反応するよう教えることができる。例えば，犬はお座りや寝返りを打ちなさいという命令に従うことができる。しかし，犬は実際，人間と同じように言葉を処理し，理解しているのだろうか。ある研究チームがこの疑問を調査しようと試みた。研究者たちは，飼い主の報告からではなく，犬自身から直接データを集めたいと考え，犬がさまざまな言葉を聞く間，画像装置を使って犬の脳をスキャンした。

スキャンを行う前に，さまざまな品種の犬に特定の言葉を教えた。犬がその装置内にいる間，教えられた言葉と知らない言葉の両方を犬に聞かせた。驚いたことに，犬の脳は，知らない言葉を聞いた後の方がより活発な動きを見せた。これは人間の反応とは逆である —— 私たちの脳は，知っている言葉に対しての方がより活発になる。

No.21 解答

（質問の訳）研究の目的は何だったか。

（選択肢の訳）
1　犬の言葉の理解を調べるため。
2　犬の異なる声への反応を調べるため。
3　犬を訓練するさまざまな方法を調べるため。
4　犬が飼い主の感情にどう反応するかを調べるため。

But do dogs actually process and understand words in the same way humans do? 「しかし，犬は実際，人間と同じように言葉を処理し，理解しているのだろうか」と疑問を投げかけた後，One team of researchers ... から，ある研究チームがその答えを探すために研究をしたことが分かる。よって，研究目的として**1**が適切。

No.22解答

質問の訳 研究者たちは犬の脳の活動について何を発見したか。

選択肢の訳 1 飼い主の報告と一致していた。
2 犬種によって異なった。
3 人間の脳の活動と逆だった。
4 知っている命令に対して活発になった。

解説 Surprisingly, ... 以下で研究結果が述べられている。This is the reverse of a human response から，**3**が正解。**3**の that は質問の brain activity のことで，reverse を opposite に言い換えている。知っている言葉に対してより活発になる人間の脳と混同して**4**を選ばないように。

F

スクリプト **Root Cellars**

Elliston is a village on the Canadian island of Newfoundland. Its long winters mean preserving and storing food has always been an important part of life there. Traditionally, local people accomplished this by using root cellars, which are tunnel-like structures in the sides of small hills. They are called root cellars because they commonly hold root vegetables, such as potatoes and carrots. The root cellars maintain the perfect temperature and moisture levels for preserving the vegetables.

Root cellars can be found in many places with long winters. However, Elliston is known as the "Root Cellar Capital of the World." For much of its history, the village was a fishing town. But when commercial fishing was banned after a decline in fish populations, Elliston's residents needed a new source of income. They decided to promote their root cellars as an attraction, and today, visitors come from all over to see them.

Questions

No.23 What is one thing the speaker says about root cellars?

No.24 What is one reason root cellars are important in Elliston today?

全文訳 **ルートセラー**

エリストンは，カナダのニューファンドランド島にある村である。そこの冬は長いため，食料の保存と貯蔵が常にその地の生活の重要な部分である。伝統的に，その土地の人々は，小さな丘の斜面にあるトンネルのような構造をしたルートセラー（根菜類貯蔵

室）を使うことでこれを実現した。それは，一般にジャガイモやニンジンなどの根菜を保存することから，ルートセラーと呼ばれている。ルートセラーは，野菜を保存するのに最適な温度と湿度を保つ。

　ルートセラーは，冬が長い多くの場所で見られる。しかし，エリストンは「世界のルートセラーの都」として知られている。その歴史の大半において，この村は漁村だった。しかし，魚の数が減少した後，商業漁業が禁止されると，エリストンの住民たちは新たな収入源を必要とした。彼らはルートセラーを呼び物として宣伝することに決め，今日では，各地から観光客がルートセラーを見にやって来る。

No.23 解答　**2** ·······················

質問の訳　話者がルートセラーについて言うことの1つは何か。

選択肢の訳　**1**　人々が冬に暖かさを保つのに役立つ。
　　　　　2　野菜を貯蔵するのに役立つ。
　　　　　3　名前はその形に由来する。
　　　　　4　1年を通して野菜を栽培するのに使われる。

解説　タイトルの Root Cellars が何かを探りながら聞き始めよう。冒頭の Elliston は村の名前で，その村では長い冬に備えて食料を保存，貯蔵するのに root cellar を使った。they commonly hold root vegetables, such as potatoes and carrots から，root cellar に保存したのは主に根菜だったので，**2** が正解。その後の preserving the vegetables もヒントになる。

No.24 解答　**1** ·······················

質問の訳　今日のエリストンでルートセラーが重要である理由の1つは何か。

選択肢の訳　**1**　地域経済を支えるのに役立つ。
　　　　　2　周辺の村に模範を示す。
　　　　　3　漁業の存続を助ける。
　　　　　4　貴重な鉱物を含むことが分かった。

解説　ルートセラーはほかの地域にもあるが，なぜエリストンで有名なのかを聞き取る。For much of its history, ... から，長い間漁村だったエリストンは，商業漁業が禁止されると，新たな収入源としてルートセラーを利用したことが分かる。各地から観光客が見にくることから，ルートセラーが地域経済活性化に貢献していると判断できるので，**1** が正解。

G

 スクリプト

You have 10 seconds to read the situation and Question No. 25.

The bus downtown leaves every half hour, and you can take a taxi from the taxi stand at any time. However, all the streets going to the center of town are very busy at this time of day. It's likely to take more than 40 minutes. The subway leaves every 5 to 10 minutes from the underground station. It's a 15-minute ride from the airport to downtown. You can also take the light-rail train. It's slower than the subway but provides a nice view of the city.

Now mark your answer on your answer sheet.

全文訳

市街地へのバスは30分おきに出ており，タクシーはタクシー乗り場からいつでも乗れます。ただ，この時間帯は街の中心部に向かう通りはどこも大変混雑しています。40分以上かかると思われます。地下鉄は地下の駅から5〜10分おきに出ています。空港から市街地までは15分の乗車です。ライトレールもご利用いただけます。地下鉄より遅いですが，街の素敵な風景を眺めることができます。

No.25 解答 ····································· 正答率 ★75%以上

状況の訳 あなたは空港に着陸したばかりである。できるだけ早く市街地に行く必要がある。案内所で次のように言われる。

質問の訳 あなたはどのようにして市街地に行くべきか。

選択肢の訳
1 バスで。
2 地下鉄で。
3 タクシーで。
4 ライトレールで。

解説 問題用紙の「状況」と選択肢から，できるだけ早く市街地に行くにはどの交通手段がよいか聞き取ろう。4の light-rail は知らなくても交通手段の1種だと分かれば問題ない。まずバスとタクシーは，道が混んでいて40分以上かかる。地下鉄は5〜10分おきで，所要時間は15分。ライトレールは地下鉄より（速度が）遅い＝時間がかかる。よって，条件に最も合うのは地下鉄。

H

 スクリプト

You have 10 seconds to read the situation and Question No. 26.

We offer several courses. Giovanni's introductory course on Monday evenings is ideal if this will be your first experience learning Italian. Martina's course on Tuesdays is for businesspeople looking to develop their written fluency in Italian to an advanced level. It's not suitable for beginners. Alfredo's intermediate course on Thursdays is suitable for people who want to improve their language skills in just a few months. Finally, Teresa's course on Fridays is for people who want to learn Italian and Italian culture through operas. This is a popular course, so I recommend registering today if you are interested.

Now mark your answer on your answer sheet.

全文訳

当校は幾つかの講座を提供しています。月曜日夜のジョバンニの入門講座は，イタリア語を学ぶのが初めての場合，最適です。火曜日のマルティナの講座は，イタリア語で流ちょうに書く能力を上級レベルまで伸ばしたいビジネスパーソン向けです。初学者の方には不向きです。木曜日のアルフレードの中級講座は，わずか数カ月で語学力を向上させたい方に適しています。最後に，金曜日のテレサの講座は，オペラを通してイタリア語とイタリア文化を学びたい人のためのものです。こちらは人気の講座なので，興味があれば今日中に登録することをお勧めします。

No.26 解答 ④

状況の訳 あなたはイタリア語を少し話すが，3カ月後のイタリアでの休暇の前に磨きをかけたいと思っている。月曜日と木曜日が空いている。語学学校の担当者が次のように言う。

質問の訳 あなたはどの講座を選ぶべきか。

選択肢の訳 1 マルティナの講座。
2 ジョバンニの講座。
3 テレサの講座。
4 アルフレードの講座。

解説 選択肢の4人の講座のうち，誰の講座が「イタリア語を少し話す」「休暇まで3カ月ある」「月曜日と木曜日がよい」の条件を全て満たすか。月曜日のジョバンニの講座は初学者向けなので不適。マルティナは火曜日なので不適。木曜日のアルフレードは数カ月で語学力の向上が期待できるのでこれが適切。テレサは金曜日なので不適。

I

スクリプト

You have 10 seconds to read the situation and Question No. 27.

Good morning, shoppers. Today is the Mayfield Mall 15th Anniversary Sale. Check out the first-floor shops for huge discounts on kids' clothing and back-to-school items. All business wear on the second floor, including suits and shoes, is 50 percent off. And don't forget the sporting goods center on the third floor, where we're offering 25 percent off every item. Remember, discounts are only available for shoppers who have registered for the sale at the fourth-floor kiosk. By registering, you will receive a card that you can present at all participating shops.

Now mark your answer on your answer sheet.

全文訳

　お買い物中の皆さま，おはようございます。本日，メイフィールドモール15周年記念セールを開催しています。子供服や新学期用品が大幅に割引されている1階の店にぜひお越しください。2階のビジネスウエアは，スーツや靴を含め，全品50%オフです。また，3階のスポーツ用品センターもお見逃しなく。そこでは全商品が25%オフとなっております。なお，割引は，4階のキオスクでセールへの参加登録をされたお客さまのみに適用されることをご承知おきください。ご登録いただくと，全参加店で提示できるカードが受け取れます。

No.27 解答

状況の訳　あなたは新しいビジネススーツを買いにショッピングモールに着いたばかりである。できるだけお金を節約したいと思っている。次のようなアナウンスが聞こえる。

質問の訳　あなたはまず何階に行くべきか。

選択肢の訳　**1**　1階。
　　　　　　2　2階。
　　　　　　3　3階。
　　　　　　4　4階。

解説　できるだけ安くビジネススーツを買うにはまず何階に行くべきか。1階は子供服や新学期用品なので不適。ビジネスウエアを扱っている2階がよさそうで，3階はスポーツ用品なので不適。続きを聞くと，Remember, discounts are ... から，割引は4階で登録した人だけに適用されると分かる。つまり，安く買うためにはまず4階へ行くべきである。

J

You have 10 seconds to read the situation and Question No. 28.

Welcome to All Adventures Park. Unfortunately, due to repairs, the walk-through reptile attraction Lizard Encounter will be closed until further notice. Our space-themed roller coaster, Into the Sky, has also suspended operation today due to strong winds. We apologize for the inconvenience. Please note, however, that our ranger-guided drive-through safari, Discovery Drive, is operating as usual, and most of the animals will be outdoors and visible. Finally, don't forget to check out the park's newest addition, Dream Fields, where guests can use VR technology to experience the game of baseball like never before!

Now mark your answer on your answer sheet.

オール・アドベンチャーズ・パークにようこそ。残念ながら，修理のため，ウォークスルー系の爬虫類アトラクション，リザード・エンカウンターは，追って通知があるまで休業します。宇宙をテーマにしたジェットコースター，イントゥ・ザ・スカイも，強風のため，本日は運行を一時停止しています。ご不便をおかけして申し訳ございません。なお，レンジャーが案内するライド系サファリ，ディスカバリー・ドライブは通常通り営業しており，ほとんどの動物が屋外の見える所にいます。最後に，パークに新しく加わったドリーム・フィールズも忘れずにチェックしてください。そこでは，来場者の皆さんは，バーチャルリアリティー技術を使ってこれまでにない野球の試合が体験できます！

No.28 解答 ② ‥‥‥‥‥‥‥‥‥‥‥‥‥‥‥‥‥‥ 正答率 ★75%以上

状況の訳 あなたは家族でテーマパークにいる。子供たちは動物と自然にとても興味がある。次のようなアナウンスが聞こえる。

質問の訳 あなたたちはどのアトラクションへ行くべきか。

選択肢の訳
1 リザード・エンカウンター。
2 ディスカバリー・ドライブ。
3 イントゥ・ザ・スカイ。
4 ドリーム・フィールズ。

解説 選択肢のアトラクションのうち，動物と自然に関するものに焦点を絞って聞こう。リザード・エンカウンターは動物と自然にかかわりそうだが，現在休業中。イントゥ・ザ・スカイも本日一時停止中。ディスカバリー・ドライブは営業中で，動物が見られるのでこれが適切。最後のドリーム・フィールズも営業しているが，動物と自然に関係ない。

K

You have 10 seconds to read the situation and Question No. 29.

Parents, I'd like to introduce the faculty members in charge of the new after-school activities. Mr. Gilbert will be teaching students table tennis once a week on Fridays. Ms. DeLuca is in charge of the swimming club, which will meet on Mondays and Thursdays. Mr. Roth will be sharing his expertise in music by giving clarinet lessons every Wednesday. And Ms. Santos will be available in the library for study group to help students with their homework on Tuesdays and Thursdays. Please speak to the appropriate faculty member for further details.

Now mark your answer on your answer sheet.

全文訳

　保護者の皆さま，新しい放課後活動を担当する教員たちをご紹介します。ギルバート先生は週に１回，金曜日に，生徒たちに卓球を指導されます。デルーカ先生は水泳クラブのご担当で，月曜日と木曜日に活動があります。ロス先生は，毎週水曜日にクラリネットのレッスンを行うことで，ご自身の音楽の専門知識を共有されます。また，サントス先生は，生徒たちの宿題を手伝う勉強会のために，火曜日と木曜日に図書館におられます。詳しくは，担当の教員とお話しください。

No.29 解答 ①

状況の訳　あなたは息子に新しい技能を習得してほしいと思っている。息子はすでに水曜日の放課後に水泳レッスンを受けている。学校の管理者が次のような発表をする。

質問の訳　あなたは誰と話すべきか。

選択肢の訳　**1**　ギルバート先生。
　　　　　　2　デルーカ先生。
　　　　　　3　ロス先生。
　　　　　　4　サントス先生。

解説　状況から，「新しい技能を習得する」「すでに水曜日に水泳レッスンを受けている」を押さえる。最初のギルバート先生の卓球は金曜日（＝水曜日ではない）ので，これが条件に合いそうである。念のため続きを聞くと，デルーカ先生の水泳はすでに習っているので不適。ロス先生のレッスンは水曜日なので不適。サントス先生の宿題の支援は，条件の「新しい技能を習得する」に合わない。よって，ギルバート先生と話すべきと決まる。

解答例 **One day, a company president was walking around the office.** He passed the break room, where a couple of employees were drinking coffee and chatting. He heard one of them say, "I've been feeling tired lately." The president was surprised to hear this. That afternoon, he was in his office reading an article. The article was saying that naps boost worker performance, and this gave the president an idea. A month later, the company president was checking on the company's new nap room. The president was happy to see that several employees were using the room to take a nap and become refreshed. The next day, the company president was in a meeting. An employee ran into the meeting room because he was late for the meeting. He looked like he had just woken up, and he said that he had forgotten to set an alarm.

解答例の訳 ある日，会社の社長が社内を歩いていました。彼が休憩室を通りかかると，２人の従業員がコーヒーを飲みながらおしゃべりをしていました。彼は，そのうちの１人が「最近疲れているんだ」と言うのを耳にしました。社長はこれを聞いて驚きました。その日の午後，彼は社長室である記事を読んでいました。その記事には，仮眠が労働者の仕事の能率を上げると書かれており，これにより社長はあるアイデアを思い付きました。１カ月後，社長は会社の新しい仮眠室の様子を見ていました。社長は，数人の従業員が仮眠を取り，気分転換するためにその部屋を利用しているのを見て喜びました。翌日，社長は会議に出席していました。１人の従業員が会議に遅れたので，会議室に駆け込んできました。彼はちょうど目が覚めた様子で，アラームをセットし忘れたと言いました。

解説 各コマで押さえるべき点は，①従業員が「最近疲れている」と言うのを社長が聞いている，②その日の午後，社長が「仮眠が労働者の仕事の能率を上げる」と書かれた記事を読んでいる，③１カ月後，社長が仮眠室の様子を見ている，④翌日，従業員が「アラームをセットし忘れました」と言って会議室に入ってくる。社長が記事から得たアイデアを実践したが，問題が生じたという展開を押さえよう。１コマ目の様子は〈hear＋O＋say〉「Oが〜と言うのを聞く」で表せる。吹き出し内のせりふは１コマ目を描写した He heard one of them say, "I've ... のようにそのまま使って直接話法で表す方法と，４コマ目を描写した he said that he had forgotten ... のように間接話法で表す方法がある。

133

No. 1

解答例 I'd be thinking, "It's natural that people need some time to get used to using the nap room. It will improve our productivity in the long term. For now, I can just send out a reminder about not oversleeping."

解説 質問は「4番目の絵を見てください。もしあなたがこの社長なら、どのようなことを考えているでしょうか」。解答例は、仮眠室に慣れるまで時間がかかるが、長期的には生産性が向上すると前向きな意見を述べた後、具体的な対策を挙げている。boost worker performance → improve our productivity のような言い換えができると高評価につながるだろう。

No. 2

解答例 No. It's more important for people to find a career that interests them personally. Being interested makes people feel passion for their work, and this allows them to become much better workers.

解説 質問は「職業を選択する際、給料は最も重要な要素だと思いますか」。No の立場の場合、質問の最上級 the most important を受けて、給料より重要だと思う要素を more important を使って表すことができる。解答例の「個人的に興味のある職業」のほか、「やりがいのある職業」「ストレスの少ない職業」などを挙げ、その理由を説明するとよい。

No. 3

解答例 Definitely. People have gotten worse at thinking for themselves. These days, people tend to believe everything that is reported in the news. People need to think more critically about the truth of media reports.

解説 質問は「人々の意見はあまりにもメディアに影響されやすいですか」。解答例の Definitely. は強い同意を表す。These days, people ... で最近の傾向を述べた後、メディア報道の真偽をもっと批判的に考える必要があることを訴えている。質問の the media は、マスメディアのほか social media などインターネットメディアの観点で述べてもよいだろう。

No. 4

解答例 Yes. In recent years, many companies have been taking advantage of their workers. It's very difficult for many workers to protect themselves, so the government needs to make sure that companies follow the law.

解説 質問は「労働者の権利を守るために政府はもっと努力すべきですか」。解答例は Yes の立場で、近年の状況を述べた後、so「だから」を用いて、政府がすべきこととして「多くの労働者にとって自分を守ることは難しいので、政府は企業が法律を守るようにする必要がある」と述べている。

解答例 **One day, a girl was walking home from school.** She passed by a skate park and looked around. Some kids were skateboarding there. There was a boy doing a big jump on his skateboard, and the girl was quite impressed. She thought that skateboarding was really cool. The next day, the girl was at home talking with her parents. She told them that she wanted to start skateboarding. Her mother looked a little worried about it, but they decided to let her get a skateboard. A month later, the girl was skateboarding at the skate park. She was practicing hard to learn how to skateboard. One of the other kids at the park was cheering her on. A week later, though, the girl was in the hospital. She had injured herself, and a nurse was putting a bandage on her head. Her mother looked very upset and said that she wasn't allowed to skateboard anymore.

解答例の訳 ある日，少女が学校から歩いて帰宅していました。彼女はスケートボード場を通りかかり，辺りを見回しました。そこでは何人かの子供がスケートボードをしていました。スケートボードで大ジャンプをしている少年がいて，少女はとても感心しました。彼女は，スケートボードは本当に格好いいと思いました。翌日，少女は家で両親と話していました。彼女はスケートボードを始めたいと彼らに言いました。母親はそれについて少し心配そうでしたが，両親は彼女にスケートボードを買ってやることにしました。1カ月後，少女はスケートボード場でスケートボードをしていました。彼女はスケートボードの乗り方を覚えようと一生懸命練習していました。スケートボード場のほかの子供の1人が彼女を応援していました。しかし1週間後，少女は病院にいました。彼女はけがをしており，看護師が彼女の頭に包帯を巻いていました。母親はとても憤慨した様子で，もうスケートボードをやってはいけないと言いました。

解説 各コマで押さえるべき点は，①少女がスケートボード場でスケートボードをしている子供たちを見ている，②翌日，少女が両親にスケートボードについて話している，③1カ月後，少女がスケートボードを楽しんでいる，④1週間後，けがをした少女が病院で手当てを受けていて，母親が「スケートボードはもう止めなさい！」と言っている。2コマ目の場面は両親への説得，4コマ目のけがはスケートボードが原因だと推測しよう。解答例を参考に，少女以外の人物の行動や表情にも着目して，各コマ3文程度で説明する練習をしておくとよい。

No. 1

解答例 I'd be thinking that it isn't fair for my mom to stop me from skateboarding. My injury isn't so serious. It's more important that I stay active and make a lot of friends at the skate park.

解説 質問は「4番目の絵を見てください。もしあなたがこの少女なら，どのようなことを考えているでしょうか」。解答例は，「スケートボードをやめさせられるのは公平ではない」と反発の気持ちを表した後，「友だちを作る」というスケートボードを続ける目的を述べている。「母親の言う通りだ」「親に心配をかけるべきではない」などの考えもあり得る。

No. 2

解答例 Yes, I think so. Children perform better in school with support from their parents. Parents can talk to their children about school, and they can give them good advice about their classes and social life.

解説 質問は「親が子供の学校生活に参加することは重要ですか」。解答例はYes の立場で，理由として「親のサポートで成績が向上する」「親は子供に授業や社会生活について良い助言ができる」などと述べている。No の立場では，親の過干渉が子供の自立を妨げるなどの理由が可能。

No. 3

解答例 Definitely. Many sports help children to learn the value of teamwork, and they also teach the importance of hard work and practice. These lessons will help them to successfully achieve their goals in the future.

解説 質問は「スポーツをすることは，若者が強い個性を形成するのに良い方法ですか」。Yes の立場では，スポーツをすることのメリットを根拠にするとよい。解答例は，子供はチームワーク，努力と練習の重要性を学ぶことができ，それらは将来目標を達成するのに役立つという意見。the value [importance] of は「～の重要性」の意味。

No. 4

解答例 No. Many different nations have to work together to hold large events like the Olympics, but such relationships are only temporary. In the end, these events don't have a lasting effect on political relations.

解説 質問は「オリンピックなどの国際イベントは国家間の関係を向上させることができると思いますか」。解答例はNo の立場で，オリンピックなどのイベントで築いた関係は一時的なもので，政治関係に永続的な影響を与えないという意見。Yes の立場では逆に，develop relations of friendship and trust「友好・信頼関係を発展させる」という観点で話せるだろう。

2022-2

解 答 一 覧

一次試験・筆記

1

(1)	2	(10)	2	(19)	4
(2)	4	(11)	1	(20)	3
(3)	2	(12)	1	(21)	4
(4)	2	(13)	1	(22)	1
(5)	4	(14)	3	(23)	3
(6)	2	(15)	1	(24)	1
(7)	2	(16)	4	(25)	3
(8)	4	(17)	4		
(9)	3	(18)	4		

2

(26)	2	(29)	2
(27)	4	(30)	3
(28)	1	(31)	2

3

(32)	4	(35)	4	(38)	4
(33)	1	(36)	4	(39)	1
(34)	2	(37)	1	(40)	3
				(41)	3

4　　解答例は本文参照

一次試験・リスニング

Part 1

No. 1	4	No. 5	3	No. 9	3
No. 2	4	No. 6	1	No.10	2
No. 3	2	No. 7	2	No.11	2
No. 4	2	No. 8	1	No.12	4

Part 2

No.13	3	No.17	1	No.21	1
No.14	1	No.18	4	No.22	1
No.15	4	No.19	3	No.23	2
No.16	3	No.20	2	No.24	4

Part 3

No.25	3	No.28	3
No.26	4	No.29	2
No.27	2		

(1) —解答 ②

訳 A：お母さん，今夜の夕食にハンバーガーを作ってくれない？

B：いいけど，まず肉を冷凍庫から出して，それを解凍しなきゃね。

解説 〈let＋O＋動詞の原形〉「O に～させる」の O ＝ it は肉のこと。ハンバーガーを作るのに肉を冷凍庫から出して「解凍する」必要があることから，thaw が適切。reckon「計算する」，stray「道に迷う」，shatter「粉々に壊れる」

(2) —解答 ④

訳 ジョセリンはいつも息子にうそをつかないよう言い聞かせた。彼女は，彼に正直であるという強い感覚を植え付けることが大切だと信じていた。

解説 it is ～ to *do*「…することは～だ」の構文で，目的語 sense「感覚」に合う動詞は instill「（主義・思想などを）植え付ける」。remodel「作り替える」，stumble「つまずく」，overlap「一部を覆う，部分的に重なる」

(3) —解答 ②

訳 ザラは彼氏にとても腹を立てていたが，彼の真剣な謝罪を聞いて彼を許した。彼女は彼が本当に申し訳ないと思っていると確信した。

解説 apology「謝罪」を修飾する形容詞はどれか。彼氏を許したことから，彼の謝罪は真剣な（earnest）ものだったと想像できる。detectable「検出できる」，cumulative「累積的な」，underlying「潜在的な」

(4) —解答 ②

訳 最初のうちは，スミス夫妻は裏庭のプールを楽しんでいたが，きれいに保つのが面倒になったので，たいていの場合カバーをしたままにした。

解説 〈such＋原因＋that＋結果〉の構造。2 つの it はプールのことで，カバーをしたままなのは，きれいに保つのが厄介（nuisance）になったから。bureau「（行政組織の）局」，sequel「続編」，metaphor「隠喩」

(5) —解答 ④

訳 歴史を通して，多くの偉大な思想家たちは，最初はその考えゆえに嘲笑されたが，最終的には真剣に受け止められた。

解説 at first と eventually の対比に着目し，嘲笑された（were ridiculed）→ 真剣に受け止められた，という流れが適切。それぞれ saturate「満たす」，flatter「お世辞を言う」，ingest「（食べ物・薬などを）摂取する」の過去分詞。なお，本文の A before B「B する前に A した」は「A し，そして B した」という意味に取るとよい。

(6) —解答 ②

訳 その少女は最初，スピーチコンテストで大勢の聴衆を前に恥ずかしく感

じていたが，1分ほどすると自信を持ち始めた。

解説 〈feel＋形容詞〉「～に感じる」が but の前にも後ろにもあり，対照的な意味になっている。confident に対比する bashful「恥ずかしがりやの」が適切。mortal「死すべき」，pious「信心深い」，concise「簡潔な」

(7) ― 解答 ②

訳 タイプライターは過去の遺物である。オフィスや家庭で一般的に使われていた時代からどれほどテクノロジーが進歩したかを思い知らされる。

解説 タイプライターは，テクノロジーが進歩した今となっては過去の物である。よって，relic「（過去の）遺跡，遺物」が適切。jumble「ごちゃ混ぜ」，fraud「詐欺」，treaty「条約」

(8) ― 解答 ④

訳 男性がトラの檻（おり）に近づくと，その巨大な動物が低くうなった。男性はその恐ろしい声に恐れをなして後ずさりした。

解説 空所には主語 the huge animal = tiger に対する自動詞が入る。第2文の the terrifying sound を手掛かりに，growl「うなる」の過去形 growled が適切。それぞれ sparkle「輝く」，leer「いやらしい目つきで見る」，disprove「反証する」の過去形。

(9) ― 解答 ③

訳 警察官は法律を守ることを約束しなければならない。もちろん，これには彼ら自身が法律に従うことも含まれる。

解説 目的語 the law に合う動詞は uphold「（法律などを）支持する，守る」。第2文の themselves は警察官のことで，uphold the law と follow the law が同義になる。gravitate「引き付けられる」，detach「分離する」，eradicate「根絶する，撲滅する」

(10) ― 解答 ②

訳 従業員は全員，毎年義務的な健康診断を受ける。各会社は，労働者全員が確実にそれを行うようにすることを法律で義務付けられている。

解説 第2文の be required by law to do は「～するよう法律で定められて［義務付けられて］いる」という意味で，medical checkup「健康診断」を修飾する形容詞として compulsory「義務的な」が適切。gloomy「憂鬱（ゆううつ）にさせる」，reminiscent「連想させる」，muddled「混乱した」

(11) ― 解答 ①

訳 生物学の学生は，細胞分裂がどのように機能しているかを学ばなければならない。その理由は，単一の細胞が2つに分裂するこの過程が自然界で一般的に見られるためである。

解説 how ... は間接疑問で，cell （ ）が S，works が V。後の a single cell splitting into two「単一の細胞が2つに分裂する」から，cell division「細胞分裂」とするのが適切。division の動詞形 divide は

split と同義。appliance「電化製品」, imposition「強制, （税などを）課すこと」, longitude「経度」

(12) – 解答 ①

訳 2つの会社が合併した後, 何人かの上級社員は不要になり, 職を失った。

解説 何人かの上級社員が職を失ったのは, 2つの会社が合併した（merged）からである。それぞれ pose「ポーズをとる」, conform「（習慣などに）従う」, flock「集まる」の過去形。

(13) – 解答 ①　　　　　　　　　　　　　　　　正答率 ★75%以上

訳 運動中に脱水症状になるのを避けるためには, 常に十分な水を飲むべきである。運動時間が長ければ長いほど, より多くの水が必要である。

解説 運動中に水を飲むのは脱水症状を避けるためである。become dehydrated で「脱水症状になる」の意味。dehydrated は動詞 dehydrate「脱水症状にする」の過去分詞（形容詞用法）。eternal「永遠の」, punctuated は punctuate「句読点を付ける」の過去分詞, cautious「用心深い」

(14) – 解答 ③　　　　　　　　　　　　　　　　正答率 ★75%以上

訳 ケンは家ではいつも行儀が良かったので, 彼の先生が彼はクラスで最も反抗的な生徒の1人だと言ったとき, 彼の母親はショックを受けた。

解説 母親がショックを受けた理由は, 行儀が良いはずの息子がクラスでは反抗的な（disobedient）生徒だと言われたからである。momentary「瞬間的な」, miniature「小規模の」, invincible「無敵の」

(15) – 解答 ①　　　　　　　　　　　　　　　　正答率 ★75%以上

訳 警察は, 近くにいた誰かが何が起こったかを見ていたことを期待して, 犯行現場の見物人に質問した。

解説 選択肢には人を表す語が並んでいる。犯行現場近くにいた人に質問したと考えて, bystanders「傍観者, 見物人」が適切。それぞれ reformer「改革者」, mourner「追悼者」, pioneer「先駆者」の複数形。

(16) – 解答 ④

訳 何人かの将軍がその国の首相を打倒しようと試みた。しかし, 彼らは成功せず, 彼は権力の座にとどまっている。

解説 However に着目し, 首相を打倒し（overthrow）ようとしたが失敗した, という流れにするのが自然。they は Several generals, he は the country's prime minister を指す。irrigate「かんがいする」, harmonize「調和させる」, outpace「追い越す」

(17) – 解答 ④

訳 カレブは, 企画書の草稿を完成させたので, 上司にそれを評価するよう依頼した。残念ながら, 彼女はまだ多くの改善が必要だと思った。

解説 文中の he は Caleb, she は his manager を指す。2つの it は a draft of his proposal のことで，上司に企画書を評価する（evaluate）よう頼んだ結果が第2文に書かれている。scrub「ごしごし洗う」，enchant「大いに喜ばせる」，prune「刈り込む」

(18) – 解答 **4** ....

訳 アメリカの大統領であるトーマス・ジェファソンとジョン・アダムズは，50年以上にわたって手紙を交換し合った。この文通は，アメリカの歴史の重要な部分である。

解説 第1文の exchanged letters with each other を名詞で表した correspondence「文通」が適切。matrimony「婚姻」，federation「連合」，horizon「地平線」

(19) – 解答 **4** ....

訳 暴動の間，町は混乱状態だった。人々は通りに出てけんかをしたり窓を割ったりし，多くの店が強盗に遭った。

解説 暴動の間の町の様子が第2文に書かれている。その内容から，町は混乱（anarchy）していたと分かる。disclosure「暴露」，admittance「入場（許可）」，attainment「達成，獲得」

(20) – 解答 **3** .... 正答率 ★**75%以上**

訳 一部の植物の花は実際に食べることができ，サラダをより美味しくするだけでなく視覚的により魅力的にするためにも使うことができる。

解説 空所後に「（一部の植物の花は）サラダをより美味しくする」とあることから，edible「食べることができる」が適切。both A and B は「A も B も」のほか，「A だけでなく B もまた」の意味にもなる。stationary「動かない」，candid「率直な」，hideous「恐ろしい」

(21) – 解答 **4** ....

訳 その有名な科学者が講演中に多くの間違いを犯したとき，誰も驚かなかった。彼は話術が乏しいことで有名だ。

解説 第2文は第1文の理由。誰もが科学者の乏しい話術を知っているので，多くの間違いを犯しても誰も驚かなかったのである。notorious は「悪名高い」の意味で，*be* notorious for で「～（悪いこと）で有名だ」。treacherous「不誠実な」，momentous「重大な」，flirtatious「軽薄な，浮気な」

(22) – 解答 **1** ....

訳 ブラッドの上司が先月彼を昇進させたとき，彼の努力や長時間労働が全て報われた。

解説 主語 ... hard work and long hours に対する動詞として，pay off「報われる」の過去形が適切。それぞれ write back「返事を書く」，chop up「～を細かく切る」，make over「～を作り直す」の過去形。

(23) 解答 3

訳 CEO の演説があまりに漠然としていたため、ジーナは会社が深刻な財政難に陥っているという事実を理解するのにしばらく時間がかかった。

解説 演説が漠然としていたという状況から、「理解」に時間がかかったと推測できる。catch on to で「～（意味など）を理解する」という意味。fill in「代理をする」、duck out「こっそり外に出る、急いで立ち去る」、give up「諦める」はいずれも〈to＋名詞〉が続かない。

(24) 解答 1

訳 チームのメンバーは各自、新しいプロジェクトのためにやるべき仕事を持っているが、彼らの努力の全てをまとめ上げる責任はマネージャーにある。

解説 each と all に着目して、but 前後の対比をつかもう。主語 responsibility「責任」と目的語 the manager に合う動詞は、fall on「（責任などが）～に降りかかる」。それぞれ square with「～と一致する」、drop by「～に立ち寄る」、stack up「～を積み重ねる」の3人称単数・現在形。

(25) 解答 3

訳 その従業員は、自分の罪を証明するファイルやその他の証拠を隠滅することで、会社からの窃盗を隠蔽しようとした。

解説 by destroying ... は、( ) his theft from the company「会社からの窃盗を( )する」ための手段である。目的語の his theft に合うのは、cover up「～（罪）を隠す」である。tuck away「～をしまい込む」、latch onto「～をつかむ」、doze off「うたた寝する」

一次試験・筆記 **2** | 問題編 p.118～121

全文訳 ナブタ・プラヤのストーンサークル

　多くの先史時代の社会がストーンサークルを建設した。これらは、太陽の動きを観測するためなど、さまざまな理由で作られた。このようなストーンサークルの中でも最古のものとして科学者たちに知られているのが、エジプトのナブタ・プラヤにある。約7,000年前のものであるこのストーンサークルは、おそらく世界で最も有名な先史時代のストーンサークルであるイングランドのストーンヘンジよりも1,000年以上前に作られた。ナブタ・プラヤの気候は現在では非常に乾燥しているが、これは常にそうだったわけではなかった。実際、ストーンサークルが建設された時期の季節的な豪雨は一時的な湖の形成につながり、これが牛を放牧する部族をこの地域に引き寄せた。

　ナブタ・プラヤの最初の入植者たちは、約1万年前に来た。考古学者たちは、これらの入植者たちが深い井戸のシステムを作って一年中水が得られるようにしたこと、また住居を真っすぐに並べて配置し、それらに保管スペースを備えていたことの証拠を発見

した。また，入植者たちは，彼らの生活に不可欠であった牛の崇拝に重きを置いた宗教を実践していた。これらの発見は，入植者たちが高度な社会を築いていた証拠である。

　研究結果は，約 7,000 年前，ストーンサークルの石の一部が 1 年で最も日が長い日に太陽に向かって一直線に並ぶようになっていたことを示している。これはストーンサークルが暦として使用されていたことを示唆している。しかし，ある宇宙物理学者は，このストーンサークルにはまた別の目的があったと信じている。彼は，ほかの石の位置が，このストーンサークルが建設された時期のオリオン座の星の位置と一致すると指摘している。このため，彼はこのストーンサークルが夜空の星の位置を示す占星術の図だったという説を提唱している。

> (語句) prehistoric「先史時代の」，predate「（時間的に）先立つ」，formation「形成」，temporary「一時的な」，cattle-grazing「牛を放牧する」，archaeologist「考古学者」，uncover「発見する，発掘する」，equip A with B「A に B を備える」，worship「崇拝」，finding「（通例複数形で）（研究や調査の）結果」，astrophysicist「宇宙物理学者」，constellation「星座」，astrological「占星術の」

(26) – 解答　**2**　　　　　　　　　　　正答率 ★75%以上

> 解説　文頭に適切な論理マーカーを補う問題。空所前の this was not the case は「この場合はそうではなかった」という慣用句で，これに not always「常に〜とは限らない」が混じった表現。「常に乾燥していたわけではなかった」と「豪雨があった」を結ぶ表現として，In fact「実際に」が適切。ここでは前述の話題について事実を加える働きをしている。

(27) – 解答　**4**　　　　　　　　　　　正答率 ★75%以上

> 解説　主語の These discoveries「これらの発見」の詳細は前述にある。「深い井戸のシステムを作って一年中水が得られるようにした」や，「住居を真っすぐに並べて配置し，それらに保管スペースを備えた」などの入植者たちの行動を「高度な社会を築いていた」と表した **4** が正解。

(28) – 解答　**1**　　　　　　　　　　　正答率 ★75%以上

> 解説　空所前の「暦として使用されていた」と空所後の「夜空の星の位置を示す占星術の図だった」は，いずれもストーンサークルの使用目的だと考えられる。よって，追加を示す another を含む **1**「また別の目的があった」が適切。対照を示す however に着目して話の展開をつかもう。

全文訳　良い道路運動

　19 世紀後期から始まった「良い道路運動（グッドロード運動）」は，同国の道路・主要路網を生み出すことに寄与し，アメリカの風景を一変させた。この運動には意外な発端があった。今日のほとんどの人は，道路網は最初，自動車を運転する人々のニーズに応えて整備されたと思っているが，これは思い込みに過ぎない。実際には，この要求は主に自転車に乗る人の間で生まれた。近代的な自転車の発明は，1890 年代のサイクリ

ングの流行につながり，何百万人ものアメリカ人が自転車に乗るためのより良い，より安全な道路を望んだ。

　自転車に乗る人たちは，きちんと整備されず，危険なことの多かった道路の質を改善するよう自治体に圧力をかけ始めた。最初，この運動は，都市部からの自転車に乗る人たちの余暇活動を支援するために税金を使われたくなかった農家たちに抵抗された。しかし次第に農家たちは考えを改め始めた。これの理由の1つが，『良い道路の福音～アメリカ農家への手紙～』と呼ばれる影響力のあるパンフレットだった。このパンフレットは，彼らが作物を市場に輸送するのが容易になるなど，道路のメリットを強調することで多くの農家を納得させた。

　自動車が一般化するにつれて，この運動は急速に勢いを増した。特に，1900年代初頭のフォードモデルTの発明によって多くの人が車を運転するようになり，これらの人々もより良い道路を熱望していた。これらの手ごろな車は何百万台と販売され，車を運転する人の増加は，道路を増やし，既存道路の質を改善するよう各自治体に圧力をかけた。

> 語句　transform「一変させる」，in response to「～に応えて」，myth「根拠のない話」，craze「流行」，〈pressure＋O＋to *do*〉「Oに～するよう圧力をかける」，resist「抵抗する」，influential「影響力のある」，convince「納得させる」，emphasize「強調する」，momentum「勢い」，*be* eager for「～を熱望している」，existing「既存の」

(29) – 解答 ②

解説　This movement「この運動」の内容は前述にある。空所後の While most people today assume ～, this is a myth. Actually, ... から，「～と思っているが，そうではない。実際には…」という展開をつかもう。道路ができたのは自動車ではなく自転車のためだったという趣旨で，これは意外な（surprising）事実である。よって，**2**「意外な発端があった」が適切。

(30) – 解答 ③　　　　　　　　　　　　　　　　　正答率 ★75%以上

解説　文中に at first が出てきたら，その後 however などが用いられて話が逆転することを予測しながら読もう。ここでは At first から Gradually, however, ... へのつながりに注目。最初，運動は農家に抵抗された→しかし次第に…→多くの農家を納得させたという趣旨から，農家の考えに変化があったことが分かる。よって，**3**「考えを改め始めた」が適切。

(31) – 解答 ②

解説　第2段落までは「自転車」のための運動の話だったが，第3段落では「自動車」の一般化によって運動が勢いを増したという話に発展する。空所後の Ford Model T の発明は自動車普及に寄与した具体例と考えられる。よって，具体例を示す In particular「特に」が適切。

全文訳 **顔の認識**

　人間は一般的に，顔を認識し，その表情を素早く読み取ることに非常に優れている。これは，顔の特徴を処理するのに特化した脳の特定領域があることにより実現されている。進化の観点からすると，この能力の発達は合理的である。というのも，初期の人類は，例えば周りの人間が怒っているのか，それゆえに潜在的に危険であるのかを判断する必要があったであろうからだ。しかし，意図せぬ結果の１つとして，人は，周囲の環境の中にある物体に顔が見えると思うことがよくある。人は，雲や木の幹から食べ物のかけらや電気コンセントに至るまで，さまざまな物体にこれらのいわゆる「偽顔」があるのに気付く。

　オーストラリアの研究者たちが最近，脳がどのように偽顔を処理するかについて詳しく知るための研究を実施した。先行研究では，本物の顔に関して言えば，顔がどのような感情を表しているかの判断は，その人が直前に見た顔に影響を受けるということが明らかになった。例えば，立て続けにうれしそうな顔を見ると，人は次に見る顔がうれしさを表していると評価しやすい。今回のオーストラリアの研究では，研究者たちは参加者たちに，特定の感情を表している一連の偽顔を見せた。彼らは，本物の顔と同様に，偽顔によって表された感情についての参加者たちの判断は，直前に見た偽顔に影響されることを発見した。この知見に基づき，研究者たちは，脳は本物の顔を処理するのと同様の方法で偽顔を処理していると結論付けた。

　研究者たちはさらに，人間の顔の配置 —— 目が２つあって口の上に鼻があるという配置 —— に大まかに似ているだけの特徴を持つどんな物体でも，脳が感情表現を読み取ろうとそれらの特徴を評価するきっかけとなり得ると指摘した。すなわち，脳の顔認識の基準は，特定のものというよりむしろ一般的なのである。研究者たちは，これは脳がこれほど素早く顔の表情を評価できる理由の１つだと言う。

語句 interpret「解釈する，（表情を）読み取る」，specific「特定の，具体的な」，process「処理する」，in terms of「〜の観点から」，unintended「意図されたものではない」，consequence「結果」，perceive「気付く」，so-called「いわゆる」，reveal「明らかにする」，a series of「一連の〜」，assess「評価する」，as with「〜と同様に」，trigger「引き起こす」，criterion「（判断）基準（複数形は criteria）」

(32) –解答 **4**

問題文の訳 第１段落で，この文章の筆者はなぜ雲などの物体に言及しているのか。

選択肢の訳 1 人の周囲の環境が，人がどれだけよく他人の感情を判断できるかに影響を与え得るという考えを裏付けるため。

2 顔を識別できない人はほかの特定の物体を識別するのにも苦労するということを説明するため。

3 周囲の環境にある日常的な物体に対する私たちの反応が，脳のさまざまな領域によって制御されていることを説明するのを助けるため。

4 そこに顔が見えると人が思い込む日常的な物の例を示すため。

解説 第1段落最終文の趣旨は「人は，さまざまな物体に偽顔（false faces）が見える」ということ。そして，この a variety of objects の具体例の1つが clouds である。よって，**4** が正解。

(33) – 解答 ①

問題文の訳 先行研究が示したことは

選択肢の訳
1 本物の顔がどんな感情を表しているかについての人の判断は，その人が直前に見たほかの本物の顔の影響を受ける。

2 人は，本物の顔よりも偽顔の方により素早く感情的な意味を結び付ける。

3 人は，本物の顔によって表された感情よりも偽顔によって表された感情の方がうれしそうで肯定的だと判断する傾向がある。

4 人は，偽顔が何も感情を表していない場合，偽顔を見分けるのにより長い時間がかかる。

解説 先行研究について書かれた第2段落第2文 Previous studies have ... から，**1** が正解。それぞれ affected を influenced に，have just seen を have seen immediately before に言い換えている。

(34) – 解答 ② ★75%以上

問題文の訳 オーストラリアの研究者たちは，顔によって表される感情を評価する脳の能力について何と言っているか。

選択肢の訳
1 この能力は，生存の面では人間にもはや利点をもたらさないため，時間の経過とともに消滅する可能性が高い。

2 脳が緩い判断基準を用いて顔を識別しているという事実により，人は，顔が表す感情を素早く判断することができる。

3 脳は，顔が非常にはっきりした特徴を持っている場合にのみ，顔が表す感情を正確に識別できる。

4 過去に人間に利益だけでなく不利益ももたらしたにもかかわらず，この能力の進化は起こった。

解説 質問文の「顔によって表される感情を評価する脳の能力」は，第3段落第1文に書かれている。そして続く In other words, ... 以下では，顔を認識するための脳の判断基準は一般的（general ≒ loose）であること，またその結果として脳が素早く表情を評価できる（assess ≒ judge）ことが分かる。これらの情報を短く表した **2** が正解。〈this is one reason SV〉→〈allow＋O＋to *do*〉という因果表現の言い換えにも着目したい。

ドリアンとオオコウモリ

　フットボール並みの大きさのドリアン果実は，その不快なにおいとクリーミーで甘い果肉でよく知られている。「果物の王様」として知られるドリアンは，ボルネオ島原産とされているが，今ではもっと広く栽培されており，世界中で消費される全てのドリアンの半分以上がタイで栽培されている。ドリアンは東南アジア全域で昔から人気があったが，その人気は今や世界各地に広がっている。ドリアンには何百もの種類があるが，ほぼマレーシアでしか栽培されていないムサンキング種は，最も価値が高い品種の１つである。ドリアンにはビタミンが豊富に含まれているため，しばしばその健康効果で宣伝されており，これが輸出の増加をもたらしている。実際，専門家たちは，次の10年間で，マレーシアから中国への出荷量だけでも50%増加すると予測している。この状況を利用するために，多くのマレーシアの農家がドリアンを生産することを選び，ヤシ油などの作物の生産をやめてしまった。

　しかし，ドリアンの木の栽培は容易ではない。ドリアンは定期的な水やりと肥料を与えることを必要とし，また温度の影響を非常に受けやすい。さらに，ドリアンは自然には群生せず，ほかの樹木や低木に混ざった方が繁茂するため，単一の作物として果樹園で栽培するのは困難をもたらす。ドリアンの木の実りを良くするために確実に花が十分授粉されるようにすることも，農家にとってはさらなる困難である。ドリアンの木の特徴の１つに，花が夜にしか花粉を放出しないという点があり，そのためミツバチなどの日中餌を求める昆虫はドリアンの受粉をしない。夜に活動する動物が受粉の役割を引き受けるが，ドリアンの木の花のうち25%ほどしか自然に受粉しない。このため，多くの農家が人の手で授粉するという多大な労働力を要する方法に頼る。

　研究によって，オオコウモリがドリアンの花の主な自然送粉者であることが分かっている。しかし，このコウモリは多くの農家に追い払われたり，駆除されたりしている。農家は，このコウモリは果実を食べることで損害を与え，利益を減らすことから，単に害獣と見なしているのだ。また，このコウモリは，食料として狩られ，売られた結果，絶滅が危惧されてもいる。というのも，東南アジアの一部の文化において，このコウモリの肉を食べることが呼吸障害を治すのに役立つと信じられているからである。オオコウモリの恩恵について人々に教えなければ，このコウモリの個体数はさらに減少する可能性があり，それはドリアン栽培に深刻な結果をもたらすことになるかもしれない。

語句 flesh「果肉」，cultivate「栽培する」，exclusively「全く，もっぱら」，take advantage of「～を利用する」，in favor of「～を選んで」，fertilizer「肥料」，*be* sensitive to「～の影響を受けやすい」，grove「小さい林」，thrive「繁茂する」，shrub「低木」，orchard「果樹園」，sufficient「十分な」，pollination「受［授］粉」，characteristic「特徴」，pollen「花粉」，pollinate「受［授］粉する」，resort to「（最終手段として）～を用いる」，labor-intensive「多大な労働力を要する」，chase away「～を追い払う」，see A as B「A を B と見なす」，pest「害虫，害獣」，threatened「絶滅が危惧されて」，decline「減少する」

(35) – 解答 4

問題文の訳 第1段落によると，ドリアンの生産について正しいのはどれか。

選択肢の訳 1 ほかの東南アジア諸国ではもはやドリアンの栽培に利用できる十分な土地がないため，現在，ドリアンは主にマレーシアで栽培されている。

2 ドリアンは，伝統的に栽培されていた場所ではよく売れているが，ほかの国々ではまだ人気を得ていない。

3 高級品種のドリアンは，より安価な品種と同じ程度の栄養価しかないため，消費者から批判を浴びている。

4 ドリアンの需要が高まっているため，マレーシアの農家はほかの作物の栽培からドリアンの栽培に切り替えつつある。

解説 第1段落中程でドリアンの人気の高まりや出荷量の増加（= the increasing demand「需要の高まり」）を説明した後，最終文で「ヤシ油などの作物の生産をやめてドリアンの生産を選んだ」と続く。正解4では最終文の内容を switch from A to B「A から B に切り替える」で表している。

(36) – 解答 4

問題文の訳 ドリアン農家が考慮しなければならない要因の1つは

選択肢の訳 1 ドリアンの木はほぼどんな温暖な気候でも栽培できるが，ほかの植物がほとんど生えていない場所で最もよく育つこと。

2 ドリアンの木がほかの植物を押し出す傾向があるため，先住植物の数が激減していること。

3 ドリアンの木は，ミツバチやほかの昼間の送粉者が容易に見つけられる場所で栽培するべきだということ。

4 ドリアンの木を自然に受粉させようと放っておくと，その木は大量の実をつける可能性が低いこと。

解説 ドリアンの栽培の難しさを説明した第2段落を参照。夜しか花粉を放出しないこと，また夜も25%ほどしか自然に受粉しないことから，多くの農家が人の手で授粉する。つまり，放っておいても受粉は困難→大量の実をつける可能性が低いと考えて，4 が正解。

(37) – 解答 1

問題文の訳 この文章の筆者がオオコウモリについて言うことの1つは何か。

選択肢の訳 1 オオコウモリがドリアンの花の受粉に果たす重要な役割に関する認識が高まらなければ，ドリアンの生産が損害を被るかもしれない。

2 東南アジアでは，一部の市場で違法に販売されたコウモリの肉を食べた結果，多くの人が病気になった。

3 オオコウモリを捕獲し，その肉を販売できるように，意図的にオオコウモリを果樹園に誘引するドリアン農家もいる。

4 多くのオオコウモリが呼吸障害で死んだため，ドリアンの花の自然送

粉者が大幅に減少している。

解説 タイトルにある giant fruit bats は第３段落で初出する。オオコウモリはドリアンの花の主な自然送粉者である（＝重要な役割を果たす）が，農家は害獣と見なして駆除し，また食用にも狩られるため，数が減少している。オオコウモリの恩恵について人々に教えなければ（＝認識が高まらなければ），個体数はさらに減少し，ドリアン栽培に深刻な結果をもたらす（＝生産が損害を被る）かもしれない。よって，**1** が正解。

全文訳 長距離砂漠挺身隊

　第２次世界大戦中，イギリスは北アフリカの砂漠でドイツやイタリアと戦った。砂漠での戦闘は，広範囲に展開した部隊間の小規模な戦闘が特徴で，探知されることと危険な日中の灼熱の両方を避けるため，素早く移動したり，夜間に移動したりする必要があった。この地域の広範な面積と砂の地形により，物資の輸送が難しく，水不足によって作戦行動は深刻な制限を受けた。

　しかし，ラルフ・バグノルド少佐という１人のイギリス陸軍将校にとっては，これらの過酷な状況は戦略的な機会を示していた。戦前，北アフリカの砂漠を何年も探検していたため，バグノルドはこの地形をよく知っており，敵軍を監視・追跡できる，小規模で機動性の高い自動車化部隊が非常に有益であると確信していた。イギリスの司令官たちは，最初，これほどの長距離情報収集には航空機の方が適していると信じ，そのような部隊を編成するという彼の提案を拒否した。しかし，バグノルドは，地上で情報収集することは有利になると主張し，彼の粘り強さは，1940 年６月にバグノルドを司令官とする長距離砂漠挺身隊（LRDG）の編成につながった。

　LRDG は，最初から異例の部隊だった。通例の階級による区別は存在せず，将校も一般兵士もファーストネームで呼び合い，彼らは全員が同じ任務を遂行することを期待された。戦場で果敢に戦う兵士を求めるよりも，バグノルドは優れた体力と機転，そして精神的な強靭さのある個人を求めた。それは例えば，飲み水の利用が限られているにもかかわらず，長期間にわたって意欲を維持し，注意を怠らずにいられる兵士たちのことだった。砂漠環境に適応させた特殊トラックを有する LRDG の偵察隊は，約３週間，1,600 キロ以上の範囲を独立して行動する態勢が整っていた。燃料，弾薬，食糧などの必需品全てが部隊によって運ばれたため，慎重な供給計画が極めて重要であった。

　LRDG の任務は，主に敵陣深くに入り込んで敵の動きを監視することを伴った。部隊はさまざまな兵器を利用でき，兵士たちは主に情報を収集する訓練を受けていたが，彼らは地雷を埋めたり，敵の飛行場や燃料庫に攻撃を仕掛けたりもした。敵陣内で急襲を行うために 1941 年に編成されたイギリス陸軍部隊である特殊空挺部隊（SAS）が，その最初の任務で敵地にパラシュートで降下して多数の死傷者を出したとき，LRDG は生存者を連れ帰る任務を負った。この救出任務は成功し，この部隊の兵士たちが持つ砂漠に関する幅広い知識のため，LRDG はその後，SAS を陸路で目的地との間を送迎する任務を任され，輸送と誘導の両方を行った。これはほぼ間違いなく，SAS がより大き

な成功とより少ない死傷者で急襲を達成することに寄与した。

　LRDG の最大の功績が生まれたのは 1943 年のことで，イギリス軍が守りの堅い敵の前線を探知されることなくうまく避けて通れるルートを同部隊が見つけ，これによってイギリス軍は敵陣の守りの弱い所を攻撃することができた。これが北アフリカにおける軍事行動で決定的な転換点となり，そこでのイギリスの勝利に大いに貢献した。LRDG は，その後も 1945 年までヨーロッパでの戦争遂行に多大な貢献をした。

> 語句　warfare「戦争，戦闘」，characterize「特徴付ける」，troop「（複数形で）軍隊」，detection「探知」，terrain「地形」，harsh「過酷な」，strategic「戦略的な」，convinced「確信して」，motorized unit「自動車化部隊」，invaluable「非常に有益な」，commander「司令官」，intelligence「（軍事的・政治的）機密情報」，advantageous「有利な」，persistence「粘り強さ」，unconventional「異例の」，from the outset「最初から」，distinction「区別」，resourcefulness「機転」，alert「注意を怠らない」，specialized「特殊な」，adapt A to B「A を B に適応させる」，ammunition「弾薬」，weaponry「兵器」，primarily「主に」，mine「地雷」，airfield「飛行場」，depot「貯蔵庫」，raid「急襲」，casualty「死傷者」，parachute「パラシュートで降下する」，crucial「決定的な」，turning point「転換点」，campaign「（一連の）軍事行動」

(38) – 解答

> 問題文の訳　ラルフ・バグノルド少佐がイギリス陸軍の司令官たちを説得できた内容は

> 選択肢の訳　1　兵士たちの砂漠での任務の成功が乏しいのは，適切な資源が供給されていないからだということ。
> 2　敵地上空を飛行したり砂漠で監視したりするのに使われている航空機には，大幅な改良が必要であるということ。
> 3　そのような環境での経験がほとんどないという事実にもかかわらず，彼は砂漠で任務を負った部隊を率いることができるということ。
> 4　砂漠で敵の行動に関する情報を収集するためには地上部隊を用いることが効果的な戦略だろうということ。

> 解説　第 1 段落で砂漠の過酷な環境に言及した後，However で始まる第 2 段落で話が好転する。バグノルドは敵軍の監視・追跡に自動車化部隊（＝a ground-based unit）を用いることを提案したが，司令官たちは最初，情報収集には航空機の方が適していると信じ彼の案を拒否した。しかし，彼の粘り強さが LRDG の編成につながった（＝司令官たちを説得できた）。よって，4 が正解。

(39) – 解答

> 問題文の訳　長距離砂漠挺身隊（LRDG）について正しいのはどれか。

> 選択肢の訳　1　部隊に選ばれた兵士の特徴や作戦行動の方法が従来の部隊と違ってい

た。

2 予算が限られていたため，ほかの部隊よりも少ない資源と古い兵器で
やりくりしなければならなかった。

3 偵察隊の兵士の数が多かったため，将校たちは管理方法の特別訓練を
受けなければならなかった。

4 その任務の成功は，敵陣の背後で定期的に LRDG へ物資が届くよう
にしてくれる部隊に大きくかかっていた。

解説 LRDG の特徴を第 3 段落から読み取る。第 1 文に unconventional
unit「異例の部隊」とあり，その具体的な説明が続く。「果敢に戦う兵
士より優れた体力と機転，精神的な強靭さのある個人を求めた」（＝兵士
の特徴）や，「砂漠環境に適応させた特殊トラックで約 3 週間，1,600 キ
ロ以上の範囲を独立して行動」（＝作戦行動の方法）などとあり，これを
抽象的に表した **1** が正解。**4** は，物資（supplies = necessary items）
は LRDG の元に運ばれるのではなく，トラックに搭載して運んでいた
ので不適。

(40) – 解答 ･････････････････････････

問題文の訳 次のうち，LRDG と特殊空挺部隊（SAS）の関係を最もよく表してい
るのはどれか。

選択肢の訳 1 両部隊は，陸と空の急襲を同時に行えるよう，統合された。

2 作戦の性質が似ていたため，両部隊の間で競争が生まれ，助け合おう
としなくなった。

3 LRDG は砂漠に関する知識を利用し，SAS が任務の有効性と安全性
の両方を向上させるのに役立った。

4 SAS が LRDG の任務に関与したことで，LRDG が敵陣に長期間と
どまることがより困難になった。

解説 SAS が登場する第 4 段落を参照。LRDG ＝陸，SAS ＝空とイメージ
しよう。LRDG の SAS 救出任務は成功だったことから，両部隊は良
い関係と推測できる。また，LRDG に砂漠に関する知識があることから，
SAS の輸送と誘導を行い（＝ effectiveness），死傷者を減らすことに
貢献した（＝ safety）。よって，**3** が正解。陸空同時襲撃や部隊統合の
話はないので **1** は不適。また，両部隊の悪い関係を意味する **2** と **4** も不
適。

(41) – 解答 ･････････････････････････ 正答率 ★75%以上

問題文の訳 この文章の筆者によると，1943 年に何が起こったか。

選択肢の訳 1 LRDG が犯したミスにより，イギリスが獲得を望んでいた領土で敵
軍が支配力を強めることになった。

2 LRDG がヨーロッパへ移ったことで，SAS は，LRDG の支援なし
に守りの堅い地域で敵軍を攻撃するしかなかった。

3 LRDGの活動により，イギリス陸軍は大きな優位性を得ることができ，その地域の敵軍を打ち負かすことにつながった。

4 イギリスの司令官たちは，LRDGは敵の行動を監視するよりも，イギリスが支配する領土を守るために使用した方がよいと判断した。

解説 1943年の出来事は第5段落参照。第1文，第2文の内容と**3**が一致。本文の the unit, them は**3**ではそれぞれ LRDG, the British army のこと。第1文で具体的に述べられている LRDG の貢献を**3**では made it possible ... a significant advantage と抽象的に表し，それによってイギリスが勝利を収めたことを述べる第2文の内容を it defeating enemy forces in the area と表している。

一次試験・筆記 **4** | 問題編 p.129

トピックの訳 **人々はインターネット上の情報を信頼すべきか。**

ポイントの訳 **・学習　・ニュース　・オンラインショッピング　・ソーシャルメディア**

解答例　In my opinion, people should trust information on the Internet. I have two reasons to support this based on news and learning.

　Firstly, Internet news sites are a fantastic source of trustworthy information. The demand for up-to-date news has led to more people submitting videos and photos of events as they happen, such as natural disasters. This information is easy to verify because it comes directly from people experiencing such events, making it easier to trust this information.

　Secondly, there are many online learning courses on the Internet with content that can be trusted. To ensure their courses are reliable, educational institutions rigorously check the content of their online resources. Moreover, these courses are widely recognized, adding to their authenticity.

　In conclusion, due to the increasing amount of news generated directly from the source and the high quality of learning resources online, we should trust information on the Internet.

解説 序論：第1段落では，トピックに対する自分の意見（主張）を簡潔に書く。模範解答は In my opinion, ...「私の意見では，…」で始め，トピックの表現を利用して Yes の立場を明らかにしている。その後 I have two reasons to support this based on「～に基づいてこれを支持する理由

が2つある」という表現を使ってポイントのNewsとLearningを提示し，本論につなげている。

本論：本論では，序論で述べた主張を裏付ける根拠・理由を，2つの観点に沿って説明する。模範解答のように，First(ly), ..., Second(ly), ...などを使って2つの段落に分けるとよい。第2段落はNewsの観点でインターネットのニュースサイトの信頼性を，第3段落はLearningの観点で信頼できるオンライン学習コースについて説明している。第2段落，第3段落を見ると，因果関係を表す句動詞lead toを用いた無生物主語構文や受動態が効果的に使われている。また，..., making it easier ... や..., adding to ... では分詞構文が用いられている。文章にバリエーションを出したいときはぜひ分詞構文も使ってみよう。

結論：最終段落は，In conclusion「結論として」などを使って，序論で述べた主張を再確認する。模範解答では，due to「〜のために」の形で2つの観点を再び取り上げて本論の内容を要約した後，we should trust ... でYesの立場を再び明らかにして文章を締めくくっている。

その他の表現　「信頼する，信頼できる」を表すのにトピックの動詞trustを繰り返し使わないように工夫したい。今回使えそうな形容詞にはtrustworthy, reliable, believable, authentic などがあり，反意語はfalse, unreliable, doubtful など，名詞にはauthenticity, reliabilityなどがある。今回のトピックはNoの立場でも書きやすいだろう。ポイントのNewsの観点ではfake news「偽ニュース」について述べることができる。Social mediaの観点では，post [spread] false information on social media「ソーシャルメディアに偽情報を投稿［拡散］する」などの表現が使えそうだ。なお，英語ではSNSではなくsocial mediaを使うようにしよう。Online shoppingの観点では，情報＝商品のレビューと捉え，Many of the buyers' product reviews are unreliable.「購入者の商品レビューの多くは信頼できない」などの視点で根拠を膨らませることが可能であろう。

No.**1**-解答 ④ ・・・・・・・・・・・・・・・・・・・・・・・・・・・・・・・・・・・ 正答率 ★**75%以上**

スクリプト ☆： Leaving for lunch already, Noah?

★： Actually, I'm on my way upstairs. We have our company medical checkups today, remember?

☆： No, I completely forgot about them.

★： You can still go. You don't need an appointment.

☆： Yeah, but I had a big breakfast this morning. You're not supposed to eat before the blood test, right?

★： Right. In fact, I'm starving. Anyway, you'll have another chance next week. They'll be back again on Wednesday.

☆： Really? I'll make sure to remember.

Question: What will the woman probably do?

全文訳 ☆： もうランチに出るの，ノア？

★： 実は上の階に向かっている途中だよ。今日，会社の健康診断があるの，覚えてない？

☆： いいえ，完全に忘れていたわ。

★： まだ行けるよ。予約は要らないから。

☆： ええ，でも今朝いっぱい朝ごはんを食べてしまったわ。血液検査の前には食べてはいけなかったでしょ？

★： そうだね。実際，僕は腹ぺこだよ。どっちにしても，来週も受けるチャンスがあるよ。水曜日にまた来るから。

☆： そうなの？　絶対覚えておくわ。

質問：女性はおそらく何をするか。

選択肢の訳 **1** 今日，血液検査を受ける。
2 朝食を食べる量を減らす努力をする。
3 ノアとランチを食べに行く。
4 来週，健康診断を受ける。

解説 オフィス内の会話。今日の健康診断を忘れていた女性に対し，男性が来週もあると言う。女性の最後のI'll make sure ... は来週の健康診断を受けるという意図なので，**4**が正解。ノアは健康診断に行くところなので**3**は不適。本問のように，本来の予定が何らかの理由でできない→予定変更という流れでは，変更後について問われやすい。

No.**2**-解答 ④ ・・

スクリプト ☆： Looks like I'll be putting in another 60-hour week. Seems like I live here at the office these days.

★ : You do live at the office these days, and they don't pay you nearly enough. Why don't you drop a hint that you'd like to review your compensation?

☆ : But I've only been working here a year.

★ : In which time they've doubled your responsibilities. Come on, Laurie! You need to stand up for yourself.

☆ : Well, maybe you're right.

Question: How does the man feel about the woman's situation?

全文訳 ☆ : また今週も勤務時間が 60 時間になりそう。最近は会社に住んでいるかのようだわ。

★ : 実際，君は最近会社で暮らしているし，会社は君に十分な給料を支払っているとはとても言えない。給料を見直したいとほのめかしてみたらどう？

☆ : でも，まだ 1 年しかここで働いていないわ。

★ : その 1 年の間に会社は君の責任を倍にしたよ。ほら，ローリー！　自分のために立ち向かわないと。

☆ : そうね，あなたの言う通りかもしれないわ。

質問：男性は女性の状況についてどう感じているか。

選択肢の訳　**1**　彼女はもっと休みを取る必要がある。
2　彼女はお金についてあまり心配しない方がいい。
3　彼女はそれほどの責任を負う準備ができていない。
4　彼女はもっと給料をもらうに値する。

解説　長い勤務時間に不満を述べる女性に対し，男性は Why don't you ～? の表現で，給料を見直したい（＝増やしてほしい）と会社にほのめかすよう提案する。後ろ向きの様子の女性だが，男性は次の発言で，行動に出るようさらに後押しする。正解は **4** で，会話中の compensation「給料」を pay で表している。

No.3 – 解答 ②

スクリプト ★ : Doctor, how were the test results?

☆ : Not bad. It's just a sprain. Nevertheless, I still think you should avoid strenuous exercise for at least a couple of weeks after you leave the hospital today.

★ : But my softball team's got a big game this Thursday.

☆ : I'm afraid you're going to have to sit that one out. You should wait till you fully recover or you may make it worse.

Question: What does the doctor tell the man?

全文訳 ★ : 先生，検査結果はどうでしたか？

☆ : 悪くありませんよ。ただの捻挫ね。とは言っても，今日病院から出た後，やっぱり少なくとも数週間は激しい運動は避けた方がいいと思います。

★： でも，今週木曜日に所属のソフトボールチームの大きな試合があるんです。

☆： 残念だけど，その試合には参加せずにいないといけませんね。全快する
まで待たないと，悪化するかもしれませんよ。

質問：医師は男性に何と言っているか。

選択肢の訳　**1**　彼はさらなる検査を受ける必要がある。

2　彼は試合でプレーすることができないだろう。

3　彼は別の運動方法を見つける必要がある。

4　彼は入院しなければならない。

解説　医師と患者の会話。医師が数週間激しい運動を避けるよう助言すると，
男性は今週ソフトボールの試合があると言う。医師は I'm afraid ... で
試合には出られないと忠告しているので，**2** が正解。that one は試合の
ことで，sit ～ out は「～（活動など）に参加しない」の意味。

No.**4**－解答　②

スクリプト　☆： Hi, Phil. I'm sorry to bother you on your day off, but I'm not
feeling well. Could you cover my shift this afternoon?

★： Unfortunately, I've already got plans.

☆： I see. Do you know who might be able to change shifts with me?

★： I'm not sure.

☆： Maybe the new guy can cover it.

★： I'd just get in touch with the manager. It's her responsibility to
deal with these issues.

☆： I know, but I hate bothering her. Maybe I should just work the shift.

★： No, don't do that. You might make everyone else sick.

Question: What does the man imply the woman should do?

全文訳　☆： こんにちは，フィル。お休みの日に邪魔して悪いのだけど，私，具合が
良くなくて。今日の午後のシフトを代わってもらえない？

★： あいにくだけど，もう予定があるんだ。

☆： そう。私とシフトを代われそうな人を知らない？

★： ちょっと分からないな。

☆： あの新人が代われるかもしれないわ。

★： 僕ならとりあえず店長に連絡を取るかな。こういう問題に対処するのは
彼女の責任だから。

☆： 分かっているけど，彼女に面倒をかけたくないの。とりあえず私がシフ
トに出るべきかも。

★： いや，それはやめて。ほかのみんなにうつしてしまうかもしれないから。

質問：男性は女性は何をすべきだとほのめかしているか。

選択肢の訳　**1**　新しい従業員に連絡を取る。

2　店長と話す。

3 彼女自身がそのシフトに出る。

4 彼とシフトを代わる。

> **解説** 電話での会話。具合が悪い女性が男性にシフトを代わってくれるようお願いするが，男性は代われない（→ **4** は不適）。男性の考える解決策 I'd just get in touch with the manager. から，**2** が正解。

No.**5** – 解答 ③

スクリプト ☆： I'm looking forward to our business trip next week.

★： Me, too. I'll double-check the flight schedule tomorrow.

☆： Thanks.

★： Have you finished putting together the presentation for our meeting?

☆： Not yet. I was planning to get it done tomorrow.

★： That's a good idea. I remember trying to finish one at a hotel last year, and I couldn't connect to the Internet.

☆： Our hotel is supposed to have good Wi-Fi, but don't worry. It'll be done before we go.

Question: What will the woman do before leaving for the trip?

全文訳 ☆： 私，来週の出張を楽しみにしているの。

★： 僕もだよ。明日，航空便のスケジュールをもう一回確認するね。

☆： ありがとう。

★： 僕たちの会議のプレゼンテーションはまとめ終わった？

☆： まだよ。明日終わらせようと思っていたわ。

★： それはいい考えだね。去年，僕はホテルで完成させようとしたことを覚えているよ。それでインターネットに接続できなかったんだ。

☆： 私たちが宿泊するホテルには安定した Wi-Fi があるはずだけど，心配しないで。出発する前に終わらせるから。

質問： 女性は出張に出かける前に何をするか。

選択肢の訳 **1** インターネット接続についてホテルに問い合わせる。

2 会議のスケジュールを確認する。

3 プレゼンテーションの準備を終わらせる。

4 航空券を買う。

> **解説** 同僚同士の会話。来週の会議のプレゼンテーションについて聞かれた女性は，I was planning to get it done tomorrow. と答える。また，最後に It'll be done before we go. とも言っているので，正解は **3**。it と It はどちらもプレゼンテーションの準備のこと。put together は「～（考えなど）をまとめる」という意味で，**3** では prepare で表している。

No.**6** – 解答 ①

━━━━━━━━━━━━━━━━━━━━━━━━━━━━━ 正答率 ★75%以上

スクリプト ☆： Shall we order some more wine?

★： I'd love to, but we should probably catch the bus home soon. It's already eleven.

☆： Eleven? Oh, dear. The last one will have left by the time we get to the bus stop.

★： We can still catch the last train.

☆： That train doesn't come for another hour. I say we treat ourselves to a taxi.

★： Works for me.

☆： Great. Let's head over to the main street. We can probably catch one there.

Question: What does the couple decide to do?

全文訳 ☆： もっとワインを頼む？

★： そうしたいけど，そろそろ家に帰るバスに乗るべきかもしれない。もう11時だよ。

☆： 11時？　あら，どうしよう。バス停に着くころには最終便は出発してしまっているわ。

★： まだ最終列車には乗れるよ。

☆： その列車はあと1時間は来ないでしょ。奮発してタクシーに乗りましょう。

★： 僕はそれで構わないよ。

☆： よかった。大通りに向かいましょう。そこでたぶんつかまえられるわ。

質問：夫婦は何をすることに決めたか。

選択肢の訳 1 タクシーに乗って家に帰る。

2 もっとワインを注文する。

3 最終列車に乗って家に帰る。

4 最寄りのバス停まで歩く。

解説 話題はレストランからの帰宅手段。バスには間に合わず，列車を却下した後，女性がタクシーを提案すると，男性は Works for me. と同意するので，**1** が正解。最後の We can probably catch one there. もヒントになる。one は a taxi のこと。本問のように，複数の候補を挙げて検討する会話では，最終的にどれに決めたかが問われやすい。

No.**7** –解答 ② .... 正答率 ★**75％以上**

スクリプト ★： Honey, did you see that the new restaurant down the block finally opened?

☆： I'm sorry, I can't chat right now. I need to start making dinner so it'll be ready by the time the kids get home from school.

★： Leave dinner to me.

☆： Really? But you don't cook. You aren't planning to order takeout, are you? We just bought groceries.

★： No. I know I'm not a good chef, but I found a cooking website for beginners. I saw a great recipe for a pasta dish I think I can make.

☆： Oh, that would be lovely!

Question: What does the man offer to do?

全文訳 ★： ねえ，1ブロック先の新しいレストランがやっと開店したの，見た？

☆： ごめんなさい，今話せないの。子供たちが学校から帰ってくるまでにできているように，夕食を作り始めないといけないから。

★： 夕食は僕にまかせて。

☆： 本当に？　でも，あなた料理しないじゃない。テイクアウトを注文するつもりじゃないわよね？　食料品を買ってきたばかりなのよ。

★： そうじゃないよ。自分は料理がうまくないことは知っているけど，初心者向けの料理サイトを見つけたんだ。僕が作れそうなパスタ料理のすごくいいレシピを見たんだ。

☆： あら，それは助かるわ！

質問：男性は何をすると申し出ているか。

選択肢の訳 **1** 子供たちを学校に迎えに行く。

2 家族のために夕食を作る。

3 今夜の夕食のための材料を買う。

4 新しくできたレストランに料理を注文する。

解説 話題は夕食の準備。男性の申し出は，Leave dinner to me. から，夕食を作ることなので，**2** が正解。I know I'm not a good chef, but ... の発言からも，男性が料理をするつもりだと分かる。

No.**8**−解答 **1** ・・・・・・・・・・・・・・・・・・・・・・・・・・・・・・・・・・・・・

スクリプト ☆： AFP Automotive.

★： Hi. I'm on Highway 5. My engine overheated, and it won't start. I need my car towed, and I could use a ride downtown. I have to be at a meeting in an hour.

☆： Could you tell me your policy number?

★： It's A735.

☆： I'm sorry. A car will arrive in about 10 minutes to take you downtown, but the system says you don't have towing coverage.

★： Really? I thought my plan included towing.

☆： Unfortunately, you'll have to pay out of pocket this time, but we can add it to your insurance policy in the future.

Question: What is one problem the man has?

全文訳 ☆： AFP自動車です。

★： もしもし。今国道5号線にいるんですが，オーバーヒートして，エンジンがかかりません。車をレッカー移動してもらう必要があって，私はダ

ウンタウンまで送ってもらえると助かります。あと1時間で会議に出なければいけないので。

☆： 保険証書番号を教えていただけますか。

★： A735 です。

☆： 申し訳ありません。お客さまをダウンタウンに送っていく車は10分ほどで到着しますが，システムによるとお客さまはレッカー移動の補償はないようです。

★： 本当に？ 私の補償プランにはレッカー移動が含まれていると思っていました。

☆： 残念ながら，今回は自己負担していただかないといけませんが，将来的に保険証書に追加していただけます。

質問：男性の抱える問題の1つは何か。

選択肢の訳 **1** 彼は予想外の料金を支払わなければならない。

2 彼は保険を解約した。

3 彼は会議に遅れている。

4 会社が彼の保険証書番号を見つけることができない。

解説 車が動かなくなった男性が保険会社に連絡を取っている場面。女性は，男性のプランはレッカー移動の補償がないことを伝え，you'll have to pay out of pocket this time と言う。pay out of *one's* pocket は「自腹で払う」という意味。また，I thought my plan included towing. の発言から，男性にとっては予想外の（unexpected）状況だと考えられるので，**1** が正解。

No.**9**‒解答 ③ ....

スクリプト ★： Excuse me, Professor Garcia. Could I ask you for some advice?

☆： Of course. Is it about our art classes?

★： Sort of. I'm thinking about changing my major from communications to graphic design, but I'm not sure if it's a good idea.

☆： Why are you considering the change?

★： It gives me career options. I could do advertising, marketing, or even web design.

☆： Those are good careers. What's your concern?

★： Well, I'm not confident that my artistic skills are good enough.

☆： I've seen your work. If you make the effort, I think you could be quite successful.

Question: What does the woman imply?

全文訳 ★： すみません，ガルシア教授。少しアドバイスをいただけませんか。

☆： もちろんですよ。芸術の授業のことですか。

★：そんなところです。専攻をコミュニケーションからグラフィックデザインに変更しようと考えているのですが，それがいい考えか確証が持てないんです。

☆：どうして変更を考えているのですか。

★：職業の選択肢が広がります。広告もマーケティングも，それからウェブデザインさえもできます。

☆：それらはいい職業ですね。何を心配しているのですか。

★：ええと，自分の芸術スキルが通用するのか自信がありません。

☆：あなたの作品を見てきました。努力すれば大成功すると思いますよ。

質問：女性は何をほのめかしているか。

選択肢の訳　**1** 男性は専攻を変えるべきではない。
2 コミュニケーション分野の仕事の方が男性に向いているかもしれない。
3 グラフィックデザインは男性にとって良い選択である。
4 男性は授業の成績があまり良くない。

解説　教授と学生の会話で，質問では教授の発言意図が問われている。専攻をコミュニケーションからグラフィックデザインに変更したい学生がその理由を説明したところ，教授は Those are good careers. と言う。その後の発言からも，変更に賛成している様子なので，**3** が正解。

No.10 解答 ②

スクリプト　★：Alicia, can I talk to you about that online meeting software we're using?

☆：Sure, Ben. What is it?

★：We've been using the free version, but I think we should consider paying to upgrade to the full version. The free version can be inconvenient at times.

☆：The participant limit has been a problem. Sometimes we'd like to have more than eight people in a meeting at once. Could you submit an official request with the cost?

★：Does that mean there's room in the budget for an upgrade?

☆：I'll see what I can do.

Question: What will the man do next?

全文訳　★：アリシア，僕たちが使っているあのオンライン会議のソフトウエアについて話せますか。

☆：いいわよ，ベン。どうしたの？

★：ずっと無料版を使っていますが，お金を払って完全版にアップグレードすることを検討すべきだと思うんです。無料版は不便なときがありますから。

☆：参加者数の制限が問題になっていたよね。一度に8人より多い人数で会議ができたらいいときもあるものね。費用を添えて正式な要望書を出し

てくれる？

★： つまり，アップグレードする余裕が予算にあるってことですか？

☆： 私に何ができるか検討してみるわ。

質問：男性は次に何をするか。

選択肢の訳　**1**　別のオンラインチャットツールを見つける。

2　ソフトウエアのアップグレードの要望書を準備する。

3　より多くの人にオンライン会議に参加してもらうようにする。

4　会社の予算を増やすよう依頼する。

解説　男性がオンライン会議のソフトウエアをアップグレードすることを提案すると，女性は納得した様子で，Could you submit an official request with the cost? と言って要望書を出すよう指示する。男性はこれに従うと考えて，**2** が正解。

No.11 解答　② ··

スクリプト　★： Carol, I have a favor to ask you.

☆： What is it?

★： Inspectors from Mexico are coming to our plant tomorrow, and our regular interpreter is on vacation. I remember you majored in Spanish in college. Do you think you could substitute?

☆： Well, I did study Spanish, but I'm not sure I can handle all the technical terms.

★： What if we asked Barbara to do your regular work today, and you spent the rest of the afternoon brushing up on vocabulary?

☆： OK. I'll do my best.

Question: What will the woman do for the rest of the day?

全文訳　★： キャロル，お願いしたいことがあるんだけど。

☆： 何ですか？

★： 明日，メキシコから調査員がこの工場に来るんだけど，いつもの通訳が休暇を取っているんだ。君が大学でスペイン語を専攻していたことを思い出したんだ。代わりをお願いできないかい？

☆： えーと，確かにスペイン語を勉強しましたが，全ての専門用語に対応できるかは分かりません。

★： 今日の君の通常業務はバーバラにやってもらうよう頼んで，君は午後の残りの時間を語彙のおさらいに充てるというのはどう？

☆： 分かりました。最善を尽くします。

質問：女性は今日の残りの時間に何をするか。

選択肢の訳　**1**　工場に行く。

2　スペイン語を勉強する。

3　バーバラと面談する。

4 通訳を探す。

解説 男性は，スペイン語の通訳が不在なので，女性にその代役を頼んでいる。女性は専門用語（technical terms）に自信がない様子だが，男性の「午後の残りの時間を語彙のおさらいに充てる」という提案（What if ...?）に同意しているので，**2** が正解。brush up on「～の能力を磨き直す」を抽象的に study と表している。

No.**12** 解答 ④ ････････････････････････････････････

スクリプト ★： Excuse me, ma'am, this is a no-parking zone.

☆： I'm sorry, officer. I felt ill while I was driving, so I stopped my car here to take a short rest.

★： Are you OK? I can call an ambulance for you.

☆： No, thanks. I'm feeling much better now, but can I rest here for another 10 minutes or so?

★： No problem. I'll stand by in the police car until you feel well enough to leave. Honk your horn if you need help.

☆： I will. Thanks.

Question: What is the police officer going to do?

全文訳 ★： すみません，ここは駐車禁止区域です。

☆： すみません，お巡りさん。運転している最中に具合が悪くなったので，ここに車を停めてちょっと休憩していたんです。

★： 大丈夫ですか？　救急車を呼びましょうか。

☆： いいえ，結構です。今はだいぶましになりました。でももう10分ほどここで休んでもいいですか。

★： いいですよ。私はあなたがここから出ていけるほど回復するまでパトカーの中で待機しています。助けが必要になったらクラクションを鳴らしてください。

☆： そうします。ありがとう。

質問：警官は何をするつもりか。

選択肢の訳 **1** 無線で救急車を呼ぶ。

2 女性の代わりに女性の車を動かす。

3 女性に駐車違反の切符を切る。

4 パトカーの中で待つ。

解説 警官が駐車禁止区域に停車している女性に声をかけている場面。女性は具合が悪くて休んでいると知った警官は，さらに10分ほど休むことを許可する。警官のこの後の行動は，I'll stand by in ... から，**4** が正解。stand by は「待機する」の意味で，**4** では wait と表している。

A

スクリプト **The P-47 Thunderbolt**

When the P-47 Thunderbolt first appeared in World War II, American pilots worried that this extremely heavy fighter plane would be at a disadvantage against smaller, lighter German planes. The P-47 was indeed slower at low altitudes, but when it was flying high, it could outrun almost any other plane. One serious weakness early on was its limited fuel supply. Eventually, however, extra tanks were fitted onto the P-47 so that it could go on longer missions.

The P-47 had eight powerful machine guns and was able to carry an impressive selection of bombs and rockets. The real reason that pilots came to love it, though, is that it was one of the most durable planes of the war and survived many hits that would have destroyed other planes. In one extreme case, a pilot was able to land his P-47 after it was shot over 100 times.

Questions

No.13 What problem did the P-47 Thunderbolt have at first?

No.14 What did pilots like most about flying the P-47 Thunderbolt?

全文訳 **P-47 サンダーボルト**

P-47 サンダーボルトが第2次世界大戦で初めて登場したとき，アメリカのパイロットたちは，この非常に重い戦闘機がより小さく軽いドイツ機に対して不利になるのではないかと心配した。P-47 は確かに低空飛行では低速だったが，高空飛行ではほかのほとんどの戦闘機を振り切ることができた。初期の深刻な弱点の1つは，燃料の供給が限られていたことである。しかし，最終的には，より長い任務を遂行できるように，P-47 に追加のタンクが取り付けられた。

P-47 は，8基の強力な機関銃を搭載し，爆弾やロケット弾を豊富に搭載することができた。しかし，パイロットたちが P-47 を大変気に入るようになった本当の理由は，P-47 が最も耐久性のある戦闘機の1つであり，ほかの戦闘機であれば破壊されたであろう多くの攻撃に持ちこたえたからである。ある極端な例では，あるパイロットは，100回以上撃たれても P-47 を着陸させることができた。

No.13 解答 ③

質問の訳 当初，P-47 サンダーボルトが抱えた問題は何だったか。

選択肢の訳
1 十分に高く飛べなかった。
2 あまりに小さくて軽かった。
3 短い距離しか飛べなかった。
4 珍しい種類の燃料を使った。

解説 P-47 の 初 期（at first = early on） の 問 題 点 は，One serious weakness early on was ... の部分から，燃料の供給が限られていた＝短い距離しか飛べなかったと考えて，**3** が正解。続く it could go on longer missions もヒントになる。

No.**14** 解答 ①

質問の訳 P-47 サンダーボルトの操縦においてパイロットが最も気に入った点は何だったか。

選択肢の訳
1 ほかの戦闘機より丈夫だった。
2 新しい種類の武器を搭載していた。
3 非常に素早く着陸することができた。
4 爆弾を正確に投下することができた。

解説 パイロットが P-47 を気に入った理由は，The real reason that pilots came to love it, ... の部分にある。「ほかの戦闘機であれば破壊されたであろう多くの攻撃に持ちこたえた」とはつまり，「ほかの戦闘機より丈夫だった」と言えるので，**1** が正解。

B

スクリプト **Ascension Island**

Ascension Island lies in the middle of the Atlantic Ocean. Originally, it was nearly treeless, and fresh water was scarce, which made for tough living conditions for the first settlers. However, in the 1840s, a British scientist named Sir Joseph Hooker started a program to transform the desert island. He started importing trees and other plants that were able to survive in the island's dry environment by absorbing water from mist in the air. His program eventually resulted in an entire mountain being covered in forest. However, Hooker's plants have been so successful that several native plant species have gone extinct.

There is now a debate about the island's future. Some people say efforts must be made to preserve the plants that were originally found on the island. Others, though, want the new ecosystem to be left as is, since it has had benefits, such as increasing available water and creating the potential for agriculture.

Questions

No.15 What was one result of Sir Joseph Hooker's program for Ascension Island?

No.16 What do people disagree about regarding Ascension Island?

全文訳 **アセンション島**

アセンション島は大西洋の真ん中に位置する。もともと，そこには樹木がほとんどなく，淡水が不足していたため，最初の入植者たちにとっては厳しい生活環境をもたらした。しかし，1840 年代に，ジョセフ・フッカー卿というイギリスの科学者がこの無人

島を改造する計画を開始した。彼は，空気中の霧から水分を吸収することで島の乾燥した環境で生き抜くことができる樹木やほかの植物の移入を始めた。彼の計画は最終的に，山全体が森に覆われる結果となった。しかし，フッカーの植物があまりに成功を収めたため，幾つかの在来種の植物が絶滅してしまった。

　現在，この島の将来について議論が起きている。島にもともとあった植物を保存する努力をすべきだという人もいる。しかし，新しい生態系は，利用可能な水を増やしたり農業の可能性を生み出したりするなどの利点があるため，そのままの状態にしておくことを望む人もいる。

No.15 解答 ④

質問の訳 ジョセフ・フッカー卿のアセンション島計画の成果の１つは何だったか。

選択肢の訳
1 水の供給量が減った。
2 大気の汚れが減った。
3 多くの人が島を離れなければならなくなった。
4 樹木の本数が増えた。

解説 Originally, However, eventually resulted in などの論理マーカーを手掛かりに，もともと樹木がほとんどなかった島だが，樹木や植物の移入を始め，山全体が森に覆われる結果になった，という展開をつかもう。山全体が森に覆われる→樹木が増えたと考えて，**4** が正解。

No.16 解答 ③

質問の訳 アセンション島に関して，人々は何について意見が分かれているか。

選択肢の訳
1 新しい生態系をどう分類するか。
2 水の供給を何のために使うか。
3 在来植物を保護すべきかどうか。
4 どこで農業を許可すべきか。

解説 質問の disagree about は「～について意見が分かれる」という意味で，意見の相違は，Some people ～. Others, ... で表されている。議論の論点は，島にもともとあった植物を保存すべきか，新しい生態系を残すべきか，であることから，**3** が適切。

C

スクリプト **Vivian Maier**

　One of the twentieth century's greatest street photographers, Vivian Maier is known for her fascinating images of people in cities like Chicago and New York. Maier worked in childcare, but her true passion was photography. She always had her camera with her, and this habit allowed her to capture unique and unusual shots of people going about their daily lives. Her photos depict everything from strangely dressed tourists to emergency workers caring for accident victims.

Despite the incredible number of photos she took, Maier was an intensely private person. Unlike most photographers, she refused to allow others to see her work. Nevertheless, a collection of her photos was purchased at an auction in 2007, and the buyers began exhibiting her unusual work. It was not until after her death in 2009, however, that she was recognized as an artistic genius.

Questions

No.17 What is one thing we learn about Vivian Maier?

No.18 How was Maier different from other photographers?

全文訳 ビビアン・マイヤー

20世紀で最も優れたストリート写真家の1人であるビビアン・マイヤーは，シカゴやニューヨークなどの都市で撮った魅力的な人物写真で知られている。マイヤーは保育分野で働いていたが，彼女が本当に情熱を注いでいたのは写真だった。彼女はいつもカメラを持ち歩き，この習慣のため，日常生活を送る人々のユニークで珍しいショットを撮影することができた。彼女の写真は，奇抜な服装をした観光客から，事故の被害者を介抱する救急隊員まで，あらゆるものを写し出している。

膨大な数の写真を撮ったにもかかわらず，マイヤーは極めて非社交的な人物だった。多くの写真家と違って，彼女は他人が自分の作品を見ることを拒んだ。とはいえ，2007年に彼女の写真コレクションがオークションで購入され，その買い手たちは彼女の珍しい作品を展示し始めた。それでも，彼女が天才芸術家として認められるようになったのは，2009年に彼女が亡くなってからのことである。

No.17 解答

質問の訳　ビビアン・マイヤーについて分かることの1つは何か。

選択肢の訳　**1** 彼女はどこにでもカメラを持っていった。

　　　　　　2 彼女は救急隊員と友だちになった。

　　　　　　3 彼女は世話をしている子供たちにカメラを貸した。

　　　　　　4 彼女は観光客として多くの場所に行った。

解説　ビビアン・マイヤーについての説明の She always had her camera with her の部分と **1** が一致する。文中の語句を含む選択肢 **2** と **4** や，worked in childcare から連想される **3** を選ばないように注意。

No.18 解答

質問の訳　マイヤーはほかの写真家とどんな点で異なっていたか。

選択肢の訳　**1** 彼女はキャリアの早い段階で有名になった。

　　　　　　2 彼女は主にオークションで写真を撮った。

　　　　　　3 彼女は非常に大規模な展覧会を開いた。

　　　　　　4 彼女は自分の写真を人々に見せなかった。

解説　後半に Maier was an intensely private person とあり，この詳しい説明が Unlike most photographers, ... に続く。refused to allow others to see her work という肯定文を did not show people her photos という否定文で言い換えた **4** が正解。refuse や avoid のような否定の意味を含む語はライティングでも生かせるので確認しておこう。

D

(スクリプト) **The Impact of Cats**

Cats are one of the most popular pets today, but like many other pets, they affect the environment through their eating habits. As carnivores, cats primarily eat meat, the production of which releases substantial amounts of carbon dioxide gas into the atmosphere and often creates air and water pollution. According to a recent study, however, the management of cats' waste may be more harmful to the environment than their diet is.

Cat owners commonly prepare boxes for their cats that contain cat litter, a material that traps the cats' waste. However, the clay that is used in most litter is usually acquired through surface mining, a process that requires oil-powered heavy machinery and can destroy large natural areas. Recently, more manufacturers have begun producing litter made from environmentally friendly materials like wood and seeds. Nevertheless, clay-based litter is still the most used type due to its low cost and exceptional odor absorption.

Questions

No.19 What is one thing the speaker says about cat-food production?
No.20 What do we learn about the process of collecting clay?

全文訳 **猫の影響**

猫は今日最も人気のあるペットの1つだが，ほかの多くのペットと同様，その食習慣を通じて環境に影響を与えている。肉食動物であるので，猫は主に肉を食べるが，肉の生産によって大量の二酸化炭素ガスが大気中に放出され，大気汚染や水質汚染を引き起こすことがよくある。しかし，最近の研究によると，猫の食事よりも猫の排せつ物の処理の方が環境に悪い可能性がある。

猫の飼い主は，一般的に，猫の排せつ物を閉じ込める素材である猫砂を入れた箱を飼い猫のために用意する。しかし，ほとんどの猫砂に使われている粘土は，通常，露天採掘，つまり石油を動力源とする重機を必要とし，広大な自然地域を破壊し得る方法で採取される。最近では，木材や種子など，環境に優しい素材を使った猫砂を製造し始めるメーカーも増えている。とはいえ，粘土を原料とした猫砂は，その低コストと優れた臭気吸収のために，最も使用されている種類であることに変わりはない。

No.19 解答 .... 正答率 ★75%以上

質問の訳 キャットフードの生産について話者が言うことの1つは何か。
選択肢の訳 **1** 真水を使う必要がない。
2 特定の気候のもとでしかできない。

3 大量のガスを発生させる。

4 昔に比べて肉の使用量が少ない。

 猫の食事や排せつ物が環境に与える影響に関する文章。質問は猫の食事について で，cats primarily eat meat, the production of which releases ... から，**3** が正解。the production of which は「肉（＝キャットフード）の生産」という意味。それぞれ本文の releases を produces に，substantial amounts of を a large amount of に言い換えている。

 No.**20** 解答 **②** ⋯⋯⋯⋯⋯⋯⋯⋯⋯⋯⋯⋯⋯⋯⋯⋯⋯⋯⋯⋯⋯⋯⋯

質問の訳 粘土を採取する方法について何が分かるか。

選択肢の訳 **1** 使用する機械が非常に高価である。

2 広大な土地に被害を与えている。

3 近隣の農地に化学物質を放出する。

4 作業員にとって危険な場合が多い。

解説 However, the clay ... natural areas. がポイント。この文を読んでいくと，「粘土」「ほとんどの猫砂に使われている」「通常 surface mining で採取される」（surface mining とは何か？）「方法」「石油を動力源とする重機を必要とする（方法）」「広大な自然地域を破壊し得る（方法）」。よって，粘土の採取方法は **2**「広大な土地に被害を与えている」と言える。

E

スクリプト **Profitable Experiences**

For many young people today, experiences have become more important than material things. This has created money-making opportunities for businesses that can provide memorable and exciting experiences. One recent example is "axe-throwing bars." While axes would normally be associated with chopping wood in a forest, now people in many cities can go to special bars and throw axes like darts. Some worry about the possible dangers of this activity, but fans argue that it is a fun way to release stress.

Such businesses that sell experiences have spread across the US, but critics argue these businesses may negatively affect communities in the long run. They say the businesses are probably a short-term trend whose popularity will not last. And, when the businesses close, their employees are left without a source of income. The critics recommend that cities encourage the development of businesses that will be popular for decades, not just a few years.

Questions

No.21 What is one reason for the popularity of "axe-throwing bars"?

No.22 What is one criticism of businesses that sell experiences?

全文訳 **有益な経験**

今日の多くの若者にとって，形のある物よりも経験が重要になっている。そのため，

記憶に残るエキサイティングな体験を提供できる商売に金もうけの機会が生まれている。最近の例の１つに「斧投げバー」がある。斧といえば通常，森でまきを割ることが連想されるが，今では多くの都市で人々が特殊なバーに行き，斧をダーツのように投げることができるのだ。この活動の潜在的な危険性を心配する人もいるが，愛好者たちはストレスを発散する楽しい方法だと言い張る。

体験を売り物にしたこのような商売は全米に広がっているが，批評家たちは，この手の商売は長期的には地域社会に悪影響を与える可能性があると主張する。彼らは，この商売はおそらく短期的な流行で，その人気は長続きしないだろうと言う。また，商売が廃業すると，その従業員は収入源を失って残される。批評家たちは，たかが数年ではなく，何十年も人気が続くような商売の発展を各都市が奨励することを勧めている。

No.21 解答

質問の訳 「斧投げバー」の人気の理由の１つは何か。

選択肢の訳 1 若者の変化する関心事。
2 若者の運動に対するニーズの高まり。
3 若者の経済状況。
4 若者の自然への情熱。

解説 今日の若者にとって「形のある物よりも経験が重要」と述べ，記憶に残るエキサイティングな体験の例として "axe-throwing bars" が挙げられる。昔の若者は「物」を重要と考えていたが，最近の若者は「体験」を重要視するように変わってきたという趣旨から，**1** が適切。理由を直接的に述べていないので判断が難しいが，消去法でも解けるだろう。

No.22 解答 ①

質問の訳 体験を売り物にする商売への批判の１つは何か。

選択肢の訳 1 長く生き残る可能性が低い。
2 都市部以外ではうまくいかない。
3 地元の人を雇用することがめったにない。
4 場所を取り過ぎる。

解説 criticism については，critics の主張を説明した部分に手掛かりがある。They say the businesses are probably a short-term trend ... から，**1** が正解。last「続く」を survive long「長く生き残る」と表している。

F

スクリプト *T. rex* **Skulls**

T. rex had two large holes at the top of its skull, which scientists used to believe held muscles that aided jaw movement. Recently, however, researchers realized that this would not have been an efficient location for jaw muscles, so they began searching for another explanation. They looked at a modern animal descended from dinosaurs: the alligator.

The researchers found that alligator skulls have similar holes. They are filled with blood vessels that help alligators control the amount of heat in their bodies. When alligators need to warm themselves, these areas absorb external heat, and they release heat when alligators need to cool down. Since large meat-eating dinosaurs such as *T. rex* likely tended to overheat, these holes and blood vessels could have functioned as a sort of internal air-conditioning system. Of course, we cannot observe living dinosaurs, but studies like this provide interesting clues as to what these prehistoric giants were like.

Questions

No.23 Why did the researchers decide to analyze alligators?

No.24 What do the researchers now think the holes in *T. rex* skulls were used for?

全文訳　**Tレックスの頭蓋骨**

　Tレックス（ティラノサウルス・レックス）は，頭蓋骨の上部に2つの大きな穴があり，そこには顎の動きを助ける筋肉があったと科学者たちはかつて信じていた。しかし最近，研究者たちは，これは顎の筋肉にとって効率的な場所ではなかったことに気付いたため，別の説明を探し始めた。彼らは，恐竜の子孫である現代の動物，ワニに注目した。

　研究者たちは，ワニの頭蓋骨にも同様の穴があるのを見つけた。その穴にはワニが体内の熱量を制御するのに役立つ血管が通っている。ワニが体を温める必要があるときはこの部分が外部の熱を吸収し，ワニが体を冷やす必要があるときは熱を放出する。Tレックスのような大型の肉食恐竜はおそらく体温が高くなり過ぎる傾向があったため，この穴と血管は体内空調システムのような役割を担っていたのかもしれない。もちろん生きている恐竜を観察することはできないが，このような研究は，これら先史時代の巨大な動物がどのようなものだったかについての興味深い手掛かりを提供してくれる。

No.23 解答 2 ⋯⋯⋯⋯⋯⋯⋯⋯⋯⋯⋯⋯⋯⋯⋯⋯⋯⋯⋯⋯

質問の訳　研究者たちはなぜワニを分析することにしたのか。

選択肢の訳　1　ワニには効率の良い顎がある。
　　　　　　2　ワニは恐竜と関係がある。
　　　　　　3　ワニは変わった場所に筋肉がある。
　　　　　　4　ワニはTレックスと同じ時期に進化した。

解説　used to *do* → Recently, however という対比に着目。以前はTレックスの頭蓋骨の上部には顎の動きを助ける筋肉があったと考えていた→最近そうではないかもしれないことに気付いた→恐竜の子孫であるワニに注目した，という流れ。ワニを分析することにした理由として**2**が正解。

No.24 解答 4 ⋯⋯⋯⋯⋯⋯⋯⋯⋯⋯⋯⋯⋯⋯⋯⋯⋯⋯⋯ 正答率 ★75%以上

質問の訳　研究者たちは現在，Tレックスの頭蓋骨の穴が何のために使われていたと考えているか。

解説　ワニの頭蓋骨にも T レックス同様の穴があり，その穴に通っている血管
は，ワニが体内の熱量を制御するのに役立つと言っている。the
amount of heat in their bodies を their body temperature と言い換
えた **4** が正解。その後のワニが体を温める・冷やす場合の穴の働きにつ
いての説明や functioned as a sort of internal air-conditioning
system の部分などもヒントになるだろう。

一次試験・
リスニング　　Part**3**　｜　問題編 p.134 ～ 135　　🔊　▶ MP3　▶ アプリ
　　　　　　　　　　　　　　　　　　　　　　　　　　▶ CD 2 **49** ～ **54**

G

スクリプト

You have 10 seconds to read the situation and Question No. 25.

Welcome to Greenville. As we approach the gate, please remain in your seats
with your seat belts fastened. We realize many of you have connecting flights,
so we have gate agents standing by who can direct you to your connecting
gates once you exit the plane. Please have your boarding passes ready to show
them. If this is your final destination, you can find your luggage on the
carousels in the main terminal. If you need to arrange ground transportation,
look for the bus service just past the baggage claim. Customer service
representatives are available throughout the airport if you need assistance.

Now mark your answer on your answer sheet.

全文訳

　グリーンビルにようこそ。ゲートに近づいていますので，シートベルトを締めてご着
席のままお待ちください。乗り継ぎ便に乗られるお客さまが多いようですので，飛行機
を降りましたら，乗り継ぎゲートまでご案内するゲート係員が待機しております。搭乗
券をご用意のうえ，係員にご提示ください。ここが最終目的地のお客さまは，メインター
ミナルの回転コンベヤーで手荷物をお受け取りいただけます。地上交通機関の手配が必
要なお客さまは，手荷物受け取り所を過ぎた所にあるバスサービスをお探しください。
サポートが必要なお客さまは，空港内のどこでもカスタマーサービス担当者がお手伝い
いたします。

No.25 解答　**3**　• •
　状況の訳　あなたは着陸したばかりの飛行機に乗っており，乗り継ぎ便に乗らなけ

れwばならない。客室乗務員がアナウンスをしている。

質問の訳 あなたは飛行機を降りた後，まず何をすべきか。

選択肢の訳　**1** 手荷物を受け取る。
　　　　　2 バスに乗って別のターミナルへ行く。
　　　　　3 ゲート係員を見つける。
　　　　　4 新しい搭乗券を印刷してもらう。

解説　問題用紙の「状況」から，乗り継ぎ便に関する情報を聞き取ろう。飛行機を降りたら乗り継ぎゲートまで案内してくれる係員が待機していることから，飛行機を降りて最初にすることは，**3**。放送文の exit を質問文では getting off と表している。**1** は，ここが最終目的地の場合のこと。

H

スクリプト

You have 10 seconds to read the situation and Question No. 26.

We sell four original incense brands. Bouquet Himalaya is a paper-type incense that features the scents of flowers from India. It has a deep, calming effect and helps relieve stress and anxiety. Next, Magnolia's Sanctuary is a stick-type incense that contains sweet-smelling substances. This incense will immediately lift your spirits and is perfect for creating an energizing mood. Akebono is a cone-type purifying incense made with sage, and it's popular among meditation practitioners. Finally, Shirley's Gift is a stick-type incense that was also developed specifically for releasing tension. The aroma calms the mind, creating a tranquil atmosphere.

Now mark your answer on your answer sheet.

全文訳

　当店は，オリジナルのお香ブランドを4つ販売しています。ブーケ・ヒマラヤは，インドの花の香りを特徴とする紙タイプのお香です。深い鎮静効果があり，ストレスや不安の解消に役立ちます。次に，マグノリアズ・サンクチュアリは，甘い香りの物質を含んだスティック型のお香です。このお香は，すぐに気分を高揚させ，活力を与えるムード作りに最適です。アケボノは，セージを原料とした浄化作用のある円錐型のお香で，瞑想する人たちの間で人気があります。最後に，シャーリーズ・ギフトは，こちらも特に緊張をほぐすために開発されたスティック型のお香です。香りが心を落ち着かせ，穏やかな雰囲気を作り出します。

No.26 解答 4

状況の訳　あなたはリラックスするのに役立つスティック型のお香を買って使いたいと思っている。店員が次のように言う。

質問の訳　あなたはどのお香ブランドを買うべきか。

選択肢の訳　**1** ブーケ・ヒマラヤ。

2 マグノリアズ・サンクチュアリ。

3 アケボノ。

4 シャーリーズ・ギフト。

「状況」から，お香の条件として「リラックスするのに役立つ」「スティック型」の2点を押さえる。また，選択肢を見て，4つの商品が順に説明されると推測しよう。ブーケ・ヒマラヤとアケボノはスティックではないので不適。マグノリアズ・サンクチュアリは「リラックスするのに役立つ」と合わないので不適。シャーリーズ・ギフトが2つの条件に合う。

（スクリプト）

You have 10 seconds to read the situation and Question No. 27.

I'm calling to confirm your appointment to set up your new Internet service. It's scheduled for this Thursday. Our technician will arrive sometime between noon and 3 p.m. If this time slot is OK, no action is necessary. However, if it's not, please contact us to reschedule. Please note that we're currently experiencing high demand, so our only available appointment times would be next week. Also, our technicians are only available Monday through Friday between 9 a.m. and 6 p.m. Remember that our offices are closed on weekends. Thank you.

Now mark your answer on your answer sheet.

全文訳

お客さまの新しいインターネットサービスをセットアップする予約確認のお電話です。今週木曜日を予定しています。当社の技術者が正午から午後3時の間に伺います。この時間帯で問題ない場合は，何もする必要はありません。ですが，そうでない場合は，ご連絡いただき，予定を変更してください。現在，需要が高まっているため，予約可能な時間帯は来週になってしまうことをご承知おきください。また，技術者は，月曜日から金曜日の午前9時から午後6時の間のみ対応しています。週末は休業となっておりますのでお忘れなく。それでは。

No.**27** 解答 ②

状況の訳 今日は月曜日で，あなたは新しいインターネットプロバイダーの担当者から音声メッセージを受け取る。あなたは今週の木曜日は正午から午後8時まで仕事をしなければならない。

質問の訳 あなたは何をすべきか。

選択肢の訳
1 今週末に予定を変更する。
2 来週の平日に予定を変更する。
3 今週木曜日の午前中に予定を変更する。
4 今週金曜日の午後6時以降に予定を変更する。

解説 選択肢より，予定を変更しなければならない状況だと推測できる。our only available appointment times would be next week から，**3** と **4** は不適。週末は休みなので **1** も不適。よって，**2** が正解。**4** は，平日の午前 9 時から午後 6 時の間のみの対応という情報でも消去できる。

J

スクリプト

You have 10 seconds to read the situation and Question No. 28.

I've checked your application, and it appears that you've submitted all of the required forms that were on our website. It looks like you also paid your application fee when you submitted those documents. And we've been contacted by your high school regarding your transcripts, which should be arriving shortly. If you aren't sure what you want to major in yet, please consider attending our open-campus event next week. Otherwise, all that's left for you to do is submit a letter from a teacher or employer recommending you. Once we receive that, we can start processing your application.

Now mark your answer on your answer sheet.

全文訳

あなたの願書を確認したところ，ウェブサイトに掲載されている必要書類は全て提出されたようですね。また，それらの書類を提出したときに，出願料も支払っているようです。あと，あなたの高校から，あなたの成績証明書について連絡がありましたので，それも間もなく届くでしょう。何を専攻したいかまだ決まっていない場合，来週のオープンキャンパスへの参加をご検討ください。そうでなければ，あとするべきことは，先生または雇用主からの推薦状を提出するだけです。私どもがそれを受け取ったら，あなたの出願手続きを開始できます。

No.28 解答 ③

状況の訳 あなたは心理学を学ぶのにある大学に出願している。入学選考事務局員があなたの願書について話している。

質問の訳 あなたは何をすべきか。

選択肢の訳
1 出願料を支払う。
2 来週の大学のイベントに行く。
3 推薦状を手に入れる。
4 高校の成績表を提出する。

解説 必要書類は全て提出し，出願料も払ったので **1** は不適。高校の成績証明書は手配済みなので **4** も不適。「状況」から専攻は決まっているので，オープンキャンパスに行く必要はない→ **2** も不適。Otherwise, ...「そうでなければ（＝希望専攻が決まっていれば）」から，**3** が正解。

K

You have 10 seconds to read the situation and Question No. 29.

There are four local tours today. Our bus tour starting at 1 p.m. takes passengers to major sites all over the city, and it costs nothing. Next, a walking tour starts at 2:30. Local volunteer guides will escort you around the downtown area, and there's no charge. If you enjoy bike riding, join the tour starting at three. It costs $35, which includes bike rental fees and refreshments. Finally, if you take our tour starting at five, you can try various kinds of local cuisine. The participation fee is just a few dollars, but you'll have to pay for what you eat and drink at food stands or restaurants.

Now mark your answer on your answer sheet.

全文訳

　本日は，現地ツアーが4つあります。午後1時発のバスツアーは，お客さまを市内各所の主要スポットに連れて行き，費用はかかりません。次に，2時30分にウォーキングツアーが出発します。地元のボランティアガイドが繁華街を案内し，無料です。自転車に乗るのがお好きなら，3時発のツアーにご参加ください。料金は35ドルで，自転車のレンタル料と軽食が含まれています。最後に，5時発のツアーに参加すると，さまざまな種類の郷土料理が試せます。参加費はわずか数ドルですが，屋台やレストランでの飲食代はご自分で払わないといけません。

No.**29** 解答 ②

状況の訳　あなたは海外旅行中で，無料の現地ツアーに参加したいと思っている。あなたは乗り物酔いをしやすい。ホテルのインフォメーションデスクで次のように言われる。

質問の訳　どのツアーがあなたにとって最適か。

選択肢の訳　**1**　午後1時からのツアー。
　　　　　　2　午後2時30分からのツアー。
　　　　　　3　午後3時からのツアー。
　　　　　　4　午後5時からのツアー。

解説　問題用紙の情報から，「乗り物に乗らない」「無料」ツアーは「何時」発か？がポイントだと推測しよう。1時のツアーはバスなので不適。2時30分のツアーはウォーキングで無料なので，これが適切。念のため続きを聞くと，3時と5時のツアーは無料ではないので不適。

解答例 **One day, a woman was talking with her husband.** They were sitting at the dining room table, and they both looked concerned. The woman was looking at a lot of bills they needed to pay, and she said that living in the city was very expensive. That night, her husband was using the computer. He had found a website inviting people to come to ABC Village. It said that housing was cheap there, and the couple thought it looked like a nice place to live. A few months later, the woman's family was moving into a traditional Japanese house in the countryside. It was surrounded by beautiful nature. Two old farmers were happily working in the field nearby, and they looked up to see the family. A few weeks later, however, the family members were sitting inside their house, and the children were complaining that they missed their friends in the city.

解答例の訳 ある日，女性が夫と話していました。2人はダイニングルームのテーブルに座っていて，2人とも心配そうな様子でした。女性は，支払わなければならない多くの請求書を見ていて，都会で暮らすのはとてもお金がかかると言いました。その夜，彼女の夫はコンピューターを使っていました。彼は，人々にABC村へ来るよう呼びかけるウェブサイトを見つけました。それにはそこは住宅が安いと書かれており，夫婦は住むのに良さそうな場所だと思いました。数カ月後，女性の家族は田舎の伝統的な日本家屋に引っ越していました。そこは美しい自然に囲まれていました。近くの畑では2人の年配の農家の人が楽しそうに作業をしていて，顔を上げて一家を見ました。ところが数週間後，一家は家の中で座っていて，子供たちが都会の友だちが恋しいと不平を言っていました。

解説 イラスト上部の情報から，「お金を節約したかった夫婦」の話である。各コマで押さえるべき点は，①女性が請求書（Bill）を見て，「都会で暮らすのはとてもお金がかかる」と言っている，②その夜，夫婦が「ABC村へお越しください。安価な住宅」と書かれたウェブサイトを見ている，③数カ月後，一家が田舎に引っ越している，④子供たちが「都会の友だちが恋しい」と言っている。画面や紙に書かれた文字は，It said (that) ～ で表せる。画面の Come to ... は，解答例では〈invite＋O＋to *do*〉「O（人）に～するよう誘う［勧める］」を使って表している。4コマ目は都会から田舎に引っ越したことで生じた問題を描写しており，however などを使って話の展開を表したい。

No. 1

解答例 I'd be thinking that I should have considered my children's needs more before moving. It's natural for them to feel lonely in a village with few friends. Perhaps we can take the children to the city on the weekends.

解説 質問は「4番目の絵を見てください。もしあなたがこの女性なら，どのようなことを考えているでしょうか」。解答例は，〈I should have + 過去分詞〉を用いて「引っ越す前に子供たちの要求をもっと考えるべきだった」という後悔を表している。解決策としては，「週末に街に連れて行く」のほか，「田舎で友だちを作る手助けをする」なども考えられるだろう。

No. 2

解答例 No, renting is better. Homeowners can't easily move to a different city to change jobs, for example. This means they might miss out on some big opportunities. Also, it's a lot of work to take care of a house.

解説 質問は「住む場所を借りるより住宅を購入する方がよいと思いますか」。2択の質問の場合，「○○の方がよい」と明確にしてからそれぞれの利点［欠点］を根拠にするとよいだろう。解答例はNoの立場で，「転職などで引っ越しにくい＝大きなチャンスを逃すかも」「家の手入れが大変」という購入の欠点を挙げている。

No. 3

解答例 Yes. It's clearly important to have nature in our surroundings. It gives people a place where they can relax and relieve their stress. Having large parks full of trees and other plants also helps to keep the air clean.

解説 質問は「日本は都市部に緑地を増やすべきか」。解答例はYesの立場で，ストレスを解消する場所の提供や，木や植物は空気をきれいに保つという緑の利点を根拠にしている。It's clearly important to ... の clearly「明らかに」のような意見を強める語を用いると説得力が増す。

No. 4

解答例 Not at all. These days, workplace culture is very competitive, so most people are under huge pressure to work hard. That leaves them with very little time to spend on hobbies or with family.

解説 「最近の人々は私生活と仕事のバランスをうまく保っているか」。解答例はNoの立場（全く保っていない）で，その理由として，職場での競争が激しいことや，それが原因で趣味や家族との時間がほとんどないことを挙げている。質問は特定の事象の真否を問うもので，should を含んでいないので「バランスを取るべきか」という質問ではないことに注意。

解答例 **One day, a couple was taking a walk by the beach.** They passed by a fenced area, where a construction worker was putting up a sign that said a new airport was being constructed by ABC Construction. The couple was shocked to learn about the plan. A few days later, the couple joined a protest against the construction project. The husband was holding a sign that said "protect ocean life," and the wife was collecting signatures from people who opposed the construction of the airport. Six months later, the couple was at the construction site with a group of people. A sign said that the construction had been canceled, and the couple and the supporters of the protest were very pleased. A year later, the couple was looking at a newspaper at home. The wife was surprised to see an article that said ABC Construction had gone bankrupt.

解答例の訳 ある日，夫婦が海辺を散歩していました。彼らがフェンスで囲まれたエリアを通りかかると，そこでは建設作業員がABC建設によって新しい空港が建設中であることが書かれた看板を立てていました。夫婦はその計画を知ってショックを受けました。数日後，夫婦はその建設プロジェクトに対する抗議活動に参加しました。夫は「海の命を守ろう」と書かれた看板を手に持っており，妻は空港建設に反対する人々から署名を集めていました。6カ月後，夫婦は集まった人々と一緒に建設現場にいました。看板には建設が中止されたと書かれており，夫婦と抗議活動の支持者たちは大喜びでした。1年後，夫婦は自宅で新聞を見ていました。妻は，ABC建設が倒産したという記事を見て驚きました。

解説 各コマで押さえるべき点は，①夫婦が「空港建設現場」と書かれた看板を見ている，②数日後，夫が「海の命を守ろう！」という看板を掲げ，妻が署名を集めている，③6カ月後，人々が「建設中止」と書かれた看板を見て喜んでいる，④1年後，夫婦が「ABC建設倒産」と書かれた記事を見ている。2コマ目は，飛行機に×が付いているので，建設反対運動の様子である。看板や紙に書かれた文字を適切な文で表すことがポイント。1コマ目のAirport Construction Siteは「建設中」と捉えてwas being constructed，3コマ目のConstruction Canceledと4コマ目のABC Construction Goes Bankruptは解答例ではhad been canceledとhad gone bankruptになっている。時制の一致による動詞の形に留意したい。

No. 1

解答例 I'd be thinking that it was partially my fault that the company went bankrupt. However, it's extremely important to protect the ocean environment, so I still think that we did the right thing by protesting the airport's construction.

解説 質問は「4番目の絵を見てください。もしあなたがこの夫なら，どのようなことを考えているでしょうか」。解答例は，「倒産は自分のせいでもあるだろう」と責任を感じつつも，However を用いて「海の環境を守ることは大事だから正しいことをした」としている。partially や extremely などの副詞をうまく使えると表現が豊かになる。

No. 2

解答例 Yes. There are many big problems in our society, so it's essential for Japanese people to feel more comfortable discussing political issues. It's the only way for us to begin solving these problems.

解説 質問は「日本人はもっと自分の政治的意見を表明すべきだと思うか」。解答例は Yes の立場で，「社会問題の解決のためにはもっと気軽に政治問題を議論できることが不可欠だ」という意見。it's ～ for A to do の形で主張を述べる際は，important や necessary の代わりに essential, crucial, significant などレベルの高い多様な語を使えるようにしたい。

No. 3

解答例 No. Businesses already provide their communities with employment opportunities, and they contribute to society by developing new products. They shouldn't be expected to do more than that.

解説 質問は「企業は社会を助けるためにもっと努力すべきだと思うか」。解答例の already は，No の立場の際に，「すでにそうだ（からその必要はない）」という意見を述べるときに有効である。Yes の立場では，同様の内容で「企業は，地域社会に雇用の場を提供したり新製品を開発したりすることで，もっと社会に貢献すべきだ」と述べることが可能だろう。

No. 4

解答例 Absolutely. Reducing the amount of electricity people use at home would reduce the amount of fossil fuels burned. Things like air conditioners use a lot of energy, so limiting their use would definitely reduce global warming.

解説 質問は「個人の行動が地球温暖化の緩和に貢献することは可能か」。Yes の立場では，個人が日常生活でできることを具体的に挙げて根拠にすればよい。この解答例のように明らかに Yes（または No）の立場を示す場合は，absolutely や definitely などの強い主張を表す語が有効である。

2022-1

解 答 一 覧

一次試験・筆記

1

(1)	3	(10)	3	(19)	2
(2)	1	(11)	1	(20)	3
(3)	4	(12)	1	(21)	1
(4)	4	(13)	2	(22)	2
(5)	3	(14)	4	(23)	1
(6)	3	(15)	4	(24)	1
(7)	2	(16)	1	(25)	4
(8)	4	(17)	1		
(9)	1	(18)	1		

2

(26)	4	(29)	1
(27)	1	(30)	3
(28)	2	(31)	4

3

(32)	4	(35)	3	(38)	2
(33)	2	(36)	2	(39)	1
(34)	1	(37)	4	(40)	3
				(41)	3

4　解答例は本文参照

一次試験・リスニング

Part 1

No. 1	1	No. 5	2	No. 9	2
No. 2	3	No. 6	1	No.10	4
No. 3	4	No. 7	1	No.11	3
No. 4	4	No. 8	3	No.12	2

Part 2

No.13	3	No.17	2	No.21	4
No.14	4	No.18	1	No.22	2
No.15	3	No.19	1	No.23	2
No.16	4	No.20	3	No.24	1

Part 3

No.25	3	No.28	4
No.26	1	No.29	4
No.27	1		

(1) —解答 ③

訳 事件を検討した後，裁判官は情けをかけることにし，その男に警告を与えただけにした。彼女は，彼が自分の犯罪に対して明らかに深く反省していると述べた。

解説 裁判官は男に何を示したか。続く「警告を与えただけ」や「すまないと思っている，反省している」から，mercy「慈悲，情け」が適切。disgrace「不名誉」，closure「閉鎖」，seclusion「隔離すること」

(2) —解答 ①   正答率 ★**75%以上**

訳 リサは双子の姉［妹］に見た目がそっくりだが，全く違う気質がある。彼女は姉［妹］と違って，とても落ち着いていて，めったに怒らない。

解説 リサと双子の姉［妹］の比較。but があるので見た目は似ているが性格は違うという趣旨だと推測できる。temperament「気質」が適切。accumulation「蓄積」，veneer「化粧板」，glossary「用語集」

(3) —解答 ④

訳 A：アナベル，宿題が終わったかどうか私が聞いたら肩をすくめるだけでは駄目よ。はっきりと答えなさい。
B：ごめんなさい，お母さん。もう少しで終わるわ。

解説 母親は don't ～ と命令文を用い，「～してはいけない，～しなさい」と注意している。shrug *one's* shoulders「肩をすくめる」は欧米人の「さあね，知らない」という仕草で，「はっきりと答えなさい」につながる。echo「（音などを）反響させる」，bow「（頭を）下げる」，dump「投げ捨てる」

(4) —解答 ④

訳 町で大規模なビジネス会議があるとき，空室のあるホテルを見つけるのはほぼ不可能だ。ほとんどのホテルはすぐに満室になる。

解説 第2文の「すぐに満室になる」から，ほぼ不可能なのは空きのあるホテルを見つけること。vacancy は可算名詞で「空室」の意味。sprain「捻挫」，segment「部分，一区切り」，transition「移行」

(5) —解答 ③

訳 刑事は何時間もそのギャングを尋問したが，彼は誰が自分の犯罪を手助けしたか言おうとしなかった。結局，刑事は彼から情報を得ようとするのをやめた。

解説 刑事はギャングから情報を得ようとしていたことから，interrogate「尋問する」の過去形が適切。それぞれ discharge「（液体・気体などを）放出する」，convert「変換する」，affiliate「提携させる」の過去形。

(6) ─解答 **3** ....

訳 けがをした足首を治療するためには，医師は圧迫を勧める。これは，けがした部分の周りに包帯をしっかりと巻くことでできる。

解説 けがをした足首の一般的な治療法を述べた文。第2文にある具体的な方法から，医師が勧めたのは compression「圧縮，圧迫」。depression「憂鬱（ゆううつ），うつ病」，progression「進行」，suspicion「疑い」

(7) ─解答 **2** ....

訳 A：家に帰る途中に突然雨が激しく降り始めてびしょぬれになってしまったよ。

B：私の忠告を聞いて傘を持って行くべきだったのに。

解説 雨にぬれて帰宅した A を，B は〈should have＋過去分詞〉「～すべきだったのに（しなかった）」を用いて非難している。heed「（助言・忠告を）聞き入れる」の過去分詞が適切。それぞれ mold「形作る」，twist「ねじる，（意味などを）ゆがめる」，yield「生み出す」の過去分詞。

(8) ─解答 **4** ....

訳 もっと多くの裕福な顧客を引き付ける方法として，その香水会社は主に裕福な人が読む雑誌に製品の広告を出し始めた。

解説 裕福な人が読む雑誌に製品の広告を出すことは，裕福な（affluent）顧客を引き付けるためである。文中の wealthy と同義の affluent が正解。theatrical「芝居じみた」，brutal「野蛮な」，frantic「狂乱した」

(9) ─解答 **1** ....

訳 先生は，幾つかのささいな間違いを除けば，その生徒のエッセーは完璧だったと言った。彼はそれに可能な限りの高い点を付けた。

解説 apart from は「～を除いて」。「エッセーは完璧だった」と続くことから，「幾つかのささいな（trivial）間違いを除けば」とする。conclusive「決定的な」，palatial「宮殿の（ような）」，offensive「不快な」

(10) ─解答 **3** ....

訳 負傷したそのサッカー選手は，自分の代わりの選手が最終戦でプレーするのをうらやましそうに見た。彼は心底プレーを続けたいと思っていた。

解説 負傷した選手が代わりの選手がプレーするのをどんな気持ちで見たか。第2文の内容も踏まえ，enviously「うらやましそうに」が適切。〈watch as SV〉は「S が V するのをじっと見る」の意味。substantially「実質的に」，previously「以前に」，relevantly「関連して」

(11) ─解答 **1** ....

訳 エイブラハムのアパートの前にある新しいホテルは，街の向こうの山々の眺めを遮るほど高くはない。彼はまだそれらをはっきりと見ることができる。

解説 第2文から，山々は実際に見えるので，ホテルは「山々の眺めを遮るほ

ど高くない」とする。not ~ enough to *do* で「…するほど~ではない」，obstruct *someone's* view で「(人) の眺め [視界] を遮る」という意味。delegate「委任する」，entangle「絡ませる」，boost「(数量などを) 増加させる」

(12) – 解答 ①

訳 白いカーペットに赤ワインをこぼしたので，マーサはせっけんと水で染みを取り除こうとした。しかし，彼女はそれを完全には取り除くことができなかった。

解説 せっけんと水で取り除こうとしたのは，白いカーペットにこぼした赤ワインの stain「染み」。slit「切り込み」，bump「衝突 (音)，(打撲でできた) こぶ」，blaze「炎」

(13) – 解答 ②

訳 戦争は 1 年間続いたが，どちらの側も勝利を得ることはできなかった。勝利は不可能に思えたため，両国は戦いをやめることに合意した。

解説 neither side は「戦っている 2 カ国のどちらも~ない」の意味。第 2 文から両国は戦いをやめることにしたので，どちらも勝つことができなかったと考える。prevail「勝つ，勝利を得る」が適切。devise「工夫する」，evolve「発展する」，reconstruct「再構築する」

(14) – 解答 ④

訳 その指導者は，自分の支配に対するいかなる反対をも阻止することを目的とした厳格な新しい法律の導入に対する口実として，国の政情不安を利用した。

解説 国の指導者が，自分に都合の良い新法律を導入しようと，政情不安を口実 (pretext) にしたと考えられる。trance「恍惚状態」，downfall「崩壊」，rampage「大暴れ」

(15) – 解答 ④

訳 容疑者は警察に無実を主張し続けた。彼は，犯罪が起こった場所からだいぶ離れた所にいたと繰り返し彼らに言った。

解説 第 2 文の「彼ら (＝警察) に繰り返し言った」から，無実を主張し続けたことが分かる。assert *someone's* innocence で「(人) の無実を主張する」という意味。conceal「隠す」，counter「反論する」，expire「期限が切れる」

(16) – 解答 ①　　　　　　　　　　　　　　正答率 ★75%以上

訳 優れた作家は自分の作品から間違いをなくすために最大限の努力をするが，時には間違いを見逃し，後で修正しなければならないこともある。

解説 but があるので「作家は作品から間違いをなくす努力をするが，見逃すこともある」という趣旨だと推測できる。eliminate A from B で「B から A を取り除く」という意味。expend「費やす」，stabilize「安定さ

せる」, oppress「圧迫する」

(17) – 解答 **1** ･･･

訳 誘拐犯らは多額の身代金と引き換えに子供を両親に返した後，その金を持って逃げようとした。しかし，警察がすぐに彼らを捕まえ，その金を夫婦に返した。

解説 誘拐犯が子供と引き換えにするのは身代金（ransom）。空所後では the money に言い換えられている。in exchange for は「～と引き換えに」。applause「拍手」, monopoly「独占」, prank「いたずら」

(18) – 解答 **1** ･･･

訳 ガスパーはある名門大学に出願した。残念ながら，成績が十分ではなかったため，あまり有名でない大学に行かざるを得なかった。

解説 対比を表す Unfortunately があるので，lesser-known「あまり有名でない」の対語となる prestigious「一流の，名門の」が適切。spontaneous「自発的な」, cordial「友好的な」, petty「わずかな，下級の」

(19) – 解答 **2** ･･･

訳 スパイらは気付かれずに軍事基地に入ろうと陸軍士官に変装した。

解説 in an attempt to *do*「～しようとして」以下の内容から，disguise *oneself* as「～に変装する」を用いる。それぞれ chronicle「年代順に記録する」, render「(人・物を)(ある状態に)する，与える」, revitalize「再活性化する」の過去形。

(20) – 解答 **3** ･･･

訳 ティモシーは非常に献身的な従業員だ。彼は信頼でき，手助けすることに熱心で，常に会社や同僚に忠誠心を示している。

解説 第2文の内容から，ティモシーは好ましい従業員だと分かる。正解は devoted「献身的な」で，後にある loyalty「忠誠心」の形容詞形 loyal と類義。grotesque「奇怪な」, defiant「反抗的な」, feeble「貧弱な」

(21) – 解答 **1** ･･･

訳 ポールが体重を減らすのを助けるため，医師は彼に食事を変えるよう勧めた。具体的には，彼女は，脂肪分の多い食べ物を減らし，もっと食物繊維を取るよう彼に提案した。

解説 医師の勧める減量方法は何か。具体的に述べた第2文の内容から，食事を変える（modify）ことである。比較級の fewer, more が変化を含意。pluck「引っ張る，(羽を)むしる」, exclaim「叫ぶ」, distill「蒸留する」

(22) – 解答 **2** ･･･

訳 A：ずっと仕事がすごく忙しいのに，今は新入社員の教育にも対応しないといけないの。
B：それはあんまりだね。代わりに誰かほかの人がそれをできるかどう

か上司に聞いてみたらどうだい。

解説 Aは，ずっと忙しい（現在完了）上に今は（now）新入社員の教育もしないといけないと不満を漏らしている。contend with「〜（困難）と闘う，〜（問題）に取り組む」が適切。turn over「〜をひっくり返す」，prop up「〜を下支えする」，count off「〜が全員いる［全部ある］かどうか数える」

(23) – 解答 ①

訳 少年は割れた花瓶のことを飼い犬のせいにしようとした。しかし，彼の母親はそのうそにだまされず，彼を部屋に追いやった。

解説 However があるので，花瓶を割ったのは犬ではなく少年だと察しが付く。fall for「〜（策略など）にだまされる」が適切。hang on「〜によって決まる」，see out「〜を見届ける」，flag down「〜（車・運転手）を合図して止める」

(24) – 解答 ①

訳 CEO（最高経営責任者）はスピーチの中で，今後5年間の会社の発展計画を打ち出した。彼は，それが会社の成長に伴い全従業員の仕事の指針となることを望んだ。

解説 map out a plan for で「〜の計画を作る［打ち出す］」という意味。第2文の this は his plan を指す。それぞれ leap in「〜に飛び込む」，rack up「〜を獲得する」，space out「〜を間隔を空けて配置する」の過去形。

(25) – 解答 ④

訳 昨年，ハロルドは全財産を費やしてさまざまな会社の株を買った。彼は今後数年間，株価が好調に推移することに賭けていた。

解説 the stock market は動名詞 performing の意味上の主語。第1文の内容を踏まえ，bet on「〜に賭ける」の過去進行形を用いて「株価が好調に推移することに賭けていた」とする。準1級では政治・経済のテーマが扱われるので語彙力を養っておこう。それぞれ cast away「〜を投げ捨てる」，put down「〜を下に置く」，step up「〜（の量［速度など]）を増やす，上げる」の -ing 形。

一次試験・筆記 **2** 問題編 p.146 〜 149

全文訳 **ピーターの法則**

　ピーターの法則として知られる理論によって，なぜ業績が悪い管理職の人が多いのかを説明できるかもしれない。この理論によると，下位職で成績の良い従業員は，自分の準備が整っていない地位にいずれ昇格する。これの理由は，従業員は通常，現職の業績に基づいて昇進するからである。この種の昇進方針は理にかなっているように見えるか

もしれないが，従業員の強みと弱みを十分に考慮することを怠ると，彼らの能力がふさわしくない地位に，彼らがゆくゆくは到達する結果になる。

　ある研究は，管理職に昇進した販売員の経歴を調べた。この研究では，予想されたように，最も優れた販売員が昇進する可能性が最も高かったことのほか，彼らが管理職では最も業績が悪かったことも判明した。この研究は，現在の業績のみに基づいて従業員を昇進させることには2つのデメリットがあることを示した。会社が最終的に無能な管理職を作り出してしまうことになるだけではなく，会社は下位職で最も優れた従業員を失うことにもなる。

　この研究を実施した研究者たちは，問題の1つは，業績の良い従業員は必然的に良い管理職になると単純に仮定してしまうという間違いを会社が犯してしまっていることだと言う。ほとんどの会社では，新入社員は仕事の仕方について専門研修を受ける。一方で，新しく管理職になった人には多くの場合において研修が全くかほとんど実施されない。これは，ピーターの法則の作用を緩和する方法の1つが新しい管理職に適切な研修を行うことであると示唆しているようである。

　(語句) principle「原理，法則」，managerial「管理者の」，result in「（結果的に）〜をもたらす」，unsuited「適さない」，solely「単に，ただ」，specialized「専門化した」，lessen「減少させる」

(26) – 解答 **4**

　(解説) 直前の who は関係代名詞で，先行詞は many people (in managerial positions)。続きを読んでいくと，下位職で成績の良い従業員が管理職（＝彼らの能力がふさわしくない地位）に昇進するという問題を論じていることが分かる。また，第2段落にも，ある研究で「管理職では最も業績が悪かったことが判明した」とあることから，**4**が適切。

(27) – 解答 **1**

　(解説)「この研究は，現在の業績のみに基づいて従業員を昇進させることには…ことを示した」という文意。空所後で not only A but also B「AだけでなくBも」を用いて「会社は最終的に無能な管理職を作り出してしまう」「会社は下位職で最も優れた従業員を失う」というデメリット（disadvantage）を2つ説明している。よって，**1**が適切。

(28) – 解答 **2** ･･････････････････････ 正答率 ★75%以上

　(解説) 文頭につなぎ言葉を入れる問題。空所前は「ほとんどの会社では，新入社員は仕事の仕方について専門研修を受ける」，空所後は「新しく管理職になった人には多くの場合において研修が全くかほとんど実施されない」という内容。most と little or no という対比に着目すると，On the other hand「一方で」が適切。

　全文訳　**近視**

　近視は世界中で急速に増加している。この状態の人は，近くの物ははっきりと見るこ

とができるが，遠くの物はぼやけて見える。多くの人がこの傾向をデジタル画面の利用のせいにする。彼らは，コンピューターやスマートフォンなどのデバイスを使うことが眼精疲労につながり，また，デジタル画面が生み出すブルーライトが眼底の感光性細胞を損傷すると主張する。しかし，デジタル画面が視力に長期的影響があるとする明らかな証拠はない。

　実際，近視の増加はデジタル画面が広く使われるようになる前から始まっていた。研究の中には，本当の問題は人々が屋内で過ごす時間が長過ぎることにあると示唆するものもある。これによって自然光にさらされることが少なくなる。近視は目の水晶体が伸びることにより起こり，これによって光を集める能力が低下する。しかし，脳内で産生される化学物質であるドーパミンの放出は，これが起こるのを防止することができ，自然光にさらされることはより多くのドーパミンの産生につながる。

　一部の専門家たちは，1日のうち3時間ほど屋外にいることが近視の予防に役立つと言う。しかし多くの人にとって，学校や仕事のスケジュールのため，これをすることは不可能である。その代わりに，人々が家の中で使う照明の種類を変える方がより現実的かもしれない。自然光の利点をいくらか提供する照明はすでに利用可能であり，研究によって将来的により多くの選択肢が提供されることが期待される。

> 語句　nearsightedness「近視」，blurry「ぼやけた」，blame A on B「A を B のせいにする」，eyestrain「眼精疲労」，light-sensitive「感光性の」，cell「細胞」，exposure to「～にさらすこと」，lens「(眼球の) 水晶体」，dopamine「ドーパミン」，practical「現実的な」，alternative「選択肢」

(29) – 解答　**①** ･･････････････････････････････ 正答率 ★**75%以上**

解説　第1段落第3文の Many people blame ... で，多くの人が考える近視の原因は「デジタル画面の利用」だと述べた後，However があるので，これに反する内容が続くと推測する。「デジタル画面が…とする明らかな証拠はない」という文意に合うのは **1** である。

(30) – 解答　**③** ･･････････････････････････････ 正答率 ★**75%以上**

解説　第2段落では，近視の原因はデジタル画面の利用以外にあると考える裏付けが書かれている。空所には「近視を増加させている本当の問題」が入る。空所後の a lack of exposure to natural light の原因として，**3** が適切。この indoors が第3段落第1文の outdoors につながる。

(31) – 解答　**④** ･･････････････････････････････ 正答率 ★**75%以上**

解説　第3段落は近視の予防について。空所前は，多くの人は近視の予防として1日のうち3時間ほど屋外にいることはできないという趣旨。空所後は，(屋外にいるよりも) 家の中で使う照明の種類を変える方が現実的だという内容。よって，Instead「その代わりに」が適切。

全文訳 **ナラタケ**

　地球上に現存する最も大きい生物は，クジラでもそのほかの大型動物でもない。それどころか，キノコや毒キノコを含む生物群にそれは属している。それはナラタケとして一般に知られる菌類の一種で，根のような菌糸がアメリカのオレゴン州の森の地中に広い面積にわたって広がっている。DNA 検査によって，この地域のナラタケ全てが同じ生物に由来することが確認されており，その年間成長率に基づき，科学者たちはそれが8 千年以上前から存在している可能性があると推定している。科学者たちはまた，仮にこれを全てひとまとめにした場合，35,000 トンほどの重さになると推定している。

　このナラタケは感銘を与えるものではあるが，森の多くの木々に問題を引き起こしている。ナラタケは木を感染させて，その根や幹から栄養を吸収し，多くの場合は最終的に枯らしてしまう。残念なことに感染した木はたいてい見つけにくく，それはナラタケが樹皮の下に隠れており，樹皮を剥がしたときに初めてその菌糸を見ることができるからである。秋の終わりごろ，ナラタケの子実体（キノコ）が木の外側に現れるが，冬の前のたった数週間だけである。木はナラタケに抵抗しようとするが，ナラタケは木の根に損傷を与えて上部に水や栄養が届かないようにするため，たいていは最終的に戦いに負ける。

　オレゴンのナラタケの完全な除去が検討されているが，費用と時間がかかり過ぎると分かるだろう。現在研究されている別の解決策は，ナラタケに対抗できる樹種を植えることである。しかし一部の専門家たちは，見方を変える必要があるかもしれないと示唆している。ナラタケの影響を否定的な観点で捉えるのではなく，むしろ人はそれを自然の成り行きの一例として考えるべきである。枯死した木々は最終的には土に返り，地域の生態系の役に立つ。

語句 fungus「菌類」, organism「有機体, 生物」, toadstool「毒キノコ」, rootlike「根のような」, filament「菌糸」, pose「(問題を) 引き起こす」, infect「感染させる」, absorb「吸収する」, nutrient「栄養素」, trunk「木の幹」, spot「見つける」, bark「樹皮」, visible「目に見える」, attempt to *do*「～しようと試みる」, resist「抵抗する」, removal「除去」, time-consuming「時間のかかる」, perspective「物事の見方」, in a negative light「否定的な観点で」, ultimately「最終的に」

(32) –解答 **4** ・・・・・・・・・・・・・・・・・・・・・・・・・・・・・・・・・・・・・・

問題文の訳 この文章によると，オレゴン州のナラタケについて正しいことの1つは何か。

選択肢の訳
1　時間をかけて一緒に成長を始めたさまざまなキノコ種の組み合わさったものである。
2　最初はゆっくりと成長したが，過去1千年でより急速に拡大している。

3 集めた栄養を，生育している木やほかの種類の植物に分け与えている。

4 木に生育し木を常食とすることで広い範囲に広がった単一生物である。

解説 第1段落から，ナラタケは，オレゴン州の森の地中を広い面積にわたって広がっている，キノコや毒キノコを含む生物群に属する菌類の一種である。また，第2段落から，菌が木に感染し，その根や幹から栄養を吸収する（＝ feed on trees）ことが分かる。よって，**4** が適切。

(33) –解答 ② ⋯⋯⋯⋯⋯⋯⋯⋯⋯⋯⋯⋯⋯ 正答率 ★**75%以上**

問題文の訳 ナラタケを見つけるのが困難である理由は

選択肢の訳
1 生育している木の種類によって，ナラタケが生成するキノコが色を変えるためである。

2 1年のある短期間に子実体を形成するときを除いて，ふつうは見えないためである。

3 ナラタケは地中で育つだけでなく，木の根のような見た目をしているためである。

4 ナラタケは，生育に必要な特定の気象条件のある地域でしか生存できないためである。

解説 第2段落参照。ナラタケが見つけにくいこととその理由は，Unfortunately, ... の文とその次の文 In the late fall, ... にある。「樹皮を剥がしたときだけ見える」「子実体が木の外側に現れる（＝見える）のは冬の前のたった数週間だけ」という内容から，**2** が適切。**3** は，地中で育つ（ので見つけにくい）は正しいが，木の根のような見た目は見つけにくい理由ではない。

(34) –解答 ① ⋯⋯⋯⋯⋯⋯⋯⋯⋯⋯⋯⋯⋯ 正答率 ★**75%以上**

問題文の訳 一部の専門家たちはどう考えているか。

選択肢の訳
1 人々は，ナラタケが木に与える影響を自然で有益なプロセスと見なすべきである。

2 ナラタケに対処する唯一の現実的な方法は，除去する試みにもっと多くの時間とお金を投資することである。

3 ナラタケに感染した木は，ナラタケがそれ以上広がるのを妨げるために利用できる。

4 ナラタケは，収穫することで人々に優れた栄養源を提供できる。

解説 第3段落の Some experts have suggested, ... を参照。問題の解決策として，（ナラタケを完全除去する，ナラタケに対抗できる樹種を植えるという）見方を変える必要があると述べた後，Rather than ... people should ... で，ナラタケの影響を「自然の成り行きの一例として考えるべき」と述べている。その一例を具体的に説明した最終文の Dead trees ... ecosystem. の内容から，**1** が適切。本文の nature taking its course は「自然の成り行き」の意味。

インテンショナル・コミュニティー

　何百年もの間，人は，しばしば「インテンショナル・コミュニティー」と呼ばれ，共通の理想，共同所有，そして資産の共同利用で特徴づけられる自立したコミュニティーを形成してきた。知られている限りの最初のインテンショナル・コミュニティーは，紀元前6世紀にギリシャの哲学者によって設立された。その後数世紀にわたって，社会の本流から離れて生きることを望む宗教団体によってこのようなコミュニティーが幾つも作られた。キリスト教修道院やイスラエルのキブツと呼ばれる集団農場など，これらの幾つかは何世代にもわたって成功が続いたが，他方で数年しか続かないインテンショナル・コミュニティーもあった。

　20世紀において，1960年代と1970年代の「大地へ帰れ」運動で見られたような哲学的観念論も，人々にインテンショナル・コミュニティーを形成する気にさせた。1970年代初頭には，アメリカ合衆国だけでもそのようなコミュニティーが何千もあったと推定されているが，その多くがその後解散した。インテンショナル・コミュニティー財団には現在，アメリカにおいて800未満のコミュニティー，世界のその他地域において250弱のコミュニティーが記載されている。失敗したインテンショナル・コミュニティーは，たいてい同じような課題に直面していた。そこにとどまるために来た人の中には仕事の分担，自分たちの食料を育てること，そして集団生活の理想に傾倒している人もいたが，それほど真剣ではない人もいた。あるコミュニティーの共同創立者は「私たちは実用性はないものの高尚なビジョンを持っていたが，それは常にただ遊びに来ただけの人たちにむしばまれた」と振り返った。

　しかし，全てのインテンショナル・コミュニティーが瓦解する運命にあるわけではない。イタリアのトリノの近くにある精神的かつ芸術的な共同体であるダマヌールの現在でも続いている成功は，オープンなコミュニケーションと実際的なアプローチによるものである。ダマヌールは，その構成員を15～20人から成る家族のようなグループに編成する。このコミュニティーでは，「家族」が25人より多いと親密さを生み出すのが難しくなることに気付いた。その一方で「家族」の構成員が少な過ぎると，効果的な意思決定を可能にするのに十分な集団的知性がない。ダマヌールの理想は，その憲法で述べられているが，選挙で選ばれたリーダーによって維持されている。そしてコミュニティー内の緊張は，塗料の入ったおもちゃの銃で戦う，遊び半分の模擬戦を開催することで対処される。

　うまくいっている全てのインテンショナル・コミュニティーには「常に先を考える能力」という共通する特徴があるように思われる。ダマヌールのある構成員はこう言う。「物事はうまくいかないときではなく，うまくいっているときに変えるべきである。」問題が起きる前に変化を起こすというこの戦略は，ダマヌールやその他のうまくいっているコミュニティーにとって功を奏しており，そのことはインテンショナル・コミュニティーが長期的にその構成員のニーズを満たすのにこれが効果的な方法であることを示唆している。

　語句 self-sustaining「自立した」，collective「共同の」，philosopher「哲

学者」, mainstream「主流（派）の」, monastery「（男子）修道院」, idealism「理想主義，観念論」, disband「解散する」, *be* committed to「～に熱心である」, cofounder「共同創立者」, noble「高貴な」, undermine「むしばむ」, *be* destined to *do*「～する運命にある」, fall apart「瓦解する」, ongoing「現在進行中の」, *be* attributed to「…の原因は～にある」, intimacy「親密さ」, decision-making「意思決定」, outline「概要を述べる」, constitution「憲法，規約」, uphold「（慣習などを）維持する」, tension「緊張」, playful「遊び心のある」, mock「模擬の」, trait「特徴」, strategy「戦略」, fulfill「満たす」, in the long term「長期的に」

(35) – 解答

問題文の訳 失敗したインテンショナル・コミュニティーが直面した共通の問題は

選択肢の訳
1 コミュニティーの大多数が誰かが参加することに賛成したが，少数の人が反対したことである。
2 人々は真の関心を持ってコミュニティーに参加したものの，効果的に貢献するためのスキルや知識が不足していたことである。
3 コミュニティーの理想に従うために一生懸命努力する構成員もいたが，共同生活に対しより軽いアプローチを取る構成員もいたことである。
4 コミュニティーは野心的なプロジェクトを完了しようと始めたが，知識と財源の不足が理由でそれを完了できなかったことである。

解説 第2段落中ほどに設問と同表現の Intentional communities that failed generally faced a similar challenge（＝ common issue）. がある。具体的には，続く Some people who ... but others were ... に「理想に傾倒している人もいたが，それほど真剣ではない人もいた」とあり，**3** が適切。**2** は「人は皆，真の関心を持って参加した」という意味になり，「ただ遊びに来ただけの人もいた」という本文の趣旨に合わない。

(36) – 解答

問題文の訳 ダマヌールの社会構造について正しいものはどれか。

選択肢の訳
1 「家族」は自由に独自のルールを作ることができ，必ずしもコミュニティーの憲法に含まれるルールに従う必要はない。
2 グループの問題を解決し，良好な関係を維持するための最良の条件を作り出すため，「家族」の人数は制御されている。
3 意見の食い違いを解決することを目的とした模擬戦は時に深刻になり，「家族」を離れる羽目になる構成員もいる。
4 コミュニティーには，構成員が大規模グループの環境で生活するか，小規模グループの環境で生活するかを選択できるよう，さまざまな規模の「家族」がある。

解説 第3段落によると，ダマヌールの「家族」は15～20人で，それは25人より多いと親密さを生み出すのが難しくなり，少な過ぎると効果的な意思決定をしにくいからである。これを「人数が制御されている」と表した**2**が適切。模擬戦による負の効果は述べていないので，**3**は不適。

(37) – 解答 ④

問題文の訳 この文章によると，ダマヌールはうまくいっているほかのインテンショナル・コミュニティーとどんな点で似ているか。

選択肢の訳
1 コミュニティーの構成員は，疲れ果てることがないように，ときどき責任を交換することが認められている。
2 構成員が新しいスキルを習得できるよう，収入を得るためにコミュニティーが行う仕事の種類が定期的に変更される。
3 コミュニティーの構成員は，共同所有の建物や設備の維持管理を交代で行う。
4 コミュニティーは，単に問題が発生したときに対応するのではなく，構成員のニーズを満たす方法を継続的に見つける。

解説 第4段落参照。ダマヌールやそのほかのうまくいっているコミュニティーの共通する特徴として，「物事はうまくいかないときではなく，うまくいっているときに変える」「問題が起きる前に変化を起こす」という戦略がある。続いて，この戦略について「長期的に構成員のニーズを満たすのに効果的な方法である」と述べている。本文の fulfill を正解**4**では satisfy と言い換えている。

全文訳 **インドのイギリス人**

　1600年に設立されたイギリス人所有の東インド会社は，2世紀以上の間，世界最大の会社の1つであった。インドや中国など，さまざまな国と海外貿易することによって，東インド会社はこれらの国々からぜいたく品をイギリスに輸入することができた。イギリス政府は，東インド会社の巨額の利益の一部を受け取っていたため，大いに喜んで政治的支援を与えた。何十万ものインド人の私兵集団を含む，その規模，権力，そして資金により，東インド会社はインドに圧力をかけて，だいたいにおいて同社の利益にしかならない貿易契約を受諾させた。1750年代に地元の支配者との戦いに勝利してからは，東インド会社はインドで最も裕福な州の1つを掌握した。その結果，東インド会社は企業としてのみ活動することをやめ，政治機関としても活動するようになり，インド国民に税金を同社に払うことを強制し始めた。

　東インド会社は，取引相手の国々の間で信頼できないという評判を得た。また，同社の不誠実な商習慣が中国との外交関係を悪化させたため，イギリス議会内でも人気を失いつつあった。それから，1850年代に，東インド会社の私兵集団の兵士の一部が，受けていた扱いに怒り，反乱を起こした。彼らはデリーまで行進してインド皇帝を権力の座に復帰させ，彼らの行動によってイギリス人に対する反乱はインド各地に広がった。

約２年後に反乱は結局鎮圧されたが，東インド会社の終焉<ruby>終焉<rt>しゅうえん</rt></ruby>の引き金となった。反乱が起こるのを許したことの責任を東インド会社に負わせたイギリス政府がインドの支配権を握り，イギリスの直接支配の時代が始まった。イギリス人は東インド会社を閉鎖し，インド皇帝を権力の座から降ろし，百年近くも続くインドの統治を始めた。

　典型的には鉄道の建設を一例として挙げて，インドはイギリス支配から恩恵を受けたと主張する人もいるが，多くの歴史家たちがインドは悪影響を受けたと主張する。イギリス文化が優れているという概念を強固なものにしようとして，インド人はイギリス人と同じ考え方や道徳，社会的選好を持つように教育された。イギリス人はまた，「分割統治」として知られる政策を実施し，これによって異なる宗教的背景を持つインド人を互いに敵対させた。イギリス政府はこの戦略を利用してインドに対する支配を維持したが，それはこれらの宗教の構成員が先の反乱時に結託したからであった。しかし，1900年代初頭からインド人の間でナショナリズムの感情が高まり，インドはついに1940年代後半に独立を獲得した。

　東インド会社が廃業したのは百年以上前のことだが，永続的な影響を及ぼしている。一部の専門家たちは，それが多国籍企業の概念の先駆けとなり，最終的には今日広まっている資本主義の経済システムにつながったと言う。さらに，イギリス政府と東インド会社の癒着は，事業目的の達成を助けるために政治的権力を利用する先例を作った。

> 語句　a portion of「〜の一部」，vast「巨大な」，*be* willing to *do*「喜んで〜する」，more than「非常に〜で」，*be* of benefit to「〜のためになる」，seize「奪取する」，province「州」，untrustworthy「信頼できない」，parliament「（Parliament で）（英国）議会」，rebel「反逆する」，〈restore＋人＋to power〉「（人）を権力の座に復帰させる」，rebellion「反乱」，trigger「引き起こす」，proceed to *do*「〜し始める」，benefit from「〜から恩恵を受ける」，in an effort to *do*「〜しようとして」，reinforce「強化する」，notion「概念」，implement「実施する」，nationalist feeling「ナショナリズムの感情」，lasting「永続的な」，pioneer「先駆けとなる」，multinational「多国籍の」，capitalism「資本主義」，precedent「先例」，objective「目的」

(38) – 解答

問題文の訳　インドが東インド会社と取引を行った結果の１つは何だったか。

選択肢の訳
1　インドは，他国と貿易取引をすることができたため，軍隊の規模を拡大する余裕があった。
2　インドには，自国にとって不利な商取引に合意する以外に選択肢がほとんどなかった。
3　インド政府は，失敗した貿易契約による損失を補うために増税しなければならなかった。
4　インド政府と中国との関係が悪化し，その結果，両国間の貿易が途絶えそうになった。

解説 第1段落の the company pressured India into accepting trade contracts that, in general, were only of benefit to the company 以降を参照。pressure A into -ing は「A に〜するよう圧力をかける」の意味。**2** が正解で，東インド会社がインドに圧力をかけて貿易契約を受諾させたことを，「ほぼ選択肢がない」と表し，また「東インド会社の利益にしかならない」を「インドにとって不利な」と表している。

(39) – 解答 ①

問題文の訳 イギリス政府がインドを支配することになったきっかけは何だったか。

選択肢の訳
1 イギリス政府は，起こった反乱の責任を東インド会社に押しつけた。
2 インド国民は，国を効果的に統治するインド皇帝の能力に対する信頼を失った結果，イギリスの支配に賛成票を投じた。
3 インド国民は，インドと中国の間の戦争を防ぐために，イギリス人の協力を求めた。
4 インド皇帝は，インドの支配を維持するための政治的戦略として，イギリス人と手を組むことを決定した。

解説 第2段落後半参照。イギリスの直接支配の時代が始まった（an era of direct British rule began）きっかけは，その前の The British government, which blamed the East India Company for allowing the rebellion to happen にある。「反乱が起こるのを許したことの責任を東インド会社に負わせた」を「起こった反乱の責任を東インド会社に押しつけた」と表した **1** が適切。本文の rebellion を uprising に，happen を occur に言い換えている。

(40) – 解答 ③

問題文の訳 イギリスの支配がインドに与えた影響の1つは

選択肢の訳
1 インド人が，自分たちの経済的・社会的ニーズを反映した政府を構築する過程に参加できたことであった。
2 学校が生徒にインドとイギリスの両文化を意識するよう教育する努力をしたことであった。
3 インド人のさまざまな集団の間に分断がもたらされ，彼らがイギリスの支配に異議を唱えるのを妨げたことであった。
4 インド政府によって建設された鉄道やそのほかの輸送システムの多くが破壊されたことであった。

解説 第3段落参照。イギリスは分割統治（統治を容易にするため被支配者の団結を妨げて分裂させること）を行い，異なる宗教的背景を持つインド人を互いに敵対させた（turned Indians from different religious backgrounds against each other）。本文 "divide and rule" の動詞 divide が正解 **3** では名詞 divisions になっている。**2** は In an effort to reinforce ... と不一致。

問題文の訳 この文章の筆者は東インド会社について何と言っているか。

選択肢の訳 1 同社は，イギリス政府がアジアのほかの国々に支配を拡大するという目的を達成するのを妨げた。

2 同社は，その時代には成功したかもしれないが，そのビジネスモデルは今日の経済では有効ではないだろう。

3 同社は，今はもう存在しないが，現在の世界経済情勢に大きな影響を及ぼしている。

4 同社が設立されていなかったとしても，おそらく別の会社が同じような政治的・経済的影響力を持つことになっていただろう。

解説 第4段落参照。東インド会社は百年以上前に廃業した（= no longer exists）が，永続的な影響を及ぼしている。また，それ（東インド会社）が多国籍企業の概念の先駆けとなり，最終的には今日広まっている資本主義の経済システム（= the present-day global economic landscape）につながったのである。

一次試験・筆記 4 問題編 p.157

トピックの訳 人の給料は仕事の成果に基づくべきか。

ポイントの訳 ・年齢 ・会社の利益 ・モチベーション ・スキル

解答例 In my opinion, from the perspectives of motivation and company profits, people's salaries should definitely be related to their job performance.

To begin with, while standardized salaries for workers in companies today are common, the level of motivation among employees can vary greatly. Rewarding enthusiastic employees who produce better work with higher salaries is not only fair but would also have the wider benefit of motivating other employees.

Additionally, the efforts that employees put into performing their work duties well ultimately benefit companies by increasing their profits. One of the responsibilities of a business is said to be the distribution of profits to those who contribute to its growth. Therefore, to fulfill this responsibility, companies must make sure that salaries match workers' job performance.

To conclude, when considering the importance of employee motivation and sharing company profits, I feel that people's salaries should be based on their job performance.

解説 序論：第1段落では，トピックに対する自分の意見（主張）を簡潔に書く。模範解答は In my opinion, from the perspectives of ... 「私の意見では，…の観点から〜」の形でポイントの Motivation と Company profits を提示した後，「給料は仕事の成果に基づくべき」という賛成の立場を明らかにしている。definitely「間違いなく」を使うと主張が強まる。

本論：本論では，序論で述べた主張を裏付ける根拠・理由を，2つの観点に沿って説明する。模範解答の To begin with, ... / Additionally, ... のように，段落を2つに分けるとよい。第2段落は Motivation の観点で，「給料は標準化されているのが一般的だが，従業員のモチベーションは千差万別だ」と述べた後，「より良い仕事をする従業員に高い給料で報いることは，公正であるだけでなく，ほかの従業員のモチベーションを高める」と説明を続けている。while A, B と not only A but also B はいずれも B が強調されるので，主張したい内容は後ろに書くこと。第3段落は Company profits の観点で，「従業員の努力は最終的に企業に利益をもたらす」と断言した後，具体的な説明が続く。is said to be「（一般に）〜だと言われている」→ Therefore「それ故に」の展開を確認しよう。Therefore（結論）以下の companies must make sure that salaries match workers' job performance「企業は確実に給料が労働者の仕事の成果に見合うようにしなければならない」の部分は，「給料は仕事の成果に基づくべき」という主張の言い換えになっている。

結論：最終段落では序論で述べた主張を再確認する。模範解答は To conclude, で始め，when considering「〜を考慮するとき」の形で2つの観点を再び取り上げ，〈I feel that + トピックの表現〉で締めくくっている。なお，序論と結論の「主張」でトピックの表現を用いる際，どちらかは表現を変える方がよい。模範解答では，序論で be based on を be related to に言い換えている。

そのほかの表現 ポイントの Age「年齢」を取り上げる場合，In Japan, salaries generally tend to increase with age, but ... 「日本では，給料は年齢とともに上がる傾向にあるが…」のような切り口が考えられるだろう。Skills「スキル」の観点では，Many companies set salaries based on skills rather than their job performance.「仕事の成果ではなくスキルを基準として給料を設定する会社も多い」などと述べて論を展開することが考えられる。

No.**1**−解答 **①**

スクリプト ☆： Hi, Vince. Nice day for a walk, huh?

★： Yeah, it is. Actually, I'm on my way to work.

☆： I thought you drove to work. Is something wrong with your car?

★： No, I've just been putting on a bit of weight recently.

☆： I guess you have to get up pretty early now, though.

★： I don't mind that. And I feel a lot healthier.

☆： Great! And I bet walking is easier on your wallet, too.

★： Definitely! I'm planning to use the gas savings to buy a new bike.

Question: What do we learn about Vince?

全文訳 ☆： こんにちは，ヴィンス。散歩日和ね。

★： そうだね。実は今仕事に向かっているんだ。

☆： 車で通勤していると思っていたわ。車に何か問題があるの？

★： いや，最近ちょっと太り気味なだけだよ。

☆： でも，今はかなり早く起きなければならないよね。

★： それは構わないんだ。それに体調がずっと良くなった気がするんだ。

☆： いいわね！　それに歩くのはきっと財布にもやさしいものね。

★： そうなんだよ！　浮いたガソリン代は新しい自転車を買うのに使うつもりだ。

質問：ヴィンスについて分かることは何か。

選択肢の訳　**1**　彼はもう車で通勤していない。

2　彼の車は修理中である。

3　彼はガソリンを買う余裕がない。

4　彼の新しい自転車が盗まれた。

解説　設問では，発言や話の展開を理解して，「つまりどういうことか」が問われやすい。最初の方の for a walk と I'm on my way to work から，男性は歩いて職場に向かっている。女性の「車通勤だと思っていた」や，walking is easier ... から，男性は車通勤をやめて歩くことにしたと判断して，**1** が正解。I thought ～「～だと思った」は実際［今］はそうではないことを示す表現。

No.**2**−解答 **③**

スクリプト ☆： Fernando, how are you getting along with your dorm roommate?

★： Oh, he's all right, Mom, I guess. He's pretty tidy, but he's not very communicative. I never know what's on his mind.

☆： Do you ever do things together?

★： Almost never. I spend more time with the other guys on my floor. They're a little crazy, but they're fun.

☆： Well, I'm glad you're enjoying yourself, but don't forget to spend enough time on your studies.

Question: What does Fernando suggest about his roommate?

全文訳 ☆： フェルナンド，寮のルームメートとはうまくいっているの？

★： うん，母さん，彼は大丈夫だよ，たぶん。彼は結構きれい好きなんだけど，あまりコミュニケーションを取ってくれないんだ。何を考えているのか，さっぱり分からないんだよ。

☆： 何か一緒にすることはないの？

★： ほとんどない。同じ階のほかのやつらと過ごすことの方が多い。彼らはちょっとクレイジーだけど，楽しいからね。

☆： そう，あなたが楽しんでいるのはうれしいけど，勉強に十分時間を割くことを忘れないでね。

質問：フェルナンドはルームメートについて何と言っているか。

選択肢の訳 1 彼は寮を出たいと思っている。

2 彼はパーティーを開くのが好きだ。

3 彼はあまり心を開かない。

4 彼はとても散らかす。

解説 息子と母親の会話で，話題は息子の寮（dorm）のルームメート。He's pretty tidy, but he's not very communicative. の部分を言い換えた **3** が正解。「communicative ではない」ことの説明となる I never know what's on his mind. の部分も参考になる。but 以下に話者が伝えたい内容がくることを意識して聞こう。

No.3 – 解答 ④ ．．．．．．．．．．．．．．．．．．．．．．．．．．．

スクリプト ☆： How are things going, Matt?

★： Not so good. I was supposed to have a job interview yesterday, but all the trains were stopped due to an accident, so I couldn't make it.

☆： But they'll give you another chance, won't they?

★： No. I called the manager as soon as I got home. He said they'd already seen enough people. Looks like I'm out of luck.

☆： That's awful.

★： Yeah, well, I guess they have a lot of good candidates to choose from.

Question: Why did Matt not get the job?

全文訳 ☆： 調子はどう，マット？

★： あんまり。昨日は仕事の面接を受けるはずだったんだけど，事故で列車

が全部運休してしまって，行けなかったんだ。

☆： でも，もう一回チャンスをくれるでしょう？

★： いや。帰宅してすぐにマネージャーに電話をかけたんだ。もう十分な数の人を面接したと言っていた。僕は運がないみたいだ。

☆： それはひどいわ。

★： うん，まあ，選べるほど良い候補者がたくさんいるんだろうね。

質問：マットはなぜその仕事を得なかったのか。

選択肢の訳 **1** ほかの候補者たちの方が適任だった。

2 彼は昨日，マネージャーに電話するのを忘れた。

3 マネージャーが彼を気に入らなかった。

4 彼は面接を受け損ねた。

解説 男性は最初の発言で，昨日面接を受けられなかった理由を but 以下で説明している。can't make it は「出席［参加］できない，（約束の時間に）間に合わない」などの意味で，これを正解 **4** では miss「逃す」を使って表している。was [were] supposed to *do*「～するはずだった」は，実際はできなかったことを示す表現。マットが適任か適任でないかは話題にないので **1** は不適。

No.**4**－解答 ④

スクリプト ☆： Professor Cranfield, can I ask you something?

★： Sure, Lucinda.

☆： It's about your intensive Spanish writing course. I feel like I'm already busy with my other classes. Doing the writing course might be too much.

★： I understand. I think you certainly have the ability, but I don't want to push you. It's not a mandatory course, but future employers would be impressed if you passed it.

☆： Thanks for your advice. I'll think it over a little more.

Question: What does the man imply about the writing course?

全文訳 ☆： クランフィールド教授，お尋ねしてもいいですか？

★： いいですよ，ルシンダ。

☆： 教授のスペイン語ライティング集中講座についてなんですが。私はほかの授業ですでに忙しいと思っていまして。ライティングの講座を受けるのは荷が重いかもしれません。

★： なるほど。私はあなたには確実にその能力があると思いますが，無理をさせたくはありません。必修の講座ではないですが，その単位を取れば，あなたの将来の雇用主も感心するでしょうね。

☆： アドバイスをありがとうございます。もう少し考えてみます。

質問：男性はライティング講座について何をほのめかしているか。

選択肢の訳 1 女性は卒業するのにその単位を取る必要がある。

選択肢の訳 1 女性は卒業するのにその単位を取る必要がある。

  2 それは女性の目標に合わない。

  3 それは女性には難易度が高過ぎる。

  4 その単位を取ることは女性が仕事を見つけるのに役立つかもしれない。

解説 教授と学生の会話で，話題はライティング講座。女性は I feel like ... の発言から受講に前向きではない様子。これに対する教授のアドバイスの future employers would be impressed ... から，**4** が正解。future employers は女性の将来の雇用主のことで，つまり就職に有利だという趣旨。

No.5 – 解答 ②

スクリプト ★： Amy, I heard you're looking for a part-time job.

  ☆： I'm thinking about working at a restaurant as a server. I could use the money to help pay for school fees.

  ★： Well, I hope you like standing for long periods of time.

  ☆： I would get breaks, you know. I doubt it would be that bad.

  ★： Well, I think you should buy some comfortable shoes, just in case.

  ☆： I need to get the job first.

  Question: What does the man imply?

全文訳 ★： エイミー，君がアルバイトを探しているって聞いたんだけど。

  ☆： 接客係としてレストランで働くことを考えているの。そのお金を学費の足しにできるわ。

  ★： そう，長時間立っているのが好きならいいけど。

  ☆： もちろん休憩はあるわよ。そんな悪くないと思うけど。

  ★： まあ，履き心地のいい靴を買っておくべきだと思うけどね，念のため。

  ☆： まずは仕事を得ないとね。

  質問：男性は何をほのめかしているか。

選択肢の訳 1 女性は学校を休学すべきだ。

  2 接客係として働くことは体力的にきつい。

  3 飲食店の店員はあまり稼げない。

  4 学生はアルバイトをするべきではない。

解説 アルバイトでレストランでの接客係をすることを検討している女性に対し，男性は，I hope you like standing for long periods of time の部分で長時間の立ち仕事を心配している。これを physically demanding と表した **2** が正解。最後の「履き心地のいい靴を買うべき」もヒントになる。男性は女性のアルバイトに賛成している様子ではないが，学生アルバイト自体を批判しているわけではないので **4** は不適。

スクリプト ☆： We still need to buy a present for Carla and Antonio's wedding. Have you checked out the gift registry yet?

★： Yes, but the only things left on the list are really expensive items, like the silver dining set.

☆： I warned you that if we didn't choose something quickly, the affordable stuff would all be gone.

★： Sorry. You were right. What should we do? Get them something cheaper that's not on the list?

☆： No. I'd rather not take any chances. We don't want to give them something they might not want.

Question: What will these people probably do?

全文訳 ☆： まだカーラとアントニオの結婚式の贈り物を買わないといけないわ。ギフト登録リストはもう確認した？

★： うん，でもリストであと残っているのはとても高価な物ばかりだよ，銀食器セットとか。

☆： 早く何かを選ばないと，手頃な物は全部なくなるってあなたに言ったわよね。

★： ごめん。君が正しかったよ。どうしたらいい？ リストにない，何か安めの物を買う？

☆： いいえ。できれば安全第一でいきたいわ。彼らが欲しくないかもしれない物をあげたくないもの。

質問： この人たちはおそらく何をするか。

選択肢の訳 　**1** リストから選んで贈り物を買う。

　　2 結婚式の招待を断る。

　　3 カーラとアントニオと話す。

　　4 銀食器セットを返品する。

解説 話題は友人の結婚式の贈り物。「リストに残っているのは高価な物だけ」「新郎新婦が欲しくない物をあげたくない」などの内容から，gift registry のリストには新郎新婦が欲しい物が載っていると推測できる。「リストにないものを買う？」という提案に女性は反対しているので，**1** が適切。not take any chances は「運任せにしない，安全第一でいく」の意味で，ここでは新郎新婦が欲しいもの＝リストにあるものを買うということ。

スクリプト ☆： Would you mind picking up some takeout on your way home?

★： No problem. How about burgers?

☆： Too greasy. I was thinking about that Korean restaurant we went to last week.

★： That's not exactly on my way home, and it's a little pricey.

☆： I know, but the servings are huge. We'd have enough for lunch tomorrow, too. Korean food is just as good the next day.

★： All right. They're usually pretty quick with orders, so I should be home by around six.

Question: What is one reason the woman suggests the Korean restaurant?

全文訳 ☆： 帰る途中で何か持ち帰りの料理を買ってきてくれない？

★： いいよ。ハンバーガーでいい？

☆： 脂っこ過ぎるわ。先週行った韓国料理店を考えていたんだけど。

★： それは帰り道からはちょっと外れるし，少し値段も高いよ。

☆： 分かってるわ，でも量が多いでしょ。明日の昼食にも十分あるわ。韓国料理は1日経っても味は落ちないし。

★： 分かったよ。あの店はたいていすぐに注文を持ってきてくれるから，6時ごろには帰れると思う。

質問：女性が韓国料理店を勧める理由の1つは何か。

選択肢の訳 1 量が多い。
2 自宅から車で近い。
3 ほかの飲食店よりも安い。
4 評判が良い。

解説 女性は冒頭で男性に，帰宅途中に食べ物を買ってきてくれるよう頼んでいる。burgers は Too greasy. と言って却下し，韓国料理店を提案する。その理由として the servings are huge と言っているので **1** が正解。serving と portion はいずれも「（料理の）1人分の量」の意味。続く発言 We'd have enough for lunch tomorrow, ... もヒントになる。

No.**8** - 解答 ③ ....

スクリプト ☆： We should start planning our vacation for this year.

★： How about escaping the cold weather and going somewhere tropical with a nice beach?

☆： I was hoping we could go skiing.

★： Well, what did we do on our last vacation?

☆： We went camping. You caught that giant fish at the lake, remember?

★： Oh, right. And you wanted to go sightseeing in town, but the kids and I outvoted you.

☆： That's right.

★： OK. Let's do what you want this time. I'll tell the kids we're headed for the mountains.

Question: What are these people going to do for their vacation?

☆： 今年の休暇の予定を立て始めるべきだわ。

★： 寒い天気を逃れて，素敵なビーチのあるどこか暑い所に行くのはどう？

☆： 私はスキーに行けたらと思っていたんだけど。

★： ええと，この前の休暇は何をしたっけ？

☆： キャンプに行ったわ。あなたは湖であの巨大な魚を釣ったわ，覚えてない？

★： ああ，そうだった。それで君は町の観光をしたかったんだけど，僕と子供たちが多数決で勝ったんだ。

☆： そうよ。

★： ああ，分かった。今回は君のしたいことをしよう。子供たちには山に行くことを伝えるよ。

質問： この人たちは休暇に何をするか。

選択肢の訳 **1** ハイキングをして過ごす。

2 湖へ釣りに行く。

3 スキー旅行に行く。

4 観光に行く。

解説 男女が休暇の計画をしている。男性の希望はビーチのある南国で，女性はスキー。前回の休暇はキャンプで，女性は町の観光をしたかったが子供たちと男性の意見が通った。outvote は「（人より）多数の票を得て勝つ」の意味。男性の Let's do what you want this time. から，今回の休暇は女性の希望を通し，スキーに行くと考えられる。we're headed for the mountains は山スキーを暗示。

No.**9** – 解答 ②

スクリプト ☆： Hey, Kenneth. I was looking at the latest post on our company's blog. The one about the release of our new earphones. The release date is wrong. It should be May 15th, not the 5th as stated in the post.

★： Really? That post was added by Jason last night.

☆： Well, we need to take care of it immediately so we don't mislead our customers. Ask Jason to do that right away.

★： I'm afraid he has the day off today. I'll handle it instead.

☆： Thanks.

Question: What does the woman say about the company's blog?

全文訳 ☆： ねえ，ケネス。会社のブログの最新の投稿を見ていたんだけど。あの新製品のイヤホンの発売についてのね。発売日が間違っているわ。投稿に書かれている 5 月 5 日ではなく，5 月 15 日のはずよ。

★： 本当ですか。あの記事はジェイソンが昨夜投稿しました。

☆： そうなの，顧客に間違った情報を与えて判断を誤らせないように，すぐに対処しないと。ジェイソンにすぐにやってもらうように頼んで。

★： あいにく彼は今日休みです。僕が代わりにやりましょう。

☆： ありがとう。

質問：女性は会社のブログについて何と言っているか。

選択肢の訳 1 一部の顧客がそれについて苦情を言った。

2 投稿の1つを修正しなければならない。

3 ケネスはその最新の投稿を編集すべきではない。

4 それはもっと頻繁に更新されるべきだ。

解説 会社員同士の会話。女性は冒頭で男性（ケネス）に，会社のブログの最新の投稿で製品の発売日が間違っていると指摘する。投稿したのはジェイソンだと分かると Ask Jason to do that right away. と指示していることから，**2** が正解。ジェイソンは不在で投稿を編集するのはケネスなので **3** は不適。選択肢の Kenneth を見て，Kenneth が話者なのか会話中に出てくる人物なのかを意識しながら聞くとよい。

No.10 解答 ④ ....

スクリプト ☆： Excuse me, sir. Has anyone turned in a train pass today?

★： I'm afraid not. Have you lost yours?

☆： Yeah. When I used mine this morning, I was certain I put it back in my wallet, but I guess I didn't.

★： I can give you the form to purchase another one.

☆： Looks like I have no choice. It makes me so frustrated, though. I had just put $50 on it. Now, I've lost it all.

★： I'm sorry. Here's the form. It should only take a couple of minutes to fill out.

☆： Thanks. I'll do that now.

Question: Why is the woman upset?

全文訳 ☆： すみません。今日，列車の定期券を届け出た人はいませんでしたか？

★： 残念ながらいないようです。ご自分のをなくされましたか。

☆： ええ。今朝使ったときには確かに財布に戻したと思ったのだけど，そうしなかったようです。

★： 新しい定期券を購入する用紙をお渡しできますが。

☆： 選択の余地はなさそうですね。でも本当にいらいらします。50 ドルチャージしたばかりだったので。今では全部失ってしまいました。

★： お気の毒です。これが用紙です。数分で記入できると思います。

☆： ありがとう。今やります。

質問：女性はなぜいらいらしているか。

選択肢の訳 1 彼女の財布が見つからない。

2 彼女の列車の定期券の有効期限が切れた。

3 彼女は列車に乗り遅れた。

4 彼女はお金を無駄にした。

解説 序盤のやりとりから，女性は列車の定期券を紛失し，届けられていないか駅係員に尋ねている場面だと分かる。女性は後半で It makes me so frustrated（＝質問文の upset）と言い，その理由として「50 ドルチャージしたばかりだった」と続くので **4** が正解。

No.11 解答 ③ .... 正答率 ★75%以上

★： Michelle, I'm sorry I couldn't make it to the piano concert last Sunday.

☆： No problem. I sold your ticket to Jasmine, so it wasn't wasted.

★： I'm relieved to hear that. Did you enjoy the concert?

☆： Well, the pianist was superb. Unfortunately, we were bothered by another audience member, though.

★： What happened?

☆： He was continuously whispering to the person next to him and playing with his smartphone. It was hard to concentrate.

★： Oh, that's a shame.

Question: What was the woman's problem?

全文訳 ★： ミシェル，先週の日曜日のピアノのコンサートに行けなくてごめんね。

☆： いいのよ。あなたのチケットはジャスミンに売ったから，無駄にはならなかったわ。

★： それを聞いてほっとしたよ。コンサートは楽しかった？

☆： そうね，ピアニストは素晴らしかった。でも，残念ながらほかのお客さんに悩まされたわ。

★： 何があったの？

☆： 彼はずっと隣の人にひそひそと話していて，スマートフォンをいじっていたの。集中しにくかったわ。

★： ああ，それは残念だね。

質問： 女性の問題は何だったか。

選択肢の訳 **1** 彼女はピアニストの演奏が気に入らなかった。

2 彼女はコンサートに遅れて到着した。

3 彼女はコンサートに集中できなかった。

4 彼女はチケットを見つけることができなかった。

解説 先に選択肢を見ると，ピアノのコンサートが話題で，どれもネガティブな内容なので，何かしら問題があったことが予測できる。女性はUnfortunately, ... でほかの客に悩まされたと言い，具体的に「ひそひそと話してスマートフォンをいじっていたから（演奏を聴くのに）集中

しにくかった」と説明する。この concentrate を focus on と言い換えた **3** が正解。

No.**12** 解答 ②

スクリプト ☆： Hello, Jenny Williams speaking.

★： Hello. I'm calling about a package I'm supposed to deliver to your house.

☆： Oh, I see. Is there something wrong?

★： When you selected your delivery option online, you asked us to use the delivery box.

☆： Yes, I won't be home until seven tonight.

★： Unfortunately, the package won't fit in the box. Could I leave it in another location instead?

☆： Sure. If you can take it around to the side of the house, there's a bicycle shelter. You can leave it there.

Question: What does the man ask the woman to do?

全文訳 ☆： もしもし，ジェニー・ウィリアムズです。

★： もしもし，お客さまの家にお届けすることになっている小包についてお電話しました。

☆： ああ，なるほど。何か問題が？

★： お客さまが配達方法をオンラインで選択されたとき，配達ボックスを使うことを指示されました。

☆： そうです，今夜は 7 時まで家に帰らないので。

★： あいにく小包がボックスに入りません。代わりに別の場所に置いておいてもいいでしょうか？

☆： いいですよ。家の横に持って回ってもらえれば，そこに自転車置き場があるわ。そこに置いてくれていいですよ。

質問：男性は女性に何をするよう頼んでいるか。

選択肢の訳 1 夜に彼に折り返し電話をする。

2 彼に新しい配達指示を出す。

3 オンラインで彼女の配達方法を変更する。

4 彼女が何時に帰宅するかを彼に伝える。

解説 Hello, 人名＋speaking. で始まる客とスタッフの電話の会話。男性配達人は女性の家に荷物を届けに来たが，女性がオンラインで指定した置き場所である delivery box に入らないと説明し，Could I leave it in another location instead? と尋ねる。別の置き場所の指示 (instructions) を求めていると考えて，**2** が正解。

A

スクリプト **International Rivers**

　Many of the world's rivers are not contained within the borders of a single country. Because of the importance of water, international laws about how neighboring countries share these rivers are essential. Typically, all countries have equal rights to use a river that flows through their lands. Also, all countries are legally forbidden from doing anything to a river that would considerably decrease its flow of water into other countries.

　However, sharing a river is not always simple. For example, the Nile River runs through a number of countries, including Ethiopia and Egypt. Ethiopia has requested international loans to build a dam on its section of the river to generate electricity. However, Egypt has used its political influence to block the loans, complaining that a dam would reduce the Nile's water flow into Egypt. At the same time, Ethiopia points out that Egypt currently uses the river for power generation, so it is unfair if Ethiopia cannot.

Questions

No.13 What is one thing the speaker says about rivers?

No.14 Why is the Nile River discussed?

全文訳 **国際河川**

　世界の河川の多くは，1つの国の境界内に収まらない。水の重要性から，近隣諸国がそういった河川をどのように共有するかについての国際法が不可欠である。通常，全ての国に自国を流れる河川を利用する平等な権利がある。また，全ての国は，他国への水の流れを大幅に減少させるようなことを河川に対して行うことを法律で禁じられている。

　しかし，1つの河川を共有することは必ずしも単純ではない。例えば，ナイル川はエチオピアとエジプトを含め，いくつかの国を流れている。エチオピアは，発電のためにナイル川の自国の部分にダムを建設するための国際融資を求めた。しかしエジプトは，ダムはエジプトに流れるナイル川の水量を減らすと訴え，その融資を阻止しようと政治的影響力を行使している。一方でエチオピアは，エジプトは現在発電のためにナイル川を利用していることから，エチオピアが利用できないのは不公平だ，と指摘している。

No.**13** 解答

質問の訳　話者が河川について言うことの1つは何か。

選択肢の訳　1　多くの河川において水位が下がっている。

　　　　　　2　河川を保護するための法律を厳しくする必要がある。

　　　　　　3　河川を共有する国々は通常，同じ使用権を持っている。

4 河川は国境を保護するのを困難にすることが多い。

 Typically, all countries have equal rights to use a river ... their lands. から，**3** が正解。typically を **3** では usually に，equal rights to use を the same usage rights に言い換えている。河川や国境を保護する話はないので **2** と **4** は不適。

No.**14** 解答 ④ ···

質問の訳 ナイル川について話されているのはなぜか。

選択肢の訳 **1** 国境問題の解決策を提案するため。

2 貧しい国々が電力を得るために河川を必要としていることを示唆するため。

3 ダムはしばしばコストがかかり過ぎることを示すため。

4 河川の使用権がいかに複雑になり得るかを示すため。

解説 設問はパッセージの目的を問うもの。後半（However, ...）で「1 つの河川を共有することは必ずしも単純ではない」と述べた後，いかに複雑かの説明が続くので，**4** が正解。not always は「必ずしも～ではない」で，**4** では simple の反意語 complicated「複雑な」を用いている。

B

スクリプト **Theriac**

For thousands of years, people believed that a substance known as theriac was a wonder drug. According to legend, it was created by an ancient king who lived in fear of being poisoned. He was said to have taken theriac daily to protect himself from all forms of poison. The use of theriac gradually spread around the ancient world, and people began to believe that it was also effective against all kinds of illnesses. Making it, however, required time and effort, as some theriac recipes contained over a hundred ingredients, some of which came from poisonous snakes.

By the fifteenth century, there were regulations in many places about how theriac could be manufactured, and in some cities, such as Venice, it had to be made in a public ceremony. Though the scientific community now believes that theriac is ineffective, the regulations on the manufacture of theriac marked an important milestone in the development of modern medicine.

Questions

No.15 What is one thing that we learn about theriac?

No.16 What is one thing the speaker says about theriac in Venice?

全文訳 **テリアック**

何千年もの間，人々はテリアックとして知られる物質を奇跡の薬だと思っていた。伝説によると，この薬は毒殺を恐れて生きていた古代の王によって作られたという。彼は，あらゆる形の毒から身を守るために毎日テリアックを飲んでいたと言われている。テリ

アックの使用は徐々に古代世界に広がり，それがあらゆる病にも効くと人々が信じ始めた。しかし，それを作るには時間と手間がかかった。というのも，テリアックのレシピには 100 種を超える成分を含むものもあり，その中には毒ヘビから採取したものもあったからだ。

　15 世紀には，各地でテリアックの製造方法に関する規制ができ，ベネチアなど一部の都市では，公の儀式で製造されなければならなかった。現在，科学界ではテリアックは効果がないと考えられているが，テリアックの製造に関する規制は，現代医学の発展における重要な節目となった。

No.15 解答

質問の訳 テリアックについて分かることの 1 つは何か。

選択肢の訳 1　毒として使うことができた。
　　　　　2　ヘビで実験された。
　　　　　3　作るのが困難だった。
　　　　　4　初の医薬品だった。

解説 冒頭の a substance known as theriac was a wonder drug に続き，have taken theriac daily や effective against all kinds of illnesses などから，テリアックは「薬」だと理解しよう。Making it, however, required time and effort, ... から，作るのが難しいと分かるので，**3** が正解。パッセージ中の語 drug，poison，snakes を含む誤答に惑わされないように。

No.16 解答 ④

質問の訳 話者がベネチアのテリアックについて言うことの 1 つは何か。

選択肢の訳 1　作るのに何日もかかった。
　　　　　2　毎日少量しか作れなかった。
　　　　　3　製造の規制が非常に甘かった。
　　　　　4　そこの人々は，それが作られるのを見ることができた。

解説 ベネチアについて，in some cities, such as Venice, it had to be made in a public ceremony と言っている。it はテリアックのこと。public は「公の（場での）」と捉え，公の場で製造しなければならなかった＝ベネチアの人々は作られるのを見ることができたと考えて，**4** が正解。

C

 Spirit Bears

Found only in parts of Canada, spirit bears are black bears that are born with white fur due to a rare gene. Scientists estimate there may be as few as a hundred of these beautiful animals in the wild. For years, native peoples did their best to prevent the bears' existence from becoming known to the outside world. Because the bears' fur is so unusual, native peoples feared it would become a great prize for hunters and collectors.

Spirit bears' bright fur also provides them with a unique advantage when hunting salmon. Unlike the fur of ordinary black bears, spirit bears' fur is difficult for fish to see, so the fish are less able to avoid the bears. Unfortunately, however, spirit bear numbers may decrease even further. Recent research has revealed the gene that results in spirit bears' white fur is rarer than once thought. Additionally, many spirit bears live outside the areas where they are protected.

Questions

No.17 What does the speaker say about native peoples?

No.18 What advantage do spirit bears have over ordinary black bears?

全文訳 **シロアメリカグマ（精霊の熊）**

　カナダの一部でしか見られないシロアメリカグマは，珍しい遺伝子のために生まれつき毛が白いクロクマである。科学者たちは，この美しい動物は野生では100頭ほどしかいないかもしれないと推定している。何年もの間，先住民たちはこのクマの存在を外部に知られないよう最善を尽くした。このクマの毛は非常に珍しいため，先住民たちは猟師や収集家の格好の獲物になることを恐れたのだ。

　シロアメリカグマの鮮やかな毛は，サケを捕る際に彼らに独自の強みも与える。通常のクロクマの毛と違い，シロアメリカグマの毛は魚には見えにくいため，魚はこのクマを避けにくいのだ。しかし残念なことに，シロアメリカグマの数はさらに減少する可能性がある。最近の研究により，シロアメリカグマの白い毛をつくる遺伝子は，かつて考えられていたよりも希少であることが明らかになったのだ。さらに，多くのシロアメリカグマは，彼らが保護されている地域の外に生息している。

No.17 解答 ②

質問の訳　話者は先住民について何と言っているか。

選択肢の訳　**1**　彼らは黒い毛を持つシロアメリカグマしか狩らなかった。

2　彼らはシロアメリカグマを秘密にしておこうとした。

3　彼らはシロアメリカグマを危険だと思った。

4　彼らはシロアメリカグマが自分たちを守ってくれると信じていた。

解説　For years, native peoples ... の部分から，**2** が正解。「外部に知られないようにする」を「秘密にする」と表している。先住民はシロアメリカグマを猟師から守ろうとしたので **1** は不適。spirit bear という名前からは分かりにくいが，このクマは生まれつき白い（born with white fur）ことから，spirit bears with <u>black</u> fur も不適。

No.18 解答 ①

質問の訳　シロアメリカグマは通常のクロクマに比べてどんな強みがあるか。

選択肢の訳　**1**　シロアメリカグマの方が容易に餌を捕まえる。

2　シロアメリカグマの方が日光に強い。

3 シロアメリカグマの方が猟師に見つかりにくい。

4 シロアメリカグマの生息地は全てよく保護されている。

 シロアメリカグマの advantage「利点，強み」については Spirit bears' bright fur also provides them with a unique <u>advantage</u> 以降にある。通常のクロクマと比較した Unlike the fur of ordinary black bears, ... から，「魚はシロアメリカグマを避けにくい」＝「シロアメリカグマは餌を捕まえやすい」と考えて，**1** が適切。対比を表す unlike「～とは違って」の使われ方を確認しよう。

D

（スクリプト）**Distributed Generation**

In many parts of the United States, the electric power industry has been shifting away from the traditional system of centralized generation to a newer system known as distributed generation. With centralized generation, electricity is generated in one central location and then delivered to homes and businesses. Distributed generation is a network of smaller energy sources, such as solar panels or wind turbines, that produce electricity close to where it is needed. This can make the distributed-generation system more cost-effective.

Distributed generation has some disadvantages, however. The required infrastructure takes up space in communities, and residents generally consider it unattractive. In fact, homes close to large solar-energy facilities often sell for less than homes that are farther away. In addition, some distributed-generation systems require water to run, which is a limitation in areas that experience water shortages.

Questions

No.19 What is true about distributed-generation systems?

No.20 What is one downside of distributed generation?

（全文訳）**分散型発電**

アメリカ合衆国の多くの地域で，電力業界は従来の集中型発電システムから分散型発電と呼ばれる新しいシステムに移行している。集中型発電では，電力は1カ所の中心的場所で生成され，家庭や企業に供給される。分散型発電は，例えばソーラーパネルや風力タービンのような，電力が必要な場所の近くで発電する，より小さなエネルギー源のネットワークである。これにより，分散型発電システムの費用対効果を高めることができる。

しかし，分散型発電には幾つかの欠点がある。発電に必要な設備が地域社会の場所を取り，住民には概して見映えが悪いように映る。実際，大規模な太陽光発電施設付近の住宅は，遠方の住宅よりも安く売られる場合が多い。さらに，分散型発電システムの中には運用するのに水を必要とするものもあり，水不足に見舞われる地域では限界がある。

No.**19** 解答

質問の訳 分散型発電システムについて何が正しいか。

選択肢の訳 **1** 電力を使用する場所付近で発電する。

2 小規模事業者に好まれる。

3 太陽エネルギーを使用しない。

4 維持費が非常に高い。

解説 分散型発電に関する説明文で，前半では集中型発電と比較して概要と利点が述べられている。Distributed generation is a network of ... that produce electricity close to where it is needed. の部分から，**1** が正解。**1** の power は electricity のことで，本文の close to「～に近い」を near と表している。

No.**20** 解答

質問の訳 分散型発電の欠点の1つは何か。

選択肢の訳 **1** 政府はおおむねその開発に反対している。

2 エネルギー会社は通常，それから利益を得ることはない。

3 資産価値に悪影響を与える可能性がある。

4 しばしば地域の水源を汚染する。

解説 欠点（disadvantage(s) = downside）は後半の however 以下で述べられる。In fact の後には重要な内容が続くのでしっかりと聞こう。「大規模な太陽光発電施設付近の住宅は，遠方の住宅よりも安く売られる場合が多い」を「資産価値（property values）に悪影響を与え得る」と抽象的に表した **3** が正解。

E

スクリプト **What Zoos Can't Do**

In recent decades, zoos have been essential to efforts to save endangered animals. Several species of frogs, birds, and turtles have been saved from extinction by conservation programs that breed endangered animals in the safe environment of zoos. Unfortunately, certain species, such as tarsiers, which are animals that look like tiny monkeys, and great white sharks, cannot survive in captivity. These animals usually die quickly after being captured, making it impossible to breed them.

For this reason, the survival of tarsiers and great white sharks depends on the conservation of their natural environments. Though many of their habitats are already legally protected, the current laws are often ignored. Governments must try harder to stop the illegal destruction of the forests where tarsiers live and breed. They must also reduce illegal fishing activities that threaten great white sharks.

Questions
No.21 Why are zoos unable to breed some endangered animals?
No.22 What does the speaker say about saving tarsiers and great white sharks?

全文訳 **動物園にできないこと**

　ここ数十年，動物園は，絶滅の危機にひんした動物を救う取り組みに不可欠となっている。動物園という安全な環境で絶滅の危機にひんした動物を繁殖させる保護プログラムにより，カエル，鳥，カメなどの幾つかの種が絶滅の危機から救われた。しかし残念ながら，小猿のような見た目の動物であるメガネザルやホホジロザメなどの特定の種は，捕獲されると生き延びることができない。こういった動物は通常，捕獲直後に死んでしまうため，繁殖させることができないのだ。

　この理由から，メガネザルやホホジロザメの生存は，自然環境の保全にかかっている。すでに生息地の多くが法的に保護されているものの，現在の法律は無視されることが多い。各国政府は，メガネザルが生息・繁殖する森林の違法な破壊を阻止するためにもっと努力しなければならない。また，政府はホホジロザメを脅かす違法な漁業を減らさなければならない。

No.21 解答

質問の訳 　なぜ動物園は一部の絶滅の危機にひんした動物を繁殖させることができないのか。

選択肢の訳 　**1** 世話にお金がかかり過ぎる。
　2 捕獲するのが難し過ぎる。
　3 深刻な病気にかかる。
　4 捕獲後長く生きることがめったにない。

解説 　メガネザルやホホジロザメなどの特定の種（＝一部の絶滅の危機にひんした動物）について，These animals usually die quickly after being captured, making it impossible to breed them. と言っている。「捕獲直後に死ぬ」を「捕獲後長く生きられない」と表した **4** が適切。

No.22 解答 ②

質問の訳 　話者はメガネザルとホホジロザメを救うことについて何と言っているか。

選択肢の訳 　**1** 動物園はそれらの繁殖方法を学ぶ必要がある。
　2 政府は確実に法律が守られるようにしなければならない。
　3 それらを新しい生息地に移動させなければならない。
　4 それらを野生で保護することは不可能である。

解説 　後半で「現在の法律は無視されることが多い」と述べた後，メガネザルとホホジロザメ保護のために政府がしなければならないこととして，森林の違法な破壊の阻止，違法な漁業を減らすことに言及している。よって，**2** が正解。**4** は「すでに生息地の多くが法的に保護されている」と合わない。

F

Written in Stone

Petroglyphs are ancient drawings or carvings on rock surfaces. For researchers in the Americas, they are an important source of information about the Native Americans who lived there before the arrival of Europeans. Some of the most famous petroglyphs are those at Castle Rock Pueblo in Colorado. These images were not drawn in the style typical of the area, but in a way that was common in another settlement hundreds of kilometers away. There are also drawings of human conflict. This suggests that there may have been contact, and likely fighting, between these two communities.

Another interesting feature of the carvings is their use of light. On the longest and shortest days of the year, the carvings create specific patterns of light and shadow. This has led researchers to conclude that they were used as a type of solar calendar.

Questions

No.23 What is one thing we learn about the Castle Rock Pueblo petroglyphs?

No.24 How do researchers think the Castle Rock Pueblo petroglyphs were used?

（全文訳） **岩石に刻まれたもの**

ペトログリフとは，岩面に刻まれた古代の線画や彫刻のことである。アメリカ大陸の研究者たちにとって，それは，ヨーロッパ人の到来以前にそこに住んでいたアメリカ先住民に関する重要な情報源である。最も有名なペトログリフとして，コロラド州のキャッスル・ロック・プエブロのものがある。その画は，その地域に典型的なスタイルではなく，何百キロも離れた別の集落でよく見られる方法で描かれた。人間同士の争いを描いた線画もある。これは，この2つのコミュニティーの間に接触，おそらく戦いがあった可能性を示唆している。

彫刻のもう1つの興味深い特徴は，太陽光の使い方である。1年で最も日が長い日と最も日が短い日に，彫刻が光と影の特定の模様を作り出す。このことから，研究者たちは，その彫刻は一種の太陽暦として使用されていたと結論付けた。

No.23 解答

（質問の訳） キャッスル・ロック・プエブロのペトログリフについて分かることの1つは何か。

（選択肢の訳） 1 典型的なものよりも数が多い。
2 遠い地域のものと似ている。
3 その地域で最大である。
4 ヨーロッパ人の姿が含まれている。

（解説） These images were not drawn in the style typical of the area, but in a way that was common in another settlement hundreds of kilometers away. の文から，**2** が正解。those は petroglyphs のことで，「何百キロも離れた別の集落」を a distant area と表している。not A but B「A ではなく B」を含む長い 1 文だが，not の後に続けて but が聞こえたらその後をしっかりと聞くとよい。

No.24 解答

質問の訳 キャッスル・ロック・プエブロのペトログリフはどのように使用されたと研究者たちは考えているか。

選択肢の訳
1 1 年の特定の時期を示すため。
2 敵に近づかないように警告するため。
3 別の集落への行き方を示すため。
4 光源を提供するため。

解説 質問は How were the Castle Rock Pueblo petroglyphs used? に do researchers think が挿入された形で，使用目的が問われている。彫刻の特徴（feature）について述べた On the longest and shortest days ... の部分から，**1** が正解。「1 年で最も日が長い日と最も日が短い日」を「1 年の特定の時期」と表している。

   Part3   問題編 p.162～163

G
（スクリプト）

You have 10 seconds to read the situation and Question No. 25.

Hi, dear. I'm sorry, I was in a rush this morning and wasn't able to do a few things. Could you take care of them? The living room is a mess. Miranda's toys are all over the place, so could you put them away? Also, Toby's new bird food arrived this morning. I know we usually store it in that box near the kitchen shelves, but when the package was delivered, I left it at the front door. Sorry. It should still be sitting there. And can you change one of the light bulbs in the garage? When I got home last night, I saw that one was flickering.

Now mark your answer on your answer sheet.

（全文訳）

もしもし，あなた。ごめんなさい，今朝は急いでいてできなかったことが幾つかあるの。それらをお願いできる？ 居間が散らかっているの。ミランダのおもちゃがあちこちにあるから片付けてもらえるかしら。あと，トビーの新しい鳥の餌が今朝届いたの。いつも台所の棚の近くのあの箱の中に保管しているのは知っているけど，荷物が届いたときに玄関に置きっぱなしにしちゃったの。ごめんね。まだそこにあるはずよ。それと，ガレー

ジの電球の1つを交換してくれる？　昨夜帰宅したとき，1つチカチカしていたの。

No.25 解答 ③

状況の訳　あなたはオウムのトビーに餌をやりたいと思っているが，その餌が見つからない。携帯電話を見て妻からの音声メッセージに気付く。

質問の訳　あなたはトビーの餌を見つけるのにどこへ行くべきか。

選択肢の訳　1　台所へ。　　　　　　　　2　居間へ。
　　　　　　　　3　玄関へ。　　　　　　　　4　ガレージへ。

解説　問題用紙の「状況」から，「トビー（オウム）の餌が見つからない」という状況をつかもう。妻はやり残した用事を順に説明して夫に頼んでいる。トビーの餌について「玄関に置きっぱなしにした」「まだそこにあるはず」と言っているので，3が正解。1は普段置いている場所なので不適。

H

（スクリプト）

You have 10 seconds to read the situation and Question No. 26.

Greta Bakken has written in various genres over her long career. I would recommend four books to a first-time reader. First, *The Moon in Budapest* is considered to be a masterpiece of romance, and it has the biggest fan base. *Along That Tree-Lined Road* is a beautifully crafted fantasy novel with a touch of mystery. If you're a travel fan, I recommend you try *Mixed Metaphors*. It's a travel journal documenting her trip to Siberia, with a number of stunning photographs she snapped along the way. Lastly, *Trishaws* is her latest book, and it has been getting great reviews from science fiction enthusiasts.

Now mark your answer on your answer sheet.

（全文訳）

グレタ・バッケンは長いキャリアの中でさまざまなジャンルの作品を書いてきました。初めて読まれる方にお薦めする本が4冊あります。まず，『ブダペストの月』はロマンスの傑作と考えられていて，最も多くのファン層を持つ作品です。『あの並木道に沿って』は，ちょっとミステリー風の，見事に作り上げられたファンタジー小説です。旅行好きでしたら，『混喩』を読んでみることをお勧めします。本書は彼女のシベリア旅行を記録した旅行記で，道中で彼女が撮った素晴らしい写真の数々が掲載されています。最後に，『人力三輪車』は彼女の最新作で，SFファンから素晴らしい評価を得ています。

No.26 解答 ①

状況の訳　あなたはグレタ・バッケン著の本を読みたいと思っている。彼女の最も人気のある本を読みたい。書店の店員があなたに次のように言う。

質問の訳　あなたはどの本を買うべきか。

選択肢の訳　1　『ブダペストの月』

2 『あの並木道に沿って』

3 『混喩』

4 『人力三輪車』

解説 「状況」から，「最も人気のある本」という条件を押さえる。店員がお薦めの本を 4 冊順番に説明する中で，1 冊目の *The Moon in Budapest* について，it has the biggest fan base と言っている。「最も多くのファン層を持っている」＝「最も人気がある」と考えて，**1** が正解。

（スクリプト）

You have 10 seconds to read the situation and Question No. 27.

The company has decided to outsource the personnel department's services to ABC Resource Systems. There will be two main changes. First, we'll be using a new website to handle all scheduling, requests for time off, and complaints. More importantly, time-off requests will now need to be submitted two weeks in advance. These changes will apply at the end of next month, so please submit requests on the website at that time. Until then, please direct all personnel issues to the manager of your department. Thank you for your cooperation.

Now mark your answer on your answer sheet.

（全文訳）

我が社は，人事部の業務を ABC リソース・システム社に外部委託することを決定しました。主な変更が 2 つあります。まず，全てのスケジュール管理，休暇の申請，クレームを処理するのに新しいウェブサイトを使うことになります。さらに重要なことに，休暇申請は今後，2 週間前に提出する必要があります。これらの変更は来月末に適用されますので，そのときはウェブサイトで申請書を提出してください。それまでは，人事に関することは全て所属部署の部長に伝えてください。ご協力をお願いいたします。

No.27 解答 ①

状況の訳 あなたの会社の社長が事務手続きの変更について発表している。あなたは来週，休暇を取りたいと思っている。

質問の訳 あなたは何をすべきか。

選択肢の訳 **1** 部長と話す。

2 新しいウェブサイトで申請書を提出する。

3 所属部署の社員たちに E メールを送る。

4 ABC リソース・システム社に連絡する。

解説 「状況」から，「来週休暇を取りたい」ことを押さえる。「主な変更が 2 つある」と前置きした後，First, ...，More importantly, ... で順に説明される。まず，休暇申請は新しいウェブサイトで行うことが分かるが，

続く These changes will apply ... から，その変更は来月末からである。来週休暇を取りたい場合の情報を期待しながら聞き進めると，Until then に続いて「部長に伝えること」と言っている。**1** が正解で，direct「（言葉などを）向ける」を speak to と表している。

スクリプト

You have 10 seconds to read the situation and Question No. 28.

The course website is now accessible. On the left side, you'll see the menu. At the top of the menu, there's a news section where I'll post event reminders and assignment due dates. I've already posted a notification about a guest lecture that you can attend for additional credit. You can click on the icon to reserve a seat. Below the news section, there's a link to a page where you can check on your weekly reading assignments. Finally, in the resources section, I put some links that might help you when working on your final research project.

Now mark your answer on your answer sheet.

全文訳

このコースのウェブサイトにアクセスできるようになりました。左側には，メニューが表示されます。メニューの上部にはニュース欄があり，そこに私がイベントのリマインダーや課題の提出期限を掲載します。追加の単位のために出席できるゲスト講義に関するお知らせをすでに掲載しました。席を予約するにはアイコンをクリックしてください。ニュース欄の下には，毎週の読書課題を確認できるページへのリンクがあります。最後になりますが，リソース欄に，最終研究プロジェクトに取り組む際に役立ちそうなリンクを幾つか貼りました。

No.28 解答 **4**

状況の訳 あなたの教授はクラスにコースのウェブサイトを見せている。あなたは成績を上げるために追加の単位を取得したいと思っている。

質問の訳 あなたは何をすべきか。

選択肢の訳 **1** ウェブサイトを通して追加の研究論文を提出する。
2 追加の読書課題を完了する。
3 クラスのためにオンラインリソースを作成する。
4 ニュース欄から講義に申し込む。

解説 「状況」から，教授がウェブサイトの画面を見せながら説明している場面を想像しよう。「追加の単位を取得したい」という条件を押さえる。ニュース欄についての説明の中で，I've already posted a notification about a guest lecture that you can attend for additional credit. と言っており，ゲスト講義に出席すれば追加単位が取得できることが分か

K

You have 10 seconds to read the situation and Question No. 29.

Hi, this is Bill. As you know, today's the deadline for your column. How is it coming along? If you've already finished it, please send the column directly to my office e-mail address. If you're likely to finish it by tomorrow morning, send the file to Paula. I'll be out all day tomorrow. However, if you're not likely to make it by tomorrow morning, could you call me on my office phone tonight? I'll be here until eight. Otherwise, you can reach me on my smartphone after eight. If necessary, I can give you another few days to finish it. Thanks.

Now mark your answer on your answer sheet.

全文訳

もしもし，ビルです。知っての通り，今日はあなたのコラムの締め切り日です。どんな感じですか。すでに書き終えているなら，コラムを直接私のオフィスのEメールアドレスに送ってください。明日の朝までに書き上がりそうな場合は，ポーラにファイルを送ってください。私は明日，一日中外出しますので。でも，明日の朝までに間に合いそうにない場合は，今夜，私のオフィスの電話に連絡してもらえませんか。8時までここにいますので。そうでなければ，8時以降は私のスマートフォンで連絡が取れます。必要なら，書き終えるのにあと数日与えることもできます。では。

No.29 解答 4

状況の訳 あなたは新聞のライターである。あなたは午後8時30分に帰宅し，編集者からの次のような音声メッセージを聞く。あなたはコラムを書き上げるのにあと2日必要である。

質問の訳 あなたは何をすべきか。

選択肢の訳
1 ファイルをビルに送る。
2 ファイルをポーラに送る。
3 ビルのオフィスの電話に電話する。
4 ビルのスマートフォンに電話する。

解説 「状況」から，「コラムを書き上げるのにあと2日必要」という条件を押さえる。メッセージは編集者＝ビルからで，執筆中のコラムについて，「～の場合，…してください」と条件別に指示が聞こえてくる。if you're not likely to make it by tomorrow morning, ...「明日の朝までに間に合いそうにない場合…」の部分に一瞬惑わされそうだが，続く Otherwise, ... がポイント。「8時以降なのでビルのスマートフォンに連絡する」→「あと数日待ってもらえるかも」と理解して，**4** が正解。

解答例 **One day, a mayor was having a meeting.** The meeting was about the decreasing number of tourists. This was a problem, and the mayor asked if her staff members had any ideas. They all looked worried. That weekend, the mayor was drinking coffee and watching TV at home. The TV show was saying that camping was popular, and this gave the mayor an idea. Six months later, the mayor and one of her staff members were visiting the new ABC Town campsite. They were happy to see that there were a lot of campers using the campsite. A few months later, the mayor and the staff member were watching TV in her office. The staff member was shocked to see breaking news that a bear had entered the campsite because there was a lot of food garbage.

解答例の訳 ある日，町長が会議を開いていました。会議は観光客の減少についてのものでした。これは問題であり，町長は職員たちに何かアイデアがないか尋ねました。彼らは皆，心配そうでした。その週末，町長は自宅でコーヒーを飲みながらテレビを見ていました。テレビ番組は，キャンプが人気だと言っており，これを聞いて町長はアイデアを思い付きました。6カ月後，町長と職員の1人は，新しいABC町キャンプ場を訪問していました。彼女らはキャンプ場を利用しているキャンパーがたくさんいるのを見て満足でした。数カ月後，町長とその職員は町長のオフィスでテレビを見ていました。職員は，生ごみがたくさんあるためにクマがキャンプ場に侵入したというニュース速報を見てショックを受けました。

解説 解答に含めるべき点は以下の4つ。①町長が会議で観光客の減少を示したグラフを見せ，職員たちに Any ideas? と尋ねている，②その週末，町長は「今，キャンプが人気」と示したテレビを見てアイデアを思い付く，③6カ月後，町長と職員が ABC Town Campsite を訪問していて，満足そうな様子，④数カ月後，2人はテレビで，クマがキャンプ場に落ちているごみを食べている様子を見ている。1コマ目について描写した解答例の This was a problem, ... は，The mayor asked her staff members, "Do you have any ideas on how to solve this problem?"「町長は職員たちに『この問題の解決方法についてのアイデアはありますか』と尋ねました」のようにせりふを利用して直接話法で表してもよいだろう。

No. 1

解答例 I'd be thinking that I should've planned the campsite more carefully. It was a good way to increase the number of tourists who come to our town, but I should've asked experts for advice about how to avoid problems with wildlife.

解説 質問は「4番目の絵を見てください。もしあなたが町長なら，どのようなことを考えているでしょうか」。解答例は，〈I should've＋過去分詞〉を用いて「もっと慎重に計画すべきだった」「専門家にアドバイスを求めるべきだった」という後悔を表している。should've は should have の短縮形。ごみを出さないなどの具体的な対策を話すこともできるだろう。

No. 2

解答例 Yes. These days, people spend a lot of time inside using computers and tablets. People should learn about the natural world, and personal experiences can be more effective for learning than the Internet or books.

解説 質問は「人々は自然について学ぶためにもっと屋外で過ごすべきだと思いますか」。解答例は Yes の立場で，最近は屋内で過ごす時間が多いという理由を述べた後，「学ぶにはインターネットや本よりも個人的な体験の方が効果的」という意見を述べている。No の立場の理由では，周りに自然がないことや屋外で過ごす時間がないなどの内容が考えられる。

No. 3

解答例 Yes, I think so. These days, many people damage their health by working too hard, so it's important for people to relax and take care of themselves. By doing so, their performance at work will naturally improve, too.

解説 質問は「企業は労働者にもっと休暇を与えるべきですか」。解答例は Yes の立場で，過労による健康被害に言及し，リラックスして自分をケアすることで仕事のパフォーマンスも上がると述べている。It's important for A to *do*「A にとって～することは重要だ」は万能に使える表現。

No. 4

解答例 I don't think so. Unfortunately, the government has more important responsibilities. Taking care of people's problems should be the priority. Besides, the government already spends a lot of money protecting endangered animals.

解説 「政府は絶滅の危機にひんした動物を保護するためにもっと努力すべきですか」という質問。Yes / No ではなく解答例のように I (don't) think so. と始めてもよい。解答例は No の立場で，「政府には（動物の保護）より重要な責務がある」「すでに多くのお金を使っている」という2つの理由を述べている。

解答例 **One day, a woman was talking with her company's CEO in the office.** He was telling her that she was promoted to manager, and she looked happy to hear that. That evening, she was at home with her husband and baby. She showed her husband that she had gotten a promotion. He said that he could pick up their baby from the day care center instead. A month later, the woman was working in her new position as manager. She got a message from her husband at 7 p.m. saying that he had picked up their baby from day care, and she was glad that she could continue working. A few days later, she was working on a project, and her husband called her at seven. He seemed very busy, and he told her that he could not pick up the baby that day.

解答例の訳 ある日，女性がオフィスで会社の CEO と話していました。彼は，彼女がマネージャーに昇進したことを伝えており，彼女はそれを聞いてうれしそうでした。その日の晩，彼女は夫と赤ん坊と一緒に自宅にいました。彼女は自分が昇進したことを夫に伝えました。彼は，代わりに託児所に赤ん坊を迎えに行けると言いました。1 カ月後，女性はマネージャーとして新しい役職で働いていました。彼女は，午後 7 時に夫から，託児所に赤ん坊を迎えに行ったと伝えるメッセージを受け取り，引き続き仕事ができることを喜びました。数日後，彼女はあるプロジェクトに取り組んでいたところ，7 時に夫から電話がありました。彼はとても忙しそうで，その日は赤ん坊を迎えに行けないと彼女に言いました。

解説 解答に含めるべき点は以下の 4 つ。① CEO が女性にマネージャーへの昇進を伝えている，②その日の晩，女性が夫に昇進を伝え，夫は「僕が（君の）代わりに赤ん坊を迎えに行けるよ」と言っている，③ 1 カ月後，女性は仕事中に携帯電話を見て，夫が託児所で赤ん坊を引き取ったことを知る，④数日後，夫は仕事が忙しそうで，電話で「今日は迎えに行けない」と女性に話している。2 コマ目の instead から，昇進前は女性が赤ん坊を迎えに行っていたことを推測しよう。3 コマ目と 4 コマ目は同じ午後 7 時の出来事であること，また，3 コマ目は携帯電話のメッセージで，4 コマ目は電話で直接話しているという違いも押さえよう。

No. 1

解答例 I'd be thinking, "Neither of us can go to pick up our baby from the day care center. The same problem is probably going to happen again. Maybe I shouldn't have accepted the promotion to manager."

解説 質問は「4番目の絵を見てください。もしあなたがこの女性なら，どのようなことを考えているでしょうか」。解答例は，〈I shouldn't have＋過去分詞〉を用いて「昇進を受け入れるべきではなかった」という後悔を表している。2人とも迎えに行けない問題に対し，「定時以降は自宅で働いてよいか交渉しよう」など具体的な解決法を話すこともできるだろう。

No. 2

解答例 I think so. Parents these days try to control every part of their children's lives, so children never get a chance to make their own decisions. As a result, the younger generation is becoming less independent.

解説 質問は「近ごろ，親は子供に対して過保護ですか」。解答例はI think so. で始まるYes の立場で，「親は子供の生活のあらゆる面をコントロールしようとしているため，子供は自分で決定を下す機会が全くない」という意見。A, so B.「A なので，B」や As a result「その結果」などの因果関係を表す表現の使い方を確認しよう。

No. 3

解答例 Yes. Especially in big cities, it seems like people never have time to relax. I think that the biggest reason is the work culture. This definitely has a negative effect on people's mental and physical health.

解説 「現代の速いペースの生活は人々に悪影響を及ぼしていますか」という質問。解答例はYes の立場。大都市に焦点を絞り，具体的な悪影響として「リラックスする時間がない」と述べた後，I think that the biggest reason is ... の形でその理由を説明している。速いペースの生活＝多忙と考えて，睡眠や食事への悪影響も根拠にできるだろう。

No. 4

解答例 I think so. The government realizes the decreasing birth rate is a problem, and it's spending money to encourage people to have more children. Also, companies provide more childcare leave these days.

解説 質問は「今後，日本の出生率は減少が止まると思いますか」。解答例はYes の立場で，政府の対策や企業の育児休暇制度を根拠にしている。「減少し続けると思う」という No の立場では，未婚化・晩婚化や子育ての負担など，少子化の原因を取り上げて説明できるだろう。

2021-3

解 答 一 覧

一次試験・筆記

1

(1)	2	(10)	4	(19)	1
(2)	2	(11)	1	(20)	4
(3)	3	(12)	1	(21)	1
(4)	2	(13)	3	(22)	1
(5)	2	(14)	3	(23)	2
(6)	2	(15)	4	(24)	1
(7)	3	(16)	4	(25)	2
(8)	1	(17)	3		
(9)	2	(18)	2		

2

(26)	2	(29)	3
(27)	4	(30)	1
(28)	1	(31)	3

3

(32)	1	(35)	4	(38)	3
(33)	2	(36)	2	(39)	4
(34)	2	(37)	1	(40)	1
				(41)	2

4　　解答例は本文参照

一次試験・リスニング

Part 1

No. 1	4	No. 5	3	No. 9	1
No. 2	1	No. 6	1	No.10	2
No. 3	1	No. 7	3	No.11	1
No. 4	1	No. 8	4	No.12	4

Part 2

No.13	3	No.17	1	No.21	3
No.14	1	No.18	2	No.22	3
No.15	1	No.19	2	No.23	2
No.16	4	No.20	1	No.24	1

Part 3

No.25	3	No.28	4
No.26	4	No.29	2
No.27	1		

(1) ─解答 ② ....

訳 ロベルトは真の愛国者だったので，自国が隣国に攻撃されると直ちに陸軍への入隊を志願した。

解説 隣国に攻撃されるという非常事態に自ら入隊して戦おうとする人はどんな人かと考えると，patriot「愛国者」が正解。villain「悪人」，spectator「観客」，beggar「物乞いする人」

(2) ─解答 ② ....

訳 「今から休憩を取りましょう」と議長は言った。「次の議題について話し合うため，約15分後に会議を再開します」

解説 休憩を取った後で次の議題について話し合うということは，約15分の中断後に会議を再開する（resume）ことになる。parody「パロディーを作る，面白おかしく真似る」，impede「妨げる」，erect「建てる」

(3) ─解答 ③ ....

訳 ダンは，初めてスキーに挑戦したときは難しいと思ったが，その後スキーに出かけるたびに上達した。今では彼はスキーの達人だ。

解説 最初は難しかったが次第に上達して今では達人だという流れから，「それに続く，その後の」（subsequent）スキー旅行のたびにと考えるのが自然。sufficient「十分な」，arrogant「尊大な」，prominent「卓越した」

(4) ─解答 ② ....

訳 その教授は自分の分野では専門家だが，常軌を逸した振る舞いがもとで同僚たちを（同僚として）恥ずかしい気持ちにさせている。「彼はいつも妙なことをしたり言ったりしている」と1人の同僚は述べた。

解説 第2文の always doing or saying strange things に相当する形容詞を考えると，eccentric「常軌を逸した」が適切。secular「世俗の」，vigilant「用心深い」，apparent「明白な」

(5) ─解答 ② ....

訳 その野菜の売店は販売している野菜がオーガニックだと証明することができなかったので，エディはそこの野菜を買うのを拒んだ。オーガニック食品だけを食べるのが彼の厳格なポリシーだった。

解説 オーガニック食品しか食べないエディが野菜を買わなかったのは，野菜の売店が野菜はオーガニックだと証明する（certify）ことができなかったから。diverge「分岐する」，evade「回避する」，glorify「美化する」

(6) ─解答 ② ....

訳 学校の進路相談員として，ペレイラさんは生徒たちが天職を見つける支援をすることを専門にしている。人は自分の個性とスキルに合ったキャ

リアを持つべきだと彼女は考えている。

解説 第 2 文の careers that fit their personality and skills がヒント。自分にぴったり合った職業を vocation「天職」と言う。boredom「退屈」，insult「侮辱」，publicity「一般に知れ渡ること」

(7) ─解答 ③
訳 そのマラソンランナーはレース後とても喉が渇いていたので，大容量のスポーツドリンクをわずか数口でがぶ飲みしてから，すぐにもう 1 本欲しいと言った。

解説 喉が渇いて 1 本では足りなかったのだから，ランナーは最初のスポーツドリンクを数口のがぶ飲み（gulps）で飲み干したと考えられる。それぞれ herd「群れ」，lump「塊」，sack「袋」の複数形。

(8) ─解答 ①
訳 眠っていた赤ん坊は，兄の部屋から聞こえる大音量の音楽にびっくりした。彼女は泣きながら目を覚まし，再び寝入るまでに長いことかかった。

解説 赤ん坊が目を覚ましたのは，大きな音に驚いたからだと考えられる。startle「びっくりさせる」の過去分詞 startled が正解。それぞれ improvise「即興的に作る」，prolong「長引かせる」，tolerate「許容する」の過去分詞。

(9) ─解答 ②
訳 A：もうこのアパートには 1 年住んでいて，賃貸契約がそろそろ切れるんだ。住み続けるべきか引っ越すべきか，決めなくちゃならない。
B：家賃が変わらないなら，契約を更新して住み続けることを勧めるよ。

解説 1 年住んだアパートに住み続けるか引っ越すかという会話なので，間もなく切れるのは lease「賃貸契約」。B の言う contract「契約」は lease のこと。token「代用貨幣」，vicinity「近隣」，dialect「方言」

(10) ─解答 ④
訳 その大統領候補は，停滞した景気は現大統領の責任だとした。当選したら景気を改善すると彼は約束した。

解説 第 2 文の it は the（　）economy を指す。それを改善する（improve）と言っていることから，景気は停滞した（sluggish）状態だと考えられる。bulky「かさばった」，functional「機能の」，ethnic「民族の」

(11) ─解答 ①
訳 A：アニー，元気だった？　去年のイタリア旅行は楽しかったかい？
B：楽しかったわよ，パブロ。実はね，すごく気に入ったので，あちらに移り住もうと考えているの。息子が高校を卒業するまで待たなければならないだろうけど。

解説 contemplate -ing で「～しようと考える」という意味。イタリアを気に入った B は移住を検討していることになる。それぞれ emphasize「強

調する」, vandalize「故意に破壊する」, illustrate「説明する」の -ing 形。

(12) – 解答 ①
〔訳〕 全上院議員がその新法を支持すると述べたので，彼らが満場一致で賛成票を投じたのは全く意外ではなかった。
〔解説〕 senator は「上院議員」。その全員が新法支持を表明したのだから，投票の際は満場［全員］一致で（unanimously）賛成したはず。abnormally「異常に」, mockingly「あざけって」, savagely「残酷に」

(13) – 解答 ③
〔訳〕 A：マーカム教授の講義に行った？
B：行ったけど，あまりに退屈で 15 分しか耐えられなかった。その後は退出してカフェに行ったよ。
〔解説〕 講義が退屈で 15 分しか「耐える，我慢する」（endure）ことができず，途中で教室を出てカフェに行ったという流れ。execute「実行する，（通例受動態で）処刑する」, discern「見分ける」, relay「伝達する」

(14) – 解答 ③
〔訳〕 寒冷地に建てられた家は，冬の間驚くほど暖かく居心地がいいことがある。暖炉と木の家具と立派なじゅうたんが，暖かくて快適な感じを家々に与えている。
〔解説〕 第 2 文の warm, comfortable に相当する cozy「暖かく居心地のいい」が適切。rigid「厳格な」, rash「向こう見ずな」, clumsy「不器用な」

(15) – 解答 ④
〔訳〕 ウィルソンさんは息子が窓を割ったとき怒ったが，やったのは別の人だと言って息子が彼女をだまそうとしたことにむしろがっかりした。
〔解説〕 息子は窓を割ったのに自分はやっていないとうそをついたわけだが，うその目的は人をだます（deceive）こと。pinpoint「正確に示す」, suppress「抑圧する」, reroute「別のルートで輸送する」

(16) – 解答 ④
〔訳〕 ワンダが 1 カ月で 3 度目の遅刻をした後，上司は時間厳守の大切さについて彼女と長時間話した。
〔解説〕 遅刻が多いワンダが上司と話して理解すべきことは，「時間厳守，時間を守ること」（punctuality）の重要性である。congestion「密集」, drainage「排水」, optimism「楽観主義」

(17) – 解答 ③
〔訳〕 その若い作家は慣習的な物語の書き方のルールには従わないと決め，自分の小説を唯一無二のスタイルで書いた。
〔解説〕 唯一無二の（unique）スタイルで書いたのだから，従わないと決めたのは慣習的な（conventional）ルールと考えられる。vulnerable「傷つきやすい」, clueless「何も知らない」, phonetic「音声の」

(18) – 解答 **2** .... 正答率 ★75%以上

訳 箱の中の品物は壊れやすいのでていねいに梱包されていたが，それでもそのうち幾つかは配達中に破損した。

解説 ていねいに梱包したのに破損したということは，それらの品物は壊れやすい（fragile）物だったと考えられる。coarse「（粒などが）粗い，（肌などが）きめの粗い」，immovable「動かせない」，glossy「つやのある」

(19) – 解答 **1** ....

訳 女王は顧問を宮殿に呼び出したが，到着まで長時間かかると激怒した。

解説 〈summon＋人＋to〉で「（人）を～に呼び出す」という意味。問題文のqueenのように，主語は権威を持つ人が普通である。それぞれhammer「ハンマーで打つ」，mingle「混ざる」，tremble「震える」の過去形。

(20) – 解答 **4** ....

訳 自軍が戦闘に負けそうだと将軍には分かっていたので，退却するよう自軍に命じた。ひとたび軍が戦場から無事に離れると，彼は敵を破るための新しい計画を練った。

解説 将軍は劣勢の軍に何を命じたか。第2文の「戦場から無事に離れると」から，命令が退却する（retreat）ことだったと分かる。entrust「任せる」，discard「捨てる」，strangle「絞め殺す」

(21) – 解答 **1** .... 正答率 ★75%以上

訳 大学に入学してから，ビルは高等数学を学ぶ能力が自分にはないとすぐに気付いたので，専攻を地理学に変更した。

解説 ビルが専攻を変えた理由を考えると，高等数学を学ぶ能力（capacity）がないと気付いたからだと思われる。capacity to *do* で「～する能力」という意味。novelty「目新しさ」，bait「餌」，chunk「塊」

(22) – 解答 **1** ....

訳 お金を盗んだと強引に認めさせるため，容疑者に暴力を振るってはどうかと相棒が言ったとき，その警官はショックを受けた。そのように暴力を用いることは許されなかった。

解説 第2文のUsing violenceから，相棒の提案は容疑者に暴力を振るう（rough up）ことで罪を認めさせることだと分かる。give out「～を配る」，break up「～をばらばらにする，～を解散させる」，take over「～を引き継ぐ，～を支配する」

(23) – 解答 **2** ....

訳 バードウオッチングの初日に珍しいワシを見ることができてジュリアスは幸運だった。しかし，彼が同じ種類のワシをもう1羽目にするまで20年が過ぎた。

解説 ～ go by before ... は「…まで～（の時間）が過ぎる」という意味。goを過去形にしたwent byが正解。それぞれhold out「持ちこたえる」，

lay off「～を解雇する」，cut off「～を切り取る」の過去形。

(24) – 解答 ①
　訳　A：週末にビーチへ出かけるのは中止するの？　台風が来ているよ。
　　　B：まだ行く可能性を排除したわけじゃない。台風がどの方向に向かうか次第だね。

　解説　B は台風の方向次第と言っているので，まだ諦めていない。つまり，ビーチに行く可能性を排除した（ruled out）わけではないことになる。それぞれ stand down「証言台を降りる」，drag into「（drag ～ into で）～を…に引きずり入れる」，scoop up「～をすくい上げる」の過去分詞。

(25) – 解答 ②
　訳　失業したら頼りにするものがあるよう，ジュンはいつもできる限り多くのお金を貯めた。

　解説　fall back on は「（最後の手段として）～に頼る」という意味。失業して収入を絶たれた場合に備えて貯金したということ。look up to「～を尊敬する」，come down with「～（軽い病気）にかかる」，do away with「～を取り除く」

一次試験・筆記 **2** 問題編 p.174 ～ 177

全文訳 **寄付者返礼品**

　近年，慈善団体が，お金を寄付してくれた人たちに寄付者返礼品 —— コーヒーマグのようなちょっとしたプレゼント —— を渡すのが一般的になっている。多くの慈善団体が返礼品を出しており，寄付者返礼品をもらう場合に人はより多くを寄付すると広く考えられている。しかし，寄付者返礼品には寄付者たちの態度を変える傾向があると研究者たちは言う。ほとんどの人が最初にお金を寄付するのは，世界をより良い場所にしたり，自分より恵まれない人たちを助けたりしたいからである。だがプレゼントをもらうと，人は利己心と欲求に動機付けられるようになり始めることがある。実際，将来的に寄付する可能性が低くなるかもしれないのである。

　しかし，この問題を避ける方法があるかもしれない。寄付した後にプレゼントをもらえると教えることは，人が将来確実に寄付するようにする最善の方法ではないことが，研究で証明されている。ある研究では，プレゼントを予想していなかったときに，寄付者たちはプレゼントをもらうことにより良い反応を示した。さらに，そうした人たちからの将来的寄付は最大 75％増えた。一方，寄付の後にプレゼントをもらえると知っていた寄付者たちは，そのプレゼントが何であるかにかかわらず，プレゼントを高く評価しなかった。

　寄付者返礼品には間接的なメリットもあるかもしれない。プレゼントは慈善団体の宣伝に役立つことがあると専門家たちは言う。例えば，慈善団体のロゴが入った凝ったデ

ザインの買い物袋といった品物は，寄付者が特別な人たちだけのグループの一員だと示す。そうしたプレゼントは寄付者たちを満足させておくだけでなく，慈善団体に対する一般大衆の認識も向上させる。

> 語句 donor「寄付者」，premium「景品，返礼品」，initially「初めは」，motivate「動機を与える」，regardless of「〜にかかわらず」，fancy「（デザインなどが）凝った」，signal「示す」，exclusive「特定の人に限られた」，awareness「認識，意識」

(26) – 解答 ② ‥‥‥‥‥‥‥‥‥‥‥‥‥‥‥‥‥‥ 正答率 ★75%以上

> 解説 第1段落前半では，返礼品は寄付を増やすという想定が述べられている。空所文は However で始まるので，空所後はその想定とは異なる内容のはず。無私の気持ちで寄付を始めた人が，返礼品をもらうと「利己心と欲求」が動機となり，寄付しなくなる可能性もあるのだから，返礼品には「寄付者たちの態度を変える」傾向があることになる。

(27) – 解答 ④ ‥‥‥‥‥‥‥‥‥‥‥‥‥‥‥‥‥‥‥‥‥‥‥‥‥‥

> 解説 第2段落では，返礼品があると知っていた場合と知らなかった場合を比較した研究が紹介されている。空所の前は，寄付者たちが返礼品を予想していなかった場合に反応が良かったという内容で，空所の後は，そうした人たちからの寄付は以後増えたという内容。前述の内容を補強する副詞 Furthermore「さらに」が適切である。

(28) – 解答 ① ‥‥‥‥‥‥‥‥‥‥‥‥‥‥‥‥‥‥ 正答率 ★75%以上

> 解説 第3段落第1文の indirect benefits「間接的なメリット」は，返礼品が寄付を増やすという直接的なメリットと対比したもの。空所後では，慈善団体のロゴ入り買い物袋の例を挙げ，寄付者の満足感を保ち，人々の慈善団体への認識を高めるという2つの効果があるとしている。これらは，「慈善団体の宣伝に役立つ」間接的なメリットだと考えられる。

> 全文訳 **政府の政策と交通安全**

シートベルトなどの安全対策の導入により，アメリカでは交通関連死が減少した。しかし，政府の政策に批判的な多くの人は，政府による規制をより厳しくすれば不慮の死者をさらに減らせるであろうと主張する。実際，制限速度に関する現在の政府の政策は危険な運転を助長するかもしれないと言う人たちもいる。これは，制限速度がしばしば「運行速度方式」を用いて設定されているからである。この方式では，制限速度はその道路を利用する車両が実際に移動する速度に基づいて決定され，危険を増大させるかもしれない道路の特徴にはほとんど注意が払われない。残念なことだが，つまり，制限は時に安全でないレベルで設定されていることになる。

車両の安全規定に関してはアメリカは他国より遅れている，とも批判的な人たちは指摘する。アメリカでは，安全規定は車両の中にいる人を守る目的で作られている。一部の車両は大型化し形状が変化したというのに，そうした車両が歩行者にもたらす危険が

231

増大したことを反映するように法律が変わっていない。批判的な人たちは，車両の乗員の安全だけを規定するのは無責任だし，歩行者の死亡防止に役立てるために取り得る簡単な対策があるのに，歩行者の死亡は増えたと言う。

　交通安全を向上させる1つの対策が，赤信号で停止しないドライバーを見つけるため，信号機でカメラを用いることである。1990年代に多くのそうしたカメラが設置され，命を救うことが証明されている。それにもかかわらず，そうしたカメラの数は近年減少している。その1つの理由は，プライバシーへの懸念から，カメラに反対する声がしばしば人々から上がることである。

> 語句 fatality「不慮の死（者）」，pose「（問題などを）投げかける」，pedestrian「歩行者」，regulate「規制する」，occupant「（乗り物などに）乗っている人」，irresponsible「無責任な」，detect「見つける，検出する」

(29) −解答 **3** ··· 正答率 ★**75%以上**

> 解説 政府の政策に批判的な人たちの主張について述べた前の文を In fact と受けていることから，空所には「制限速度に関する現在の政府の政策」を批判する内容が入ると分かる。道路の危険要因を考慮せずに設定されている制限速度は安全なレベルではないこともある，という記述から，現在の政策は「危険な運転を助長する」可能性があると考えられる。

(30) −解答 **1** ···

> 解説 第2段落では別の批判が述べられている。空所後によると，法律は車両の変化による歩行者への危険の増大に対応しておらず，歩行者の死亡は増えている。つまり，vehicle-safety regulations（第1文）は vehicle occupants（第4文）を守るための規定である。**1**の those inside vehicles は vehicle occupants の言い換え。

(31) −解答 **3** ··· 正答率 ★**75%以上**

> 解説 空所の前は，1990年代に多くのカメラが信号機に設置され，交通安全に役立っているという内容で，空所の後は，最近はカメラの数が減っているという内容。カメラが有用であれば増えてもよさそうであるがその想像に反する内容なので，**3**「それにもかかわらず」が適切。

一次試験・筆記 **3** | 問題編 p.178〜184

全文訳 **カリグラ**

　「狂気の皇帝」としても知られるローマ皇帝カリグラはあまりに悪名高くなったので，その人生に関する事実と伝説とを区別するのは難しい。カリグラは在位中に，「脳炎」と言われているものを患った。この病気が原因で彼は正気を失ったとしばしば言われてきたが，この主張は，病後の一見不合理な彼の振る舞いに裏付けられている。しかし今日では，彼の行動はよく練られた，巧妙で恐ろしいほど暴力的な政治戦略の一部だった

のかもしれない，と主張する歴史家たちもいる。

　カリグラは病気の後，膨大な数の市民を，軽い犯罪であっても拷問にかけ処刑するようになった。また彼は，自分は生ける神だと主張した。これらの行動は精神的不安定を示唆するのかもしれないが，別の解釈としては，自らの地位を守ることを意図したものであったとも考えられる。カリグラが病気の間，生き延びることはないであろうと思われていたので，彼を（別の人を皇帝にして）交代させる計画が立てられ，その結果おそらく彼は裏切られ脅かされていると感じたのだろう。同様に，自分は神であると主張することは確かに狂気の兆候のように思われるが，多くのローマ皇帝は死ぬと神になると考えられていたのであり，カリグラは敵に暗殺を思いとどまらせるためにその主張をしたのかもしれない。

　一般的に信じられているように，カリグラが愛馬インキタトゥスを政府の有力な地位に任命しようとしたさまの話も，彼に精神疾患があった証拠として挙げられることがある。しかしカリグラは，動きにくい服を着て彼の戦車の前を走るといったことをさせて，ローマ元老院の議員たちにしばしば屈辱を与えたと言われている。愛馬を彼らよりも高位に昇進させることは，自分が無価値だと元老院議員たちに感じさせる別の方法だったのだろう。しかし最終的に，カリグラの振る舞いは度を越し，彼は殺害された。彼を歴史から消し去るために精力が注がれ，現代の歴史家たちが研究するための信頼できる資料はほとんど残っていない。その結果，彼が本当に狂気の皇帝だったのかどうかは決して分からないかもしれない。

　　　　語句　infamous「悪名の高い」，reign「在位期間，治世」，insane「正気でない，狂気の」，irrational「不合理な」，deliberate「計画的な，故意の」，horribly「恐ろしく，ひどく」，torture「拷問にかける」，offense「（軽微な）犯罪」，instability「不安定」，betray「裏切る」，insanity「狂気」，assassinate「暗殺する」，supposedly「おそらく，推定では」，humiliate「恥をかかせる」，senate「(the Senate で) 元老院」，chariot「（馬が引く 2 輪の）戦車」，elevate「昇進させる」，go too far「度が過ぎる」，erase「（記憶などから）拭い去る」

(32) – 解答　

問題文の訳　一部の現代の歴史家たちは次のように主張する。

選択肢の訳
1　カリグラの一見正気でない行動は，実際は入念に考え抜かれた計画の一部だったのかもしれない。
2　カリグラが患った「脳炎」は，当初考えられていたより重かった。
3　カリグラは精神疾患があった期間に基づいて判断されるべきでない。
4　カリグラが実行したと伝えられる暴力行為の多くは，ほかのローマ皇帝たちが行ったものだった。

解説　第 1 段落最終文に，問題文とほぼ同じ some historians argue という表現がある。この文の his actions は前文の his seemingly irrational behavior を指す。つまり，カリグラの狂気は，実際はよく練られた戦

略の一部だったというのが一部の歴史家たちの主張である。**1** では本文
の irrational を crazy と，deliberate を carefully thought-out と言
い換えている。

(33) – 解答 ②

問題文の訳 何がカリグラの病気の１つの結果だったかもしれないか。

選択肢の訳
1 死にかけたことが原因で，彼は神々と宗教以外は何にも関心を持たな
くなった。
2 彼はもう誰も信頼できないと感じ，その結果統治するやり方を変える
ことになった。
3 やはり彼は死ぬだろうとローマ市民は思っていたので，彼は神々が自
分を守ってくれると彼らに示そうと試みた。
4 彼はローマ皇帝に関する古い考えに疑問を抱き始め，それが政府のほ
かのメンバーたちとの深刻な対立につながった。

解説 第２段落の「裏切られ脅かされていると感じた」を「もう誰も信頼でき
ないと感じ」と言い換え，多くの市民を拷問・処刑し自分は神だと主張
したことを「統治するやり方を変えた」とまとめた **2** が正解。

(34) – 解答 ②

問題文の訳 この文章によると，カリグラはローマ元老院の議員たちのことをどう感
じていたか。

選択肢の訳
1 彼を敵から守るためなら彼らは何でもするのだから，民衆は彼らを
もっと尊敬すべきだと彼は感じていた。
2 彼は彼らに対する支配力を見せつけたかったので，自分には価値がな
いと彼らに感じさせる方法をしばしば見つけた。
3 彼らは身体的に弱くファッションセンスに乏しいと彼は感じていたの
で，彼は彼らが嫌いだった。
4 彼は彼らの支援に感謝していたので，彼らをたたえるために戦車競走
などのイベントを催した。

解説 第３段落第２文の humiliated「屈辱を与えた」が，元老院議員たちへ
のカリグラの考え方を端的に示している。馬を高位に就けようとする，
議員たちに戦車の前を走らせるといった行為は，「支配力を見せつけ」
る方法だったと考えられる。**2** の no value は本文の worthless に相当。

全文訳 **エディ・コイルの友人たち**

1970 年にアメリカの作家ジョージ・V・ヒギンズは，小説第１作『エディ・コイル
の友人たち』を発表した。この犯罪小説はヒギンズが弁護士として働いて過ごした年月
に着想を得たもので，彼はその期間，自身がかかわった事件に関連する何時間もの警察
の監視カメラのテープと口述の書き起こしを精査した。彼が聞きそして読んだのは普通
の犯罪者たちの日常の話し言葉で，当時テレビの犯罪ドラマの台本に書かれたせりふと

は全くの別物に聞こえた。ヒギンズは本物の犯罪者たちの話し方を覚え，彼らの独特でしばしば乱雑な言葉遣いのパターンは『エディ・コイルの友人たち』の基礎となった。この小説の生々しいリアリズムは，当時ベストセラーリストの上位を占めていた洗練された犯罪小説から大きくかけ離れていた。ヒギンズは罪を犯す登場人物の人生を美化したり，警察や連邦捜査官たちをことさら英雄的に描いたりはしなかった。

　『エディ・コイルの友人たち』をほかの犯罪小説から際立たせる１つの側面は，ほぼ全編が会話で書かれていることである。犯罪ものというジャンルがサスペンスを作り上げる綿密に組み立てられた物語に依拠することを考えれば，これは非常に独創的な手法だった。重要な出来事は直接述べられず，その代わり，小説の登場人物たちの会話を通して紹介される。従って読者は，エディ・コイルとその犯罪仲間たちの話をこっそり盗み聞きしているという感覚になる。アクションシーンすら会話で描かれ，地の文が必要なところでは，ヒギンズは言葉をわずかしか用いず，読者が筋を追うのに必要なだけの情報しか与えない。焦点は主に登場人物たち，彼らが住む世界，そして彼らが従う行動規範に当てられる。

　ヒギンズの最初の小説はたちまちヒットしたものの，全ての読者が著者の文体 —— 彼が続く著作でも用いた文体 —— を好んだわけではなかった。多くの人は，彼のその後の小説には分かりやすい筋がなく，アクションが少な過ぎると不平を述べた。だがヒギンズは，物語を語る上で最も人を引き付ける方法は登場人物たちの会話を通してで，そうすれば読者は話されていることに細心の注意を払わざるを得ないからだ，という信念に忠実であり続けた。ヒギンズは多くの小説を書いたが，デビュー作の成功を再現することはかなわなかった。晩年に近づくと，彼は自分の著作が注目と評価を受けないことに落胆しいら立った。それにもかかわらず，『エディ・コイルの友人たち』は，これまでに書かれた犯罪小説の大傑作の１つだと今では多くの人に見なされている。

　(語句) surveillance「監視」，transcript「（口述などの）書写」，scripted「台本のある」，messy「汚い，雑な」，gritty「生々しい，どぎつい」，removed「かけ離れた」，polished「洗練された」，dominate「支配する」，glamorize「美化する」，portray「描写する」，heroic「英雄的な」，dialogue「対話，会話」，given「～を考慮すれば」，reliance「依存」，plot「（小説などの）筋を組み立てる；筋」，listen in on「～を盗み聞きする」，depict「描く」，narration「語り」，sparingly「控えめに」，inhabit「住んでいる」，code of conduct「行動規範」，(be) committed to「～に献身する，～に忠誠を誓う」，engaging「人を引き付ける」，replicate「繰り返す」，appreciation「評価」

(35) – 解答 **4** 正答率 ★75%以上

(問題文の訳) この文章によると，ジョージ・V・ヒギンズが『エディ・コイルの友人たち』を書いたのは，

(選択肢の訳) **1** この小説がベストセラーになり，弁護士業を辞めて作家活動に専念できると考えたからである。

235

21年度第3回　筆記

2 アメリカの犯罪活動の規模に関する意識が普通のアメリカ人に欠けていることにいら立った後のことである。

3 犯罪の被害者たちを守るために弁護士たちがどれだけ熱心に働いているかを読者に教えたかったからである。

4 彼が弁護士だったころに行った調査中に見つけたことに着想を得た後のことである。

解説 第1段落によると，ヒギンズは弁護士時代に犯罪者が実際に使う言葉を知り，それを基にして小説を書いた。事件に関連する警察の監視カメラのテープと口述の書き起こしから犯罪者の言葉遣いを知ったという本文の内容を，選択肢4では「調査中に見つけたこと」と漠然と言い換えている。

(36) – 解答 ② ･････････････････････････････････ 正答率 ★75%以上

問題文の訳 第2段落から『エディ・コイルの友人たち』について何が分かるか。

選択肢の訳 1 ヒギンズは，犯罪小説に関する伝統的ルールが現代でもなお有効だと証明する小説を生み出したかった。

2 この小説が普通と違うのは，特定の出来事を詳細に描写するのではなく，登場人物たちの言葉のやりとりを通してヒギンズが物語を語っているからである。

3 ヒギンズが小説全編を通して会話に大きく依拠したのは，長い地の文を書く自信がなかったからである。

4 この小説は犯罪世界を忠実に描写しているが，ヒギンズは真の犯罪小説とは見なしていなかった。

解説 第2段落冒頭に書かれているように，この小説の特徴はほとんどが登場人物の会話で成り立っていること。2ではそれを interactions「言葉のやりとり」と表している。2の「特定の出来事を詳細に描写するのではなく」は本文の「重要な出来事は直接述べられず」に対応している。narration が少ないのは，第3段落で述べられている通りヒギンズが会話を重視していたからで，3のように自信がなかったからではない。

(37) – 解答 ① ･･

問題文の訳 この文章の筆者は以下の記述のどれに同意する可能性が最も高いか。

選択肢の訳 1 文体を変えればヒギンズはより広い読者層を引き付けることができたかもしれない可能性があったにもかかわらず，彼は自分の創造的ビジョンに忠実であり続けた。

2 ヒギンズが生み出した最初の著作は出来が悪かったが，彼の作品の質はそれに続く年月で着実に向上した。

3 犯罪小説作家たちがほかのジャンルの作家たちと同レベルの名声と称賛を得ることが決してないのは必然である。

4 最初に出版された数十年後になっても自分の作品が読者に受けるであ

236

ろうと犯罪小説作家たちが考えるのは非現実的である。

解説 第3段落では，ヒギンズのその後が書かれている。独特の文体が多くの読者に不評だったのに，彼はそれを変えようとしなかった。つまり，文体を変えれば読者が増えたかもしれないのに，会話を通して物語を語ることにこだわる「創造的ビジョン」を守り抜いた，というのがこの文章の筆者のヒギンズ評と考えられる。**1** の true は本文の committed の言い換え。

全文訳 **マミーブラウン**

　数千年もの昔，古代エジプト人は mummification（ミイラ製作）—— 死者の体を完全に乾燥させ，さまざまな物質で処理し，保存するためにくるむ手順 —— を行い始めた。これは死者の魂が来世に入るのを助けると考えられていた。しかし，12世紀から，ミイラの部位を用いて作った薬の需要がヨーロッパで生じると，多くの古代のミイラが奇妙な目に遭った。人々は，ミイラの色が黒なのは瀝青（れきせい）—— 中東で天然に産出し，古代社会が病気の治療に用いた黒い石油由来の物質 —— で処理されていたからだと思い込んでいた。しかし，確かに古代エジプト人はミイラを瀝青でコーティングして保存したこともあったが，この手法はヨーロッパに運ばれたミイラの多くには使われていなかった。さらに，アラビア語の原典が不正確に翻訳された結果，ミイラの処理に使われた瀝青は実際にミイラの体内に入ると誤って信じられた。

　18世紀になるころには，医学的知識が進歩したことで，ヨーロッパ人はミイラ由来の薬の使用をやめていた。それにもかかわらず，フランスの指導者ナポレオン・ボナパルトがエジプトで軍事作戦を率いると，ヨーロッパ大衆のミイラへの関心は新たな高みに達した。軍事作戦には大規模な科学調査遠征も含まれており，重要な考古学的発見と古代の人工遺物の記録をもたらした。裕福な観光客たちは，私的コレクション用に古代人工遺物を入手しようと，エジプトを訪れさえした。実際，私的なパーティーでミイラを包んだ布を解きミイラを見せることが，人気の催しになった。ミイラは，作物の肥料や鉄道機関車の燃料に変えるといった，さまざまなほかの方法でも用いられた。

　ミイラの特に珍しい1つの利用法が，茶色の絵の具を作るための顔料としてであった。すりつぶしたミイラを用いて作られたこの顔料はマミーブラウンとして知られるようになり，その需要が伸びたのはナポレオンのエジプト戦役の時代前後だが，早くも16世紀には使われていた。その色は一部のヨーロッパの芸術家たちに称賛され，彼らは今日美術館で見ることのできる芸術作品にこの顔料を使った。それでも，この顔料を批判する人たちの方が熱狂的な支持者たちよりも多かった。多くの芸術家たちは，この顔料の乾く力が弱いことやほかの好ましくない特性について不平を述べた。さらに，亡くなった人で作った顔料で絵を描くことは非礼だと次第に考えられるようになった —— マミーブラウンを使ったある有名な英国人画家は，その製造に本物のミイラが用いられていたと知ると，持っていた絵の具のチューブを直ちに地面に埋めた。

　死んだ動物の体の部位がミイラの部位として売られることもあったので，マミーブラ

237

ウンに異論のない芸術家たちですら，それが本物のミイラから作られたものだと常に確信できたわけではなかった。また，いろいろな製造業者がミイラのいろいろな部位を使って顔料を製造していたことは，販売されているさまざまなバージョンの間にほとんど一貫性がないことを意味した。加えて，死体を保存するために使われる物質を含めてミイラ製作の手順それ自体が，時とともに変化を経た。まさにこれらの要因が，特定の絵画におけるマミーブラウンの存在を今日の研究者たちが検出することをほぼ不可能にしている。しかし，顔料の物議を醸す出所を考えると，自分たちが称賛する絵画のどれかにこの顔料が使われたと知ったなら，もしかすると芸術愛好家たちはショックを受けるかもしれない。

(語句) mummy「ミイラ」，dry out「～をすっかり乾かす」，afterlife「来世」，bitumen「瀝青」，fascination with「～に魅了されること」，military campaign「軍事作戦」，expedition「遠征（隊）」，archaeological「考古学的な」，documentation「文書［資料］による裏付け，（収集した）参考資料，証拠書類提出」，artifact「人工遺物」，unwrapping「包装を解くこと」，fertilizer「肥料」，pigment「顔料」，ground-up「すりつぶした」，artwork「芸術作品」，deceased「死去した」，disrespectful「礼節を欠く，失礼な」，genuine「本物の」，consistency「首尾一貫性」，undergo「（変化などを）経る」，controversial「物議を醸す」

(38) – 解答 ③

(問題文の訳) この文章の筆者によると，なぜ古代エジプトのミイラはヨーロッパで薬を作るために使われたのか。

(選択肢の訳)
1 当時ヨーロッパでは病気がまん延していたので，ヨーロッパ人はよく効く薬を作るためなら何でも試すことをいとわなかった。
2 ミイラは大昔のものであるにもかかわらず黒く変色していなかったので，健康にメリットがあるかもしれないとヨーロッパ人は思い込んだ。
3 ヨーロッパ人は，医学的メリットがあると考えられる物質が全てのミイラに存在すると誤って信じた。
4 ミイラが古代エジプト人にとって宗教的意義を持っていたことが原因で，ヨーロッパ人はミイラに特別な力があると信じた。

(解説) 第1段落後半に，ヨーロッパ人がミイラで薬を作るようになった経緯が書かれている。瀝青は，古代社会で病気の治療に用いられ，ミイラの処理に使われることもあった。しかし，「ヨーロッパに運ばれたミイラの多くには使われていなかった」。この事情に合う説明は**3**で，瀝青を「医学的メリットがあると考えられる物質」と言い換えている。**2**は「黒く変色していなかった」が本文の記述と食い違う。

(39) – 解答 ④

(問題文の訳) ナポレオン・ボナパルトのエジプトでの軍事作戦について分かることの1つは何か。

選択肢の訳 **1** 数人の指導者たちが，これは自分たちもエジプトを侵略する理由になると考え，そのため多くの古代人工遺物が破壊されることになった。

2 ミイラから作った薬についてのヨーロッパ人の見解を変えさせることとなった，古代エジプト文化に関する情報を明らかにした。

3 自分たちの古代人工遺物コレクションが破壊される結果を招くと思った裕福なヨーロッパ人に反対された。

4 ミイラへの関心を高まらせるとともに，幾つかの目的にミイラを利用するようヨーロッパ人を触発した。

解説 第2段落によると，ナポレオンのエジプトでの軍事作戦はヨーロッパ人のミイラ熱を再燃させた。ミイラは，富裕層の私的展示物にされたり，肥料や燃料といった「さまざまなほかの方法」で利用されたりした。これを「幾つかの目的」と表した**4**が正解。**2**の「古代エジプト文化に関する情報を明らかにした」は正しいが，第1文に書かれているようにヨーロッパ人はすでにミイラから作った薬を使わなくなっていたのだから，見解が変わったのはナポレオン以前のことである。

(40) – 解答 ①

問題文の訳 この文章の筆者が英国人画家に言及しているのは，

選択肢の訳 **1** マミーブラウンの使用が死者に対する敬意の欠如を示すということで，一部の人たちから反対されたさまを例示するためである。

2 技術的性能が良くないにもかかわらず，マミーブラウンが有名な芸術家たちの間で人気があり続けた理由を説明するためである。

3 マミーブラウンは独特な成分のためほかの絵の具顔料より優れていたという説に裏付けを与えるためである。

4 一部の芸術家たちが，当初は使うのを拒んだが後にマミーブラウンについて肯定的な見解を持つようになった1つの理由を説明するためである。

解説 第3段落後半はマミーブラウンを批判する人たち（= critics）に関する記述で，英国人画家はその流れの中で登場する。彼がミイラを使った絵の具を地面に埋めた理由は，「亡くなった人で作った顔料で絵を描くことは非礼だ」と考えたからである。従って**1**が正解。選択肢では本文のdeceased peopleをthe deadと，disrespectfulをa lack of respectと言い換えている。

(41) – 解答 ②

問題文の訳 絵画がマミーブラウンを含むかどうかを確定するのを難しくしていることの1つは何か。

選択肢の訳 **1** 色を良くするため顔料に加えられた物質が，検証すれば検知できた可能性のあった一切の生物学的証拠を破壊した。

2 古代エジプト人がミイラをつくる方法が変化したので，顔料の内容物

が一貫していなかった。

3 芸術家たちはその顔料を絵に塗る前にほかの種類の絵の具と混ぜたので，顔料はごくわずかな量しか存在しないだろう。

4 その結果が絵画の価値に影響するかもしれないという懸念から，芸術業界は研究者たちに絵画の検証を行わせないようにしてきた。

解説 第4段落では，マミーブラウンの検出をほぼ不可能にしている These same factors「まさにこれらの要因」として次の3つが挙げられている。①ミイラではなく死んだ動物が用いられた顔料もあった，②顔料は製造業者によってばらつきがあった，③保存用の物質を含めてミイラ製作の手順は変化を繰り返していた。**2** の内容が③と一致する。「顔料の内容物が一貫していなかった」の部分は，保存用の物質も含めて変化したという記述に相当する。

一次試験・筆記 4 | 問題編 p.185

トピックの訳 人々は動物から作られた商品の使用をやめるべきか。

ポイントの訳 ・動物の権利　・絶滅危惧種　・製品の質　・伝統

解答例　　I believe that the quality of alternative products and respecting animal rights are reasons why people should not use goods made from animals.

Many products made from animals are being replaced by artificial goods, and technological advancements have greatly improved the quality of these man-made goods. For example, the quality of fake fur is almost the same as that of real fur. Such high-quality alternative goods mean that using animal products is unnecessary.

Furthermore, some animal products come from animals living in conditions that restrict their freedom. However, animals deserve the right to live freely, and this right should not be ignored for the sake of commercial gain. Therefore, stopping the use of animal-based goods is an effective way to protect animal rights.

In conclusion, the high quality of other types of products and the importance of protecting animal rights mean that people should stop using goods made from animals.

解説 序論：第1段落では，トピックに対する自分の意見を簡潔に書く。模範解答は，ポイントの Product quality と Animal rights を用いている。

これらに alternative「代替の」や respecting「尊重すること」という語を加えて本論での記述を先取りし，トピックに賛成だと表明している。I believe that 〜 are reasons why ...「私は〜が…である理由だと考える」は序論で最も使いやすい表現の1つで，〜に2つのポイントを，...に自分の意見を表す文を入れる。模範解答のように，トピックの stop using「使用をやめる」を not use「使わない」に言い換えたり，that are を省略したりといった工夫ができるとよい。

本論：本論では，序論で述べた主張の理由・根拠を説明する。Product quality を取り上げた第2段落では，序論で alternative という語を用いているように，動物を使わない代替製品について述べている。科学技術の進歩によって artificial「人工の」あるいは man-made「人造の」商品の品質が大幅に向上しているので，動物から作る商品は不要だという意見である。フェイクファーの品質は本物の毛皮の品質とほぼ同じだ，と具体例を示していることで説得力が増している。Animal rights を扱う第3段落は Furthermore で始め，自由を制限された状況で生きている動物から作られた製品もあるという問題を指摘している。そこから，動物には自由に生きる権利がある，動物由来の商品の使用をやめることは動物の権利を守るのに有効だ，という展開となっていて分かりやすい。第2文の冒頭に However，第3文の冒頭に Therefore という副詞を置いていることも，論理の流れを明快にしている。

結論：最終段落では，トピックに対する自分の意見を再び主張する。模範解答は In conclusion「結論として」で始めて，序論・本論で使った alternative を other types of「ほかの種類の〜」と言い換えた上で2つのポイントに改めて言及し，トピックの表現を繰り返してまとめている。第2段落でも用いられている A mean(s) that B「A は B ということを意味する，A ということはつまり B ということである」は，理由（A）と結果・結論（B）をシンプルに結ぶ表現として使えるようにしておきたい。

(そのほかの表現) 模範解答では，動名詞を用いた主部が，respecting animal rights，using animal products，stopping the use of animal-based goods と3つ登場する。第3段落の stopping the use of ... は，it を使って it is an effective way to protect animal rights to stop the use of animal-based goods とすると，to 不定詞が2つあってやや分かりにくい文になる。

No.1 – 解答 ④

スクリプト
★： Dr. Jenkins, could I speak with you for a moment?

☆： Sure, Eric. What's on your mind?

★： I'm embarrassed to say this, but I'm having a hard time keeping my eyes open in class. I have to work two part-time jobs to make ends meet, and your class is so early in the morning.

☆： So are you thinking about dropping the class? That would be a shame, considering that your test scores have been pretty good.

★： No, not that. I need this class in order to graduate next year. Actually, I was wondering if you could arrange your seating chart so I'm sitting right up in front. That should help me pay better attention in class.

☆： I think I can probably do that.

Question: What is the student concerned about?

全文訳
★： ジェンキンズ先生，ちょっとお話しできますか？

☆： いいわよ，エリック。気になることでもあるの？

★： こんなことを言うのは恥ずかしいんですが，授業中目を開けているのがつらいんです。お金のやりくりをするのにアルバイトを2つしなければならなくて，先生の授業は午前中のすごく早い時間なんです。

☆： じゃあ，授業に出るのをやめようと考えているの？ ずっとテストでかなりいい点を取っていることを考えると残念だわ。

★： いいえ，そうじゃないんです。来年卒業するためにはこの授業が必要です。実は，僕が最前列に座れるよう，座席表を調整していただけないかと思いまして。それならきっと授業中注意力が上がると思うんです。

☆： それならたぶんできると思う。

質問：この学生は何を心配しているか。

選択肢の訳
1 最近のテストの点数。

2 その授業に出るのをやめなければならないこと。

3 仕事を見つけること。

4 授業中目を覚ましていること。

解説 男子学生が相談に来たのは，アルバイトで忙しいのに教師の授業が「午前中のすごく早い時間」なので，「授業中目を開けているのがつらい」から。そのため，注意力が上がるよう最前列に座らせてもらえないかと依頼している。keeping my eyes open を Staying awake と言い換えた **4** が正解。seating chart は「座席表」。

No.2-解答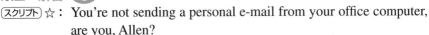

スクリプト ☆： You're not sending a personal e-mail from your office computer, are you, Allen?

★： It's just a quick note to my mom — it's her birthday tomorrow.

☆： Didn't you read the memo from the CEO? Using office computers for private communications could get you fired. I heard they're looking for excuses to cut staff.

★： I doubt if they'd take a birthday message that seriously, but thanks for the warning.

☆： Better safe than sorry.

Question: Why is the woman concerned?

全文訳 ☆： 会社のパソコンから私用Eメールを送っているんじゃないよね，アレン？

★： 母にさっと短信を書いただけだよ — 明日は母の誕生日なんだ。

☆： CEOからの回覧を読まなかった？　会社のパソコンを個人的通信に使うと首になるかもしれない。人員削減する口実を探しているらしいよ。

★： 誕生日のメッセージをそんなに深刻には考えないだろうと思うけど，ご忠告には感謝するよ。

☆： 用心するに越したことはないわよ。

質問：女性はなぜ心配しているのか。

選択肢の訳　**1**　男性は失業するかもしれない。

2　男性は母親の誕生日を忘れた。

3　男性は彼女のEメールに返信しなかった。

4　男性はCEOに好かれていない。

解説　会社のパソコンで母親にEメールを送ることについて，男性本人は大したことだとは思っていないが，女性はcould get you fired「首になるかもしれない」と心配している。これをcould lose his jobと表した**1**が正解。Better safe than sorry. は「後で悔やむより今安全策を取った方がいい」という意味のことわざ。

No.3-解答

スクリプト ☆： Sam, next week, it's my turn to drive us to work, but my car's in the shop.

★： What's wrong with it?

☆： Oh, I had an accident over the weekend.

★： Nothing too serious, I hope.

☆： No. Just a fender bender.

★： OK. Well, why don't I do the driving next week, and you can take your turn once your car's fixed?

☆： That would be great. Thanks a lot.

21年度第3回　リスニング

243

Question: What do we learn about these people?

☆： サム，来週は私があなたを乗せて車で出勤する番なんだけど，車が修理中なのよ。

★： 車がどうかしたの？

☆： うん，週末の間に事故を起こしちゃって。

★： それほどひどい事故じゃなかったのならいいけど。

☆： うん，大丈夫よ。ほんのちょっとした事故なの。

★： 分かった。そうだね，来週は僕が運転を担当するのはどうだろう，そして，車の修理が済み次第君の番にすればいい。

☆： そうしてもらえると助かるわ。どうもありがとう。

質問：この人たちについて何が分かるか。

1 交替で車を運転する。

2 大きな事故を起こした。

3 自動車修理工場で働いている。

4 ２人とも来週は運転できない。

女性の「来週は私があなたを乗せて車で出勤する番」や男性の「来週は僕が運転を担当する」などから，２人は毎週交替でそれぞれの車に相手を乗せて通勤していると分かる。従って **1** が正解。fender bender は「（フェンダーが曲がる程度の）ちょっとした事故」なので **2** は誤り。

No.**4** - 解答 ··· 正答率 ★**75%以上**

☆： I'm sorry, sir, but your credit card was declined.

★： I don't understand why. It was fine yesterday.

☆： Perhaps you've reached your limit. It happens quite often.

★： I don't know. That's certainly possible, I suppose.

☆： Anyway, I suggest you call your card issuer. Do you have a debit card or a personal check you'd like to use for today's purchases?

★： No, I'll just pay with cash.

Question: What's the man's problem?

☆： 申し訳ございませんが，お客さまのクレジットカードは通りませんでした。

★： 理由が分かりません。昨日は大丈夫だったんですよ。

☆： もしかすると限度額に達したのかもしれません。ありがちなことです。

★： どうでしょう。確かにそれはあり得るとは思いますが。

☆： ともかく，カードの発行会社に電話することをお勧めします。本日のご購入分にお使いになりたいデビットカードか個人小切手はお持ちですか？

★： いいえ，現金で払います。

質問：男性の問題は何か。

1 クレジットカードを使えない。

2 カードの発行会社に連絡するのを忘れた。

3 今日は現金が足りない。

4 デビットカードを紛失した。

解説 女性の your credit card was declined がポイント。*be* declined「断られる」はクレジットカードについて用いると，カードを読み取り機に通しても利用が承認されないという意味になる。つまり，男性はクレジットカードが使えなかったと分かる。

No.5 – 解答 ③

スクリプト ☆： How's the job-hunting going, Tyler? You know your dad and I can't support you forever.

★： Actually, I've been offered a second interview for a call-center job. I'm not sure it's my thing, though.

☆： It doesn't have to be. The more jobs you try your hand at, the more you'll learn about the working world.

★： But what if I take it and end up missing out on my dream job?

☆： You can keep applying to other places while you work.

★： Fair enough. I'll call them back and schedule the second interview.
Question: What is the woman's opinion about her son?

全文訳 ☆： 職探しの調子はどう，タイラー？　お父さんも私も，いつまでもあなたを養うわけにはいかないんだからね。

★： 実は，コールセンターの仕事で二次面接に呼ばれているんだ。それが自分向きかは分からないけど。

☆： そうである必要はないわ。チャレンジする仕事が多ければ多いほど，それだけ仕事の世界のことをたくさん学べるもの。

★： だけど，その仕事に就いたあげくに夢の仕事を逃すことになったら？

☆： 働きながら別のところに応募し続ければいいじゃない。

★： もっともだ。こちらから電話して二次面接の予定を決めるよ。
質問：息子に関する女性の意見は何か。

選択肢の訳 **1** コールセンターの仕事に向いていない。

2 間違った面接のテクニックを学んでいる。

3 呼ばれている面接に行くべきだ。

4 夢の仕事を見つけることを優先すべきだ。

解説 求職中の息子はコールセンターの仕事が自分に向いているか分からないと言っているが，母親は，とにかくいろんな仕事をやってみることを勧めている。最後に息子も二次面接を受けることに決めているので，**3** が正解。*one's* thing「一番好きな[合っている]こと」，try *one's* hand at「～を初めてやってみる」といった表現を理解できるかどうかがポイントになる。

スクリプト ☆： Hello, Sergio. What brings you to the clinic today?

★： My energy's been really low recently, so I thought I should have a checkup.

☆： Any major changes since your last appointment?

★： I got promoted to a new position that's pretty stressful and requires a lot of business trips. I've been eating unhealthy food, too.

☆： I see. Getting adequate nutrition can be a challenge when you're traveling.

★： What should I do?

☆： Let's get a few tests done, and then we'll look at your options once the results come in.

Question: What is the doctor going to do next?

全文訳 ☆： こんにちは，セルジオ。今日はどういったことで来院されたんですか？

★： 最近全然元気が出ないので，健康診断を受けた方がいいと思いまして。

☆： 前回の予約から何か大きな変化は？

★： 結構ストレスがたまって多くの出張が必要な新しいポストに昇進しました。ずっと不健康な食事もしています。

☆： なるほど。出張のときは，十分な栄養を取るのが難しいこともありますね。

★： どうすればいいでしょう？

☆： 幾つか検査を終わらせて，それから結果が出次第，選択肢について検討しましょう。

質問：医師は次に何をするか。

選択肢の訳 **1** 男性に幾つか検査を受けさせる。

2 もっと運動するよう男性に促す。

3 仕事に関連するストレスについて男性にアドバイスする。

4 専門医に行くよう男性に勧める。

解説 元気が出ないという男性の話を聞いた医師は，最後に Let's get a few tests done と言っている。これを言い換えた **1** が正解。検査結果が出たら options「選択肢」を検討すると言っているが，次にするのは検査である。

No.7 - 解答 ③

スクリプト ☆： Jasper? I thought you were on vacation this week.

★： Officially, I am. My manager was planning to take some time off, so I thought I'd do the same. Unfortunately, she's still working, which means she's asking me to do stuff.

☆： She's making you work during your vacation? You should complain to the personnel department.

★： But I've only been here a year. I want to prove I'm committed to the company.

☆： Well, be sure to set aside a little time for yourself this week. You are technically on vacation.

★： I will. Thanks.

Question: What is one thing we learn about the man?

全文訳 ☆： ジャスパー？　今週は休暇を取っていると思っていたけど。

★： 表向きにはそうなんだ。上司が少し休みを取る予定だったので，僕も同じようにしようと思ったんだ。あいにく彼女はまだ仕事をしていて，ということは，あれこれするよう僕に頼んでいるというわけ。

☆： 休暇中にあなたを働かせているの？　人事部に苦情を言った方がいいよ。

★： だけど僕はここに来てまだ１年だし。会社に忠誠心があると証明したいんだよ。

☆： うーん，今週は必ず自分のために少し時間を取りなさいよ。厳密に言うとあなたは休暇を取っているんだから。

★： そうするよ。ありがとう。

質問：男性について分かることの１つは何か。

選択肢の訳
1　今年もっと後になってから休暇を取る。
2　人事部長と面談する。
3　上司からするように頼まれたことをする。
4　女性に助けてくれるよう頼む。

解説 休暇中なのに会社にいる男性を見て女性は驚いている。男性は，休暇を取りやめて働いている上司に仕事を頼まれていると言い，まだ入社１年なので I'm committed to the company「会社に忠誠心がある」と証明したいと説明している。つまり，**3** のように，男性は上司に頼まれたことをやろうと思っていることになる。technically は「規則を厳密に適用すると」という意味。

No.**8** – 解答 ④

スクリプト ★： What do you think of the proposed design for our new company logo?

☆： I quite like the style of the lettering, but the logo doesn't have enough impact. How about you?

★： The colors are appealing, but I think the shape of our current logo represents our company better.

☆： I heard there's a trend toward simplicity these days, but the designers have gone too far in that direction.

★： Agreed. We should talk to them again.

Question: What do these people think about the proposed logo?

★： うちの会社の新しいロゴだけど，提案されたデザインについてどう思う？

☆： 文字のスタイルはとても好きだけど，ロゴ（マーク）に十分なインパクトがないわ。あなたはどう？

★： 色使いは引き付けるものがあるけど，今のロゴの形の方がうちの会社をよく表していると思う。

☆： 近ごろはシンプルさを求めるのがトレンドらしいけど，デザイナーたちはそっち方面に行き過ぎたわね。

★： 同感だ。デザイナーたちともう一度話した方がいいな。

質問：この人たちは提案されたロゴについてどう思っているか。

選択肢の訳 **1** もっと明るい色が必要だ。

2 会社のイメージに合っている。

3 現在のロゴに似過ぎている。

4 デザインのやり直しが必要だ。

解説 提案された新しいロゴのデザインについて，女性は文字のスタイルは好きだがロゴにインパクトが足りないと言い，男性は色はいいがロゴの形は今の方がいいと言っている。これらから，最後に男性が言っている We should talk to them again. は，デザインを再考するようデザイナーたちに話すという意味だと考えられる。それを redesign という動詞で表した **4** が正解。

No.9 – 解答

スクリプト ★： Sheena, are you going to Alice's book-launch party on Wednesday?

☆： Of course. It's taken her a decade to write, but the book turned out great!

★： You've already read it? That's not fair! But I suppose you two have been friends since kindergarten.

☆： And I helped with research for one of the chapters.

★： I guess I'll just have to read it when it's available to the general public.

☆： You only have to wait a few days.

Question: What is one thing we learn about the man?

全文訳 ★： シーナ，水曜日のアリスの出版記念パーティーには行くの？

☆： もちろん。彼女は執筆に10年かかったけど，本は素晴らしい出来なのよ！

★： もう読んだの？ 不公平だよ！ だけど君たち2人は幼稚園からの友だちなんだよね。

☆： それに私は章の1つの調査を手伝ったの。

★： 一般の人たちが読めるようになったら，僕も読まなきゃなあ。

☆： 2，3日待つだけでいいわよ。

質問：男性について分かることの1つは何か。

1 まだアリスの本を読んでいない。

2 アリスのパーティーに出席できない。

3 アリスとはもう友だちではない。

4 アリスの本にがっかりした。

解説 book-launch party は launch a book「本を刊行する」から来た表現で，「出版記念パーティー」のこと。アリスの本について，男性は You've already read it? That's not fair! と言っているので，まだ読んでいないことが分かる。手に入るようになったら読むと言っていることからも裏付けられる。従って **1** が正解。

No.10 解答 ②

スクリプト ☆： Morning. Sorry to be late.

★： No problem. Was your train delayed again?

☆： Yes, for the third time this month. I take an early train, but there are always big delays on weekdays during rush hour.

★： Isn't there another train line in your area?

☆： Yes, but the station on that line is a 45-minute walk from my house.

★： Perhaps you could ride your bicycle there.

☆： That's an idea. If I did that, I could catch a later train than I do now.

★： Cycling would be good exercise, too.

☆： Good point. I think I'll give it a try.

Question: What will the woman probably do in the future?

全文訳 ☆： おはよう。遅れてごめん。

★： 構わないよ。また電車が遅れたの？

☆： うん，今月3度目。早い電車に乗るんだけど，平日のラッシュアワーはいつもすごく遅れるのよね。

★： 君の住んでいる地域に別の路線はないの？

☆： あるけど，その線の駅はうちから45分歩くの。

★： そこまで自転車で行くのもありかもしれない。

☆： いい考えね。そうすれば，今より遅い電車に乗れる。

★： サイクリングはいい運動にもなるだろうし。

☆： 確かに。やってみようかな。

質問： 女性は今後おそらく何をするか。

選択肢の訳 1 確実にもっと早い電車に乗るようにする。

2 違う路線を使う。

3 自転車で会社に行く。

4 週末に会社に入る。

解説 電車がよく遅れるので遅刻が多い女性に，男性は別の路線の駅まで自転車で行くことを提案している。女性は男性の提案に乗り気である。選択肢の中でこの内容に合致するのは **2**。男性は自転車で会社まで行くのがいいとは言っていないので，**3** は誤り。

No.11 解答 ①

スクリプト ☆： What're you doing with those garbage bags, Ronan?

★： I was just about to put them outside. Wednesday is collection day, right?

☆： Actually, they've switched over to a 14-day schedule. There was an announcement in the local paper last month.

★： They're only collecting every two weeks now? I sometimes wonder what we pay our taxes for.

☆： I know what you mean, but I guess the city needs to reduce spending. They're also talking about lowering the number of bags you can put out.

Question: What is one thing we learn from the conversation?

全文訳 ☆： そのごみ袋，どうするの，ローナン？

★： 外に出そうとしていたんだ。水曜日は収集日だよね？

☆： 実はね，14 日間のスケジュールに切り替わったの。先月地元紙に告知があったよ。

★： 今じゃ隔週にしか収集してないってこと？　何のために税金を払っているんだろうとときどき思うよ。

☆： 言いたいことは分かるけど，市は支出を減らす必要があるんだと思う。外に出せる袋の数を減らそうという話もしているよ。

質問：この会話から分かることの 1 つは何か。

選択肢の訳 1　ごみ収集の頻度が減った。

2　ごみ袋の価格が高くなる。

3　地方税が間もなく上がりそうだ。

4　新聞の配達スケジュールが変わった。

解説 Wednesday is collection day だと思ってごみ袋を外に出そうとしている男性に，女性は they've switched over to a 14-day schedule と言っている。その後で男性が every two weeks と言い換えているように，毎週水曜日だったごみの収集日が，2 週間に 1 回に減ったことが分かる。それを less frequent と表した **1** が正解。

No.12 解答 ④

スクリプト ★： Hey, Sharon. Are you OK? You look exhausted.

☆： Hi, Ranjit. Yeah, I can't sleep because of my upstairs neighbors. They're awake at all hours of the night. Even earplugs haven't worked, so I'm going to complain to the landlord.

★： Have you thought about writing a polite note to them first? They might get upset if you go directly to the landlord.

☆： I hadn't thought about that. Have you ever tried something like that?

★： No, but I've read online that it can be quite effective.

☆： Thanks. I think I'll do that.

Question: What will the woman most likely do?

全文訳 ★： やあ，シャロン。大丈夫？　疲れ果てた顔だよ。

☆： こんにちは，ランジット。うん，上の階の住人のせいで眠れないの。夜の間ずっと起きているんだもの。耳栓をしても効き目がなかったから，大家に苦情を言うつもり。

★： まずその住人にていねいな手紙を書くことは考えた？　大家のところに直行すると，住人は腹を立てるかもしれないよ。

☆： それは考えなかった。そういったことをしてみた経験があるの？

★： ないけど，かなり効果的なこともあるってネットで読んだんだ。

☆： ありがとう。やってみようと思う。

質問：女性は何をする可能性が最も高いか。

選択肢の訳 1　耳栓を使ってみる。

2　ランジットに彼女の上の階の住人と話してもらう。

3　大家について苦情を言う。

4　上の階の住人にメッセージを書く。

解説 上の階の住人が夜の間ずっと起きていて眠れないので大家に苦情を言うつもりだ，と話す女性に対し，男性は Have you thought about writing a polite note to them first? と別の方法を提案している。その後はこの提案に関するやりとりが続くので，女性が最後に言っている I think I'll do that. の that は男性の提案ということになる。note を message と言い換えた **4** が正解。

一次試験・リスニング Part2　問題編 p.188 ～ 189

▶ MP3 ▶ アプリ
▶ CD 3 42 ～ 48

A

スクリプト **Picky Eaters**

Some children are picky eaters. They will only eat a few foods and refuse to eat anything else, and this is generally considered unhealthy. Researchers have found that genetics may be one cause of this behavior, but the environment in which children are raised may also be important. Parents, for example, serve as role models for their children, so it can be damaging if their children see them following limited, unhealthy diets.

Once children form such eating habits, how can they be changed? Parents often use rewards. For example, they will tell their children they can have ice cream if they eat their vegetables. However, some experts warn against doing this. They say it does little to change children's negative attitudes toward foods they dislike. Instead, these experts recommend involving children in the growing, purchasing, and preparation of these foods. This may help children develop a positive relationship with healthy meals.

Questions

No.13 What may be one reason children become picky eaters?

No.14 What is one thing that some experts recommend?

全文訳 **偏食家**

　偏食家の子供がいる。食べるのは数種類の食べ物だけで，ほかのものは一切食べようとせず，これは健康に悪いと一般に考えられている。遺伝的体質がこの行動の１つの理由かもしれないと研究者たちが発見したが，子供が育つ環境も重要かもしれない。例えば，親は子供のロールモデルとなるので，親が限られたものしか食べない不健康な食生活を送るのを子供が見れば有害なことがある。

　子供がそうした食習慣を身に付けてしまったら，どうしたら変えられるのだろう。親はしばしば褒美を用いる。例えば，出された野菜を食べたらアイスクリームを食べてもいいと親は子供に言ったりする。しかし，そういうことはしないように警告する専門家たちもいる。嫌いな食べ物に対する子供の否定的態度を変えるのに，これはほとんど役に立たないと彼らは言う。代わりにこれらの専門家たちはこうした食べ物の栽培と購入，そして調理に子供を関与させることを勧める。これは，子供が健康的な食事と前向きな関係を築くのに役立つかもしれない。

No.13 解答

質問の訳 子供が偏食家になる理由の１つかもしれないのは何か。

選択肢の訳
1 手に入る食べ物の選択肢が多過ぎる。
2 学校がしばしば面白味のない食べ物を用意する。
3 子供は親の食習慣を真似る。
4 子供には減量したいという願望がある。

解説 picky eaters の意味が分からなくても，They will only eat a few foods ... と説明されているので慌てないこと。子供が偏食家になる理由として，２つの可能性が挙げられている。１つは genetics「遺伝的体質」。もう１つは the environment in which children are raised で，続けて具体例が紹介されている。親は子供のロールモデルなので，親の偏食を見ることは子供に有害な影響を与え得る。それを copy「真似る」と

いう動詞を使って表した **3** が正解。

No.14 解答

質問の訳 一部の専門家たちが勧めることの１つは何か。

選択肢の訳
1 子供に自分の食事を作る手伝いをさせること。
2 もっと多くのスポーツをするよう子供に促すこと。
3 ときどき子供に不健康な食べ物を食べさせてやること。
4 野菜を食べたことで子供に褒美を与えること。

解説 these experts recommend 以下が専門家たちが勧めることの内容。嫌いな食べ物の the growing, purchasing, and preparation に子供をかかわらせることを勧めている。このうち preparation「食事の準備」，つまり「調理」にかかわらせることに相当する **1** が正解。

B

スクリプト **Ching Shih the Pirate**

It is sometimes said that a Chinese woman named Ching Shih was one of history's most successful pirates. Her husband was also a pirate. Following his death in 1807, Ching Shih took control of their pirate operations, which grew rapidly. The Chinese government then ordered its navy to capture her. The sea battle that followed, however, went badly for the government. Ching Shih's pirates captured several naval vessels, which increased Ching Shih's power.

However, it is thought that Ching Shih began having difficulty controlling her huge forces. In 1810, therefore, she came to an agreement with government officials in which she promised to end her operations. In exchange, she was allowed to keep her wealth, and she and most of her followers were given their freedom. While many pirates throughout history died violently, Ching Shih avoided that fate.

Questions

No.15 What was one result of the sea battle?

No.16 What did Ching Shih do in 1810?

全文訳 **海賊・鄭氏**

鄭氏という名の中国人女性が歴史上最も成功した海賊の１人だったと時に言われる。彼女の夫も海賊だった。1807 年に夫が死んだ後，鄭氏が彼らの海賊業の支配権を握り，海賊業は急速に成長した。すると中国政府は，彼女を捕らえるよう海軍に命じた。しかし，それに続く海戦は政府に不利に運んだ。鄭氏の海賊たちは軍艦数隻を捕獲し，それが鄭氏の力を増大させた。

しかし，鄭氏は自身の巨大な軍勢の制御に苦労するようになったと考えられている。そのため，彼女は 1810 年に，海賊業を終わりにすると約束する協定を政府の役人たちと結んだ。引き換えに，彼女は財産の保持を許され，彼女と手下のほとんどは自由を与えられた。歴史を通して多くの海賊が惨死した一方で，鄭氏はその運命を免れたのだ。

No.15 解答

質問の訳　海戦の結果の１つは何だったか。

選択肢の訳　1　鄭氏の海賊たちが船を何隻か手に入れた。
　　　　　　2　多くの海賊の指揮官たちが捕らえられた。
　　　　　　3　海賊たちのほとんどが死んだ。
　　　　　　4　鄭氏が中国海軍を助けることに同意した。

解説　海賊と中国海軍の間の海戦は went badly for the government なので，海賊側が優勢だったことが分かる。captured several naval vessels を gained a number of ships と言い換えた **1** が正解。

No.16 解答 ④

質問の訳　鄭氏は 1810 年に何をしたか。

選択肢の訳　1　処罰を逃れるため中国を去った。
　　　　　　2　財産を差し出した。
　　　　　　3　新たな海賊組織を作った。
　　　　　　4　海賊業をやめることに同意した。

解説　1810 年に鄭氏は政府の役人たちと協定を結んだが，その内容は she promised to end her operations というものだった。operations は前半に出てくる pirate operations のことなので，**4** が正解。

C

スクリプト　**The Canada Lynx**

The Canada lynx is a type of wildcat found mainly in Canada and the northern United States. The animals are skilled at avoiding humans, so they are rarely seen in the wild. However, lynx sightings increase roughly every 10 years. This is because the population of animals called snowshoe hares rises and falls in a roughly 10-year cycle. Lynx hunt snowshoe hares, and when there are more hares to hunt, the lynx population tends to grow.

It was long believed that Canada lynx live their whole lives in one particular area. However, scientists have discovered that lynx can journey thousands of kilometers to establish new territories. Some scientists think it is likely that these animals are following hares. However, lynx have also been observed making long journeys at other times, so there may be another reason why they travel.

Questions

No.17 What does the speaker say about Canada lynx?

No.18 What did scientists discover about Canada lynx?

全文訳　**カナダオオヤマネコ**

カナダオオヤマネコは，主にカナダとアメリカ北部に生息するヤマネコの一種である。この動物は人間を避けるすべにたけているので，野生ではめったに見られない。しかし，

オオヤマネコの目撃例はおよそ 10 年ごとに増加する。これは，カンジキウサギという動物の個体数が，およそ 10 年周期で増減するためである。オオヤマネコはカンジキウサギを狩り，狩るウサギが多いほどオオヤマネコの個体数は増える傾向がある。

　カナダオオヤマネコは生涯ある特定の地域に生息すると長い間考えられていた。しかし，オオヤマネコは新たなテリトリーを築くために数千キロの旅をすることができると科学者たちが発見した。一部の科学者たちは，おそらくこの動物はウサギを追っているのだろうと考えている。しかし，オオヤマネコはほかのときにも長旅をしているのが観察されているので，彼らが移動する別の理由があるのかもしれない。

No.17 解答

質問の訳 話者はカナダオオヤマネコについて何と言っているか。

選択肢の訳 1　ある特定の時期に数が増える。
2　人間に狩られている。
3　生息地が最近狭くなった。
4　食べるカンジキウサギの数が減ってきている。

解説 話者がカナダオオヤマネコについて話している情報は，主にカナダとアメリカ北部に住んでいること，ほとんどない目撃例が約 10 年ごとに増えること，それは餌となるウサギの数が増えるのでカナダオオヤマネコも増えるからだということ。個体数が約 10 年ごとに増えることについて，**1** が population を numbers と言い換え，「約 10 年ごとに」を at certain times と抽象的に表している。

No.18 解答

質問の訳 科学者たちはカナダオオヤマネコについて何を発見したか。

選択肢の訳 1　食べ物を探すときだけ移動する。
2　時に長距離を移動する。
3　ほかのヤマネコよりずっと長生きする。
4　常に最初のテリトリーに戻る。

解説 scientists have discovered that 以下が科学者たちが発見した内容。「新たなテリトリーを築くために数千キロも旅をすることができる」と述べられている。この内容を journey → travel, thousands of kilometers → long distances と言い換えた **2** が正解。**1** は，ほかのとき（＝食べ物を探す以外のとき）にも長旅をするのが観察されているので誤り。

D

スクリプト **The Catacombs of Priscilla**

In Rome, there are networks of tunnels that were built around the beginning of the second century AD. These tunnels were used as burial places for people of many religions. However, the tunnels became especially important for

Christians. Their religion was not officially recognized at the time, so Christians used the tunnels to hold religious ceremonies.

One famous section of tunnels is called the Catacombs of Priscilla. In this section, there are some early Christian paintings. One of the paintings seems to show a woman dressed in a priest's robe, and others show women performing religious ceremonies. Some people believe the paintings are proof of female priests in the church in ancient times. This is significant because some Christian churches today do not allow women to become priests. Other observers, however, say that we cannot be sure exactly what the paintings show.

Questions

No.19 What is one thing we learn about the tunnels?

No.20 What do some people believe the paintings show?

全文訳 **プリシッラのカタコンベ**

ローマには，紀元2世紀初頭前後に造られた地下トンネル網がある。これらのトンネルは，多くの宗教の人々の埋葬所として用いられた。しかし，トンネルはキリスト教徒にとって特に重要になった。彼らの宗教は当時公式には認められていなかったので，キリスト教徒は宗教儀式を行うためにトンネルを用いた。

トンネルのある有名な区画は，プリシッラのカタコンベと呼ばれる。この区画には，幾つかの初期キリスト教絵画がある。絵の1つは，祭服に身を包んだ女性を描いているように思われ，ほかの絵は宗教儀式を執り行う女性たちを描いている。これらの絵は古代の教会に女性聖職者がいた証拠だと考える人もいる。今日のキリスト教の教派には女性が聖職者になることを許さないところもあるのだから，これは重要なことである。しかし，ほかの評者たちは，これらの絵が何を描いているのか，はっきりとは分からないと言う。

No.**19** 解答 ② ･･････････････････････････････････････ 正答率 ★75%以上

質問の訳 トンネルについて分かることの1つは何か。

選択肢の訳 1 現代の埋葬所はそのトンネルの設計に基づいている。
2 宗教的目的で用いられた。
3 非キリスト教徒によってのみ用いられた。
4 入り口はつい最近見つかったばかりだ。

解説 catacomb は「地下墓所」の意味で，特に初期キリスト教のものは「カタコンベ」と呼ばれる。ただし，この語の意味が分からなくても問題はなく，トンネルの話だと理解できれば十分である。そのトンネルは多くの宗教の burial places「埋葬所」で，またキリスト教徒は religious ceremonies「宗教儀式」に用いたと言っていることから，**2**が正解となる。

No.20 解答

質問の訳 　絵が何を描いていると一部の人は考えているか。

選択肢の訳 　1　昔は女性が聖職者だった。
　　　　　　2　トンネルは教会として用いられなかった。
　　　　　　3　初期キリスト教徒に女性はほとんどいなかった。
　　　　　　4　かつては聖職者たちが絵を制作していた。

解説 　トンネルにある絵には祭服を着た女性や宗教儀式を行う女性が描かれているように見える，という話に続いて，絵が proof of female priests in the church in ancient times だと一部の人は考えている，と言っている。この内容から 1 が正解。

E

スクリプト **Happiness and Success**

Many people believe that only by working hard and having a successful career can they find happiness. However, trying to make a lot of money or get promoted at work may not make people truly happy. People who focus on such success often prioritize work over other activities. Consequently, they may lose opportunities to enjoy the things that make life truly enjoyable, such as simple, relaxing times with their families.

After reviewing many studies, researchers recently concluded that success may actually follow happiness. They believe that happy people are more energetic and confident because they experience frequent positive moods, and that this leads to success. Of course, success also depends on factors such as intelligence and social support. More research is needed, but it may be that those whose happiness leads them to success are more likely to stay happy.

Questions

No.21 What does the speaker say about people who focus on success?
No.22 What did researchers recently conclude about happy people?

全文訳 **幸福と成功**

　多くの人は，一生懸命働いてキャリアで成功を収めることによってのみ幸福を見いだすことができると考えている。しかし，大金を稼ごうとしたり仕事で昇進しようとしたりすることは，人を真に幸福にはしないかもしれない。そうした成功に注力する人は，ほかの活動より仕事を優先することが多い。それゆえ，家族と過ごす飾らないほっとする時間といった，人生を真に楽しいものにする物事を楽しむ機会を失ってしまうかもしれない。

　多くの研究を精査した後，最近研究者たちは，成功は実際には幸福の後に来るのかもしれないという結論を出した。幸福な人は前向きな気分をしばしば経験するので，より活力と自信があり，これが成功につながると研究者たちは考えている。もちろん，成功は知能やソーシャルサポートといった要因にも依拠している。さらなる研究が必要だが，

幸福によって成功に導かれる人たちの方が幸福でい続ける可能性が高いのかもしれない。

No.21 解答 ③

質問の訳 話者は成功に注力する人について何と言っているか。

選択肢の訳 1 しばしば成功した家族がいる。
2 しばしばストレスレベルが低い。
3 飾らない喜びを楽しむチャンスを逃しているかもしれない。
4 周囲の人を幸福にするかもしれない。

解説 People who focus on such success 以下で，そういう人は仕事を優先することが多く，家族と過ごすといった人生の楽しみを味わう機会を失ってしまうかもしれないと言っている。**3**がそれと一致する。放送文の lose opportunities を miss chances と言い換え，the things that make life truly enjoyable を pleasures の1語でまとめている。

No.22 解答 ③

質問の訳 最近研究者たちは幸福な人についてどんな結論を出したか。

選択肢の訳 1 幸福でい続けるために家族の支援を必要としない。
2 収入はおそらく多くない。
3 前向きな気分が彼らをより活動的にする。
4 不幸な人より知能が高い。

解説 研究者たちの結論は success may actually follow happiness で，続けて詳しく説明されている。すなわち，幸福な人の前向きな気分が活力と自信を生み，それが成功につながる，と述べている。energetic を active と言い換えた**3**が正解である。なお，social support は行政による金銭的・制度的支援というより，家族や友人など社会的なつながりがある人たちからの精神的支援という意味合いが強い。

F

スクリプト **Ancient Oysters**

For thousands of years, Native Americans along what is now called the US East Coast used oysters as a food source. Today, however, oyster stocks have been greatly reduced. Overharvesting, pollution, and disease have caused oyster populations to fall, especially since the late 1800s, when European settlers introduced new harvesting methods. These methods included dredging, which involves removing huge numbers of oysters from the seabed. This process also damages the ecosystem in which the oysters live.

In recent years, archaeologists have studied Native American harvesting practices. The archaeologists found that Native Americans did not harvest young oysters. Instead, Native Americans waited for oysters to grow and reproduce before they harvested them. The archaeologists also discovered that average shell size increased until the 1800s, which indicates that Native American practices helped ancient oysters to become larger. This finding surprised the archaeologists, who expected oyster shells to gradually get smaller in response to being harvested.

Questions

No.23 What do we learn about oysters along the US East Coast today?

No.24 What is one thing the archaeologists discovered?

全文訳 **古代のカキ**

　数千年の間，今ではアメリカ東海岸と呼ばれる所に沿って住んでいたネイティブアメリカンは，カキを食料源として利用していた。しかし今日では，カキ資源は大きく減少している。乱獲と汚染，そして病気が原因で，特にヨーロッパからの入植者が新しい収穫方法を持ち込んだ1800年代後期以降，カキの個体数が落ち込んだ。これらの方法には桁網漁業（漁具で海底を引っかいて漁獲する漁法）も含まれていたのだが，桁網漁業は海底から膨大な数のカキを取り去ることを伴う。このプロセスは，カキがすむ生態系にもダメージを与える。

　近年，考古学者たちがネイティブアメリカンの収穫のやり方を研究している。ネイティブアメリカンは若いカキを収穫しなかったことを考古学者たちは突き止めた。その代わり，ネイティブアメリカンはカキを収穫する前に，カキが成長して繁殖するのを待った。考古学者たちは平均的な殻のサイズが1800年代までは大きくなっていたことも発見したが，これは，ネイティブアメリカンのやり方が古代のカキの大型化を助けたことを示している。カキの殻は収穫されるのに対応して次第に小型化するはずだと考古学者は思っていたので，この発見は彼らを驚かせた。

No.23 解答 **2** ....

　質問の訳　今日のアメリカ東海岸沿いのカキについて何が分かるか。

　選択肢の訳　**1**　病気と闘うのがよりうまくなってきている。

　2　数が以前より少ない。

　3　カキの多くは食用に収穫されない。

　4　カキがすむ水域がきれいになってきている。

　解説　東海岸のカキの現在の状況については，oyster stocks have been greatly reduced や have caused oyster populations to fall と言っていることから，数が減っていると分かる。それを「以前より少ない」と表した**2**が正解。減った理由として disease を挙げているので**1**は不適。pollution や生態系へのダメージを挙げているので**4**も不適である。

No.24 解答 **1** ....

　質問の訳　考古学者たちが発見したことの1つは何か。

　選択肢の訳　**1**　ネイティブアメリカンの収穫のやり方はカキが大きくなるのを助けた。

　2　ネイティブアメリカンの収穫方法は桁網漁業を含んでいた。

3 ネイティブアメリカンは今でもカキを収穫する。

4 ネイティブアメリカンは若いカキしか収穫しなかった。

解説 考古学者たちの発見は2つ。1つは，ネイティブアメリカンは若いカキ
を収穫せずカキが成長するのを待ったこと。もう1つは，そうしたやり
方がカキの大型化を助けたことである。2つ目の発見の大型化（become
larger）を**1**がgrowと言い換えている。

G

スクリプト

You have 10 seconds to read the situation and Question No. 25.

This bus goes around town all day, so you can just hop on and off anytime. The castle can be accessed from stop 4, and the medieval library is also just a five-minute walk away from that stop. If you're interested in the San Giovanni church, stop 7 is the nearest. It's also normally the meeting place for our 30-minute guided walking tour, but please note that due to an ongoing construction project, that tour will begin from stop 9, just in front of Montalto Gardens. Stop 13 offers access to famous sights like the Gravina Bridge and the town fountain.

Now mark your answer on your answer sheet.

全文訳

このバスは終日町を巡りますので，いつでも乗り降りしていただけます。お城は4番バス停からアクセスでき，中世の図書館もそのバス停からわずか徒歩5分の距離です。サン・ジョバンニ教会に興味がおありなら，7番バス停が最寄りです。そこは通常は当社のガイド付き30分徒歩ツアーの集合場所でもありますが，進行中の建築事業のため，そのツアーはモンタルト庭園の正面，9番バス停から始まります。13番バス停からは，グラビーナ橋や町の泉などの名所にアクセスできます。

No.25 解答 ....

状況の訳 あなたはイタリアで町を巡るツアーバスに乗るところである。ガイド付きの徒歩ツアーに参加したい。次のようなアナウンスが聞こえる。

質問の訳 あなたはどのバス停で降りればよいか。

選択肢の訳 **1** 4番バス停。

2 7番バス停。

3 9番バス停。

4 13番バス停。

解説　状況から，「ガイド付きの徒歩ツアー」がポイントになる。stop 7 が教会の最寄りのバス停であるという説明に続いて It's also normally the meeting place for our 30-minute guided walking tour と言っているが，normally「通常は」から，今は違う事情があるのだと予想できる。すると続けて，建築事業のためツアーは 9 番バス停から始まるとアナウンスしているので，**3** が正解となる。なお，hop on は「飛び乗る」，hop off は「飛び降りる」だが，途中で乗降可能なツアーバスについて「乗る」「降りる」の意味でも用いられる。

H

スクリプト

You have 10 seconds to read the situation and Question No. 26.

You can apply online to renew your working-holiday visa. However, there are some things you should prepare before you apply. You'll need to provide proof that you've had a medical examination by a qualified doctor and have no serious health issues. Once you've done that, you'll also have to present evidence of your employment until now. You mentioned you had all of your salary statements, so those should be sufficient. Since you're applying from within the country, proof that you've saved enough to cover your living costs will not be required this time around.

Now mark your answer on your answer sheet.

全文訳

ワーキングホリデービザの更新はオンラインで申請できます。ですが，申請する前に用意しておいた方がいいものが幾つかあります。有資格医師から健康診断を受け，健康に重大な問題がないことの証明を提出する必要があります。それが済んだら，現在までの雇用の証拠も提示しなければなりません。給与明細は全てお持ちだというお話でしたから，それで十分でしょう。国内から申請することになるので，生活費を賄うのに足りるだけのお金を貯めたという証明は，今回は必要とされません。

No.26 解答

状況の訳　あなたはワーキングホリデープログラムで外国にいる。ビザの更新について入国管理事務所に電話し，次のような話をされる。

質問の訳　あなたはまず何をすべきか。

選択肢の訳　1　オンラインで申請書に記入する。
2　雇用主に給与明細を要請する。
3　貯蓄の証明を見せる。
4　健康診断証明書を取得する。

解説　「まず」何をすればいいかに集中して聞く。話者は before you apply「申請する前に」用意するものを幾つか挙げ，まず medical examination の証明が必要だと言っている。Once you've done that 「それが済んだら」雇用の証拠の提示だが，すでに持っている salary statements で足りる。貯蓄の証明は不要だと最後に言っている。従って，まず **4** をしてから申請に移ることになる。

I

（スクリプト）

You have 10 seconds to read the situation and Question No. 27.

The new security cameras, warning signs, and staff training have all worked. Shoplifting of most products is much lower than in the last quarter. However, stock records for low-cost fruit items like bananas and oranges and expensive things like avocados and mangoes don't match the sales records. This usually means some customers at the self-checkout registers are entering false information to get costly items at a cheaper price. I recommend extra guidance for staff observing the self-checkout stations. If this doesn't work, you may have to think about checking customers' receipts at the exit.

Now mark your answer on your answer sheet.

（全文訳）

　新しい監視カメラと警告の掲示，そしてスタッフの訓練は全て効果が出ています。ほとんどの商品の万引きは，前の四半期よりかなり減っています。ですが，バナナやオレンジなど低価格の果物の品目と，アボカドやマンゴーなど値の張るものの在庫記録が，販売記録と合いません。これは普通，セルフレジの一部の客が，高価な商品をより安い価格で手に入れるため，偽りの情報を登録していることを意味します。セルフレジコーナーを見張るスタッフに追加の指導をすることをお勧めします。それでも効果がなければ，出口で客のレシートを調べることを検討しなければならないかもしれません。

No.**27** 解答　①

（状況の訳）　あなたはスーパーマーケットの店長である。窃盗が原因の損失を減らしたいと思っている。警備アナリストが次のように言う。

（質問の訳）　あなたはまず何をすべきか。

（選択肢の訳）　**1**　スタッフの一部にもっと訓練を受けさせる。
　　2　もっと多くの監視カメラを設置する。
　　3　出口で客のレシートをよく調べる。
　　4　果物の価格をはっきりと表示する。

（解説）　アナリストは，セルフレジで高い果物を安い果物だと偽って登録する客がいるため損失が起きている可能性があると指摘している。それに対する提案は extra guidance for staff observing the self-checkout stations なので，extra guidance を more training と言い換えた **1** が正解。staff training はすでに効果が出ていると最初に言っているが，

それでは足りないということになる。**3**は**1**でも効果がない場合の対策。

スクリプト

You have 10 seconds to read the situation and Question No. 28.

Welcome to our summer sale. We're offering great discounts on all brands, including Rannexe and Duplanne. Interested in a new vacuum cleaner? Use the coupon available on our smartphone app to get $50 off any brand. How about a new washing machine? This month, exchange your used Rannexe washing machine for a $100 credit toward any new Rannexe product. During the month of August, exchange any old Duplanne appliance and get $150 off a new one. Finally, we are offering $75 cash back on any new dishwasher until the end of August.

Now mark your answer on your answer sheet.

全文訳

当店の夏のセールにようこそ。ラネックスとデュプランを含め，全ブランドを大幅値引き中です。新しい掃除機に関心がおありですか。当店のスマートフォンアプリで手に入るクーポンをご利用いただくと，どんなブランドも50ドル引きになります。新しい洗濯機はいかがですか。今月は，お使いのラネックスの洗濯機を，ラネックスのどんな新しい製品にも使える100ドル分のクレジットと交換してください。8月の間は，古いデュプランの家電製品をどれでも交換していただくと，新しいものが150ドル引きになります。最後に，8月末まで，新しい食器洗い機にはどれも75ドルのキャッシュバックをご提供中です。

No.**28** 解答　

状況の訳　あなたは新しい洗濯機が欲しい。現在はデュプランの洗濯機を所有している。7月に電器店を訪れ，次のようなアナウンスを聞く。

質問の訳　お金を最も節約するには，あなたは何をすべきか。

選択肢の訳　**1**　店のスマートフォンアプリをダウンロードする。
2　キャッシュバックがある得な買い物を申し込む。
3　今月洗濯機を交換する。
4　8月に新しいデュプランの洗濯機を買う。

解説　Duplanne の洗濯機を所有していることだけでなく，今は July だということもポイントになると予測して聞く。スマホアプリのクーポンが使えるのは掃除機だけ。100ドル分のクレジットは，Rannexe の洗濯機と交換と言っているので該当しない。続いて，8月中に Duplanne の製品を買い替えると150ドル引きになると言っている。最後のキャッシュバックは食器洗い機のみ。以上から，最も節約になるのは8月に Duplanne の洗濯機に買い替えることである。**3** の this month は7月

なので不適。credit は，その店で使える金券やポイントなどのこと。

スクリプト

You have 10 seconds to read the situation and Question No. 29.

This suit is a clearance item, so we only have what's here on the shelves. Our other location may still have one in your size, though. If you'd like, I can check online for you. If our other store has one, you could go there, if you don't mind driving out of town. The other option would be to reserve one for you and have it sent over to this store at no extra cost. That might take a few days, but if you give me your number, I can call you when it arrives.

Now mark your answer on your answer sheet.

全文訳

このスーツは売り尽くしの商品なので，ここの棚のものしかありません。ですが，ほかの店舗ならお客さまのサイズがまだあるかもしれません。よろしければ，オンラインでお調べできます。ほかの店にあれば，車で町の外まで行っていただいても差し支えなければ，そちらに行かれるのがいいでしょう。もう１つの選択肢は，スーツを取り置きして，追加料金なしで当店に送ってもらうことになります。2，3日かかるかもしれませんが，お電話番号を教えていただければ，届いたら電話でお知らせできます。

No.29 解答

状況の訳　あなたは近所の店で欲しいスーツを目にするが，あなたのサイズのスーツがない。町の外には出かけたくない。店員が次のように言う。

質問の訳　あなたは何をすべきか。

選択肢の訳　**1**　店が新しい在庫を入れるまで待つ。
2　店員にほかの店を調べてもらう。
3　オンラインストアにスーツを注文する。
4　スーツを自宅に配達してもらう。

解説　スーツは clearance item だと店員は言っており，**1** の可能性はない。他店舗ならあるかもしれず，オンラインで調べられると言っていることから **2** が正解。If our other store has one 以下では他店舗にあった場合のことが詳しく述べられているが，それに該当する選択肢はない。**3** は放送文の online を使った引っかけ。スーツがあったら this store に送ってもらうと言っているので，**4** も不適。

解答例 **One day, a husband and wife were going on a walk together.** They saw a group of volunteers picking up garbage in the park. The husband and wife looked pleased to see them cleaning up the area. The next day, the couple was walking around their neighborhood again, and they saw a poster. It said that volunteers were wanted to help at the city marathon. The couple thought it was a good opportunity for them, so they decided to volunteer. At a volunteer staff meeting, the couple was listening to an explanation about their duties at the marathon. A man was explaining that volunteers would help with tasks like working at water stations and at the information booth. The couple seemed to be looking forward to volunteering at the marathon. The day before the marathon, however, the wife was speaking with her manager at work. He told her that she needed to meet a client the next day.

解答例の訳 ある日，夫婦が一緒に散歩に出かけていました。彼らはボランティアたちが公園でごみ拾いをしているのを見かけました。彼らが地域をすっかりきれいにしているのを見て，夫婦はうれしそうでした。翌日，夫婦はまた近所を散歩していて，ポスターを見かけました。市のマラソン大会を手伝うボランティアを募集していると書かれていました。自分たちにとっていい機会だと夫婦は思ったので，ボランティアをすることにしました。ボランティアスタッフの打ち合わせで，夫婦はマラソン大会での自分たちの任務に関する説明を聞いていました。ボランティアは給水所や案内所で働くといった作業の手伝いをする，と男性が説明していました。夫婦はマラソン大会でボランティアをするのを楽しみにしているようでした。しかしマラソン大会の前日，妻は職場で上司と話していました。翌日彼女は顧客と会う必要がある，と彼は彼女に告げました。

解説 解答に含めるべき点は以下の4つ。①散歩中の夫婦がボランティアの清掃活動を見かける，②翌日，夫婦はマラソン大会のボランティア募集のポスターを見かける，③ボランティアスタッフの打ち合わせで，マラソン大会での任務の説明を夫婦が聞いている，④マラソン大会の前日，妻は，翌日は顧客に会う必要があると上司に言われる。人物の表情や発言，掲示物の内容などを基に，夫婦の気持ちを想像しよう。解答例は，1コマ目について pleased，3コマ目について looking forward to と，前向きな気持ちを示す表現を用いている。

No. 1

解答例 I'd be thinking that I should have talked about becoming a volunteer with my boss first. Now I can't fulfill my responsibilities to both my work and the marathon. I should be more careful about my schedule in the future.

解説 質問は「4番目の絵を見てください。もしあなたがこの妻なら，どのようなことを考えているでしょうか」。解答例は〈I should have＋過去分詞〉を使って上司にあらかじめ話しておかなかった後悔を表している。

No. 2

解答例 Yes. It's a chance for parents to better understand their children's relationships with their classmates. This is good for building strong family relationships. It also gives parents and teachers an opportunity to communicate.

解説 質問は「親は運動会などの学校行事に参加すべきだと思いますか」。解答例は Yes の立場で，自分の子供とクラスメートの関係をより良く理解できる，家族の関係が強まる，親と教師の意思疎通の機会になる，と3つの利点を挙げている。No の立場では，親は仕事を優先しなければならないこともある，行事の数が多過ぎる，といった理由が考えられる。

No. 3

解答例 No. The purpose of public libraries is to give people access to information, but I think we can achieve the same goal using digital libraries online. That way, we don't need to spend a lot of money maintaining library buildings.

解説 質問は「公共図書館は今でも地域社会で重要な役割を果たしていますか」。解答例は No の立場で，デジタル図書館で情報を提供することができるのだから，図書館の維持に大金を費やす必要はないとしている。That way「そうすれば」というつなぎ言葉を効果的に使っている。Yes の立場では，誰もが気軽に情報を得たり，子供に読書習慣をつけたりなどの機能は今でも有効だ，などと述べることができる。

No. 4

解答例 Definitely. It might not be realistic for some companies, but I think in many cases having a more flexible schedule is an easy way to increase employee satisfaction. This will especially help employees who have young children.

解説 質問は「より多くの企業が従業員に柔軟な仕事のスケジュールを提供すべきですか」。Definitely.「絶対にそうです」は Yes. より強い肯定表現。従業員の満足感を高め，特に小さい子供のいる従業員は助かるとしている。ほかに，仕事の効率が上がる，在宅勤務はコスト削減につながる，などの理由も考えられる。

解答例 **One day, a woman was talking with her friend.** They were sitting at a table, and her friend was holding a brochure for a beach resort. The woman's friend suggested they go together, but the woman looked worried about the price. Later that evening, the woman was looking at her computer, and she saw that she could earn money by doing some part-time work before the trip. According to the calendar, the woman's trip was just a few weeks away. Two weeks later, the woman was working at a restaurant. She was taking an order while her manager looked on. A few days later, the woman's suitcase was almost packed, and she was nearly ready for her trip. She was talking on the phone with her manager. The manager had an injured leg and was telling her that the restaurant would need her help the next day.

解答例の訳 ある日，女性が友人と話していました。彼女らはテーブルに座り，友人はビーチリゾートのパンフレットを持っていました。女性の友人は一緒に行くことを提案しましたが，女性は料金が心配そうな表情でした。その後その日の晩，女性はパソコンを見ていて，旅行の前にパートタイムの仕事をしてお金を稼ぐことができると知りました。カレンダーによると，女性の旅行はわずか数週間先でした。2週間後，女性はレストランで働いていました。店長がそばで見ている中，彼女は注文を取っていました。数日後，女性のスーツケースはほぼ荷造りが終わっていて，彼女は旅行の準備がほとんどできていました。彼女は店長と電話で話していました。店長は脚をけがしていて，レストランは翌日彼女の手伝いが必要になると彼女に話していました。

解説 解答に含めるべき点は以下の4つ。①女性の友人がビーチリゾートに一緒に行こうと誘うが，女性はお金の心配をしている，②その日の晩，女性はパソコンを見ていて，パートタイムの仕事でお金を稼げばいいと思い付く，また，カレンダーによると旅行まで半月ほどある，③2週間後，女性はレストランで働いている，④数日後，旅行の前日になって，荷造り中の女性に店長から電話があり，脚をけがしたので翌日手伝ってほしいと言われる。1コマ目の友人の Let's go together! を suggest を使って言い換えているが，その後の動詞が they go と仮定法現在になることに注意。3コマ目の描写のように接続詞 while を用いると，同時に起きている2つのことを1つの文ですっきりと表現できる。

No. 1

解答例 I'd be thinking, "I'm sorry to hear that my manager hurt his leg, but it's impossible for me to work tomorrow. I've already booked everything for the trip, including the plane ticket and hotel reservation."

解説 質問は「4番目の絵を見てください。もしあなたがこの女性なら，どのようなことを考えているでしょうか」。解答例は，店長のけがは気の毒だが，航空券やホテルなどをすでに予約してあるのだから，明日仕事をするのは無理だ，という内容。ほかには，旅行のことを店長に伝えていなかったので話しておくべきだった，などの考えがあり得るだろう。

No. 2

解答例 It depends. Classwork should always come first. However, some university students have a lot of free time. In such cases, getting a part-time job is a good way to earn extra money and learn responsibility.

解説 質問は「大学生がアルバイトをするのはいいことだと思いますか」。解答例は It depends.「状況次第だ」という立場。学業第一であるべきだとした上で，自由な時間があるのならアルバイトをするのもよい，と述べている。ほかにも，社会経験は将来役に立つ，親の経済的負担を減らせる，といった Yes の立場などが考えられる。

No. 3

解答例 No. These days, there are many different types of theft on the Internet. Even large online businesses have had their information stolen by hackers. Traditional, face-to-face businesses are safer.

解説 質問は「オンライン企業に個人情報を渡すことは安全だと思いますか」。解答例は No の立場で，インターネット上では情報が盗まれるので従来の対面式が安全だという意見。Yes の立場では，企業のコンプライアンスは向上した，ネットの安全対策は強化された，などの理由が考えられる。

No. 4

解答例 I don't think so. Companies should only hire as many employees as they need. Hiring too many workers would mean the companies become less efficient. In addition, the unemployment rate in Japan is not so bad.

解説 質問は「日本の雇用率を上げるために政府はより多くのことをすべきですか」。解答例は，過剰に従業員を雇用するとその会社の効率が下がることになるという考えと，日本の雇用率は悪くないという現状認識から，政府の積極的介入に反対する立場である。

MEMO

英検受験の後は 旺文社の

英検® 一次試験 解答速報サービス

PC・スマホからカンタンに自動採点！

- ⭕ ウェブから解答を入力するだけで，リーディング・リスニングを自動採点
- ⭕ ライティング（英作文）は観点別の自己採点ができます

大問別の正答率も一瞬でわかる！

- ⭕ 問題ごとの ○× だけでなく，技能ごと・大問ごとの正答率も自動で計算されます

英検® 一次試験 解答速報サービス
https://eiken.obunsha.co.jp/sokuhou/

※本サービスは従来型の英検 1 級〜 5 級に対応しています
※本サービスは予告なく変更，終了することがあります

旺文社の英検®合格ナビゲーター https://eiken.obunsha.co.jp/

英検合格を目指す方には英検®合格ナビゲーターがオススメ！
英検試験情報や級別学習法，オススメの英検書を紹介しています。

2024年度版

文部科学省後援

英検®準1級 過去6回全問題集　別冊解答

Obunsha